WORLD DRUIDRY
A Globalizing Path of Nature Spirituality

WORLD DRUIDRY
A Globalizing Path of Nature Spirituality

Larisa A. White, M.S.Ed., Ph.D.

Simurgh Books
Journeys of Discovery

Simurgh Books
2533 Lincoln Avenue
Belmont, CA 94002 U.S.A.
publisher@simurgh-books.com

100% human authored

No concept, text or image used in this book
was suggested, generated or edited by AI.

First Edition

ISBN-13: 978-1-7367792-0-0 (Hardcover)
ISBN-13: 978-1-7367792-1-7 (Trade Paperback)
ISBN-13: 978-1-7367792-2-4 (ePub)

Library of Congress Control Number: 2021904656

TABLE OF CONTENTS

LIST OF TABLES, CHARTS & ILLUSTRATIONS

POP QUIZ

Q: Which of the following images represent modern-day Druids, engaged in sacred activity? (Check all that apply.)

☐ A mother and her six-year-old son race out into pre-dawn twilight, dressed in pajamas and bathrobes, to sing and dance in the first real rain, at the end of a seven-month drought.

☐ An aged man in a long white robe blesses mistletoe harvested from an ancient oak.

☐ A hiker stops atop a mountain in high desert. He closes his eyes to breathe for a time, then sits with his back against a rock and meditates on mesquite.

☐ A musical quartet sits in the grass at the edge of a forest clearing, playing music for the trees.

☐ A circle of white-robed people at Stonehenge declares peace to the four directions.

☐ A woman with grubby blue-jeans and work-gloves digs compost into a planting bed and blesses seeds for a permaculture food forest.

☐ A lawyer strides into a court house and files a law suit to protect a wild space from development.

☐ All of the above

☐ None of the above

And the survey says…

AN OFFERING OF GRATITUDE

A survey-research project of this scale would never have been possible without the support, encouragement, advice, and assistance of a global village of dedicated Druids.

First, I would like to thank the Druidry discussion-board denizens who brought the perennial questions to my attention. The questioning, doubting, and civilized discourse that characterize internet-based Druidry communities were the inspiration for this study.

I am also indebted to Philip Carr-Gomm, Chosen Chief of the Order of Bards, Ovates, and Druids (emeritus), for his encouragement to pursue this area of inquiry, and for his invitation to be the 2021 Mount Haemus scholar, and to present the findings of this research as part of the 2024 Mount Haemus Awards program. The Mount Haemus scholarship was instrumental in offsetting the direct expenses of administering the survey.

When formulating questions for the survey instrument, and developing strategies for maximizing the global reach of the survey, I sought input and advice from the leadership of all major Druidry groups, so as to ensure fair and balanced treatment of the various flavors of world Druidry. I am grateful for the thoughtful suggestions and insights provided by Philip Carr-Gomm of the O.B.O.D., as well as from: Gordon Cooper, Grand Archdruid of the Ancient Order of Druids in America (emeritus); Philip Shallcrass and the Circle of Elders of the British Druid Order; Geoff Boswell and Aurora Stone, Trustees of The Druid Network; Jean Pagano, Archdruid of Ár nDraíocht Féin; Malcolm Brown, of the Isle of Wight Order of Druids; and Jeffrey Keefer, Morgan Glover, and Atilio Baroni Filho of the World Fellowship of Druids.

Translation of the survey instrument into all major world languages was key to making the survey accessible and welcoming to Druids from all parts of the world. I am grateful for the generous, careful, and thoughtful work of my wonderful, international team of volunteer translators: Rebecca Trinidad of the U.S.A. (Spanish); Eva Leenknegt of Belgium (Dutch/Flemish); David Olivier Creuze of France (French); Atilio Baroni Filho of Brazil (Portuguese); and Uta Frieling of Germany (German).

I owe a debt of gratitude to the 725 Druids who completed the survey and took the time to answer so many questions with such vivid detail. Most survey participants spent well over an hour of their time responding to difficult and highly personal essay-questions about their living environments, religious beliefs, and spiritual practices, creating the richest dataset on contemporary Druidry the world has yet to see.

Peter White coded all the custom-software and macros I needed to wrangle my giant data-set (which overwhelmed the capabilities of all the standard, mixed-methods analytic software packages!). He, along with Melanie Narish and Louise Naples, offered valuable feedback on the structure and tone of the developing book, and then proofread the final manuscript. Jon Grundy offered his advice and assistance, digging up references and definitions for some of the more obscure terms listed in the glossary. Michael Tenenblatt helped me wrangle the cover art into its final form, converting files into all the appropriate formats and color spaces in preparation for printing. I owe them all a debt of gratitude.

Finally, more than words can convey, I am grateful to my husband, Peter, and my son, Steven, who were unfailingly encouraging and supportive, and patient with me while I worked. They cheered me on, and provided smiling, desk-side deliveries of food and coffee when I lost track of time and missed family meals. Without them, this project would not have been possible.

This project has truly been a labor of love, with the world community of Druids and myself working together to understand ourselves more fully. Blessings of Land, Sea, and Sky to you all.

Larisa A. White
Belmont, California
Flower Season 2021

CHAPTER 1:
CONCERNING "DRUIDS"

What does it mean to be a Druid, circa 2020 c.e.?

The word *Druid* has been used by a variety of different people in recent times, to mean a variety of different things, all of which were inspired in some fashion by the very limited historical data that exists regarding the ancient historical Druids of Europe. Setting aside the multitude of role-playing gamers who play characters of the "Druid Class" in fantasy dungeon crawls, three major varieties of Druid still exist in the real world, today:

1. those belonging to fraternal/charitable organizations that use the term *Druid* as a title of honor;

2. those engaged in study, revival, or continuation (as far as possible) of ancient Celtic cultural traditions; and

3. those belonging to the Nature-based, new religious movement that has been spreading rapidly since the early 1990s.

All three groups are worthy of study (and the groups are certainly not mutually exclusive), however, numerous books have already been written, exploring, interpreting, re-interpreting, and debating the historical and archae-ological evidence pertaining to the evolution of those first two groups, and their relationship (or lack thereof) to the ancient historical Druids of Europe. The last dozen years, alone, have seen the publication of three new scholarly works, updating and enriching the robustly researched academic record for those first two groups: Ronald Hutton's book, *Blood and Mistletoe*[1]; Miranda Aldhouse-Green's book, *Caesar's Druids: Story of an Ancient Priesthood*[2]; and Barry Cunliffe's book, *Druids: A Very Short Introduction*[3]. The one group which has not yet received any substantial scholarly attention is the group of Druids, alive today, who are actively engaged with some form of Druidry or

Druidism as their primary religious/spiritual path. The above-mentioned works do speak to the origins of this new religious movement, and to the nature of its various organizations, founders, and early organizational leaders, but they do not delve into any significant detail pertaining to the religious beliefs and spiritual practices of contemporary world Druids.

Even within this narrowly defined group of contemporary Druids, the definition of the word *Druid* can be problematic. As pointed out by several *World Druidry Survey* respondents, depending upon whom one asks, the term *Druid* might be interpreted as meaning any one of the following:

- any practitioner of a Druidic religion or spiritual path;
- a person engaged in one specific field of endeavor within a Druidic religion or spiritual path (i.e. Druid as opposed to Bard or Ovate);
- a person who has completed the third of three levels of training within a Druidic religion or spiritual path; or
- the honorific bestowed upon (only) ordained Druidic clergy, serving leadership roles within their communities.

There is also a semantic problem posed by the term *Druidry* versus *Druidism*. Which is the proper term denoting the Druidic religion or spiritual path that is currently followed by living Druids? As with the definition of *Druid*, the implications of the terms *Druidry* and *Druidism* differed depending upon whom was asked. For some, the difference was seen as that between a religion defined by what one does and a religion defined by what one believes. For others, it represents a division between practices inspired by the Druid Revival Movement, and practices inspired by modern efforts to reconstruct various Indo-European systems of polytheistic worship.

Even the term *religion* poses a problem for many Druids, who came to Druidry from religious traditions in which powerful, centralized, religious organizations acted in direct opposition to the values they hold dear. For those Druids, the term *religion* is associated with forced adherence to prescribed beliefs and ritual forms. However, the meaning of the word *religion* is also a subject of ongoing academic debate[4]. According to J.D. Bettis, prior to the 1799 publication of Schleiermacher's book, *On Religion*[5], the preferred term was not *religion*, but *religious tradition*, and it was defined in a much broader sense than it is now, as a...

> *"...cultural tradition that provided the fundamental means of individual and social identification. Traditionally, religion referred to the basic guiding images and principles of an individual and a culture. Religion was identical with a style of life."*[6]

For the sake of simplicity, clarity, and inclusiveness in this study, I have opted to use the term *religion* in the broader cultural sense outlined above. I have opted to use *Druidry* as the more broadly applicable and more widely accepted term for the modern-day Druidic religion, and the term *Druid* in its broadest sense, to refer to any practitioner of that religion. It is to this community of Druids, and their cultural, spiritual, and religious practices, that I now direct your attention.

There are many how-to books, currently in print[7], offering advice on how to become a Druid. In addition, several of the larger Druid orders have published curricula to help guide new Druids along their developing spiritual paths. Many of these books and curricula were written by highly articulate and charismatic leaders within the modern Druid community, and offer a variety of well-considered perspectives on what modern Druidry is, what it has been, or might have been in the past, and what it could or should be in the future. However, very little research has been done, as yet, to determine the extent to which what is written in those books and curricula is actually put into practice.

Contemporary Druidry is a relatively new religious/spiritual path, and is still in the process of defining itself as a global movement. There are many Druidic organizations, each promoting a slightly different variation of contemporary Druidry, and each claiming a certain number of Druids among their memberships. However, there is also substantial overlap in those memberships, as well as substantial fluidity in terms of which organization(s), if any, an individual Druid will call home at a given moment in time. In addition, many Druids practice as *solitaries* — Druids who remain unaffiliated with any organized Druidry group(s).

Druids hold varied beliefs about the nature of Divinity: monotheism, assorted forms of polytheism, pantheism, animism, or sometimes simply the scientist's devout reverence for the universal powers and laws of Nature. Druids draw their inspiration and ritual traditions from varied sources: nature study, books of science, philosophy, history, world myths and legends, major world religions, aspects of modern Paganism, esotericism, curriculum materials drawn from one or more of the teaching orders, etc. Contemporary Druids also hail from diverse cultural backgrounds, and from countries scattered around the globe.

Given the enormous diversity that exists among self-identified Druids, and given that each Druid will tend to adapt his or her personal practices over time, the question arises: what, if anything, forms the spiritual common core of contemporary world Druidry? What do modern-day Druids believe? What are their religious and spiritual practices? How do their beliefs and practices vary over time, and over distance? What if anything do the Druids of the world hold in common?

A Brief Review of Existing Literature

Until now, there have been only two, broad sociological studies of contemporary Druidry. The first of these was Michael T. Cooper's 2010 book, *Contemporary Druidry: A Historical and Ethnographic Study.*[8] The second was Ellen Evert Hopman's 2016 book, *A Legacy of Druids.*[9] A third publication, Adam Anczyk's, *The Golden Sickle: An Introduction to Contemporary Druidry*[10], provides an excellent summary of the documents relevant to the new religious movement that is Druidry, and bridges between the historical works cited earlier, and the sociological research at hand.

Adam Anczyk's book begins where the works of Hutton, Cunliffe, and Aldhouse-Green leave off, with a summary of the early history of Druidry as a new religious movement. Anczyk explores the beliefs and practices of modern Druids, as set forth in the books, pamphlets, and internet literature produced by the major Druidry organizations and their leaders. He considers interview transcripts and articles published in popular news media, to complement those sources, and clarify certain points. Drawn from a wide range of academic and popular sources, this information serves as an excellent starting point for exploring the beliefs and practices of modern Druids. However, it is limited in scope. Only the perspectives of highly visible, vocal Druid leaders are represented in these sources, and so the results are not necessarily representative of the broader world community of practicing Druids. To fully understand the beliefs and practices of contemporary Druidry, as practiced "on the ground," broad, sociological or ethnographic studies are needed to supplement this information.

Michael Cooper's book was the first to attempt to serve this function. It is divided into two main parts: a brief overview of the history of Druidry, and an ethnographic study based on a combination of field observations and interviews with 80 practicing Druids, primarily members of Ár nDraíocht Féin and the Order of Bards, Ovates, and Druids, but also including 7 members of the Loyal Arthurian Warband. The study focused on Druidic perspectives on the meaning of life, death, well-being, and misfortune; and on Druidic methods of seeking guidance, and relating to the unknown. He also included chapters on the relationship between certain contemporary Druids and Stonehenge, and on pathways to conversion from other religious paths to Druidry.

Interesting as these research questions might be, they are relevant primarily to religions defined by shared systems of theological belief. Theology, as it turns out (see *Chapter 5*), is the one area in which Druids are least likely to share an opinion. Furthermore, the concept of "conversion" does not apply to people who so often identify with multiple, sometimes seemingly conflicting, simultaneous religious belief systems.

Another weakness in Cooper's study stems from its small sample size, coupled with a strong sampling bias — both artifacts of Cooper's outsider status, and his identity as a Christian scholar. As will be seen in *Chapter 3*, privacy and safety considerations are a major issue for modern Druids. Most would never speak to a non-Pagan about their personal religious practices and beliefs, due to fears of humiliation, harassment, persecution, and/or physical violence (Christians being the most-feared group). In light of this, Cooper's study will have inadvertently excluded Druids with significant privacy and safety concerns — concerns which frequently lead to variations in Druidic beliefs and practices. His study also excludes solitary practitioners, and Druids affiliated with the majority of world Druidry groups. As a result, his study's findings are necessarily biased, and of limited value as a general study of contemporary Druidry.

Ellen Hopman's book takes an entirely different approach. Rather than attempting a broad sociological study, Hopman focused on conducting in-depth interviews with 30 modern-day Druid leaders, purposefully chosen to represent a wide variety of Druid orders, and diverse experiences and perspectives on Druidry. Her sources included spiritual leaders, scholars and writers, political activists, artists, and bards. The interviews had been conducted some twenty years prior to the publication of her book, which makes the material somewhat dated, however, it provides a robust set of stories from the time at which Druidry was first beginning to grow into a global movement.

As a self-identified Druidess, Ellen Hopman was able to ask questions that were more relevant to Druidry qua Druidry, and to elicit richer and more deeply considered responses from her sources than Cooper's study was able to achieve. Rather than filtering those diverse views through her own lens, and reporting only fragments that supported her own hypotheses, Hopman presents the full interview texts, verbatim, allowing the reader to fully experience the details of each Druid leader's perspective. *A Legacy of Druids* is not a book that can be easily summarized. It is fascinating to read, but its strength lies in its representation of the diversity of perspectives and spiritual experiences that existed among the founding members of modern Druidry. As a reader wondering what, if anything, contemporary Druids hold in common, I found myself wanting more.

Hence, the current study: *The World Druidry Survey* of 2018-2020.

CHAPTER 1 NOTES & REFERENCES

1 Hutton, R. (2009). *Blood and Mistletoe: The History of the Druids in Britain*. New Haven; London: Yale University Press.

2 Aldhouse-Green, M. (2010). *Caesar's Druids: Story of an Ancient Priesthood*. New Haven; London: Yale University Press.

3 Cunliffe, B.W. (2010). *Druids: A Very Short Introduction*. New York: Oxford University Press.

4 Harrison, V.S. (2006). "The Pragmatics of Defining Religion in a Multi-Cultural World." *International Journal for Philosophy of Religion* 59: 133-152

5 Schleiermacher, F. (1893). *On Religion: Speeches to Its Cultured Despisers* (John Oman, B.D., Trans.). London: Kegan Paul, Trench, Trübner & Co., Ltd. (Original work published 1799)

6 Bettis, J.D. (1975). *Phenomenology of Religion*. London: SCM Press, pg. 170

7 See *Chapter 4* for a list of the most influential titles among them.

8 Cooper, M.T. (2010). *Contemporary Druidry: A Historical and Ethnographic Study*. Salt Lake City: Sacred Tribes Press.

9 Hopman, E.E. (2016). *A Legacy of Druids: Conversations with Druid leaders of Britain, the USA and Canada, past and present*. Winchester, U.K.: Moon Books.

10 Anczyk, Adam. (2014). *The Golden Sickle: An Introduction to Contemporary Druidry*. Katowice, Poland: Sacrum Publishing House.

CHAPTER 2:
THE WORLD DRUIDRY SURVEY

The book you hold in your hands contains the results of *The World Druidry Survey* — a global, multi-lingual survey of practicing Druids, exploring the ways in which Druidry is evolving both in the traditional lands of the ancient Druids, and elsewhere, as it spreads and takes root in other countries and cultures of the world. It is a project sparked by my curiosity about that perennial question, regularly posted by newcomers to Druidry discussion boards: How does one know if one is, in fact, a Druid?

Responses to that question are typically fraught with uncertainty, and always seem to include some version of, "A Druid is as a Druid does." But what does a Druid do? And where do they do it? And when? And how? And why? There seemed to me to be quite a bit of diversity in responses to these questions, depending upon whom was asked, their group affiliation, and the nature of their place of residence.

The obvious solution was to ask *everybody* in the world Druidry community, then look for commonalities and differences among the responses. It was an ambitious goal. One might say absurdly so. To derive any meaningful results from the effort, it would be necessary to locate and contact Druids from all over the world, including both unaffiliated solitary practitioners and Druids affiliated with a wide variety of Druid organizations, and entice them all to respond, in depth, in a variety of languages, to a lengthy series of questions about highly personal matters.

Given the anticipated diversity of participants in terms of geographic location, linguistic fluency, cultural identity, and Druid group affiliation, it would also be necessary to achieve a very large sample size. Otherwise, there would be insufficient data to make any valid claims regarding the broader applicability of any patterns which might emerge. In order to include a large, diverse, and widely scattered population of Druids in the study, in a manner that would not favor certain groups over others based upon ease of contact, a survey seemed the most pragmatic approach to gathering the necessary data.

Participant-Researcher Background & Motivations

Before delving into the details of research design, survey questions, analysis and results, it is important to consider my personal background and motives for conducting this research. I am a practicing Druid. Therefore, my role in the *World Druidry Survey* would necessarily be that of a participant-researcher — a role that brings with it both potential benefits and potential biases. The trick is to maximize the former while minimizing the latter, which among other things requires transparency in reporting.[1]

I was raised as a global nomad, moving every two years throughout my childhood, as my father's company moved us from country to country, and my father designed international airports. Rather than becoming rooted in any one place, my childhood was spent in the interstices between cultures, learning to navigate the spaces between. I learned local languages, attended local schools, participated in local religious celebrations, and adapted to local customs. By the time I had reached adulthood, I had participated in religious observances and celebrations with Catholics, Southern Baptists, Latter-Day Saints, Muslims, Zoroastrians, Sikhs, Anglicans, Wiccans, Russian Orthodox Christians, and Reformed and Orthodox Jews. I had read books about world religions, in addition to reading their sacred texts (when applicable). I learned hymns and prayers in local languages. I was by no means a religious scholar. I was what one might call a religiously well-educated atheist — knowledgeable about many religions, but a true adherent of none.

My upbringing left me with a sense of deep respect for all cultures and systems of belief, because I saw, first hand, how much they had in common: all religions seemed to stand for basic human values and virtues, a stance which each religion liked to claim was uniquely its own. The differences, to me, were simply differences in culture, stemming from differences in national histories. That, in itself, is a potential bias.

As a result of my globally nomadic upbringing, I consider histories, always in the plural, merely to be the sets of stories that groups of people like to tell themselves about themselves, and about other groups of people. In my experience, those stories — whether factually accurate or not — are the things that drive human behavior, as well as being used to identify people as belonging or not belonging to any particular group. Therefore, I have little interest in the accuracy, or lack thereof, of the various histories used to connect or separate modern Druids from the ancient Druids of Europe. I am only interested in what the Druids of today currently believe, theologically, and how they currently practice their religion. This bias can be seen in the form of an omission: I chose not to ask any questions in this study pertaining to who may or may not be "rightfully" permitted to call themselves a Druid, or the reasons behind that permission or prohibition. I have taken the position that, since the word *Druid* is already used by so many people, in so many different parts of the world, the horse is out of the proverbial barn, and there is no point in attempting to close that door. I believe the only meaningful questions to be asked must be asked of all people who currently self-identify as Druids in the spiritual or religious sense of the word. These questions are:

- What do people who currently self-identify as Druids do and believe?
- What do people who currently self-identify as Druids hold in common?
- In what ways do the religious beliefs and practices of self-identified Druids vary?

The reason for my interest in these questions is not purely academic. In 1994, I had a mystical experience at the Chalice Well in Glastonbury, which catapulted me out of my atheistic belief system, and set me on a long, winding path in search of a spiritual home. It was many years later when I first stumbled upon the word *Druidry* in my readings of world religions. As with many others who walk this path, my experience of coming to Druidry was less a matter of studying how to become a Druid, and more a matter of discovering a label that actually seemed to fit who I was. My introduction to the world of Druidry was J.M. Greer's *Druidry Handbook*[2].

As a long-time ecosystem restorationist and naturalist, I was pleased to find a religion that seemed to value "hands in the dirt" and the planting of trees as a valid means of spiritual expression. I was pleased to see a religious path focused on deeds rather than beliefs: go outside and study nature; change your habits to live in harmony with nature; practice meditation; study and learn; celebrate the seasonal cycles of nature, as they actually manifest in the land where you live. As a global nomad, I was also very encouraged by the Druidic philosophical tradition of using ternary thinking to resolve problems created with binary thinking. Druidry seemed a very good fit for me, and so I decided to explore it further.

I read more books. I joined the Ancient Order of Druids in America (AODA), the Order of Bards, Ovates, and Druids (OBOD), Ár nDraíocht Féin (ADF), the British Druid Order (BDO), The Druid Network (TDN), and the Order of the Yew. I studied, practiced, and completed the full first-year curriculum materials provided or suggested by AODA, OBOD, ADF, and the BDO. I read the Mount Haemus papers. I interacted with Druids on internet forums, and face-to-face at Pagan gatherings.

I began to notice what seemed to be authentic cultural norms among Druids. Druids I met all seemed to say that it is what you do rather than what you believe that makes you a Druid. Druids I met expressed open-mindedness toward Druids with beliefs and ritual practices different from their own. Druids I met actively encouraged others to pursue multiple, diverse avenues of learning, and to explore diverse flavors of Druidry, in order to find or create a path of Druidry that was uniquely their own. And when differences of opinion did arise, for the most part, Druids adhered to a cultural norm of civilized discourse — in stark contrast to the nature of public discourse in the world at large, today.

All of it seemed too good to be true. Was Druidry truly my long-sought spiritual home? Or had I simply stumbled upon a small handful of likeminded outliers, who were not "real Druids" any more than I was? Was there any such thing as a "real Druid" in the modern world? One danger of a group being too openminded about inclusiveness is that, if a label can be applied to anyone, then the label becomes rather meaningless. Perhaps all that modern Druids shared was a desire to use the word *Druid* as a title? My personal goals in undertaking this research project were: to find out whether or not there actually exists a coherent religious path of Druidry, and if so, to find out whether or not I had found a spiritual home in it.

Although my motive for undertaking this research project was not purely academic, my approach to executing the research was. I am an educator and independent scholar with over 30 years' experience using a variety of qualitative and quantitative research methods to shed light on the ways in which people learn, grow, and change under the influence of changing social and educational contexts. During that time, I came to appreciate that the use of a rigorous, mixed-methods research approach yields far more interesting and useful results than any particular method, used alone. Therefore, the design for this study of contemporary Druidry also involved a rigorous, mixed-methods research approach.

Research Design

The World Druidry Survey project was developed as a convergent, mixed-methods research design.[3] This means that the research project would include both qualitative (story-based) and quantitative (things you can count) research strands, the data-gathering for which would be pursued simultaneously. The data gathering phase of the project would be completed by way of a long-form questionnaire designed as a hybrid of typical, categorical (check-box and rating scale) survey-style questions, interspersed with open-ended, essay-style questions of a kind more typically associated with interview research.

The benefit of using this kind of mixed-methods approach is that one is able to gather data that allows for both breadth and depth in analysis, in a relatively short span of time, and within a very limited budget. The categorical data allows for objective measurement and statistical analysis of demographic distributions, as well as the prevalence and/or strength of beliefs and behaviors that might be expected of a population. The open-ended/essay questions allow for deep exploration of participant motives, religious experiences, and individual variations in religious belief and practice. In addition, simultaneous collection of two types of correlated data allows for triangulation within each participant's responses, to verify and clarify meanings, and to check for completeness within a participant's responses.

There are two potential downsides to this mixed-methods research design. First, the mere presence of the open-ended essay questions is likely to frighten off potential respondents, yielding a lower response rate than might otherwise be obtained. Second, with a respondent base so much larger than would typically be targeted for purely qualitative research, it would not be feasible to probe more deeply with follow-up questions or follow-up interviews, to explore emergent themes. However, the mixed-methods approach would be able to identify interesting lines of questioning, to be further explored in future research.

In addition to general research design considerations, it was important to consider potential biases caused by my status as a participant-researcher in the project, and to ensure that data-gathering, analysis, and reporting were completed in a manner that was credible, valid, transparent, and useful.[4] In order to make any credible claims about how Druidic beliefs and practices vary, and what they have in common, it was necessary to target as broad and varied a population of Druids as was possible, given high levels of uncertainty regarding the overall number of Druids on the planet, and their geographic distribution. This meant that a diverse group of Druids in leadership positions would be needed as advisors to the project, to ensure that the survey questions were formulated in a manner that would be equally welcoming and inclusive of many diverse approaches to Druidry, to help locate and contact Druid groups and solitaries in different regions of the world, to make introductions, and to encourage participation among Druids of their various communities.

Questionnaire Development Process

Development of the questionnaire began with a session of discursive meditation on my own Druidic practices and beliefs: Which of these were part of my Druidry, rather than part of just being myself, as a person? Could I even differentiate the two? Which beliefs and practices did I bring to my Druidry? Which of them did I take from Druidry? And if I learned it from my Druidry studies, what were the primary sources of that learning? Nature? Insights derived from practice? Curriculum materials from AODA? OBOD? ADF? BDO? Books on the history or practice of Druidry?

I returned to the books and curricula I had previously studied[5], and began to generate lists of practices, suggested areas of study, and shared beliefs that appeared in those printed materials. Then, I generated lists of topics, and lists of potential questions within each topic, based upon emergent themes. I generated a draft questionnaire from these questions, and added demographics questions that could be used to screen for respondent self-selection biases, and which would later serve as predictor-variables for statistical analyses.

Once I had a completed draft questionnaire, knowing that it would be biased by my own narrow experience of Druidry, I sent discussion copies to the heads and governing bodies of several Druidry groups, as well as to several practicing Druids, of no particular level of prominence, hailing from different parts of the world, and engaged in some lengthy phone conversations and e-mail exchanges with them, in order to answer the following questions:

- Have I omitted asking about any major/important aspects of modern Druidry that you believe are likely to change or vary with the physical and cultural environment in which a person's Druidry is practiced?

- Have I included or omitted or worded something in a manner that you think is likely to be taken as having mistreated or neglected someone's (or some Druidry organization's) central beliefs or practices?

- Which countries of the world do you believe to currently have an active Druid population that should be invited to participate in the study?

I received feedback from Geoff Boswell and Aurora Stone, Trustees of The Druid Network, Gordon Cooper, Grand Archdruid of The Ancient Order of Druids in America (emeritus), Philip Carr-Gomm, Chosen Chief of The Order of Bards, Ovates, and Druids (emeritus), Philip Shallcrass and the Circle of Elders of The British Druid Order, Rev. Jean Pagano, Archdruid of Ár nDraíocht Féin, Malcolm Brown, of the newly founded Isle of Wight Order of Druids, and several members of the World Fellowship of Druids — scattered about the globe.

Their responses helped me reformulate the questionnaire. For example, it became clear from their responses that the various Druid organizations used the terms *Bard, Ovate,* and *Druid* to refer to slightly different categories and/or levels of endeavor. To use those terms in the survey, at all, might alienate one or more groups of Druids — something I very much wanted to avoid. As a result, I restructured the questionnaire, eliminating the *Bard*, *Ovate*, and *Druid* references, and instead using descriptive categories: nature related activities; artistic activities; educational and activist activities; leadership activities; and areas of study or scholarship. In addition, I learned of several areas of Druidic work and practice of which I had been unaware, and these were added to the questionnaire. In its final form (see *Appendix A* for a reproduction of the survey instrument), the questionnaire comprised 189 items, organized into 42 sets of questions, including 18 open-ended/essay questions.

Once the content of the questionnaire had been made as inclusive as possible, I turned my attention to its tone. I wrote an introduction to the *World Druidry Survey,* which I hoped would be welcoming and encouraging to Druids of all persuasions. In it, I introduced myself as a fellow Druid (a member of multiple Druid organizations, with no particular group-affiliation bias). I disclosed the fact that the OBOD's Mount Haemus Award program had provided seed funding for the project, and gave a brief overview of my professional qualifications for executing this type of research. I also described the measures taken to ensure the privacy and safety of all participants. The website for the survey described the diverse group of Druid leaders who had advised me on the project, as evidence of my efforts to avoid bias both in question formulation and in the solicitation of survey participants.

All survey questions were phrased in a neutral manner. Closed-ended questions included options for, "none of the above," and, "other (please specify):_____," with spaces provided for participants to add choices that I had failed to include, and to answer questions that I had failed to ask. In every decision pertaining to wording and tone, my goal was to encourage all Druids, of all types and affiliations, to participate in the survey and share their stories.

Encouraging Global Participation

Once the questionnaire was finalized, I began to prepare to administer the survey to the Druids of the world. The first step was to identify which nations were most likely to have a population of practicing Druids. The second step was to arrange for translation of the questionnaire into all the necessary languages, so that Druids of different nationalities would have the option of reading and responding in the language with which they felt most comfortable. Finally, there was a need for an outreach strategy.

According to the membership rosters of the four largest Druid organizations (OBOD, ADF, AODA, and BDO), there were 31 nations in which Druids were known to have lived, in recent years. The largest populations of Druids seemed to be concentrated in the English speaking nations of Britain/U.K., Ireland, Australia, New Zealand, Canada, and the United States. However, a substantial number of Druids were also located in Brazil, Portugal,

Spain, Mexico, France, Germany, Belgium, and the Netherlands, with an odd few scattered in other countries. This meant that, at the very least, I would need to translate the questionnaire into five other world languages: Portuguese, Spanish, French, German, and Dutch/Flemish.

Translation of the questionnaire would be key to making the survey accessible and welcoming to Druids from all parts of the world. Even the best computer-translation software will make mistakes, and it was important that the questions — which ask people to think about and express their ideas about very personal issues — would be clearly and politely formulated, which is not merely a matter of linguistic accuracy, but also requires careful consideration of local customs and culture. I therefore posted a request on the OBOD and AODA forums for volunteers who could help me with the translation effort. I ended up with a wonderful, international team of volunteer translators: Rebecca Trinidad of the U.S.A. for Spanish; Eva Leenknegt of Belgium for Dutch/Flemish; David Olivier Creuze of France for French; Atilio Baroni Filho of Brazil for Portuguese; and Uta Frieling of Germany, who not only did the German translation work, but also asked all the difficult, cross-cultural questions that I did not know I needed to ask.

With polished questionnaires in six major languages in hand, the next step was to plan the logistics of administering the survey. Once again, I needed to consider that not all Druids are computer savvy, nor do they all have easy access to the internet. While the bulk of the data was likely to arrive through the SurveyMonkey web interface, I wanted to ensure that Druids who preferred pen and paper to computers, or computer print-outs to smartphone screens, would also feel welcomed and encouraged to participate. Copies of the questionnaire, in all six languages, were therefore made available via internet links to the SurveyMonkey interface, via fillable-PDF forms that could be downloaded, filled out, and returned via email, and via paper forms that could be completed by hand, and returned to me via postal mail.

Then began the long process of announcing the survey. Direct contact was attempted first, by posting announcements, in all six languages, to the internet forums for each of the major Druid orders, and sending email invitations to the leaders of each of the local Druid seed groups, groves, or sub-groups associated with each of those orders. In the email invitations, local leaders were invited to participate personally, and were asked to share information about the survey with the other members of their local groups, and any other, unaffiliated Druids they happened to know, in their area. They were also asked to post the announcement in local newsletters, and on any and all social-media accounts through which they typically interacted with other Pagans or Druids.

In the second stage, I compiled a listing of all Druid groups that I could find mentioned in academic texts on the subject of Druidry, or via internet searches on the subjects of Druidry and Druidism, as well as the translation of those terms into the most common languages spoken in countries rumored to have been, at least at one time, the residence of people claiming to be Druids. Multilingual invitations were sent to all such groups that still seemed to have an active internet presence. A number of groups that I found on lists dating from the early 1990s seem to have vanished entirely. A few responded that the organization had officially dissolved, but had maintained their web sites for historical purposes. For those organizations, I sent invitations to peripheral sub-groups still listed on the archival website, under the assumption that even if the central organization was no longer formally active, there might still be a network of Druids to be accessed via those contacts.

Articles about the *World Druidry Survey* were published in Pagan and Druid magazines, including *The Wild Hunt,* and *Dryade.* Articles about the Survey were also included in the quarterly newsletters of several major Druid organizations.

In addition to these direct attempts to reach the practicing Druids of the world, I engaged in what I call "six degrees of separation" advertising. At the end of every questionnaire, in every language and format, respondents were asked to share copies of the questions, in any format they desired, with all other Druids with whom they regularly interacted. Druids whom I had never met apparently worked heartily on behalf of the *World Druidry Survey,* spreading the word and encouraging others to participate. The announcement inviting survey participation was posted and re-posted on Pagan and Druidry-related social media accounts. It was discussed on Druid order forums. It was talked up at private Druid gatherings, at which stacks of paper questionnaires were distributed to attendees.

The effort seemed to be quite successful, as a substantial number of survey responses were returned in every language, and by way of all three modes of delivery — email, snail-mail, and SurveyMonkey form — over the course of the six-month data-gathering period.

Protecting Participant Privacy and Data Security

Anonymity and privacy considerations were of utmost importance for my own safety as a researcher, as well as for that of survey participants. I wanted to encourage those who might otherwise decline to participate for fear of harassment or discrimination. For that reason, Druids were given the option to return an anonymous survey form via postal mail. Responses submitted via postal mail or email were transcribed into the database, associated with only an anonymous respondent identification number. For responses collected by the SurveyMonkey system, an email address was used to track progress and collate pieces of an individual's responses, so that participants did not have to complete the entire survey in a single sitting, but could come and go at will.

Once the completed survey was submitted, the response data was transferred to the database with an anonymous respondent identification number in place of the email address. After the data collection phase of the survey was complete, all data was downloaded to a secure, private computer for analysis, and the SurveyMonkey account was purged of all data and deleted.

The Unprecedented Response

The response to the *World Druidry Survey* was overwhelming. After eliminating all responses that fell into each of the following categories:

- email addresses with no data attached; or
- duplicate responses from different email addresses, in which every check-box and long-answer was repeated, verbatim; or
- responses that included only predictor-variable (demographic) data, but no response data pertaining to Druidry beliefs and practices; or
- the one person who responded to every question with the words, "This is too personal a question; I am not going to answer it."

I was left with 725 completed questionnaires, including 128,325 check-box survey responses, and 1,500 pages of essay-question responses, with over 375,000 words of rich, detailed, anecdotes regarding the spiritual and religious practices of 725 living Druids, scattered around the globe. According to the SurveyMonkey statistics, the average Druid spent well over an hour typing in their responses to the questions, not counting the time they may have spent offline, downloaded PDF questionnaire in hand, pondering what to write.

A brief review of the demographics data shows that the outreach effort succeeded in enticing a substantial number of diverse Druids to participate in the *World Druidry Survey*. Druids responded from 34 countries around the world, and hailed from many diverse physical and cultural environments. Response distributions were well balanced along lines of gender, age, level of experience with Druidry, and Druidry group membership, if any.

Completed surveys were returned by Druids in 34 different nations, including all 31 nations initially targeted by the outreach effort (see table, at right). As expected, the majority of the responses came from English-speaking nations, with smaller, but meaningful turnouts (N>20) from the Netherlands and Germany. The response rates from Ireland, France, Belgium, Portugal, Spain, Brazil, and Mexico were too small to allow for any valid statistical analyses to be made of the responses from those countries on an individual basis; however, the responses I did receive from Druids in those countries are still quite valuable, because they enrich the emerging picture of modern world Druidry as a whole. There was substantial variation in the response rates from the English-speaking nations (see *Appendix B* for detailed analysis). The British Isles, Canada, and Australia all had survey response rates of about 3-4% of the estimated national population of Druids. New Zealand and Ireland had response rates of 12-15%. The United States had the lowest response rate, at 0.69% of the estimated national population of Druids; however, the absolute number of U.S. respondents was sufficiently large to allow for reasonable statistical analyses, despite the low response rate.

The gender distribution of respondents to the *World Druidry Survey* (see charts on page 18) was 56% female, which is roughly in line with 2011 census statistics for Pagan religions, as a whole. Census data for pagan religions generally indicate that females comprise between 55% and 65% of the overall Pagan population.[6] Historically, the Druid path has been reported as more male-centric than this, however, so much world census data is comprised of counts for groups of Druid-like, Pagan and other nature religions, rather than for Druids as a distinct group, that it is only possible to make valid comparisons of general Pagan numbers, as a whole.

The age distribution of survey respondents was well balanced, with reasonable representation in all age groups. Most Druid respondents

Geographical Distribution of Druid Respondents

Nation of Residence	# Druids
Europe	
British Isles	137
Netherlands	27
Germany	24
Ireland	11
France	7
Belgium	5
Austria	4
Czech Republic	2
Italy	2
Norway	2
Portugal	2
Sweden	2
Switzerland	2
Denmark	1
Gibraltar	1
Poland	1
Spain	1
Americas	
United States	358
Canada	44
Brazil	11
Mexico	1
St. Lucia	1
Uruguay	1
Oceania	
Australia	42
New Zealand	24
Asia	
India	1
Japan	1
Malaysia	1
Russia	1
Saudi Arabia	1
Africa	
Kenya	1
South Africa	1

Druid Gender Distribution

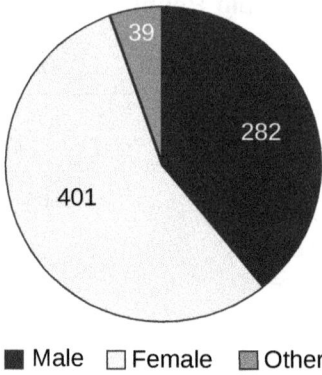

39
282
401

■ Male □ Female ▤ Other

Druid Birth Decade

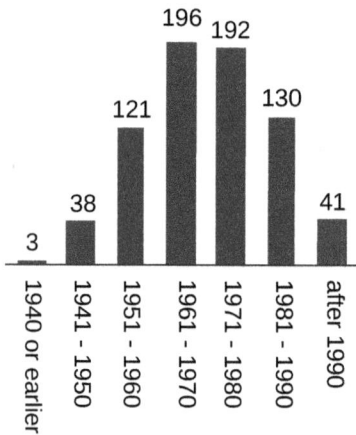

196 192

121
130

38
41
3

1940 or earlier
1941 - 1950
1951 - 1960
1961 - 1970
1971 - 1980
1981 - 1990
after 1990

Time Practicing Druidry

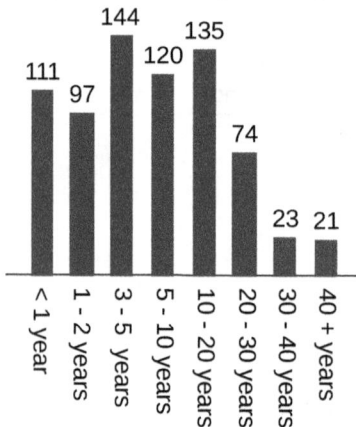

144
135
111
120
97
74
23 21

< 1 year
1 - 2 years
3 - 5 years
5 - 10 years
10 - 20 years
20 - 30 years
30 - 40 years
40 + years

were middle aged, with representation tailing off among older adults, and among people at the start of their independent adult lives.

Respondents also reported a broad range of experience levels with Druidry. As would be expected of a new and growing religious tradition, the response distribution shows geometric growth over time; the number of practicing Druids has doubled with each decade, since 1990.

Survey participants reported being members of 147 distinct Druidry groups, large and small, local and international (see *Appendix C* for the complete list). Although many of the smaller groups were technically subgroups of other, more global, parent organizations, 6% of Druids reported belonging to the subgroups, while not being members of the larger, global organizations. These smaller groups might therefore develop their own unique, local flavors of Druidry, quite different from those of their parent organizations. Many Druids (26%) belonged to more than one group; and 18% of Druids reported being unaffiliated, solitary practitioners.

Respondents were also fairly evenly distributed among rural (33%), suburban (36%), and urban (28%) communities, with a small number residing in small towns, urban fringe areas, and military bases.

Given popular assumptions and beliefs about contemporary Druids' presumed connections to the ancient Druids of northern and western Europe, and given the Celtic cultural origins of the modern religious tradition that is Druidry, it comes as no surprise that the majority of contemporary Druids claim at least some ancestral connection to the Celtic cultures of Europe. When asked to describe their personal, cultural heritage, only 11% of world Druids reported having ancestries derived — entirely, or in part —from non-European peoples and nations. Other nations cited by Druids as forming part of their personal, ancestral heritage included: Brazil, assorted Brazilian-Amerindian nations, Chile, Mexico, Uruguay, North American First Nations (Cherokee, Choctaw, Wendat/Huron, Algonquin, Lumbee, Comanche, Apache, Wyandotte, Miami, and unspecified others), Jamaica, Puerto Rico, Algeria, Kenya, other unspecified African nations, Lebanon, Iran, India, Bangladesh, Indonesia, the Philippines, Singapore, Malaysia, Japan, New Zealand's Māori, or Australian aboriginal peoples. Nearly all Druids with non-Celtic ethnic backgrounds reported having come to Druidry within the past ten years. So, while the ethnic diversity of the Druid path is clearly limited at this time, it has also, apparently, been growing over time.

There may yet be some other kind of hidden, self-selection bias in the response data; however, by all obvious measures of diversity — aside from ethnic background — the Druids who responded to the *World Druidry Survey* are a reasonably well-balanced representation of the current, world population of Druids.

Making Sense of the Stories

Most of the 725 participating Druids completed the questionnaire in its entirety, but occasionally, a Druid would skip, or overlook, a few questions. I did not want to introduce a bias by presuming intentions for omitted responses, so the database cells for missing responses were filled with the code word, "blank," so that omitted responses could be identified and omitted from tallies and percentage calculations.

Then, I cleaned up the data-set, in preparation for analysis. The first step was to review the complete set of responses from each anonymous Druid, using a process called triangulation to verify the responses to each question, checking to ensure the responses in each Druid's questionnaire were complete, internally consistent, and parsed into the proper question-columns for coding and analysis. For example, there were several cases in which a respondent failed to tick a "polytheist" box in a check-box/check all that apply question pertaining to categories of religious belief, but in the next question provided details of their personal pantheon of gods, along with a rich description of polytheistic practice. In such a case, the "polytheist" category was added to their other check-boxes, to more accurately represent their religious beliefs. In other cases, respondents gave detailed responses in one question, which also answered a later question on the survey form — which was left blank. In such cases, the response was duplicated in the "blank" box for the later question, so that the data would not be lost when coding the relevant question column.

During the data-cleaning phase, I added English translations to the cells for all responses that had been submitted in other languages. I also corrected spelling and capitalization errors for accuracy, and changed some of the spelling variations found in participant responses, to ensure consistency throughout the database, so that things like nations, deities, and holiday names, or author names and book titles, could be searched for and tallied by computer. In addition, this simplified the task of creating a *Glossary* that would be more easily searchable by readers less familiar with both the terms, and the many linguistic and spelling variations that are so commonly found among them.

Responses to all open-ended questions were coded for conceptual content[7], with code words or short phrases used to identify both anticipated categories and emergent themes. Coded excerpts from Druids' narrative responses were then sorted into response categories. The categories are reported using frequency counts for each code, along with thick descriptions, heavily illustrated with quotations pulled from the relevant responses. This method of reporting allows readers to decide the extent to which they agree or disagree with my interpretation of the qualitative data.

In selecting quotations to illustrate emergent themes, I chose a small subset of the quotes that I felt most clearly illustrated the theme in question. The number of quotes used to illustrate each theme was dependent upon the theme's prevalence within the data set. For themes that were evident in the responses of a majority of responding Druids within a given category, I use 7-9 representative quotes. For minor themes, I offer only 3-5 quotes by way of illustration.

Occasionally, when Druids had written long, stream-of-consciousness essays in response to a survey question, it was necessary to correct a bit of spelling or grammar to facilitate comprehension, or to omit irrelevant tangents within a response that had wandered off topic before returning to a key point. In addition, in order to guarantee the privacy and safety of survey participants, I omitted any information, contained within the quotations, which might be used to identify a specific individual as the source of the quotation. In the presentation of survey results, any omissions are indicated by the inclusion of an ellipsis enclosed in square brackets, thus:

> "The beginning of a relevant quotation [...] the end of the relevant bits of this quotation."

Any added words or grammatical corrections are printed in regular text, within square brackets, within the body of the italicized quotation, for example:

"In the middle of this quote [a correction is made by the researcher] *and then, the quote continues."*

For simplicity in reporting, the quantitative, rating-scale response data pertaining to the importance of, or level of influence of, various factors were condensed into *percentages of maximum possible importance/influence,* within each specified Druid subgroup. To achieve this, I generated a weighted average of each rating-scale response distribution, such that: if everyone in a subgroup responded "not important" or "not an influence", the result would be a zero; if everyone in the subgroup responded "moderately important" or "moderate influence", the result would be 50%; and if everyone in the subgroup responded "essential" or "major influence", the result would be 100%.

When analyzing cross-tabulated codes, to check for the statistical significance, if any, of observed, qualitative variations in sub-group practices and beliefs, I used chi-squared tests of independence[8]. This is a widely applicable approach to examining associations between two sets of independent, categorical variables, when the overall sample size is sufficiently large to ensure that the expected response distributions would have at least five people in each category. Statisticians will be familiar with the technique. For readers less mathematically inclined, I offer the following, plain English translation:

The chi-squared test allows me to calculate the probability that an apparent difference in the data may have occurred by random chance. All probabilities fall somewhere between zero ($p = 0.00$) and one ($p = 1.00$). A chi-squared test result of "$p = 0.00$" means that there is zero possibility that the observed difference is due to random chance; there really is a significant difference between the groups being compared. A result of "$p = 1.00$" means that there is no meaningful difference between the groups; and any apparent differences can be considered random static in the data. P-values closer to zero are more likely to represent a meaningful difference than p-values closer to one.

Given a statistical result for a chi-squared test of independence, the researcher can then choose a numeric threshold for the p-value, below which they would consider the results to be "significantly different." The threshold p-value I chose for this study is $p \leq 0.01$, which means: if I discuss a difference between Druidry subgroups, I am at least 99% sure that the apparent difference is due to something real, and is worthy of discussion.

For most of the analyses presented in this book, the chi-squared tests were performed on distributions of straight-forward response counts. However, when considering sacred activities in everyday life, the survey data contained hundreds of highly specific activities, including both those listed in the original survey, and many that had been added by respondents. This meant there were too many activities, and too few Druids associated with each activity, to allow for valid chi-squared tests. To allow for meaningful analysis and discussion,

I used cluster analysis[9] to condense the activities into thematically related clusters for discussion. This was achieved by combining thematically-related items for which the response distributions were either identical, or highly similar. Then, when performing the chi-squared tests for intergroup variations, I focused on the clusters, rather than on the component activities for which there had been insufficient data to perform valid tests. The statistical results are reported for each cluster, accompanied by a description of the sub-items that had been included in that cluster. For example, activities such as "growing vegetables," and "planting a permaculture food forest," and "organic gardening," and "growing my own food," and "keeping a kitchen-garden," might be combined into a cluster called "gardening," for statistical analysis, while the specific varieties of gardening would be described, qualitatively, in the discussion.

In the interest of readability, when discussing statistically significant differences, I have chosen not to include the statistical results in the main text. All relevant percentages and p-values can be found in the *Notes & References* section of each chapter.

Armed with these basic analytic tools and techniques, we are now ready to begin to make sense of the stories, and to learn what there is to learn from the Druids of the world.

CHAPTER 2 NOTES & REFERENCES

1 Roller, M.R. and Lavrakas, P.J. (2015). *Applied Qualitative Research Design: A Total Quality Framework Approach*. New York: The Guilford Press.

2 Greer, John Michael. (2006). *The Druidry Handbook: Spiritual Practice Rooted in the Living Earth*. San Francisco, California: Red Wheel/Weiser LLC.

3 Creswell, J.W. and Plano Clark, V.L. (2018). *Designing and Conducting Mixed Methods Research* (3rd Ed.). Thousand Oaks, California: SAGE Publications.

4 Roller, M.R. and Lavrakas, P.J. (2015). *Applied Qualitative Research Design: A Total Quality Framework Approach*. New York: The Guilford Press. p. 21-47

5 Books and curriculum materials referenced, while generating first-draft survey questions:

ADF's *Dedicant Path Manual* (2018)

AODA's *New Candidate Guide* (2018)
AODA's *Apprentice Guide* (2019)

BDO's *Bardic Course* curriculum booklets (2018-2019)

OBOD's *Bardic Grade* curriculum booklets (2018-2019)

Billington, Penny. (2011). *The Path of Druidry: Walking the Ancient Green Way*. Woodbury, MN: Llewellyn Publications.

Greer, John Michael. (2006). *The Druidry Handbook: Spiritual Practice Rooted in the Living Earth*. San Francisco, California: Red Wheel/Weiser LLC.

Greer, John Michael (2011). *The Druid Grove Handbook*. Traverse City, MI: Lorian Press.

Hopman, Ellen Evert. (2016). *A Legacy of Druids: Conversations with Druid leaders of Britain, the USA, and Canada, past and present*. Winchester, UK: Moon Books.

Nichol, James. (2014). *Contemplative Druidry: People, Practice and Potential*. CreateSpace Independent Publishing.

Nichols, Ross. (1992). *The Book of Druidry: History, Sites and Wisdom*. San Francisco, CA: Aquarian Books.

6 Lewis, J.R. and Bårdsen Tollefsen, I. (2013). "Gender and Paganism in Census and Survey Data." *The Pomegranate* 15.1-2 (2013) 61-78

7 Saldaña, Johnny. (2016). *The Coding Manual for Qualitative Researchers* (3rd Ed.). Thousand Oaks, California: SAGE Publications.

8 Agresti, A. (2019). *An Introduction to Categorical Data Analysis* (3rd Ed.). Hoboken, NJ: John Wiley & Sons, Inc. pg. 36-42

9 ibid. pg. 306-310

CHAPTER 3:
A GEOGRAPHY OF WORLD DRUIDRY

Twenty-first century Druids are a diverse group. They hail from many different countries. They include people of all ages, genders, and levels of experience, ranging from those just discovering Druidry, to those who have been practicing for over 40 years. They also reside in many different kinds of physical, social, and cultural environments. Given the importance of such things in helping define who people become as individuals, and given that Druidry is, after all, a nature-based spiritual tradition, it is worth considering the various geographical contexts in which contemporary Druids live and work to develop their personal paths of Druidry.

Modern Druids and their Natural Environments

Druids can be found living and practicing in biomes ranging from the mistletoe and oak filled temperate forests depicted in history and fantasy, to tropical rainforests, blistering deserts, maritime fishing villages, and urban

Countries with Resident Druids

canyons. One third of *World Druidry Survey* respondents live in agricultural grazing or croplands — rural lands so transformed by human activity that there is little or no trace left of what was once the naturally occurring biome. One third are urban Druids, who face similar challenges when attempting to connect with a truly natural environment on a regular basis.

Despite these challenges, 80% of modern Druids are able to identify the naturally occurring biome(s) in which they reside. The majority live in biomes characterized by four seasons — winter, spring, summer, and autumn — with seasonal cycles driven primarily by variations in light and heat. In contrast, 17% live in biomes where seasons are driven by cyclical variations in precipitation, and in terrestrial and atmospheric moisture, instead. These biomes may have pronounced wet and dry seasons, but rarely, if ever, does the ambient temperature drop to freezing. As will be seen in later analyses, this fundamental difference in the nature of Druids' home biomes corresponds with some of the most pronounced variations in Druidic beliefs and practices.

Which Biomes Do Druids Inhabit?

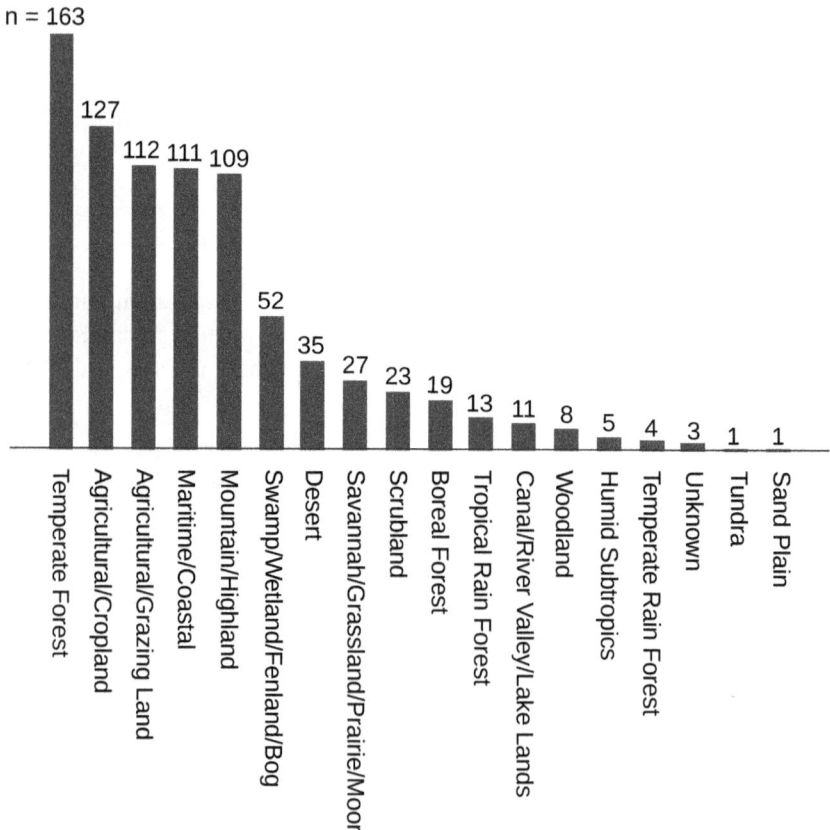

n = 163

Temperate Forest: 163
Agricultural/Cropland: 127
Agricultural/Grazing Land: 112
Maritime/Coastal: 111
Mountain/Highland: 109
Swamp/Wetland/Fenland/Bog: 52
Desert: 35
Savannah/Grassland/Prairie/Moor: 27
Scrubland: 23
Boreal Forest: 19
Tropical Rain Forest: 13
Canal/River Valley/Lake Lands: 11
Woodland: 8
Humid Subtropics: 5
Temperate Rain Forest: 4
Unknown: 3
Tundra: 1
Sand Plain: 1

Connections to Celtic Culture and the Lands of Ancient Druids

Modern Druids currently reside in many countries and cultures of the world. Only 32% of survey responses were submitted by Druids living in European nations located within the areas historically inhabited by Celts. The remainder came from countries, and continents, very far removed from there. Given this wide geographical distribution of Druids, one cannot help but wonder at the extent to which modern Druids are influenced by perceived connections to Celtic culture, or to the lands that may once have played host to the ancient Druids of Europe.

Two survey questions addressed this topic. The first of these asked Druids to rate the importance of Celtic language, culture, and/or traditions to their personal path of Druidry. The second question asked them to describe their personal connection, if any, to the traditional, Celtic lands of the ancient Druids. A summary of their responses is presented in the charts found below, and on page 28.

Less than one-third (only 28%) of Druids reported having been born and bred in lands of Celtic heritage. The majority (61%) reported being part of what might be called a Celtic diaspora — people with a family heritage that derives from those regions of Europe, but with little or no direct, personal connection. Only 11% of Druids reported having no genealogical ties to any land of Celtic heritage. It follows that most Druids consider Celtic language, culture, and/or traditions to be of some importance to their Druidry practice.

The percent of maximum possible importance[1] attributed by modern Druids to Celtic languages and/or cultural traditions was 60% overall — more than *moderately important* but neither *very important* nor *essential*. Druids with no genealogical ties to Celtic lands rated Celtic traditions as less important to their practice, with a score of 51%.[2] There was no difference between Druids born and bred in Celtic areas, and Druids who were part of the Celtic diaspora, with one exception: members of the Ancient Order of Druids in America tended to attribute significantly less importance to Celtic traditions (just 45% of maximum possible importance)[3]. This was the only statistically significant intergroup variation.

Importance of Celtic Culture

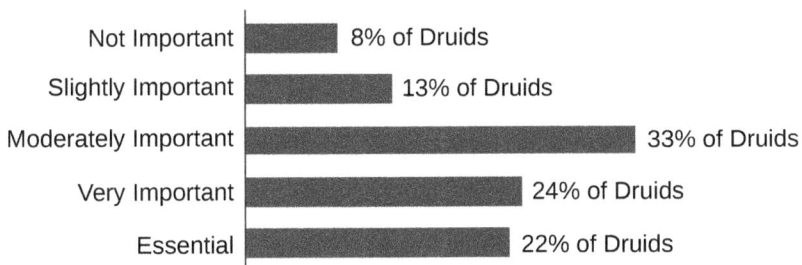

Category	Percentage
Not Important	8% of Druids
Slightly Important	13% of Druids
Moderately Important	33% of Druids
Very Important	24% of Druids
Essential	22% of Druids

Personal Link to Celtic Lands

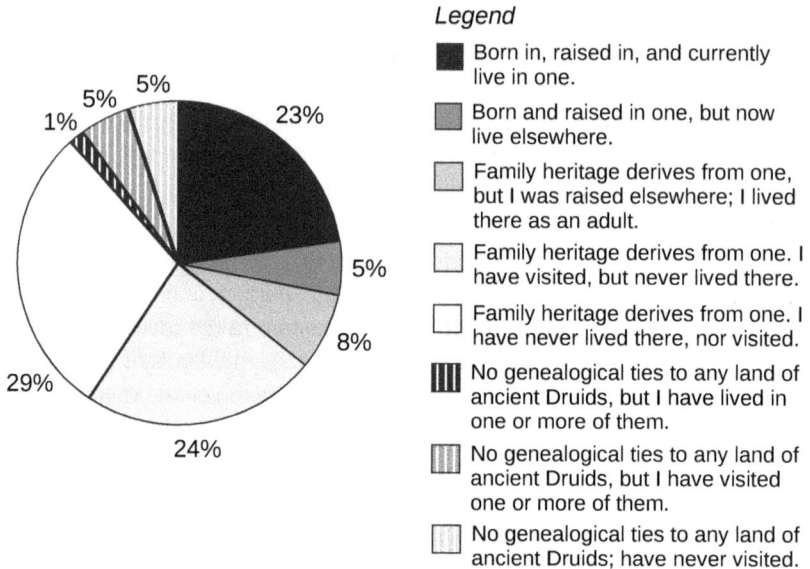

Legend

■ Born in, raised in, and currently live in one.

▨ Born and raised in one, but now live elsewhere.

▧ Family heritage derives from one, but I was raised elsewhere; I lived there as an adult.

□ Family heritage derives from one. I have visited, but never lived there.

□ Family heritage derives from one. I have never lived there, nor visited.

▥ No genealogical ties to any land of ancient Druids, but I have lived in one or more of them.

▥ No genealogical ties to any land of ancient Druids, but I have visited one or more of them.

▥ No genealogical ties to any land of ancient Druids; have never visited.

The most interesting finding in this area came from calculating the average importance-of-Celtic-culture scores for each biome currently inhabited by Druids, and then sorting the biomes by those scores. The result was a perfect split between biomes with seasonal cycles driven by light and temperature (e.g. temperate and boreal forests, North American prairies, mountains and highlands, etc.), and those with seasons driven by variations in precipitation and moisture (e.g. scrublands with Mediterranean climates, tropical rain forests, humid subtropical areas, etc.). Druids in the light/warmth-driven biomes tended to rate Celtic traditions as more important (61%), while those in biomes driven by precipitation/ moisture cycles tended to rate Celtic traditions as less important (47%) than the norm. There were also significant differences in the qualitative ways in which Druids from these two groups practiced their Druidry, and the extent to which Celtic traditions played a role in those practices. This will be discussed more fully in the sections on geography and wildcrafting in Druidry, and on cultural studies and preservation work, in *Chapters 4, 5, 6, and 7.*

Modern Druids and their Local Communities

In addition to the natural environment and Celtic cultural traditions, Druidry practices have frequently been influenced by the presence of other people, both inside and outside of the Druid's home. Unrelated housemates, extended family members, spouses, children, and strangers in the home, have all influenced the nature of Druidic practice. This impact is most pronounced when the Druid's home community is comprised primarily of intolerant members of other religions, and when access to private gardens is limited.

Nearly all participating Druids (95%) reported living in majority-Christian communities. The next most prevalent external religious communities were Muslim (14%) and Jewish (8%), closely followed by Atheist communities (6%). Less than 5% of Druids live among followers of other faiths. Among these, the most frequently cited faith communities were: various Neopagan traditions, Buddhism, Hinduism, indigenous/shamanistic traditions, Sikhism, New World African-Matrix religions, Baha'i Faith, and Unitarian Universalism. As will become evident in the next few sections, the prevalence of intolerant Abrahamic religious beliefs and attitudes within local communities has had a significant impact on the practices of many Druids, who feel unsafe worshipping outside the confines of a private garden.

Just over half of survey respondents (55%) reported having access to a private garden or wild space, in which to practice their Druidry. Fifteen percent had access to only a public park or public garden, in which they would attempt to find a less-trafficked area in which to conduct their spiritual practices. The remaining 30% — nearly one third of all Druids — had no regular access to any kind of garden or natural wild space. While this may seem like a simple matter of separating the "haves" from the "have nots," the implications for the practice of a nature-based religion are important. Considering the significant privacy and safety concerns reported by a majority of modern Druids, lack of access to private gardens and/or wild spaces often meant the difference between being able to safely practice one's religion, and feeling forced to abandon it.

Privacy & Safety Concerns of Modern Druids

Practicing a new religion has always involved risks for the early adopters of those religions, and Druidry is no exception. Though there were some within the Druid community (26%) for whom privacy and safety were not of concern, the majority of respondents reported that privacy and safety considerations played a significant role in their practice of Druidry.

Some Druids were comfortable acting upon the popular notion that Druidry should be "practiced in the eye of the Sun," rather than in darkness and secrecy, so as to avoid the fear and anger that are so often provoked by occult practices. (Only two Druids mentioned the need to protect initiation secrets, or rituals specific to a particular Druidic Order.) This type of open, trusting situation does occur in some places, as described by a survey respondent who wrote:

> *"I lead a group of Druids in the Minneapolis area who gather in public parks for rituals and post photo & video to social media. Our goal is to raise awareness of Druidry, demonstrating that our brand is not sinister or covert, and contribute to the normalization of Druidry and Paganism. This part of Minnesota is very progressive and many people are civil and polite. Because of this, we have not been harassed and feel relatively safe. We always extend an open invitation to respectful observers and participants."*

Another Druid wrote, in similar vein:

> *"The tendency of those who do not know about Druidry to assume that what I do is dangerous or malevolent. The three most common assumptions, in order of frequency, are that I torture goats (not sure why that animal is chosen, but it is), that I am a Satanist, and that I am interested in making human sacrifices. Since none of these are accurate, I sometimes grow tired of educating people on the realities of my practice when I have important ritual work to do. In those cases, privacy is very beneficial. That being said, I am fairly open about being a Pagan and Druid in public and do not feel that I am threatened very often where I live. There are a very large number of Pagans in this area, and the scholarship and dedication that my way of practicing Druidry requires are generally respected by those I talk to."*

In situations such as these, the worst a Druid risks is the inconvenience of a rude interruption, or a distraction from spiritual practice. The trade-off is in having an opportunity to educate the broader community about the realities of Druidic practice, and to begin the process of normalizing public perceptions of modern Druidry.

In contrast, the vast majority of survey respondents (74%) reported at least some level of concern with privacy and safety in their Druidry practices. The nature of their concerns, and the extent to which those concerns affected their lives and spiritual practices, was addressed in the responses to the open-ended question:

Question:
What (if anything) causes privacy or safety in your Druidry practice to be a matter of concern for you?

The overall level of concern for privacy and safety in the practice of Druidry varied little from place to place. However, when I coded the different

Level of Privacy Concern

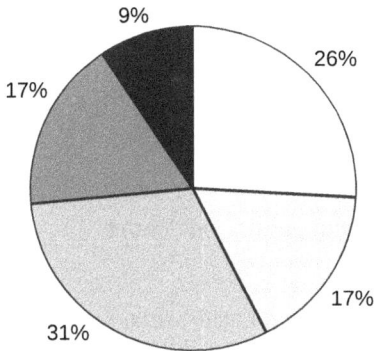

9%

26%

17%

17%

31%

Legend

■ Major   □ Almost None

■ Moderate   □ None

□ Minor

Privacy & Safety Concerns of Modern Druids

Cause of Concern	%**
General Shyness	30%
Fear of Discrimination	19%
Fear of Harassment	17%
Fear of Assault	8%
Fear of Disruptions	8%
Preference for Solitude	6%
Environmental Fears	4%

**Percentages are of all 725 Druids.

types of concern, and analyzed them separately, pronounced international variations began to emerge. Aside from the two people who mentioned secrecy as their primary concern, all cited reasons for concern about privacy or safety fell into one of seven categories (see table, and pie-chart, above).

The most prevalent causes of concern were a general sense of shyness, a fear of being harassed by passers-by, and a fear of discrimination or persecution within the local community. Less prevalent, but still of significant concern were fears of physical violence or hate-crimes, fear of disruptions to ongoing rituals, and a general preference for solitude. A number of Druids also expressed concerns about the environment, either dangers to themselves posed by elements of the wild, or harm that might come to the natural world, due to ritual elements gone awry.

Each of these causes of privacy and safety concern is worthy of separate discussion, both to provide an in-depth description of what is included in each category, and to examine the international variations in the relative prevalence of each concern. I will address each, in turn, in order from least to most worrisome.

A Preference for Solitude

The least worrisome reason that Druids gave for wanting privacy while engaged in spiritual practices was a simple preference for solitude. For these people, there was no real worry or concern, just a preference for keeping private, personal matters private and personal. Examples of responses that fell into this category included:

> *"I suppose I find my religion to be a private affair between myself and the universe, so other than sharing with like-minded people, I tend to be very reserved about sharing details of my religion with those outside of it."*

> *"What happens sometimes is personal gnosis and doesn't apply to others."*

> *"Privacy is necessary for self reflection and meditation, which are some of my core beliefs and practices. To me, to be alone with nature is to be one with it."*

> *"My study and practice are quiet and solitary. I have no need to keep it a secret or anything, it's just something I keep to myself."*

> *"I am deeply private about my spiritual practices, so I prefer to be alone and unobserved when I undertake rituals and meditation. If there were a group of practicing Druids in my area, I might work with them occasionally, but I would still prefer to practice primarily alone."*

Others in this category were simply conscious of wanting to maintain a clear separation between personal, spiritual practices, and public ritual performances, for example:

> *"Spirituality has always been a private thing for me so I don't feel the need to publicly display symbols, nor to perform public rituals."*

> *"Privacy is important for me for my rituals, it is a personal choice/decision. I would like to practice in the forest, or at least in one of our parks full of trees but I don't do it because these places are public and I have no interest in people watching my rituals or ceremonies."*

> *"I see my Druidic practice as being a private engagement in personal spiritual disciplines. While I don't generally assume that anyone would necessarily bother me, I prefer to engage in these practices outside of watching eyes."*

This preference for quiet and solitude during spiritual practice was mentioned by 6% of survey respondents, and was relatively evenly distributed throughout the world.

Fear of Disruptions

The second reason Druids gave for wanting privacy in their practice was a concern that the presence of onlookers might disturb or distract them from their spiritual work. In such cases, there was no fear of potential danger posed by onlookers, but rather, a perceived risk of interruptions while engaged in meditations, visualizations, and other energy work requiring deep focus and careful attention. Examples of responses in this category included:

> *"No safety concerns, but I consider privacy necessary to avoid distractions (people talking outside the circle of celebration, mobile phones ringing, passersby taking photos, etc)."*

> *"Being interrupted during meditations or solo ceremonies while out in public. Both annoying, and in the case of meditation, disorientating."*

> *"There have been abundant questions I will say, mostly as to what I'm doing and why. I prefer to do so in my own space, as the explanation is either long and disturbs the work, or becomes vague and brings further queries."*

> *"I don't feel unsafe as a practicing Druid; however, I am less likely to practice in an outdoor space where I feel that I may be observed, as this can affect how I connect with the earth, and the energy that I give and receive."*

> *"Meer zorgen over privacy dan veiligheid. Voelt niet prettig om in een publiek stuk natuur een ceremonie te houden - je moet dan je omgeving managen ipv. dat je concentreert op je doel.*
> [Translation:]
> *More about privacy than security. It doesn't feel good to hold a ceremony in a public piece of nature – you have to manage your environment instead of concentrating on your goal."*

These kinds of concerns were cited by 8% of Druid respondents, also evenly distributed throughout the world.

General Shyness

Many Druids (30% of respondents) expressed concerns about being observed — and possibly judged — by strangers, or unsympathetic friends and family, while engaged in Druidic practices and rituals. Most of these Druids expressed worries about what others might think of them, a concern related to their personal discomfort when in the presence of others. They wrote, for example:

> *"I tend to feel more self-conscious than I ought to when depositing gifts outdoors, meditating outdoors, praying aloud to nature spirits, etc."*

> *"Privacy is important for solitary rituals so your actions are not misinterpreted as sheer lunacy."*

> *"The biggest concern for me is that my connection to Druidry is not ancestral (I am a person of color.) and so I'm concerned about people judging me for that. The second consideration is most of the people I associate with are either Christian (nominally or otherwise) or agnostic/atheist."*

> *"[My] garden is a little overlooked by other homes. This can inhibit ritual practice. Social media use is also a concern. In addition to Druidry I also attend a church and church groups. I feel some of my Christian friends may not be accepting of my Druidry. So I worry about my mix of Pagan and Christian friends on social media and being 'outed'. My Pagan friends are very accepting of my various spiritual practices."*

> *"I live and work in what is still a 'man man's world' in which men do not think that much about their deeper relationship to Nature (let alone scribe poetry from spirit words whispered on the wind). No, here men grunt a lot and talk about huntin', fishin', and trucks. Closed conservative ways are slowly loosening up here, but [...] I feel that it is still too soon to be too open about my spiritual practice or poetic works and roots."*

In other cases, the concern was primarily for the potential discomfort of others, when observing practices which they did not understand — practices which those others may have been taught to fear as potentially evil or dangerous. Examples of such responses included:

*"No real safety concern for myself, however, if I were to
bring someone into a public gathering, I would be
worried about their comfort level based on my own
experience with the public."*

*"I'm living temporarily in the home of my friend's parents
and I believe at least one of them would be uncomfortable
knowing I was carrying out rituals in my bedroom."*

*"I am careful not to wear the kind of 'traditional' robes I
see in British groups. White-hooded white people in the
USA make people think of the KKK."*

For all responses in this "general shyness" category, the concern was
for the thoughts or unspoken judgements of others, and did not include any
kind of concrete, harmful action or intent. There were no differences in the
prevalence of shyness in any of the Druid subgroups.

Fear of Harassment

Fear of harassment, that is, a fear of being confronted with angry,
threatening, or unkind words, should others discover that one is a practicing
Druid, was a concern reported by 17% of Druids. Unlike the vague worries
expressed in the "general shyness" category, these fears were typically grounded
in experience. Many Druids reported having been harassed about their Druidry
practices in the past, and wishing to avoid further harassment. Others had directly observed other people in their communities being harassed about their
religious beliefs, and feared becoming the next target.

Three subcategories were evident in the responses that fell into this
"harassment" category. The first was the irritation caused by proselytizing
Christians, for example:

*"I was raised in a fairly strict religious Christian house-
hold so there's always the small feeling that I'm doing a
bad thing and blahblahblah. My brother and sister-in-law
leave fundamentalist Christian tracts on my bedside table
when I visit, which I do find amusing. Somehow
pamphlets will keep me from the fires of Hell, I guess."*

*"There are still people who are intolerant of different
religious and spiritual paths, especially in the middle of
the USA. I experience frequent proselytizers in my
community when I wear Neopagan jewelry and garments
(logo t-shirts included). This has caused me to scale back
somewhat how open I am with my faith."*

> *"There are a fair* [number] *of evangelical Christians in my area. I don't fear for my safety so much as I would rather not be 'witnessed' to, or be told I'm going to burn for eternity for denying the gospel."*

The second subcategory was a concern about being scorned or loudly and publicly ridiculed for the simple fact of being a Druid, for example:

> *"The people of no-faith around me are frequently and loudly contemptuous of faith/spiritual traditions. These comments are aimed at dominant culture religions (Christianity, mostly) but I am afraid if I were open about my Druidry they would lose respect for me."*

> *"People are not used to vivid and profound spirituality. I have been gifted with some psychic abilities and I practice Druidry and Shamanism. It* [must seem] *too exotic, weird, irrational and un-modern,* [because] *I have been accused of being mentally ill, antisocial, etc."*

> *"More than anything, it's the disdain that people seem to have for any sort of Pagan practice; most just roll their eyes and tell me I won't be practicing in a few years. That makes me not want to share with anybody."*

Finally, there were fears of verbal threats and bullying, for example:

> *"I do not want my work colleagues to have knowledge of my practices for fear of ridicule and bullying."*

> *"There are a lot of bigots in the area but mostly they verbally harass* [people]. *Physical violence is not a major concern."*

> *"I live at home with my parents still, and they have been openly hostile to religion and spiritual practices."*

> *"Since, where I live, people have little (or no) experience of other religions, it's not unusual for people to call the authorities when they see something going on that is unfamiliar to them."*

> *"We get the occasional, semi-threatening message on our Grove Facebook and whatnot."*

Fear of harassment was reported in all areas of the world, however, it was more prevalent in the United States (20% of United States Druids reported fear of harassment, versus 14% of Druids in other countries).[4]

Fear of Discrimination & Persecution

The next major category of concern with respect to privacy and safety among Druids was a fear of discrimination or persecution within their broader communities. Druids were worried that they would be subjected to harmful and unkind actions such as: shunning or exclusion from community activities; gossip or public shaming leading to loss of a job, business, or professional reputation; vandalism of personal property; and separation from or endangerment of their children. In two cases, the worries about persecution were related to official government policies of repression. Overall, concerns about religious discrimination and persecution were cited by 19% of respondents. As with the above-mentioned fears of harassment, these fears were grounded in realities that had been directly observed, or experienced.

Four subcategories were evident in the responses in this "discrimination and persecution" grouping, the first of which was a general sense of social exclusion or shunning. Druids wrote, for example:

> *"Opposition from the community through negative media, subtle discrimination, and resistance to public activities. Religious freedom holds strongly enough in this area (in urban, northeastern USA) that no one is actively protesting our events or attacking practitioners, but Pagans and Pagan events are usually treated with disdain, being ignored or excluded from advertising, discouraged from public spaces, and disfavored in private organizations (e.g. Prayer Breakfasts or Day of Faith). Part of this is not having a physical presence, i.e. real-estate, to meet the usual category of 'religion', but some is a religious directive to oppose Paganism and Witchcraft whenever possible. Individual members sometimes ask not to be named in media or depicted, because of possible repercussions in employment, domestic relations (e.g. adoption or custody issues) or family relationships."*

> *"I converted to Islam many years ago, and my wife is Muslim. Actively practicing the rituals we practice as Druids would take me outside of Islam, in the Islamic religion's view. I do privately practice these rituals. They [are] my path of spiritual practice now. If I were to do this openly, my wife would be put under tremendous pressure by her family and Muslim community to divorce me."*

*"We are definitely afraid of being ostracized by
community organizations, such as 4H, if it were known
we were not Christian."*

*"I want to adopt children in the future. Pagans don't
always get cleared to foster or adopt."*

*"I am weary of being outcast and isolated because of this,
although I am mostly solitary anyway."*

The second subcategory involved fears of job loss, or harm to one's
professional reputation and work opportunities, due to prejudices against non-
mainstream religions. Examples of this included the following:

*"I am a public school teacher and the community is not
open to Druidry due to a Christian Fundamentalist
mentality. They think I am practicing or working with evil
or Devil worship. There was an issue at my old school
where, because I read Harry Potter, they thought I was
teaching Witchcraft and found ways to get me in trouble."*

*"Não é uma prática aceite na universidade em geral, espaço
onde eu desenvolvo o meu trabalho e pode ser um motivo
para me descredibilizarem.
[Translation:]
It is not an accepted practice in the university in general,
a place where I develop my work, and so it can be a
reason to be discredited."*

*"The default in my area is evangelical Christianity, with
no shortage of fundamentalists. My main concern is for
my livelihood. As a physician, I have little doubt that my
patient volume would fall."*

*"I was ridiculed (repeatedly) in a previous job after I
shared with another staff member that I followed a Druid
path. This person mentioned this scoffingly, to discredit
me in important business meetings when I was not present
to reply. (I heard from another party, who was present.)"*

*"I am working on my doctorate in clinical psychology. In
my field there is quite a bit of scientific orthodoxy [against
having a] Pagan worldview, especially [that of] a magic-
using polytheist. I am concerned, based on some
comments from professors, that being too open about my
practice could lead to gatekeeping and questioning my
fitness to practice."*

The third subcategory pertained to the physical safety and emotional well-being of Druids' children, should it be discovered that the parents of those children were Druids. This included the potential for the children being targeted by school bullies, or by extended family and child "welfare" services personnel who, convinced of the evil of a parent's Druidic beliefs, might try to separate children from their parents. Examples of such responses included:

> "My youngest child goes to a Church of England school
> (the only school in my neighbourhood), and I fear
> hostility and discrimination, especially for my children.
> The school has already [called] social services on us, and
> I believe they may not have [done so] if our beliefs were
> different."

> "I am currently a public-school teacher, and work at a
> school with a lot of conservative families who might
> persecute me or my kids if they knew I was practicing
> Druidry. I also don't talk about my practice with my
> in-laws for the same reason. I'm worried they will give
> my husband a hard time, or try to evangelize my kids."

> "Threats to have my child taken away for exposure to
> what people judge as an evil craft. Having my child
> ostracized because of Druidry."

> "Where I live, if I were to publicly flaunt it, I know the
> Muslim community would target me with rude comments
> and racism, as I saw it happen to my children in the
> school system. I had to quickly teach my children to keep
> it private and not talk about our beliefs at school."

> "Nederland is een open en vrij land met een vrijheid op
> religie en vrij meningsuiting. Echter in een dorp gaan
> verhalen snel in de rondte. Ik wil niet dat mijn kinderen erop
> aangekeken worden, of gepest worden omdat ik met
> paganisme bezig ben.
> [Translation:]
> The Netherlands is an open and free country with freedom
> of religion and free speech. However, in a village stories
> circulate quickly. I don't want my children to be looked at,
> or bullied for being Pagan."

Finally, there were two situations in which government actions to suppress pagan religions were the cause of concern, rather than random actions of neighbors or co-workers:

"There is 'The law on protecting the religious feelings' in Russia which is a matter of concern for me."

"Living in a Christian country that frowns upon anything connected with the Occult, certain aspects of my belief may be seen as 'evil'. Obeah is practiced here, but definitely in private, and in the 6 months I have been here I haven't met anyone who would admit to practicing Paganism. Had any Occult material been found in my belongings when we moved over at the beginning of 2018, we could have faced a large fine or deportation (I left a lot of books behind in the UK, and had to do some strategic packing for the ones I wasn't sure about!)."

It is interesting to note that more Druids, worldwide, were concerned about discrimination and persecution than were concerned about harassment and verbal abuse. As with harassment, the fear of discrimination and persecution was also more prevalent in the United States (20% of United States Druids, versus 17% of Druids in other countries).[5] On a happier note, Druids in the British Isles were significantly less likely to be concerned about religious discrimination and persecution (4% versus 21% for other parts of the world).[6]

Fear of Physical Violence

Hate crimes, physical attacks, or other acts of violence perpetrated by those ignorant or intolerant of Druidic beliefs and practices were mentioned as a privacy and safety concern by 8% of world Druids. For some, this concern was driven by the angry tenor of modern-day discourse and social interactions, for example:

"People are so divisive and angry and feel so entitled to dictate who and how others must be, and to use violence to enforce that."

"Lack of acceptance for non-Christian religious practices is a real issue where I live. Protestors and threats of violence have occurred at public events near by, so it's something we consciously pay attention to."

"There are enough angry, vehement Christians around here who find other faiths threatening that I have safety concerns."

For others, the concern was due to the prevalence of hostile, threatening and intimidating behaviors by weapon-wielding Christians:

"The Evangelical Christians in the region where I live occupy a position of political and social dominance, and are becoming increasingly radicalized with time. Many are heavily armed with military-style weapons and are openly and aggressively hostile to non-Christians."

"Although technically illegal, some dominant Christians (who oddly enough think they're victims) like to impose their beliefs on people who are of different religions, sometimes with great cruelty. Because of this risk, being too overt about my Druidic practice seems somewhat dangerous."

"Armed Christian Dominionists claiming their god gives them the right to suppress and even kill unbelievers who do not submit to them. (No different from Islamists.)"

Finally, a number of people expressed deep concerns regarding the potential for violent physical attacks, due to prior attacks against members of minority religions, which had happened within their local communities, for example:

"I'm in the Bible Belt. [...] Our neighbors are conservative Christians, some belonging to religious right wing groups, and would not look kindly upon our faith. (I'm on a committee in town that is tracking hate group movement with the Southern Poverty Law Center, and I know for a fact that there is a small cluster of hate group members within 1/2 mile of where I live). There have been various hate incidents in our area for non-Christians (including the recent bombing of the Jewish Synagogue in Pittsburgh) and it's not a good thing to stand out as something else. We try to be open, as we are both leaders in the Druid community, but there are various levels of openness. We don't have anything overtly Druid or Pagan outside of our home, but we do have a grove tucked in the woods. It's a serious concern here."

"I still own the farm I grew up on and it is precious to me. I have concerns that there could be nut jobs that would burn the house or otherwise vandalize the farm if they found I am no longer Christian. My experience is 90+% of Christians aren't Christian."

"Some police are poorly educated in matters of religion and have a reputation for violence. Members of the public may call the police with outlandish claims and the police act without first checking facts."

"O preconceito religioso, que na minha cidade é latente, especialmente por parte dos cristãos. Nos últimos 3 anos alguns santuários de religiões de matriz africana foram destruídos criminalmente.
[Translation:]
The religious prejudice, which in my city is latent, especially on the part of Christians. In the last 3 years some sanctuaries of African religions have been criminally destroyed."

"People have been murdered in this country for adherence to Pagan spiritual practices."

In addition, several female Druids reported a fear of physical harm by men, who might prey on women they discovered alone and unprotected in the out-of-doors, for example:

"You never know when someone is potentially going to freak out if they think you're a 'witch,' and get all fundamentalist on you, or, if you're out alone in nature, potentially harm you. That is a risk anyway if you're a woman, but perceiving someone as a 'witch' or as 'doing weird things' out in public could be enough of an excuse for someone inclined towards malfeasance anyway."

"I do worry about being a woman alone going out to camp in public forest land, where people go four wheel driving and riding motorbikes a lot. Generally I walk in forest but stick to camping on private land, my own or someone else's. I also worry about going out into certain areas of forest by myself by day. Here at home I do have neighbours and cars going by so I stick to more wooded areas of our land to wear my cloak, etc."

"As a woman, I am currently afraid to go out into the woods alone. The news is filled with stories of women getting assaulted, kidnapped, or murdered just while they are out running or hiking. In our local news, we've had two women recently assaulted in our local parks. I've asked my husband to come with me and sit at a distance while I work with trees, and that has been nice, but we need to make time for that on weekends as he works late on weekdays. If I do my practice on my own, I stay close to home or use my inner grove inside the safety of my house."

Fear of physical violence was reported by 8% of survey respondents. Druids in the United States and Druids in Brazil were both more likely to report this fear (11% in both the USA and Brazil, versus 6% for the rest of the world).[7]

Environmental Fears & Concerns

The final category of concern for privacy and safety in the practice of Druidry pertained not to interactions with other people, but to interactions with the natural environment. For some, who live in areas that are still quite wild, the concern was for the safety of Druids, given the very real dangers posed by the untamed, natural world around them. Examples of this type of response included:

> *"In the mountains where I go to see Oaks, [there] are mountain lions and bears."*

> *"My Druidry practice often takes me to bushland where I need to be mindful of typical bushwalking hazards, and some concerns regarding wildlife, mainly snakes."*

> *"Cold temperatures and high winds are considerations [...], especially ice and snow conditions. [...] We are usually indoors to prevent hypothermia or frostbite."*

For others, the environmental dangers were not due to nature, but the built, urban environment in which they lived, as some Druids explained:

> *"I am concerned about [...] people with mobility issues as it's an older building with no handicapped access."*

> *"Safe practice, i.e. lighting fire, incense and extinguishing safely, trip hazards etc."*

> *"General safety concerns of living in an urban setting."*

Finally, several Druids expressed concerns regarding potential harm to people or to nature, caused by elements of ritual gone awry, for example:

> *"High fire danger area with stressed trees."*

> *"Safety more than privacy: we use fire, after all, and frequently hold rituals near open water. Ritual garb needs to be safe around candles. Be careful when making oil or alcoholic offerings to the fire. Things like that."*

"Safety - with children and a cat I have to be careful with candles, incense etc. "

Concerns about dangers emanating from, or posed to, the natural environment was the least-common cause of concern. It was cited by only 4% of Druids, and did not vary noticeably with differences in geography.

As so many other new religious movements have done throughout history, Druidry now faces significant challenges due to the repressive words and actions of the world's mainstream religions and dominant culture. These effects are most pronounced in the United States, which no doubt accounts for the anomalously low response rate to the *World Druidry Survey*. However, despite these challenges, Druidry is still growing rapidly. What remains to be seen is how it is growing, and how it is developing as a new world religion.

Modern Druids at Home

Considering the safety and privacy concerns that most Druids have about their communities, it should come as no surprise that most Druids arrange either to live alone, or to share their homes only with people tolerant of Druidry. According to the survey results (see bar-chart and table on page 45), 85% of Druids share their home with housemates or children. Only 4% of respondents have housemates that *"are unaccepting and disrespectful of my religious/ spiritual beliefs and practices (or would be, if they knew)."* Most of these Druids are young adults, who have not yet left their parents' homes. Twelve percent of Druids reported living with people who *"tolerate my religious/ spiritual beliefs and practices, with some sense of forbearance or trepidation."* The rest live among children and adults who are either accepting and respectful of Druidry, or are themselves Druids.

Of the 617 Druids who reported having housemates or children living at home, the majority (55%) indicated that the presence of those housemates had no effect on their personal practice of Druidry. The rest described one or more of the following effects: needing to exercise discretion regarding what, if anything, a Druid allows his or her housemates and children to observe; limiting or abandoning certain aspects of Druidry practice; thinking more deeply about Druidry, in order to be able to explain it more clearly to others, and; making the most of opportunities to teach others about Druidry.

Exercising Discretion in Druidry Practice

No matter how Druid-tolerant or Druid-friendly their housemates might be, 34% of Druids with housemates still thought it necessary to keep their practices and sacred objects subdued or out of sight. In part, this was due to a desire to secure privacy and quiet for Druidry practices; in part, it was due to a desire to minimize any inconvenience or irritation posed to others.

For most Druids, exercising discretion merely entailed scheduling practices and formal rituals for times when housemates were asleep or away from home, for example:

> *"I have to work around my toddler's schedule as I am a stay at home parent."*

> *"I normally practice when my teenaged daughter is at school or out. Only sometimes when she is home but in another room. It's a distraction from my end, not hers."*

> *"I do my meditation early in the morning. This suits me as the house is quiet and it means that others don't have to [be] quiet whilst going about their day's activities."*

In other cases, Druids sought alternate venues for their practices, to avoid the issue of disturbing or being disturbed by housemates. Most frequently, they

The Most Prevalent Types of Druid Housemates

n=363

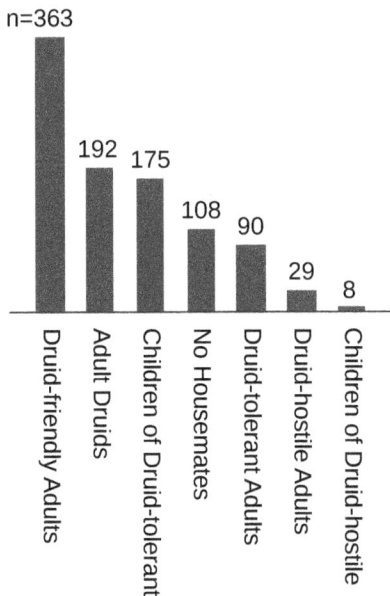

Bar chart values: Druid-friendly Adults (363), Adult Druids (192), Children of Druid-tolerant (175), No Housemates (108), Druid-tolerant Adults (90), Druid-hostile Adults (29), Children of Druid-hostile (8)

Effects of Housemates and Children on Druidry

Effect	%**
Forces me to be discrete.	34%
Limits my Druidry practice.	6 %
Causes me to think deeply.	6 %
Lets me teach non-Druids.	4 %

**Percentages are of the 617 Druids with housemates & children.*

moved their practices to outdoor spaces like gardens or parks, or wild areas such as forests or mountaintops. They wrote, for example:

> *"My wife is not a Druid, but is supportive. I mostly practice outside in my little part of the garden or in my office/sanctuary, where I keep my altars and shrines."*

> *"Je ritualise quand je suis seul à la maison ou lorsque je me promène en foret.*
> [Translation:]
> *I perform rituals when I am alone at home, or while I walk in the forest."*

> *"[I] find that even when [I] ask [my] husband to be left alone, he will walk in ('Oh sorry, forgot.'), or pop his head in to ask a question! I found when I did my Druid self-initiation and went outside at night for a couple of hours onto our front deck, he did understand to leave me alone, but when I'm indoors during the day, or just in another room he can't see that it will hurt to just pop in and out occasionally."*

When neither of these choices was possible, Druids adapted their Druidry practices and rituals, to make them quieter, tamer, or less obvious to the non-Druids sharing their space. Examples of this type of response included:

> *"I am by necessity very private and somewhat toned-down in my practice. I carry out my practices in whispers, and* [I don't use] *incense at present. I only have a very small, very discrete altar up, which is unusual for me."*

> *"My faith is understood, however ceremony has had to be scaled down due to their qualms. I don't begrudge as this isn't only my home, but the extent I can practice is certainly constrained - something I hope to change."*

> *"Rituals tend to be small, short and quiet."*

At times, when even this approach was insufficient, Druids opted to focus on inner work and contemplative practices rather than on overt ceremonies, as Druids explained:

> *"[It] has changed my personal ritual practice from one that's more concrete and experiential to one that's more meditative."*

> *"I practice in solitude, mostly in my mind (inner grove, astral temple) or outside. I also keep my experiences to myself."*

> *"I have to do more internal work and less open ritual."*

Another common act of discretion is to keep obviously Druidic art, ritual tools, and altars tucked away in unobtrusive corners, or hidden away in private rooms of the house, for example:

> *"In our home, my wife and I tend not to have overtly Druid (or Pagan) material on open display. It avoids awkward situations with visitors or family who do not share our views or who might feel threatened by them."*

> *"I don't leave things (like an altar) out. They're organized in drawers, and pulled out as needed. [...] My partner is accepting and respectful. He even accepted the altar and such as being visually nice to have. [But] others who come through, (the housekeeper who comes weekly, the garden help, locals who come to repair or modify things) are almost all Evangelicals. I hide things so that I don't have to talk to them about it."*

> *"My altar is tucked away on top of a desk in the attic, whereas if I shared my living space with other Druids (or spiritually-inclined people) I would probably have it in the main living area. I would probably also have more relevant objects and artworks displayed around the house."*

While these techniques for exercising discretion in Druidry practice do change the outward expression of Druidry, they do not necessarily limit the spiritual essence of Druidry practice, as one Druid explained:

> *"I don't do* [formal] *ritual if anyone else is at my house, but Druidry is a way of life for me, an attitude that I carry with me all the time."*

However, for some, the obstacles posed by housemates was more limiting.

Limitations on Druidry Practice

For a small number of Druids (5%), the presence of non-Druids in their homes was such a hindrance that they severely curtailed their Druidry practices, or abandoned formal practice entirely. Some indicated that this was due to a perceived need to keep their Druidry secret, for example:

> "I have actively kept my practice a secret. Other than the tree of life necklaces I keep wearing and buying and my plants there is nothing about me or my living space that says 'Druid'. I feel unable to celebrate the holidays, and have [resigned] myself to reading about Druidry solely through online sources so there is no physical evidence to be found. [...] I would love to sign up for the [OBOD] course, or even just check out a couple books from the library, but I don't want my parents to happen across these materials and confront me about it. Not until I'm ready to deal with whatever they'll say."

> "It's really taken a toll. When I lived alone I worked and studied hard at Druidry. I do not celebrate hardly at all now that I have to share space."

> "I feel that I can't practice any ritual because it would be weird to them."

Others cited the competing goals of wanting to spend time with family or housemates, and wanting to spend time in solitary, spiritual practice:

> "Sometimes I find it hard to find time to study/practice between work and spending time with my partner."

> "None other than family time taking precedence on some occasions."

> "My husband is accepting of my practices, but I feel a need to balance out my spiritual time with non-spiritual, relational time. On my own, I tend to be very devoted to rituals, but I can't always do that and maintain my relationship obligations."

Learning & Encouragement from non-Druids

In direct contrast to those who felt stifled by their housemates, an equal number of Druids (5%) reported that non-Druids at home were a source of support and encouragement. They wrote, for example:

> "My partner was raised Christian but has practiced Paganism. She is not Druid, but actively encourages my daily practice."

> *"My wife often wants to join in, and she encourages me in practicing ritual because she particularly likes the effect it has on me. She also notes that 'things seem to go well when I am connected'. She also likes the other Druids with whom I practice. This makes ritual mostly very easy to do and she is happy to be the liaison with the neighbours on 'neighbourhood issues', so I am blessed."*

> *"My wife accepts my practice and is encouraging that I explore my beliefs even though she does not share them."*

In several cases, non-Druid housemates provided the Druid with opportunities for blended practice and spiritual exploration, for example:

> *"Surprisingly enough, this has influenced my practice in a positive way. I recently moved in with my girlfriend, who is pursuing a Yogic brand of spirituality, and not only is she supportive of my own path (while she doesn't share all of its tenets, and definitely acknowledges the things she finds 'weird'), she actively encourages me to pursue it, and even works with me to develop shared practices, like deepening my meditation, etc. We share a room dedicated to our spiritualities, with a yoga mat, both of our incense/crystals, an altar, my accoutrements for Wheel of the Year ceremonies, and my Druid books."*

> *"Wonderfully. My mate is a Sundancer and pipe carrier, and we often create blended rituals where I call in the directions and create a circle, Wren leads the water ceremony or pipe ceremony, I bring in my Druidic elements, and we close the circle."*

> *"My husband [...] is very respectful and supportive and shares my belief that I am a Druid, but he is not a Druid. He is a Bard, but does not believe that being a Bard is a step toward becoming a Druid. He is an actor, a singer, a musician, has [...] degrees in Theater, but he does not feel energy like I do. He knows an incredible amount of lore and history and, as I am reading and studying more about Druidry, whenever I come across something I find interesting or intriguing, we'll talk about it. Often, he can add more insight or history to what I've read. He has helped me learn and grow as a Druid."*

Housemates who did not encourage or participate in Druidry often helped Druids develop, as well, by forcing them to think more deeply about their

practices, in order to explain themselves to others in conversation. Examples
of these responses included:

> "Het uitleggen aan anderen wat voor mijn druidisme/
> druiderij inhoudt was waardevol om mijn eigen gedachten
> te structuren.
> [Translation:]
> Explaining to others what my Druidism/Druidry means
> was valuable to structure my own thoughts."

> "Sie ermöglichen mir, mich und meinen Weg immer wie-
> der kritisch zu hinterfragen. Ansonsten sind sie eher
> neugierig.
> [Translation:]
> They enable me to critically question myself and my path
> again and again. Otherwise they are rather curious."

> "She has made me conscious of my beliefs, views and
> methods of working with Druidry, not only in a supporting
> way but also a critical view on things: how real are
> things, is this logic, am I true to myself, etc."

Even hostile, non-Druid housemates occasionally had a positive effect on the
pursuit of Druidry, by way of negative example — as one Druid explained:

> "The Christian holidays (such as Easter and Christmas)
> are practiced in my house, and during these times I
> always feel so frustrated and annoyed because I have to
> watch my parents celebrate and decorate the house [and
> observe] traditions of food and [gift-giving.] The spiritual
> reasons behind [these holidays] have been neglected, and
> [the holidays have become] over-commercialized. [...]
> This is why I prefer to celebrate the natural occurrences
> in the wheel of the year, because they honour the very
> earth we stand on as well as those who came before us,
> human or not. It feels much more tangible and sincere."

Most responses in this section on *Learning & Encouragement from
non-Druids* also serve to illustrate a theme that emerges repeatedly throughout
the *World Druidry Survey*: a Druidic habit of seeking wisdom everywhere —
even within the words and actions of those skeptical of or hostile to Druidry.
It is one emanation of the cultural norm among Druids to respect, and remain
open to learning from all systems of spiritual practice and religious belief.

Educating non-Druid Housemates and Guests

The final effect of housemates on Druidry involved educating non-Druids about Druidic philosophical principles, practices, and beliefs. For the most part, Druids refused to proselytize, or share information without being asked; however, they would respond to direct questions, as Druids explained:

> *"For adult non-Druids, I make no changes to my personal in-home practices. Since (to me) Druidry is a highly personalized quest for knowledge that is contemplative, experiential, and introspective, if one was to ask a question or inquire about my practice, I would answer them. I [neither] aim to draw in converts, nor [to] recruit people to Druidry."*

> *"I am not evangelical at home or in public. I do not promote my Druidry unless someone is interested, but I also do not hide it at home or in public. I am totally open with my grown children and with my grandchildren."*

> *"Family respectfully tolerate my spiritual beliefs. Though not interested in learning or participating, there is a measure of curiosity. When visiting or staying, discussions are deep and meaningful without any attempt to proselytize. Though Druidry and Shamanism are not mentioned, the principles are discussed and there are occasional moments when it is relevant. Softly, softly is best approach."*

Some were more eager to demystify Druidry, and to normalize perceptions of their practices and beliefs among family and friends. However, even then, it was handled with tact, via casual conversation, or by including friends and family in the more mundane elements of Druidry practice, for example:

> *"When family visits I show them how I 'practice.' I used to tone it down, but no longer do I hide who I am from anyone. But just like anyone, I don't shout out about it at work etc. I do share as others share."*

> *"I always have to make certain people understand what I mean or intend because there is so much misinformation about Druidry in our modern culture."*

> *"For feast days, I do the religious, magical parts myself and later invite guests to a simple ritual they can join in*

*on, such as jumping over a purifying fire and then we
have a big feast and party."*

Both approaches to educating non-Druids support the Druidic habit
of seeking wisdom everywhere — by supporting that habit from the opposite
direction; both approaches allow others to explore Druidry as a prospective
source of wisdom, without in any way pushing the seeker into a particular
system of spiritual practice or belief.

Druidry, with Children

According to *World Druidry Survey* demographics, 25% of practicing
Druids had one or more underage children living at home. As with all other
things when one becomes a parent, Druids with children typically found that
the time, space, and quiet moments of privacy needed for the practice of
Druidry were significantly limited, due to the presence of children in their
lives. They wrote, for example:

> *"[I] have a somewhat feral toddler so plans for a family
> altar are on hold. No personal altar and no time to use it
> if I did (see: toddler)."*

> *"Because I have children it is harder for me to do longer,
> more complicated rituals or journey work. I have to fit my
> religious practice around my family's needs."*

> *"Just timing takes a toll on practices, having 3 active
> teenagers in the house tends to take up a considerable lot
> of my time."*

In addition to these obstacles to personal practice, there is the "baby-proofing"
aspect of life with young children, as Druids explained:

> *"Some adjustments* [must be] *made to ensure personal
> safety of small children: no smudging* [or] *incense burn-
> ing inside, and limiting access to the altar, due to small
> objects."*

> *"Preciso ser mais cuidadoso para evitar incêndios ou
> outros acidentes.*
> [Translation:]
> *I need to be more careful to avoid fires or other
> accidents."*

"I do live with children which limits the placement of dis-
plays/altars to places they cannot be disturbed, but this is
of little consequence - I have to do the same thing with
candy :)"

Despite these difficulties, 86% of Druids with children find ways to
teach elements of Druidry to their children in a manner that is age-appropriate,
safe, and comprehensible to young minds. This is particularly challenging,
given the dearth of Druid parenting resources, and the absence of other Druid
families within the local community, as one Druid parent explained:

"Modern Druidry is still relatively young, and many
adherents are adults (who are often solitary). But it is old
enough now that there are families. Yet there aren't nearly
as many resources geared towards families (although
there are some). This connects to what I said before about
thinking about how to teach children the beliefs and
practices of Druidry. […] It has also caused me to think
about how to present ourselves to the community we live
in. I am pretty introverted and don't have a significant
amount of social interaction. If I was alone I probably
wouldn't have to think much about how I am perceived by
others, but my children will obviously want to be social
and have friends as they are growing up. So it has caused
me to think of the ways it will impact them growing up in
a Druid home [within] *a conservative Christian*
community, and the ways they may have to navigate
friendships and other social interaction. It has also
helped me see some of the ways that the Druid community
could improve in terms of family resources."

Since there does not yet exist a coherent source of educational materials and
parenting advice for raising young Druids, Druids with children have been
forced to think deeply and creatively about how to address this important
issue, on their own.

For 23% of Druid parents, Druidry has merely become the normal
backdrop for life at home, with no special effort made to explicitly teach or
adapt Druidry practices for children or young adults. Altars are visible, rituals
happen, and children are welcome to watch and participate, if and when they
choose to do so — learning primarily by osmosis — as Druids explained:

"I live with my son, who is 6, and […] for him, it is
normal to live with the presence of altars in the house.
It is normal to make prayers and give thanks and make
offerings to ancestors and supportive spirits."

> *"Our son doesn't seem interested in Druidry at all, but he is quite accepting and enjoys sitting around our fires and outdoor rituals."*

> *"Our children have grown naturally with our beliefs. They are welcome to explore any paths that call them."*

Nearly half of Druid parents (45% of them) consciously work to find family-friendly ways of introducing their children to Druidic values, myths and legends, and age-appropriate ritual practices. In some cases, this means thinking about how to simplify practices, to make them more accessible to young people, as they explained:

> *"I have rewritten rituals so my daughter can be included and not be overwhelmed by superfluous pageantry."*

> *"We all celebrate the seasonal festivals with typical crafts, symbols and dishes for each, we teach the children to respect and honour nature and different kinds of people/ belief systems/ religions, we tell them stories, we lead them into religious practice (with silence exercises, prayer, visiting religious places), we teach them songs, we initiate creative processes, we teach them to prepare [meals], and to care for each other."*

> *"My husband watches our son while I do the more religious/spiritual/meditative bits, and then the entire family (and non-Druid friends) participate in the more secular aspects of our seasonal celebrations, such as Yuletide wassailing, Flower Season flower-crown weaving, Fire Season rain dances, etc."*

> *"I often tell them stories from mythology, talk to them about different gods and ancient peoples, nature and the cycles of nature, the aboriginal names for things and teach them meditation. So I feel I am raising them with a Druid understanding."*

> *"Our child participates in our worship rites when she wants to and so we have also adapted them to make them more inclusive for her. Our liturgy when she takes part involves a lot more singing and moving meditations. It's also far shorter."*

Rather than focusing on formal Druid lore and ritual practice, 24% of Druid parents focused on teaching their kids about nature, for example:

"I always feel that I practice Druidry when I explore the garden or any other nature space with my daughter."

"Trying to teach my children the name of plants."

"Discuss general Earth-caring practices with children, and practice (largely) what I preach."

Being Druids, this nature study often took on a spiritual aspect, focused on helping children develop a reverent relationship with the natural world, and helping them to understand the metaphorical aspects of the Wheel of the Year, in terms of the rhythms and cycles of life, as they explained:

"Rather than being quietly in tune with nature and engaging in my own private worship when we are in parks and nearby forests, I realize that I need to be able to talk about and explain things like the Earth Mother, and nature spirits and how to interact with and offer to them."

"I talk about natural history, animism, and similar Druidic themes in daily life."

"When my kids were at home we practiced together. We focused on the wheel of the year and marking the seasons and cyclic changes along with rites of passage."

"We did a lot when they were little to ensure all the festivals of the year were celebrated so they were set up with an understanding of the rhythm of life as it works here."

"Spending time in nature together is very special. We love to garden together and make offerings. My daughter is very sensitive to how we treat nature and Mother Earth as a result of the values I share with her."

For Druids who engaged in more rigorous magical and shamanistic practices, care was taken to keep children away from ritual practices for which they were not yet ready, for example:

"It rarely stops us and in fact, we enjoy teaching them when they show interest however, more private rituals (mainly nudity or complicated debates) are something we keep to ourselves until the right age."

"I avoid evocations of spirits, and have increasingly turned to ancestor-focused prayer. When they're older, I'll reintroduce this."

"I do not perform ritual or magic in front of children."

"Sjamanistisch werk doen we niet in bijzijn van kinderen.
[Translation:]
Shamanic work is not done in the presence of children."

"I don't discuss my unverifiable experiences with him."

Given the often antagonistic attitudes toward Druidry exhibited by members of the wider community, some Druid parents also focused on the need to be seen as exemplary role-models of what Druids are, and ought to be. They wrote, for example:

> *"A presença de crianças e não druidas influencia a minha prática porque existe uma preocupação constante em demonstrar para eles que o que eu faço é bom, é algo de que me orgulho e é algo que eu quero que seja uma referência positiva para todos que me conhecem, logo eu busco aprimorar a mim mesma constantemente para me relacionar melhor com as pessoas, sendo um bom exemplo como mulher e druidesa.*
> [Translation:]
> *The presence of children and non-Druids influences my practice because* [I want] *to show them that what I do is good,* [that it] *is something I am proud of.* [...] *I want to be a positive reference for everyone who knows me, so I try to constantly improve myself to relate better with people, being a good example as a woman and Druidess."*

> *"Mijn kinderen (en die van anderen) zijn een spiegel die laat zien was druiderij wel is en wat niet.*
> [Translation:]
> *My children (and those of others) are a mirror that shows what Druidry is and what it is not."*

In contrast to the parents working to gently teach and share Druidry with their children, there was a second group of parents (27% of Druid parents) who worked just as hard to keep their Druidry hidden from their children — also for their long-term safety and well-being. Two reasons were given for these acts of secrecy. The first was that young children could not be expected to exercise appropriate discretion about Druidry, when in public or when in the presence of intolerant, extended family members. These parents were protecting their children from the potential repercussions of juvenile indiscretion, as several Druid parents explained:

> *"My 5 year old daughter doesn't know that I'm a Druid. I don't speak much about it because I know she will repeat it in public, and to anyone with the purest intentions, and I fear the consequences."*

> *"I try to be respectful of my children, who are not necessarily Druids themselves, and avoid putting them in spot where they might have to defend or explain my beliefs or practices to friends."*

> *"I want to be able to demonstrate and explain it in a more coherent way before I involve my children. The likelihood of the kids* [discussing] *things with potentially hostile in-laws is also a concern. So, for now my Druidic practice stays out of their sight and space."*

The second reason for keeping Druidry from children was the Druid tradition of allowing every individual (including one's own children) to identify and define their own, personal, spiritual path in life. These parents wished to avoid 'brainwashing' their children with Druidry, before those children had a chance to choose their own paths. Examples of their responses included:

> *"I tend to practice behind closed doors or after he goes to bed. It's not really an issue for him. He knows. It's just a matter of respecting his ability to form his own spiritual identity when he is ready for it."*

> *"My husband and I did not practice until our daughter was 9. We felt it would be difficult for her to make her own religious choices if she was raised from infancy, practicing* [Druidry]*."*

> *"I have a child, whom I would never force into any religion, however I am trying to raise her with as much knowledge of all religions so she can make her own, informed choice when she is old enough to choose a path for her own life."*

The final theme that emerged from responses to the question of practicing Druidry with children was the joy of learning and growing as a Druid, as a direct result of practicing with children. This was cited by 13% of Druid parents, for example:

> *"I feel the children are wonderful teachers. They are good 'friends' in celebration, and curiosity, and crafting."*

> *"I have tried to teach my daughter and grandchildren the ways of Druidry. It has opened many avenues that I wouldn't have encountered remaining solitary."*

> *"Having children has made my Druidry complete. I am watching life that was created in the womb of my wife from my seed. My twins (boy and girl) are the reason I am able to comprehend magic as something real and tangible. I am watching it grow and transform little bits of me and my wife into two new people who are unique and brilliant."*

> *"It's made me more aware of seasonal aspects as it's something she can easily join in with."*

> *"Children encouraged me to be more creative and fun with it to encourage their interest. My teenage son now identifies as a Druid too and comes to ceremonies, which encourages me to get to them despite my chronic illness making it challenging."*

While the broader community's influence on Druidry practice was often limited to affecting the extent to which, or the location in which Druidry was practiced, the home life of a Druid often affected the very nature of that practice. It caused Druids to think more carefully about the essential elements of their practices, and about how to communicate that essence to non-Druid adults and children. It caused Druids to simplify their practices, and shift their emphasis away from formal ceremony and ritual, toward more contemplative practices, such as nature study, nature connection, and the celebration of local seasons, particularly when in the presence of others. In doing so, it sowed the seeds for the evolution of Druidry from a simple migration of Celtic cultural and ritual traditions into a global spiritual tradition, more broadly applicable to diverse physical and cultural environments. The specific ways in which geography affects the development of one's personal path of Druidry will be further explored in *Chapter 4: Crafting a Personal Path of Druidry.*

CHAPTER 3 NOTES & REFERENCES

1 For an explantation of this calculated statistic, please see *Chapter 2: Making Sense of the Stories.*

2 This difference in the percent of maximum possible importance attributed to Celtic language, culture, and tradition (51% for Druids of non-Celtic heritage versus 60% for Druids overall) was statistically significant with p = 0.00

3 This difference in the percent of maximum possible importance attributed to Celtic language, culture, and tradition (45% for AODA members versus 60% for Druids overall) was statistically significant with p = 0.00

4 20% of Americans fear harassment, versus 14% for Druids in other countries, this difference is statistically significant with p = 0.01

5 20% of Americans fear discrimination or persecution, versus 17% for Druids in other countries, this difference is statistically significant with p = 0.00

6 4% of Druids resident in the British Islands fear discrimination or persecution, versus 21% for Druids in other parts of the world, this difference is statistically significant with p = 0.00

7 11% of Druids in the USA and Brazil feared physical violence, versus 6% for the rest of the world. This difference was only statistically significant at a 96% confidence level (p = 0.04), however, I felt the need to mention it because the severity of this fear has such a profound effect on Druidry practice.

CHAPTER 4:
CRAFTING A PERSONAL PATH OF DRUIDRY

How does one become a Druid? Until recently, there were very few modern-day Druid families in which a child might be raised within a Druidic tradition. Most Druids came to it on their own, as adults. But how? As we saw in the preceding chapter, Druids generally do not proselytize; in fact, most Druids make a conscious effort to avoid influencing the spiritual journeys of others — unless answering a direct question. There are no Druid temples, churches, synagogues, or mosques, no obvious ceremonial locations at which to pick up a leaflet about the religion, or to learn about its central practices and beliefs. Druidry has no canonical sacred text akin to the *Bible, Torah, Vedas*, or *Koran*. So, how do those new to Druidry learn about Druidry? What factors influence them and help them to define their spiritual paths?

Six questions in the *World Druidry Survey* focused on this issue. The first was a rating-scale response question, listing a wide variety of possible sources of inspiration and information, and asking Druids to decide the extent to which each had inspired them, or helped them shape and define their personal paths of Druidry. Response options ranged from *not an influence* to a *major influence.* At the end of the list, there was a space available for Druids to list and rate the relative importance of any other influencing factors, which had played a role in their spiritual development but had not already been included in the survey question.

Five open-ended questions probed for additional detail regarding several major sources of potential influence. These questions asked about the influence, if any, of: Druidry group affiliations; Druidry group curricula; books, media, and other online resources; myths, legends, and traditional tales from various world cultures; and the natural and cultural environments in which individual Druids lived and studied. The responses to these six questions, taken together, begin to paint a vivid picture of how most modern Druids learn to be Druids.

Factors Influencing Druids' Spiritual Paths

An overview of the factors influencing Druids' spiritual paths, and their relative importance to the developing spiritual paths of world Druids is presented in the graphic on the facing page. The percentages listed next to each factor are the "percent of maximum possible influence" (MPI) scores described in *Chapter 2: Making Sense of the Stories*.

As can be seen in the graph, by a very wide margin, the most influential factors in Druids' developing practices were direct inspiration from nature, and direct inspiration from spirits of nature or place. Inspiration from deities, was the only other external, non-human influence on Druidry. Although deities may seem to be far less influential, the apparent influence gap between spirits of place and deities corresponds to a difference in Druid theology — between those who primarily identify as animists or pantheists, and those who identify primarily as polytheists. Overall, 99% of world Druids were influenced by nature; 97% of world Druids were influenced by spirits of nature or place; and 96% of Druid polytheists were directly influenced by their deities.

The second-most important set of factors were the books and media that Druids read. This included books on Druidry, and books philosophically aligned with Druidry. A detailed analysis of the specific books, authors, and media that Druids found informative and inspirational is presented later in this chapter. Overall, 98% of world Druids reported that books had influenced their personal paths of Druidry.

The third-most important set of factors were related to the Druidry groups to which respondents belonged. This included curriculum materials provided by or recommended by Druidry groups; websites, periodicals and podcasts produced or supported by those Druidry groups; online interactions with Druids via Druid group forums or Facebook; face-to-face interactions with Druids at group-sponsored gatherings; and one-on-one interactions with Druidry mentors or tutors. While these factors were of less importance to most Druids, as compared with direct interactions with nature, spirits of place, deities, and even books, they were at least of minor importance to a majority of survey respondents (between 67% and 90% of world Druids, depending upon the factor).

Some Druids' spiritual paths were also influenced by other, highly personal, and/or localized experiences, such as dreams or past-life memories; ancestral family traditions; and the ancestral traditions of places in which they had lived. These were rated as less important, overall, and included a smaller, but still meaningful proportion of world Druids (between 55% and 75%). The role of ancestors (of all kinds) in Druidry practice is discussed in more detail in *Chapter 5*. The other factors are either quite rare, or very private and personal, and therefore unlikely to vary with Druidry subgroup. No further analysis of these factors is possible, given the limited data at hand.

Extent of Influence on my Druidry Path Caused by...

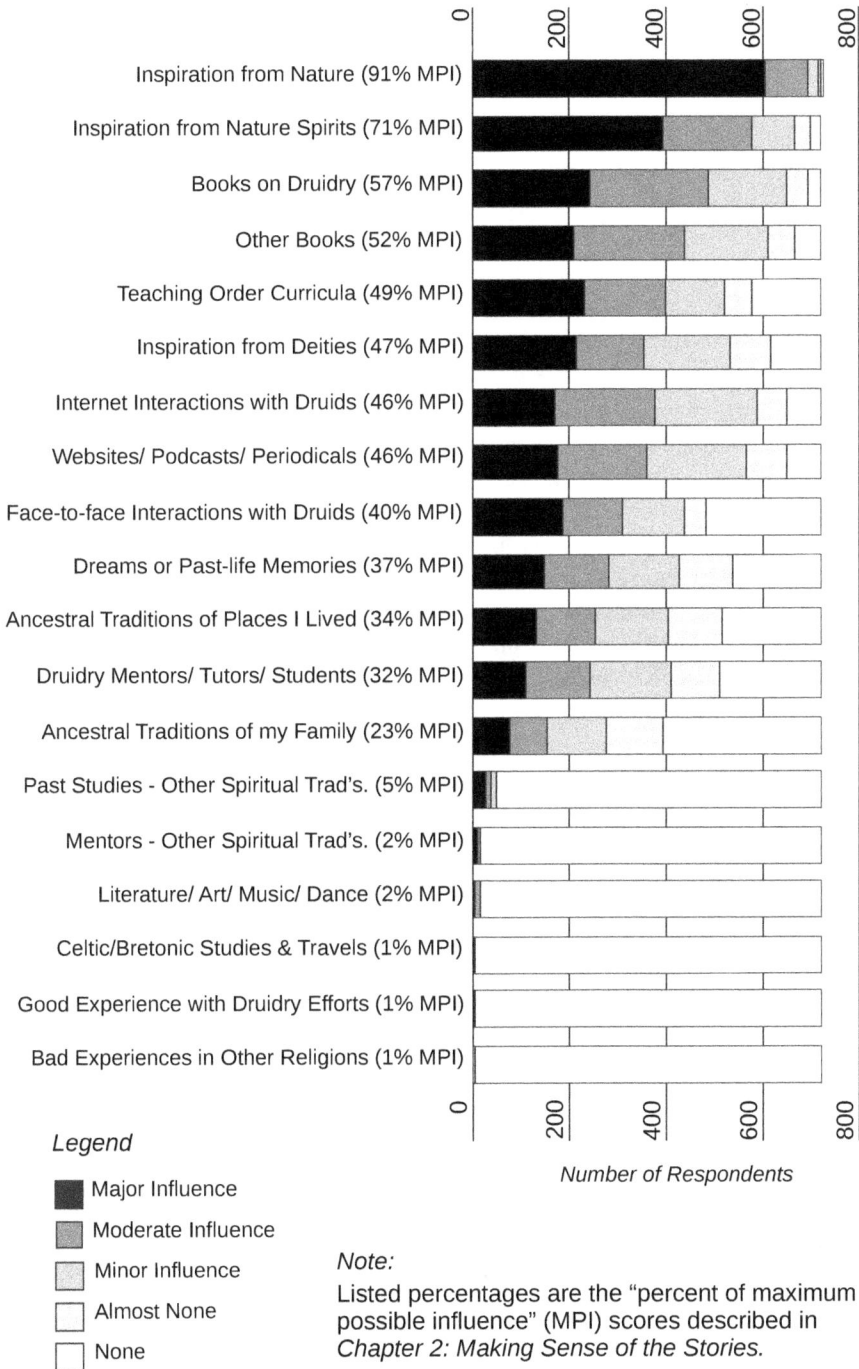

Inspiration from Nature (91% MPI)
Inspiration from Nature Spirits (71% MPI)
Books on Druidry (57% MPI)
Other Books (52% MPI)
Teaching Order Curricula (49% MPI)
Inspiration from Deities (47% MPI)
Internet Interactions with Druids (46% MPI)
Websites/ Podcasts/ Periodicals (46% MPI)
Face-to-face Interactions with Druids (40% MPI)
Dreams or Past-life Memories (37% MPI)
Ancestral Traditions of Places I Lived (34% MPI)
Druidry Mentors/ Tutors/ Students (32% MPI)
Ancestral Traditions of my Family (23% MPI)
Past Studies - Other Spiritual Trad's. (5% MPI)
Mentors - Other Spiritual Trad's. (2% MPI)
Literature/ Art/ Music/ Dance (2% MPI)
Celtic/Bretonic Studies & Travels (1% MPI)
Good Experience with Druidry Efforts (1% MPI)
Bad Experiences in Other Religions (1% MPI)

Number of Respondents

Legend

■ Major Influence
▣ Moderate Influence
▢ Minor Influence
□ Almost None
□ None

Note:
Listed percentages are the "percent of maximum possible influence" (MPI) scores described in *Chapter 2: Making Sense of the Stories.*

Several regional variations were evident in the relative importance of factors influencing Druids' spiritual paths.[1] Druids of the British Isles and Ireland were significantly more likely to be influenced by face-to-face interactions with other Druids, Druidry curriculum materials and mentors, and local deities and ancestors-of-place. They were less likely to be influenced by books of their own choosing, or internet interactions. Druids of continental Europe were significantly more likely to be inspired by curriculum materials, websites, Druidry mentors, dreams and past-life experiences, and less likely to be inspired by nature spirits, deities, or ancestors-of-blood. Druids in North America were less likely to be inspired by curricula, face-to-face interactions, or ancestors-of-place, but more likely to be inspired by almost everything else. Druids in Oceania were less likely to find inspiration on the Internet, but more likely to be influenced by dreams, Druidry mentors, face-to-face interactions with other Druids, ancestors-of-blood, and ancestors-of-place.

There were also intergenerational trends in the data pertaining to the relative importance of two factors.[2] Those newer to Druidry were more likely to be influenced by websites than more experienced Druids. There was also a trend in the data correlating more years of experience with a greater focus on ancestors-of-blood. Since this focus on ancestors-of-blood did not correlate with age differences among Druids, this finding indicates that the importance of ancestors-of-blood in world Druidry practice is fading over time. The importance of a Druid's connection with the natural world is taking precedence over ancestry, with increasing frequency in each passing generation of Druids.

The Impact of Druidry Groups & Curricula

The closest Druidry comes to having religious or spiritual organizations akin to churches, synagogues, temples, or mosques, are an assortment of local and international Druidry groups and organizations. Druidry does not have dedicated, physical locations in which to meet, and so these groups play a vital role in organizing physical gatherings of Druids to celebrate holidays. They also provide virtual networking venues for Druids wishing to organize study groups, or social gatherings of like-minded Druid folk. In addition, many of these organizations disseminate information to their members in the form of newsletters, informational websites, podcasts, and curriculum materials.

World Druidry Survey respondents reported being members of 147 different Druid groups, worldwide. The only Druid groups for which more than 25 survey respondents reported being active members were: The Order of Bards, Ovates, and Druids (OBOD); Ár nDraíocht Féin: A Druid Fellowship (ADF); The Ancient Order of Druids in America (AODA); The British Druid Order (BDO); and The Druid Network (TDN). Thus, these were the only Druid groups for which it was possible to perform valid statistical analyses of the effects of group membership on Druidry practices. Each of the other groups were mentioned by fewer than 2% of respondents. A complete list of organizations represented by *World Druidry Survey* participants can be found in *Appendix C*. Twenty-five percent of participating Druids belonged to multiple Druidry groups; 57% belonged to just one group. The remaining 18% of world Druids were solitary practitioners, not affiliated with any group.

Intergroup Comparison of Factors Influencing Druidry

With 82% of world Druids belonging to one or more Druidry groups, it makes sense to ask the extent to which group membership influences the importance of the various factors affecting a Druid's practice. Analyses of the response distributions for each of the factors listed in the graph on page 63 showed no statistically significant differences among the major Druidry groups, with a few notable exceptions.

ADF members were, on average, less likely to be inspired by nature, and more likely to be inspired by deities, which is consistent with the ADF's emphasis on being a *"Pagan church based on ancient Indo-European traditions,"*[3] rather than a broad, all-encompassing Druidry order. ADF Druids were also more likely to be influenced by both internet and face-to-face interactions with other Druids.[4]

AODA members were significantly more likely to rely upon non-Druidry books philosophically aligned with Druidry, to help them define their personal Druidic paths.[5]

OBOD members were, on average, more likely to rely upon the teachings of their order's curriculum materials.[6]

The Role of Druidry Group Curricula & Media

Druidry group curriculum materials played a significant role in shaping the spiritual paths of 59% of world Druids. However, not all curricula were equally influential. If one considers the percentage of an order's membership who considered that particular order's curriculum and teachings to be important to their practice, the ratings ranged between 57% and 88%, as indicated in the table on page 66. Several other Druidry groups provided instructional materials that were cited as having had a major influence on the developing practices of a very small number (<<1%) of world Druids. These can be found listed in the chapter end notes.[7]

Informational websites hosted by various Druid groups — websites which did not require group membership in order to access the materials — also played a small role in educating those new to Druidry, though far less of a role than the curriculum materials provided by those same groups. Only five

Influence of Druid Order Teachings & Curricula

Druid Order Teachings & Curriculum	% Order Members	% World Druids
New Order of Druids (NOD)	88%	2%
Order of Bards, Ovates, and Druids (OBOD)	87%	49%
British Druid Order (BDO)	78%	4%
Anglesey Druid Order	62%	1%
Ár nDraíocht Féin: A Druid Fellowship (ADF)	59%	7%
Ancient Order of Druids in America (AODA)	57%	4%

Druidry websites were cited more than once as being influential: druidry.org (OBOD), adf.org (ADF), druidnetwork.org (TDN), aoda.org (AODA), and druidry.co.uk (BDO). Smaller groups that hosted influential websites included: the New Druid Order (NOD), the Isle of Wight Druid Order, the Order of the White Oak, Hermandad Druida Dun Ailline (Spain), Orden Druida Fintan (Spain), and Sternenkreis (Germany).

Internet forums and Facebook groups hosted by Druid groups allow Druids to interact with others following a similar spiritual path. This can be particularly important when member Druids are few and far between. Eleven percent of Druids reported participating in one or more online communities, and 31 different internet community groups were cited as being influential. However, only ten of these communities were mentioned by more than one Druid, and the two most influential forums (hosted by AODA, and OBOD) were each cited by just 2% of Druids.

A few periodicals issued by Druidry groups were cited as influential to Druid spiritual journeys, in specific, OBOD's *Touchstone* magazine, the OBOD-sponsored *Mt. Haemus Research Papers*, ADF's *Oak Leaves* journal, AODA's *Trilithon* journal, *Druid* magazine, and the *SerpentStar Newsletter*. However, taken together, these publications were cited by fewer than 2% of respondents, and so did not play a significant role in shaping World Druidry.

Far more influential than any of these were the OBOD audio podcast, *Druidcast*, hosted by Dahm the Bard (cited by 15% of Druids), and the video podcast, *Tea with a Druid*, hosted by Philip Carr-Gomm (cited by 4%).

Influential Authors, Books, and Media

More important to most Druids' developing spiritual paths than any Druidry-group publications or curricula were the personal libraries of books and media which Druids curated to fit their spiritual interests and personal needs. This includes both books and media explicitly about Druidry, and books and media philosophically aligned with or otherwise related to elements of Druidry practice. Only 4% of survey respondents said that books and media had played no role in defining their personal path of Druidry. Most who did so explained that, while they might enjoy such books, their Druidic beliefs and practices were not derived from textual sources, for example:

> *"I enjoy myths, legends, and traditional tales and understand that they can be a wonderful teaching tool, but I'm not sure I consider any of them influential or inspirational."*

> *"De vraag is weldegelijk relevant maar toch zijn er geen mythen etc die mijn persoonlijke pad hebben bepaald. Als ik een verhaal moet noemen dan is dat het verhaal dat ik zelf vertel over mijzelf als druide.*
> [Translation:]
> *The question is very relevant but there are no myths etc. that have defined my personal path. If I have to name a story then that is the story I tell about myself as a Druid."*

> *"Celtic mythology and history. I read The Tain and The Mabinogi, and I am familiar with other old Celtic literature and stories. I'm a big history buff... I love reading about European Celtic history; Hallstatt and La Tene cultures, and later Gaul and Brythonic cultures. Also history of the Roman Empire and British and European medieval history. I also love reading the Norse Eddas and sagas. Fascinating stuff. While this stuff got me interested in the history of Druidry, it didn't really shape my beliefs within Druidry."*

The vast majority of Druids (96%), however, did find myths, legends, books, and media to be inspirational and educational in ways that were relevant to their spiritual paths. About 10% were such avid readers that they said they simply could not decide which ones to list, for example:

> *"Oh my gosh, this is a complicated question. My current spirituality has evolved through MANY influences…"*

> *"There are too many to list. I have been a Pagan for twenty years and have been influenced by many books."*

> *"I am a Jungian and a feminist and a bibliophile. Literally hundreds of books have illuminated my path."*

Categories of Influential Authors, Books & Media

Creative Works	# cited
Myths / Legends / Tales	1559
Novels	116
Music, Art, and Film	50
Poetry	33
Children's Literature	21
Total:	**1774**

Popular Spirituality	# cited
Druidry	377
Other Pagan Paths	188
Celtic Spirituality	139
Shamanistic Topics	104
Magic & the Occult	95
Mainstream Religions	14
Total:	**924**

Scholarly Works	# cited
History / Archaeology	139
Anthropology / Sociology	71
Linguistics/ Ancient Texts	35
Theology	13
Jungian Psychology	10
academic books / articles	27
Total:	**295**

Popular Non-Fiction	# cited
Science & Nature	86
Ecological Philosophy	53
Total:	**139**

In such cases, Druids typically named only authors, or broad categories of reading materials. When counting just named authors, and specific titles cited, the survey data yielded a list of 390 unique authors, and 634 unique titles.

To make sense of this extensive list, I sorted titles, authors, and subjects into categories of reading material. The list of categories, with the total number of citations in each, is presented in the table at left. In the next few pages, the specific books and media included in each category are described in some detail, with lists of the most commonly cited authors (and titles cited for each of these authors — when titles had been provided by survey respondents) within each category. In order to merit a listing in these pages, a specific author, title, or translator must have been mentioned by at least two Druids.

Influential Myths & Legends

Creative works of story, poetry, music, and art were, by far, the most influential sources of inspiration for Druids around the world. In particular, the myths and legends of a variety of world cultures served as fodder for meditation, reflection, and learning, surpassing all other types of media. The ways in which Druids work with the gods, goddesses, and legendary figures portrayed in these myths and legends will be further discussed in *Chapter 5: Themes and Variations in Druid Theology.* For the moment, let us simply consider the range of creative works that Druids turn to for inspiration — addressed in descending order of prevalence.

The myths and legends of Wales accounted for 30% of the mythology citations. Of these, *The Mabinogion*, and the tale of *Cerridwen and Taliesin* were the most frequently cited tales. Druids typically read popular retellings of these tales, with far too many versions to count, but a few Druids also studied scholarly translations of early Welsh manuscripts such as: the *Black Book of Carmarthen*, the *Red Book of Hergest*, the *Peniarth Manuscripts*, the *White Book of Rhydderch*, and poems from the *Book of Taliesin*.

Localized myths and legends, specific to the landscapes, seascapes, and skyscapes of the region in which a Druid happened to live, accounted for 17% of the mythology citations. The specific tales cited in this subcategory were mentioned by only a few Druids each, but when considered together, as localized myths of place, they played a significant role in inspiring modern Druids. For Druids in peripheral areas of the British Isles, this included legends specific to places such as the Isle of Wight, the Isle of Man, the Scottish highlands and islands, and Cornwall. Druids in continental Europe cited German and Austrian alpine legends; Grimm's fairy tales, and works by Hans Christian Andersen; northern legends specific to Denmark, Norway and Sweden; and Russian, Slavic, and Galician folktales. North American Druids found inspiration in the myths and legends of the Ojibwe, Navajo, Lakota, Dakota, Cherokee, and Cheyenne nations. Druids in and around Mexico, looked to Aztec and Mayan tales for inspiration. In South America, the focus was on Peruvian and Brazilian myths and legends. Druids in Brazil and New Orleans also cited legends from the mixed, African-matrix religions practiced in those areas, and Druids in the Appalachians wrote of Southern folk-magic traditions. Hawaiian myths and legends inspired Druids in Hawaii. Māori, and Australian aboriginal stories played an inspirational role in New Zealand and Australia. In Japan, Druids looked to the traditions of Shinto. As for those Druids who actually reside in Wales and Ireland — if they cited Welsh and Irish mythology, then those citations were counted in this subcategory, as well.

Myths and legends from Ireland accounted for 13% of the mythology citations, overall. As with the Welsh, translations were too many and varied to count. These citations focused on tales from the *Book of Invasions* (especially tales of the Tuatha Dé Danann), the *Ulster Cycle* (especially the tales of the *Táin Bó Cúailnge*, *The Birth of Cú Chulainn*, *King Conchobar mac Nessa*, *Queen Medb*, *Fergus mac Róich*, and *Deirdre*), the *Fenian Cycle* (tales of Fionn mac Cumhaill), and assorted tales of the Irish deities, Lugh, Dagda, Brigit, and Morrigan.

Other myths and legends that Druids found inspirational included the Arthurian legends, undifferentiated "Celtic myths", Greek and Hellenic myths, Norse myths (especially the *Poetic & Prose Eddas*, and tales of the mythical tree, Yggdrasil), and the epic poem, *Beowulf*. Each of these mythological subcategories accounted for only 4%-8% of the mythology citations.

Finally, 4% of Druids found inspiration in stories from other major, modern world religions. These included Bible stories, and tales from Taoist, Buddhist, and Hindu traditions.

Modern Works of Fiction & Art

Novels, children's literature, and other modern works of creative writing also inspired many Druids. The 137 citations of this kind included 49 authors and 45 specific titles and book series. The most influential of these writers, along with the specific books, if any, that were mentioned in the survey

Influential Authors & Books:
FICTION

Author / Title(s)	Cited by
J.R.R. Tolkien	**24**
"The Lord of the Rings"	
"The Hobbit"	
Marion Zimmer Bradley	**20**
"The Mists of Avalon"	
Holling Clancy Holling	**6**
"Paddle to the Sea"	
"Pagoo"	
"Minn of the Mississippi"	
"Seabird"	
"Tree in the Trail"	
Brian Bates	**5**
"The Way of Wyrd"	
Ursula LeGuin	**4**
The "Earthsea" series	
Morgan Llywelyn	**4**
"Druids"	
"Finn Mac Cool"	
"Brian Boru"	
J.K. Rowling	**4**
The "Harry Potter" series	
Monica Furlong	**2**
Herman Hesse	**2**
"Steppenwolf"	
C.S. Lewis	**2**
Astrid Lindgren	**2**
Juliet Marillier	**2**

responses, are listed in the table on page 70. The "cited by" numbers in the table refer to the number of Druids who cited each author. Titles are listed in descending order of prevalence within those citations.

Inspiration for Druidry practice and belief was also found in assorted works of art, comic books and graphic novels, video games, television shows, and movies. However, no specific work was cited by more than one person. Music was also a noted source of inspiration, especially Celtic music and folk music. One musician was mentioned by five different Druids: Dahm the Bard, and his *Antlered Crown and Standing Stone* album.

Thirty-three citations were for poetic sources of Druidic inspiration. Favorites included works by William Butler Yeats, poems from the *Book of Taliesin*, and the poetry of Mary Oliver.

Books & Media on Spiritual Topics

The second most influential category of books and media were those which explored spiritual and religious themes, but were written or produced for a mainstream audience. This includes books and media about Druidry, other Neopagan spiritual paths, Celtic spirituality, shamanistic spiritual practices, occult, magical, and New Age topics, as well as a few mainstream religious writings. The most influential authors and books in these categories are listed on pages 72-76.

Popular books and media written explicitly about Druidry were cited 377 times in the survey. Authors and bloggers in this category wrote about Druid ritual forms, seasonal celebrations, and magical practices, Druid myths and lore, Druidic prayer and meditation techniques, and Druidic techniques for forging spiritual connections with the landscape. Several popular Druid blogs were also mentioned, including: Dana O'Driscoll's *Druid's Garden Blog*, Danni Lang's *Esoteric Moment Blog & YouTube Channel*, M.A. Phillips' *The Ditzy Druid Blog*, Ryan Cronin's *Wrycrow Blog*, and *ADF's Three Cranes Grove's YouTube Channel*.

Books, magazines, and blogs about Paganism were cited 188 times in the survey. These writings focused on topics such as: Witchcraft and Wicca; Northern, Heathen and Ásatrú traditions; Goddess traditions; green, or natural magic; and Neopagan forms of ritual, celebration, and prayer. Popular blogs in this category included: John Beckett's *Patheos* blog posts; Car, Gwyn & Ode's *3 Pagans and a Cat* podcast, Gordon White's *Rune Soup* blog and podcast, the *Patheos* blogs, *Dandelionlady*, and *Between the Shadows*, and the *Pagan Perspective* YouTube channel.

Books and media focused on Celtic spiritual traditions — especially those of Ireland, Scotland, and Wales — formed another important category of influence. These 139 books, blogs, and websites were not about Druidry,

Influential Authors & Books:
DRUIDRY

Author / Title(s)	Cited by
Philip Carr-Gomm	**162**
"Druid Mysteries: Ancient Wisdom for the 21st Century"	
"DruidCraft: The Magic of Wicca & Druidry"	
"The Druid Way: A Journey through an Ancient Landscape"	
"What Do Druids Believe?"	
"In the Grove of the Druids: The Druid Teachings of Ross Nichols"	
"The Elements of the Druid Tradition"	
"The Druid Renaissance"	
"The Rebirth of Druidry: Ancient Earth Wisdom for Today"	
John Michael Greer	**124**
"The Druidry Handbook: Spiritual Practice Rooted in the Living Earth"	
"The Druid Magic Handbook: Ritual Magic Rooted in the Living Earth"	
"The Celtic Golden Dawn: An Original & Complete Curriculum of Druidical Study"	
"The Dolmen Arch: A Study Course in the Druid Mysteries"	
"The Druid Grove Handbook"	
"The Gnostic Celtic Church"	
Emma Restall Orr	**76**
"Living Druidry: Magical Spirituality for the Wild Soul"	
"Spirits of the Sacred Grove: The World of a Druid Priestess"	
"Principles of Druidry: The Only Introduction You'll Ever Need"	
"Perennial Course in Living Druidry"	
"Druid Priestess: An Intimate Journey through the Pagan Year"	
"Druidry"	
Penny Billington	**62**
"The Path of Druidry: Walking the Ancient Green Way"	
Joanna van der Hoeven	**34**
"The Awen Alone: Walking the Path of the Solitary Druid"	
"Zen Druidry: Living a Natural Life with Full Awareness"	
"Dancing with Nemetona: A Druid's Exploration of Sanctuary and Sacred Space"	
Isaac Bonewits	**25**
"Bonewits's Essential Guide to Druidism"	
Ross Nichols	**22**
"The Book of Druidry"	
"Das Magische Wissen der Druiden"	
Kristoffer Hughes	**12**
"Natural Druidry"	
Nimue Brown	**8**
"Druidry and Meditation"	
Danu Forest	**8**
"Celtic Tree Magic: Ogham Lore and Druid Mysteries"	
"Gwyn ap Nudd: Wild God of Faery, Guardian of Annwfn"	
"The Magical Year: Seasonal Celebrations to Honor Nature's Ever-turning Wheel"	
"The Druid Shaman: Exploring the Celtic Otherworld"	

Influential Authors & Books:
DRUIDRY (cont'd)

Author / Title(s)	Cited by
Robert (Skip) Ellison	6
"The Solitary Druid: Walking the Path of Wisdom and Spirit"	
"Ogham: The Secret Language of the Druids"	
Ellen Evert Hopman	6
"A Druid's Herbal for the Sacred Earth Year"	
"A Druid's Herbal of Sacred Tree Medicine"	
Ivan McBeth	6
"The Bardic Book of Becoming: An Introduction to Modern Druidry"	
Erynn Rowan Laurie	5
"Ogham: Weaving Word Wisdom"	
John Matthews	4
"The Druid Sourcebook: From Earliest Times to the Present Day"	
"Secrets of the Druids"	
"The Bardic Sourcebook: Inspirational Legacy & Teachings of the Ancient Celts"	
Douglas Monroe	4
"The 21 Lessons of Merlyn: A Study in Druid Magic and Lore"	
Philip Shallcrass	4
"Druidry: A Practical and Inspirational Guide"	
Maya Magee Sutton	4
"Druid Magic: The Practice of Celtic Wisdom"	
Julie White & Graeme Talboys	4
"The Path through the Forest: A Druid Guidebook"	
"Arianrhod's Dance: A Druid Ritual Handbook"	
Julie Brett	3
"Australian Druidry: Connecting with the Sacred Landscape"	
Ian Corrigan	3
"Sacred Fire, Holy Well: A Druid's Grimoire"	
Kevan Manwaring	3
"The Bardic Handbook: The Complete Manual for the 21st Century Bard"	
Iolo Morganwg (a.k.a. J. Williams Ab Ithel)	3
"Barddas: A Collection of Original Documents, Illustrative of the Theology Wisdom, and Usages of the Bardo-Druidic Systems of the Isle of Britain"	
Graeme Talboys	3
"The Druid Way Made Easy"	
Gordon Cooper	2
"Wild-crafting the Modern Druid" (article)	
James Nichol	2
"Contemplative Druidry: People, Practice, and Potential"	
Amber Wolfe	2
"Druid Power: Celtic Faerie Craft & Elemental Magic"	

Influential Authors & Books:
OTHER PAGAN PATHS

Author / Title(s)	Cited by
John Beckett	23
"The Path of Paganism: An Experience-Based Guide to Modern Pagan Practice"	
Emma Restall Orr	14
"Living with Honour: A Pagan Ethics"	
"Kissing the Hag: The Dark Goddess and the Unacceptable Nature of Women"	
"Ritual: A Guide to Life, Love, and Inspiration"	
Scott Cunningham	13
"Wicca: A Guide for the Solitary Practitioner"	
"Living Wicca: A Further Guide for the Solitary Practitioner"	
"Magical Herbalism: The Secret Craft of the Wise"	
Ceisiwr Serith	12
"Deep Ancestors: Practicing the Religion of the Proto-Indo-Europeans"	
"A Book of Pagan Prayer"	
Starhawk	12
"The Spiral Dance: A Rebirth of the Ancient Religion of the Goddess"	
"Dreaming the Dark: Magic, Sex, and Politics"	
Margot Adler	6
"Drawing Down the Moon: Witches, Druids, Goddess-Worshippers, and Other Pagans in America"	
Ian Corrigan	6
"The Book of Visions: A Manual of Pagan Meditation & Trance"	
Isaac Bonewits	4
"Real Magic: An Introductory Treatise on the Basic Principles of Yellow Magic"	
"Rites of Worship: A Neopagan Approach"	
Marian Green	4
"A Witch Alone: Thirteen Moons to Master Natural Magic"	
Kirk S. Thomas	3
"Sacred Gifts: Reciprocity and the Gods"	
Alaric Albertsson	2
"Travels through Middle Earth: The Path of a Saxon Pagan"	
Rae Beth	2
"Hedge Witch: A Guide to Solitary Witchcraft"	
Luisa Francia	2
Gerald Gardner	2
Francis Hitching	2
"Earth Magic"	
Lora O'Brien	2
Jhenah Telyndru	2
"Avalon Within: A Sacred Journey of Myth, Mystery, and Inner Wisdom"	

Influential Authors & Books:
CELTIC SPIRITUALITY

Author / Title(s)	Cited by
Caitlín & John Matthews	**45**
"The Encyclopedia of Celtic Wisdom: A Celtic Shaman's Sourcebook"	
"The Western Way: A Practical Guide to the Western Mystery Tradition, v. 1 & 2"	
Caitlín Matthews	
"The Celtic Devotional: Daily Prayers and Blessings"	
John Matthews	
"Taliesin: The Last Celtic Shaman"	
"The Celtic Shaman: A Practical Guide"	
"The Book of Celtic Verse: A Treasury of Poetry, Dreams & Visions"	
Kristoffer Hughes	**20**
"From the Cauldron Born: Exploring the Magic of Welsh Legend & Lore"	
"The Book of Celtic Magic: Transformative Teachings from the Cauldron of Awen"	
"The Journey Into Spirit: A Pagan's Perspective on Death, Dying & Bereavement"	
Morgan Daimler	**10**
"Fairies:: A Guide to the Celtic Fair Folk"	
"Brigid: Meeting The Celtic Goddess Of Poetry, Forge, And Healing Well"	
"Where the Hawthorn Grows: An American Druid's Reflections"	
Frank MacEowen	**8**
"The Mist-Filled Path: Celtic Wisdom for Exiles, Wanderers, and Seekers"	
Alexei Kondratiev	**7**
"The Apple Branch: A Path to Celtic Ritual"	
"Celtic Rituals: An Authentic Guide to Ancient Celtic Spirituality"	
Mara Freeman	**4**
"Kindling the Celtic Spirit: Ancient Traditions to Illumine Your Life Through the Seasons"	
John O'Donohue	**4**
"Anam Cara: A Book of Celtic Wisdom"	
Wolf Dieter Storl	**4**
"Die Pflanzen der Kelten"	
Lunaea Weatherstone	**3**
"Tending Brigid's Flame: Awaken to the Celtic Goddess of Hearth, Temple, and Forge"	
Clann Bhríde	**2**
"Book of Hours: For Daily and Seasonal Practice"	
Barbara Meiklejohn-Free	**2**
"Scottish Witchcraft: A Complete Guide to Authentic Folklore, Spells, and Magickal Tools"	

Influential Writers & Books:
SHAMANISTIC TOPICS

Author / Title(s)	Cited by
David Abram	8
"The Spell of the Sensuous: Perception and Language in a More-Than-Human World"	
"Becoming Animal: An Earthly Cosmology"	
Tom Cowan	6
"Fire in the Head: Shamanism and the Celtic Spirit"	
Juliet Batten	5
"Celebrating the Southern Seasons: Rituals for Aotearoa"	
"Dancing with the Seasons: Inspiration and resilience through times of change"	
D.J. Conway	4
"By Oak, Ash, & Thorn: Modern Celtic Shamanism"	
Michael Harner	4
"The Way of the Shaman"	
John Michael Greer	3
"Mystery Teachings from the Living Earth: An Introduction to Spiritual Ecology"	
Sandra Ingerman	3
Sandra Kynes	3
"Whispers from the Woods: The Lore and Magic of Trees"	
Emma Restall Orr	3
"The Wakeful World: Animism, Mind and the Self in Nature"	
Elen Sentier	3
"Elen of the Ways: British Shamanism - Following the Deer Trods"	
Ted Andrews	2
"Nature-Speak: Signs, Omens and Messages in Nature"	
"Animal Speak: The Spiritual & Magical Powers of Creatures Great and Small"	
Penny Billington	2
"The Wisdom of Birch, Oak, and Yew: Connect to the Magic of Trees for Guidance & Transformation"	
Carlos Castaneda	2
Steven D. Farmer	2
"Earth Magic: Ancient Shamanic Wisdom for Healing Yourself, Others, and the Planet"	
John G. Neihardt	2
"Black Elk Speaks: Being the Life Story of a Holy Man of the Oglala Sioux"	
Evelyn Rysdyk	2
"The Norse Shaman: Ancient Spiritual Practices of the Northern Tradition"	
"Spirit Walking: A Course in Shamanic Power"	

Influential Writers & Books:
SCHOLARLY WORKS

Author / Title(s)	Cited by
Ronald Hutton	**34**
"Blood and Mistletoe: The History of the Druids in Britain"	
"Stations of the Sun: A History of the Ritual Year in Britain"	
"Pagan Britain"	
"The Druids: A History"	
Peter Berresford Ellis	**20**
"A Brief History of the Druids"	
Joseph Campbell	**10**
"The Power of Myth"	
"The Hero's Journey"	
"The Hero with a Thousand Faces"	
Ellen Evert Hopman	**8**
"A Legacy of Druids: Conversations with Druid Leaders of Britain, the USA and Canada, Past and Present"	
"Being a Pagan: Druids, Wiccans, and Witches Today"	
Miranda J. Aldhouse-Green	**7**
"The World of the Druids"	
Alexander Carmichael	**6**
"Carmina Gadelica, Vol. 1 & 2"	
John Michael Greer	**6**
"A World Full of Gods: An Inquiry into Polytheism"	
Barry Cunliffe	**4**
Mircea Eliade	**4**
"Patterns in Comparative Religion"	
"The Sacred & the Profane: The Nature of Religion"	
Alwyn Rees	**4**
"Celtic Heritage: Ancient Tradition in Ireland and Wales"	
Anne Ross	**4**
Sharon Paice MacLeod	**3**
"Celtic Myth and Religion: A Study of Traditional Belief, with Newly Translated Prayers, Poems and Songs"	
Dáithí Ó hÓgáin	**3**
"The Sacred Isle: Belief and Religion in Pre-Christian Ireland"	
Nora Chadwick	**2**
Clarissa Pinkola Estés	**2**
"Women Who Run with the Wolves: Myths and Stories of the Wild Woman Archetype"	
Prudence Jones & Nigel Pennick	**2**
"A History of Pagan Europe"	
Kuno Meyer	**2**
"The Triads of Ireland"	

Influential Writers & Books:
POPULAR NON-FICTION

Author / Title(s)	Cited by
John Michael Greer	7
"After Progress: Reason and Religion at the End of the Industrial Age"	
"The Blood of the Earth: An Essay on Magic and Peak Oil"	
"Green Wizardry: Conservation, Solar Power, Organic Gardening, And Other Hands-On Skills From the Appropriate Tech Toolkit"	
"The Ecotechnic Future: Envisioning a Post-Peak World"	
Robin Wall Kimmerer	5
"Braiding Sweetgrass: Indigenous Wisdom, Scientific Knowledge, and the Teachings of Plants"	
David Attenborough	4
"Planet Earth" BBC video documentaries	
"Blue Planet" BBC video documentaries	
Glennie Kindred	4
"Letting in the Wild Edges"	
Brendan Myers	4
"The Earth, the Gods and the Soul"	
"The Other Side of Virtue: Where Our Virtues Come From, What They Really Mean, and Where They Might Be Taking Us"	
Bill Plotkin	4
"Nature and the Human Soul: Cultivating Wholeness and Community in a Fragmented World"	
Peter Wohlleben	4
"The Hidden Life of Trees: What They Feel, How They Communicate"	
"The Inner Life of Animals: Love, Grief, and Compassion"	
Thomas Berry	3
"The Dream of the Earth"	
"The Great Work: Our Way into the Future"	
Wendell Berry	3
"The Unsettling of America: Culture and Agriculture"	
Aldo Leopold	3
"A Sand County Almanac"	
Brian Swimme	2
"The Universe Story: From the Primordial Flaring Forth to the Ecozoic Era — A Celebration of the Unfolding Cosmos"	

per se, but were certainly applicable to Druidry. This category also includes books on Celtic Christian spiritual traditions, and on the folk-magic and ritual traditions specific to Ireland, and the British Isles.

Books focused on shamanistic spiritual practices comprised another significant category of influence, with 104 unique citations. These works taught about methods for understanding and spiritually connecting with nature and natural forces, including trees, plants, animals, and other elements of the land, sea, and skyscape. They also taught about methods for connecting with the world(s) of spirit, and for deriving wisdom from the resulting connections.

Another cluster of books and media related to magical, occult, and New Age topics, such as various forms of divination, astrology, dowsing and ley lines, and occult studies such as the Kabbalah and the Hermetic tradition. Although 95 citations fell into this broad category, none was cited by more than one Druid, with the exception of: books by Dion Fortune (3 citations), and *The Kybalion* by The Three Initiates (2 citations). In addition, several oracle and tarot card decks were cited as being particularly inspirational: Will Worthington & Philip Carr-Gomm's *Druid Plant Oracle, Druid Animal Oracle,* and *Druid Craft Tarot*; Mark Ryan & John Matthews's *Wildwood Tarot*; Barry Brailsford's *Wisdom of the Four Winds - Shamanic Wisdom* Card Set; Caitlín Matthews' *Celtic Book of the Dead* Card Set; and Caitlín & John Matthews' *Hallowquest: The Arthurian Tarot.*

The final category of popular books and media written about spiritual topics involved books from other, mainstream religions: Buddhism, Taoism, and Christianity. The only authors cited more than once in this category were Thich Nhat Hahn (for books on Buddhism), and Mark Townsend, for his Christian-Pagan books: *The Path of the Blue Raven, Jesus through Pagan Eyes*, and *Diary of a Heretic.*

Scholarly Works

Scholarly works of research and analysis also informed the spiritual development of many modern Druids. In particular, Druids cited works of history and archaeology; anthropology and sociology; linguistics and translations of early texts; theology; and Jungian psychology. The majority of these citations were for general categories of academic research, unspecified academic journal articles, materials from college curricula, or unspecified *"academic books on"* particular subject areas. However, some specific titles and authors were mentioned in survey responses, the most influential of which are listed in the table on page 77.

Popular Non-fiction Authors & Titles

The final category of books and media that modern Druids turned to for inspiration and information were popular works of non-fiction (see table, page 78). One group of 86 books in this category focused on science and nature writings pertaining to Earth's biosphere. These included naturalist training programs, books on medical herbalism, gardening, permaculture, ecology, and the like. The other 53 books in this category were works of what I have termed *ecological philosophy* — studies that bridge between the fields of philosophy, economics, politics, and ecological sustainability. These books all present arguments in support of the need for humanity to reconsider and restructure its relationship with the natural world.

Along with these book titles, Druids were also influenced by J.M. Greer's blogs, *The Archdruid Report, Well of Galabes,* and *Ecosophia*; and the *Gods and Radicals/A Site of Beautiful Resistance* website.

Meditations on Druid Reading Habits

As evident in the vast number of books, authors, and subject areas that Druids have cited as being influential to their developing spiritual paths, most Druids love to read. But does that love of reading speak to any particular theme within modern Druidry? If one considers that only 15 titles were cited by more than 1% of survey respondents, it seems unlikely. *The Mabinogion,* which was, by far, the single most popular title, was cited by only 16% of Druids. The most popular instructional book about Druidry, John Michael Greer's *Druidry Handbook,* was cited by only 7% of Druids, followed by Penny Billington's *The Path of Druidry,* which accounts for nearly another 7%. Clearly, there are no specific books that are a shared source of inspiration or information for all Druids. If one considers just authors, irrespective of any specific book titles, one is left similarly disappointed. The most influential author among modern Druids, Philip Carr-Gomm, was mentioned or referenced by only 19% of world Druids — and that is when taking all of his many pub- lications, together. The second most influential author was John Michael Greer, referenced by 13% of respondents, all told.

If one considers broad categories of reading material, the results are a bit more cohesive: 77% of Druids look to myths and legends for inspiration; 28% look specifically to myths and legends from their local environments; 59% look to instructional books on spiritual topics; 26% look to creative works of fiction, music, or art; 16% look to non-fiction books in the sciences, ecology, or ecological philosophy; and 16% focus on academic works of anthropology, history, and linguistics. At this level of analysis, some variations among Druidry group memberships become apparent.[8] Localized myths and legends, derived from the land in which a Druid resides, were less likely to have inspired ADF members, members of the Celtic diaspora, and North American Druids. They were slightly more likely to have inspired members of OBOD, BDO, and TDN, and Druids born, raised, and resident in the British Isles and Ireland. OBOD Druids are more likely to find inspiration in creative works of music, art, poetry, and fiction. AODA members are more likely to find inspiration in non-fiction works of science, ecology, and ecological philosophy, as well as instructional books on spiritual topics.

An even more interesting theme emerges when one considers how and why Druids read, rather than focusing on the content of that reading. Although this was not something the survey explicitly addressed, many Druids offered long explanations and justifications for their lengthy lists of influential reading materials. In their responses, it became evident that — at least for these Druids — reading was less a search for simple answers, and more a search for seed-topics for meditation. They read to challenge themselves, to explore new possibilities, to understand competing opinions, and re-view their own beliefs and practices from different perspectives. Druids used the resulting cognitive dissonance as the impetus to learn and grow, or to clarify for themselves the reasons why a suggested path was not one they would choose to pursue. Examples of their comments included:

> *"Even the parts that didn't quite work for me were super helpful, as they forced me to articulate WHY I didn't agree. That's HUGE."*

> *"I like to make sure to read a lot of competing opinions, so I often don't agree with some of these, but it contributes to an overall mixture of sources to work with, as well as prompting me to define exactly why I might not agree to myself. I tend to read around an hour a day on average, which makes this list pretty long!"*

> *"I read widely, but it's impossible to say what has had the greatest influence for me. My reading has included nature writing of all kinds, nature poetry, and a wide variety of spiritual and personal development books. [...] I tend to take the approach that anything I read or study might be meaningful, and might inform my path, if I am open to it. I have also studied nature connection as an academic, with a particular focus on people's relationships with places in nature that are important or meaningful to them. This has brought me into contact with a wide range of writing and research which, although rarely explicitly spiritual, has profoundly shaped and informed my worldview."*

> *"No one book. All of them have grains of truth."*

"Rather than pick a specific book and relying on its teachings I prefer to see all written material as opinions. I like Ronald Hutton and Miranda Green's opinions more than, say, that knob who wrote 'Witta' but I don't think anyone has the wrap on truth."

"ALL myths and folktales affect me, as they help me to see my spiritual path from different angles and different cultural lenses. I crave reading myths and folktales from all over the world."

"The curriculum has been the primary external source of inspiration and influence. The interaction with my internal thoughts and feelings, which I can best describe as unordered and abstract, has allowed me to grow spiritually and otherwise. A visual to explain [this] is a library full of books, but they are not on shelves. They are scattered about on the floor in no order. The OBOD curriculum and other sources have allowed me to start putting the books on the shelves in order, which allows access to the wisdom within."

This focus on meditation, and deep reflection upon reading materials — regardless of whether or not one agrees with the content — is consistent with the study practices recommended in the curriculum materials of ADF, AODA, BDO, and OBOD all of which emphasize practicing some form of meditation, not only as a tool for calming body and mind, but also as a tool for learning, and developing inner wisdom, as described by J.M. Greer, in *The Druidry Handbook*:

"The core process of meditation, no matter what system you're discussing, is focused attention. The Druid meditator focuses attention on thinking itself, directing thought steadily onto a chosen subject. The mind thus unfolds its inner potential, as in any other kind of meditation, and the meditator also comes to understand more about the subject of the meditation.

This form of meditation is called discursive meditation, because it takes the form of an inner discourse or dialogue. It can be defined as the continued movement of thought toward a chosen theme." [9]

The chosen theme might be the metaphorical implications of a character's role in a myth, or a vivid line of poetry, or an excerpt from a spiritual text, or the ecological role of an indigenous tree. The specific content matters less than the practice, which is the gradual training of the Druid's mind to calmly, deliberately, and fully consider any topic brought to his or her attention.

The Role of Geography in the Evolution of Druidry

Having considered the influence of books, media, and Druidry groups on Druids' developing spiritual paths, we now turn our attention to the influence of geography. By *geography*, I mean not only the locations and basic features of a landscape, but also its indigenous ecologies, including its flora and fauna, cultural norms, legends, lore, deities, and spirits of place.

Any transplanted cultural tradition is likely to be changed in the process of migration. This is particularly true if the new physical or cultural environment is significantly different from the one in which that tradition was born. In the case of Druidry, a tradition born in the forests and farmlands of northern Europe, one might expect significant changes as the tradition was brought into places as culturally and ecologically diverse as the tropical rain-forests of Brazil, the mesas of the North American Southwest, and the bushlands of Australia and New Zealand. Even within Europe, variations in local culture and microclimate might affect the particularities of Druidic practice from place to place. To explore variations in Druidic practice attributable to variations in geography, the *World Druidry Survey* included the two open-ended questions:

> *Question:*
> *In what ways (if any) has your natural or cultural en-*
> *vironment influenced the form of your Druid rituals?*

> *Question:*
> *In what ways (if any) has your natural or cultural en-*
> *vironment influenced the way in which you celebrated*
> *your Wheel of the Year?*

In 13% of the responses to these questions, either due to hostile weather patterns or Druidry-hostile neighbors, physical and cultural environments were seen only as impediments to Druidic practice, as discussed in *Chapter 3: Privacy & Safety Concerns of Modern Druids*. Other environmental effects on Druidry practice tended to fall into one of four main categories (see table on pg. 84): a focus on nature connection; a tendency toward *wildcrafting* Druidry practices from the local ecology (a process that will be discussed in detail, later in this chapter); a factor reinforcing traditional practices; and an enticement to simplify or eliminate formality. Less than 2% of respondents indicated that their physical and/or cultural environments had played no role in either the form of their rituals or the celebrations of their wheel of the year.

Effects of Physical & Cultural Environment on Druidry

Effect	%**
Invites nature connection.	76%
Encourages wildcrafting of rituals & celebrations.	32%
Reinforces ritual and holiday traditions.	24%
Encourages simplification of rituals & celebrations.	15%

**Percentages are of the 716 Druids who were influenced by their physical and/or cultural environments.

Nature Connection

The most frequently mentioned influence on Druidry emanating from Druids' physical environments was an enticement to connect, deeply and spiritually, with the natural world. This influence was described in a variety of ways, by 76% of survey respondents, overall, and 93% of Druids in Oceania[10]. The mere presence of trees, and waters, and wild lands was a constant reminder that they were a part of the natural world, rather than apart from it. Nature invited them into sacred relationships, and facilitated the process of forging connections. Druids wrote, for example:

> *"I live in a very beautiful village, and the natural environment (many trees, parks etc.) makes it very easy to connect with nature, seeing it as divine, with healing energy. I live close to a river that is swimmable."*

> *"I have trees (and therefore birds) all around my house. We live across the road from 120 hectares of native bush reserve. This influences me. I feel very much part of the natural environment living where I do. I feel like I am part of the forest a lot of the time not just an observer. I sometimes do a meditation or short ritual in a secluded part of the bush reserve. [...] Every morning I can open a door upstairs and welcome in the day and the deities: the gods of earth and sky, forest and sun and moon. We have regular conversations and interactions with the birds."*

> *"I intentionally bought a home where the yard is natural (trees, bushes, flowers, paths) so that I see nature out of every window, I hear and smell it constantly (I leave a window open partially all year round for this purpose). It keeps me centered."*

"It's called me in and invited me to see its bounty despite being so dry and what I previously thought of as limited."

"We live completely surrounded by dense native NZ forest, 9 km away from a wild black-sand surf beach. This enhances and reinforces my relationship with nature many times every day."

"I live at the edge of the wilderness. Bear, porcupine, eagles & many ravens are my neighbors. It gives a very different perspective on the powerful beauty - & dangers - of the wild places. I find it is less necessary to actually walk in the forest; because its spirit is all-pervasive, I can feel it in the comfort of my own garden, with the towering pines above me."

"Having relatively easy access to natural spaces makes it easier for me to do rituals and walk in nature and feel the energetic connections."

Taking the work of nature connection one step further, many Druids also discussed efforts they were making to actively connect with Nature. They saw nature connection as a two-way, reciprocal relationship, and worked to develop the skills and practices that would enable them to comprehend, and respond to Nature, rather than merely consuming its boons. This sometimes involved learning to interpret animal language, or plant language, or the local legends about landscape features and constellations. It also involved ritual practices derived from conversations with spirits of place, rather than simply on written traditions imposed upon the land. Druids wrote, for example:

"In moving to rural Italy I have been able to forge a far closer connection with the natural world. The area in which I now live is very wild and untamed and because it is also very remote (2km to the nearest neighbor) I feel far more free to practice my Druidry out in the woods surrounding my house. I have also formed a greater appreciation of the teachings surrounding Elen of the Ways and the lifestyle of the deer trods so my practice now includes regularly following the tracks of deer, boar and other animals to seek guidance and inspiration in my day to day life."

"Naturally I always greet the sun and moon (when I can see them!), I have recently started doing a full moon peace meditation. I am actively trying to improve my plant, tree and bird identification skills."

"Ich versuche, in Zwiesprache mit dem Geist des jeweiligen Ortes zu treten, um seine Energie in den Ritualen zu nutzen. Ebenfalls die Kräfte der Elemente, die besonders präsent sind - z. B. an einem Fluss oder See, am Meer oder im Wald die entsprechenden Bäume, die den Platz umgeben. Die besondere Magie von heiligen Kultstätten, wie dem Long Man of Wilmington oder den Frauensteinen bei Düsseldorf verleiht den Ritualen eine ungeheuere Tiefe. In gleicher Weise wie meine anderen rituellen Handlungen. Ich versuche stets in Kontakt mit dem Geist des Ortes zu treten und die präsenten Elemente, wie Fluss/Regen/Sonne/Sterne etc. in ihrer Kraft in die Zeremonie einfließen zu lassen. Die Bäume sind wichtige Zeugen der Rituale.

[Translation:]

I try to enter into dialogue with the spirit of the respective place in order to use its energy in the rituals. Also the powers of the elements that are particularly present — e.g. at a river or lake, at the sea or in the forest the corresponding trees that surround the place. The special magic of sacred places of worship, such as the Long Man of Wilmington or the Frauensteinen near Düsseldorf, lends the rituals a tremendous depth. In the same way as my other ritual acts. I always try to get in contact with the spirit of the place and to let the present elements like river/rain/sun/star etc. flow into the ceremony in their power. The trees are important witnesses of the rituals."

"Trees figure strongly in my practice; I am blessed with ancient oaks, a silver birch and a horse chestnut in my garden, and within walking distance is a wild space with very ancient trees. Trees are my connection with the earth and with the universe. If possible I celebrate outside with my trees"

"Der Boden, auf dem Haus und Garten sind, war jahrhundertelang nur Schafweide und Ziegelstein-Lehmboden und ist energetisch total tot. Wir bemühen uns seit Jahren, das zu verändern. Es gelingt in winzigen Schritten.

[Translation:]

The ground on which house and garden are, was for centuries only sheep pasture and brick-clay soil and is energetically totally dead. We have been trying to change this for years. It succeeds in tiny steps."

"I am working to befriend the spirits in the more urban area that I now live in, as well as those in the agricultural

*areas outside of the city. They seem so foreign to me,
being not of the forest, but I am excited to learn from
them."*

*"I spend 6 months a year in Africa, living in the Zambian
bush, working as a safari guide and camp manager. We
have up to 8 guests at a time and so each evening around
the campfire we get to tell stories of old folklore or recent
interesting sightings. We also spend time looking up at the
stars and explaining the ancient stories associated with
constellations. When I return to the UK, I spend a lot of
my time in our small woodland, planting, maintaining and
watching the wildlife. The two environments are very
different, but both allow me to be completely 'in touch'
with the natural world on a daily basis."*

When discussing the impacts of the natural environment on ritual
forms and celebrations, many Druids explained that practicing deep nature
connection was their primary form of ritual. They wrote, for example:

*"Because I live by the ocean and feel a deep connection
to it, the beach and oceanfront profoundly influence my
rituals. I feel in deepest connection with nature when I am
physically at one particular beach I frequent – which is
part of a larger public park with many groves of trees,
small bits of woodland, and open space. This beach has
become part of my inner world and is the one from which
I access my inner Grove."*

*"Door mijn buitenwerk sta ik vaak midden in het seizoen,
waardoor de natuur me veel metaforen aanrijkt voor
zingeving of reflectie.*
[Translation:]
*Because of my outdoor work I am often in the middle of
the season, so nature enriches me with many metaphors
for meaning or reflection."*

*"As an animist, my entire Druid practice is founded on
my relationships with the land where I live and the ancestors of this land and of my bloodline. [...] Tracking the
seasons is a foundational element of my practice, so the
eight festivals of the wheel of the year have my appreciation and attention."*

*"My natural environment is how I celebrate the wheel of
the year. I spend a lot of time in the wild desert with my
family."*

"Living in an urban environment (and an apartment) has prevented me from setting up a permanent outdoor grove in which to practice. I use any natural setting to connect with the spirits of the Earth. It also means that I more often practice spiritual awareness when I am outdoors rather than doing a specific ritual."

Others used elements taken from the local, natural environment to enhance and enrich their formal rituals and ceremonies, for example:

"The Olympic National Forest and surrounding region is a sacred place. It's hard to deny it when you're in its presence. I have made it a goal to practice outdoors more often, among the trees and near the water. In fact, I changed jobs and moved to this area (from a larger town further away) so that I could be closer to nature. I also will collect water from special places for ritual use - from the ocean, the sound, hot springs, etc."

"We celebrate outside no matter the weather and make use of it. For instance during Imbolc ritual, we take the snow and melt it as a metaphor for the ground thawing. If it rains, we stand in the rain. One time at Samhuinn it was threatening to rain. I prayed to Manannán to keep it at bay during ritual. He kept responding with 'don't worry about it.' As soon as we started ritual it started to rain. But I didn't worry about it. LOL"

"The local natural environment is the bedrock of my practice - I go to the fields, the woods and send messages down the stream outside the front door. We use all local things in the ceremonies, from props to circle adornments, and often delineate the circle with flowers or leaves."

"I lived on the coast and did rituals on the beach for half the year and then moved inland and so use the woods around my home now. gathering of representative items for land, sea and sky change accordingly. I change the ritual items to suit the surroundings, things that would be natural to the area, leaves and twigs or sea shells and found feathers and sea weeds."

"I live in oak woodlands - I work with the things I find there. I also have a natural stone circle that I work in. I live in the mountains with a natural stone circle (four medium boulders) on my property with a circle of oaks and cedars at the back of my property. I have a cloughtie

tree (a manzanita) as well. I also have another very large boulder that I place offerings on - we call it the 'offering stone' and it has a natural seat in it."

"The UK is rich in 'ritual space'. The land holds our space. Trees provide groves or shelter as well as ritual firewood. Caves give access to the underworld, or historical places of spirit. Sea and streams provide places to clean, bathe, and ritually wash. Fields and meadows are places to be in nature. I use them all."

"My natural environment influences my celebrations in that I work with native plants and animals that are active at a given time. For example, at Winter Solstice I will work with Great Horned Owl as they are pairing for mating during this time."

Wildcrafting

Druids new to Druidry, or new to a microclimate different from those of northern Europe, often expressed keen awareness of and frustration with the fact that the ritual forms and celebrations presented in Druidry books and curricula did not fit the realities of their local environments, for example:

"At this time, I am following the ritual practice most commonly practiced by the AODA/OBOD in the celebration of the eightfold Wheel of the Year. While these seasonal holidays are suited for temperate climates, I live in a tropical/subtropical environment that tends to have two seasons (hot and rainy; less hot and no rain). I would eventually like to 'wildcraft' my own druid practice, which Gordon Cooper discusses, but I have not been able to do that yet. As part of my candidate year, however, I am required to learn a great deal about my local environment, which I believe will provide fruitful information in adapting my practice to the local land. Certainly, I will say that living very close to the ocean has had a fairly significant influence. Almost all of my visualizations of the elements occur at the beach (focusing on the winds coming off the ocean for air; standing in the water as it crashes onto the shore for water; noonday sun with a bonfire on the beach, etc.)."

"I am examining the possibility of moving the dates of celebration of the Wheel of the Year due to climate change."

"Being in a place with very few trees has changed me in some way but I cannot pinpoint it. Certainly more attentive to other features of the land. Missing salmon. Missing the sense of water moving always in the land. [...] The move to Iowa has had an enormous impact. I'm not sure I can even explain how much it has shifted my practices. Still celebrate but it's become less natural, somehow."

"My natural environment definitely plays a part - when you get flowers sprouting in early February, it changes the meaning of Imbolc a bit. Likewise, it's almost always still warm here at Samhain, so the feeling is somewhat different. Having three 'harvest' festivals makes a bit more sense here, though, since something is pretty much always being harvested for at least half the year."

"Temperate climate. The seasons tend to last around 3-4 months. Currently going into winter. Terrible summer heat, rain in Spring and Winter. Autumn isn't really discernible. The problem for me is that still, after 20 years here, I become confused. My body, my soul, my conscious and unconscious being responds to the pull of the North, to the seasons of the Northern Hemisphere. Yes, I understand, intellectually, that I am in another hemisphere, that the times of festival and recognition of nature are opposite to the North, but with the best will in the world, I cannot bring this knowledge into me. I suppose its cognitive dissonance really."

"When I envision the elements of air, water, and earth, I picture flora and fauna from my current environment. I would like to learn stories about the land from our local Native American tribes but haven't yet found any books on the subject. [...] I would like to come up with more locally-specific ritual elements but haven't done so yet."

"Since my move to the Caribbean I have had to gradually get used to a totally different environment, a different nature spirit so to speak. [...] As a Celt in the Caribbean I still find I need to celebrate my own Celtic rituals. Once I have settled to the culture here in St. Lucia, [and] understood its natural rhythms and spirits I'm sure rituals will develop."

Although these Druids expressed a desire to develop new rituals and celebrations, to better connect with the landscape and seasonal cycles of their homes, they had not, as yet, been able to do so.

Other Druids (32% of survey respondents), who had spent more time contemplating and connecting with their local environments, had begun the process of *wildcrafting* their Druidry, as described by Gordon Cooper, in his 2012 article, *Wild-crafting the Modern Druid*.[11] There were several notable intergroup variations in the prevalence of wildcrafting.[12] Druids resident in moisture driven, wet/dry climates were much more likely to wildcraft (56%), as were Druids resident in Oceania (69%). Druids of the AODA, which at the time of the survey was under the direction of Gordon Cooper, were also more likely than others to wildcraft (53%). Druids born, raised, and residing in traditionally Celtic lands were much less likely to engage in wildcrafting.

The first stages of wildcrafting typically involved adapting bits of traditional rituals and celebrations to the local landscape, swapping out traditional tree, animal, or other ritual elements or symbols, and substituting comparable symbolic elements indigenous to the local environment. For some, this also included shifting celebration dates a bit, when the seasons refused to cooperate with the calendar. Examples of this type of response included:

> *"In Canada, we always tailor ritual to the weather. In Alberta, where I live, the seasons are not normal, given our proximity to the Rocky Mountains. (Snow in July, +25 C in December) Therefore, it's dress accordingly! Again, our seasons are screwed up here in Alberta, so I tend to go with the lunar or calendar dates for celebrating. Beltane, for instance, is usually seen as the start of summer. By May 1, we usually do not have a single leaf on a tree. In fact, it's usually still cold and snowy. When the trees blossom, I celebrate true Beltane, which could be anywhere between May 15 and June 10."*

> *"OBOD coursework references flora and fauna in the UK and Europe. I am in Michigan. So, when we celebrate Imbolc on Feb 1, we don't use snowdrops as a sign of Spring but rather the maple tree whose sap is just starting to run (or about to start). We celebrate the sacredness of maple and honor its gifts: sap for syrup and wood for musical instruments, furniture and sports equipment."*

> *"I live in the Arizona desert, and virtually none of the traditional trees, herbs, etc. grow around here, so I have had to substitute desert plants (of the same genus when I have been able), grow some of them myself, or order them online. We have no standing stones, but we DO have ley lines, and the energy around them is just a potent as any in Europe. I also use rain water in my rituals."*

"The structure of most of my rituals is still pretty much as given [in] AODA's Grove Ritual Handbook, apart from some small modifications that allow me to act out the symbolism informed by my biome. In addition to the above mentioned, I've also appointed 4 different myths, one to each gate, from my cultural environment. The fruits that serve as symbolic offerings in each holy day (and are ready for harvest at roughly the appropriate time) are:
New year: Pitanga (Eugenia Uniflora)
Light: Mango (Mangifera indica)
Old Year: Avocado (Persea americana)
Heart: Cacao (Theobroma cacao)"

"Altering the animals for the directions given in the OBOD-rituals, because the hawk/ stag/ salmon/ bear are not native to these lands; I use instead the rowan/ deer/ toad/ fox. Prayers/ songs/ stories of Christian or generally German background. Daily practice connected to the forest/ the river/ the sun, moon and stars. Morning ritual in a grove at a riverside or while being in a train along the course of a river valley."

"[The environment influences my wheel of the year...] *Primarily in terms of ritual timing: you don't want a Summer Solstice ritual during the crushing heat of the day in the desert, so ritual is after dark. Winter Solstice *may* actually be outside. Spring Equinox may be inside because of high winds/sandstorms. Summer Solstice may be rained out. However, when it rains, because of the preciousness of water in our bioregion, the Gods and the spirits of the rains get thanks offerings."*

"I have made one major change, however in the Order's Sphere of Protection. I have reversed the location and seasons of Air and Water so that Air is in the West and Water in the East. All of the main bodies of water, from our closest creek to the Delaware River to the Atlantic Ocean are to the east and our rainiest months are in the spring. By contrast, our prevailing winds are westerly and northwesterly and they blow most steadily in the fall. Also the windiest place I ever lived was Iowa, far west of SE Pennsylvania, and when I visualize windy places, I always see the prairie."

Druids who had been wildcrafting their practices for a longer period of time had often carefully researched the myths, legends, and seasonal ritual traditions of local indigenous peoples. In addition to incorporating local symbolic elements from nature, these Druids often looked for ways to blend local cultural traditions and lore with their Druidry practice, to enrich that practice, and ground it more deeply in the local culture and landscape. Some of the most vivid examples of this came from Druids in Sweden, North America, Russia, Japan, New Zealand, and Australia, for example:

"Living in a place where I see all seasons, and where the weather changes dramatically within the season, I wanted to be connected to it. Not being connected to the Wheel of the Year made me feel disconnected and suffocated. This was the first year that I celebrated Samhain in any deeper sense. it meant a lot to me to be able to see the energy of my ancestors and to show my respect and gratitude toward them. I've grown up with celebrating the four equinoxes as this is common practice in Sweden. Winter is celebrated with processions of candlelights, eating saffron baked goods and drinking mulled wine. Spring is celebrated with making a huge bonfire and singing, from sunset and into the night. Prior to the Spring equinox, we bring birch branches into the house and decorate them with coloured feathers. Summer is celebrated with what is now world famous via IKEA: Midsummer. You dance - often there are at least 2-3 circles around it - around a pole that is very phallic and dressed in flowers and leaves. Dance until you are tired, then have a dish made with seafood or fish of some kind. Dessert is fresh berries - and a lot of drinks... At night, maidens and bachelors pick 7, 9 or 11 different kind of flowers (it varies what people want but it is always an odd number), lay them under their pillow, and if they are lucky, they will see their future spouse in a dream. Autumn equinox; I can't remember doing much for it. I think it's been forgotten over the years in Sweden or replaced with a Christian holiday. My grandmother used to highlight it by dressing her home in yellow/ochre/golden textiles and bring branches into the house. And from that day onwards, she would light a lot of candles."

"Local trees and spirits of place have helped me adjust my Druid practice to North America where I live. Native Abenaki names and practices in New England feature in my personal ritual and blessing. Work with a general Pagan group over the course of a year for seasonal festivals influenced my personal practice away from a formal OBOD ritual format into more varied and some-times freer practice. [...] New England climate and regional foods shape rituals indoors and out, and the kinds of foods at feast and offered in ritual."

"Imbolc goes very close to a Russian pagan feast called Maslenitsa which has almost the same meaning. So, I try to combine two these traditions - the Celtic and Russian - so I can enjoy coming of the Spring with my Slavic pagan friends."

"I have a lot of trouble with the traditional Wheel, because it doesn't reflect my environment AT ALL. My natural environment is functionally completely opposite— the 'dark time' when everyone huddles indoors is summer, not winter. In my personal work I actually follow the ancient Greek calendar more closely in terms of the significance of the seasons--Persephone emerges from the underworld in September/October to initiate the rainy season, which is when things grow, and goes back down before the summer, when it's too hot for agriculture. The Wheel is also backwards in terms of my day-to-day life. I pretty much exist on the academic calendar--New Year is late August/September, fall, winter, and spring are the busiest times (in my particular field, especially October/November, because our annual conference is near American Thanksgiving), and summer is, not rest time, but down time, where the behind-the-scenes work gets done. I'm not much of a solitary, and the eight festivals are important to me mostly for the community aspect, so this doesn't affect the way I practice too much, but it does affect the way I think about seasons, time, and the symbolism of birth/ life/ death that always comes along with the Wheel. I never quite feel like I fit into it."

"Because I am in Japan, the main religions could be said to be mainstream paganism if you like. However, as they are organized religions and have a set way of doing things. [...] My wife and mother-in-law seemed concerned at first that I was not doing enough to remember my own ancestors of blood, and reminded me to pray for them when we visit a shrine and the shrine at my mother-in-law's house. So, I practice only some of my Druid rituals with family. I try to make a big deal when the moon is out and make sure my son and wife get a good look. I get my three year old son to say hello to the moon, and think about whether they see a rabbit (the Japanese tradition) or a face (the Western tradition) in the moon. I tell him as he goes to sleep that the moon will be watching over him. My wife can't argue against that because Shinto says kami are in nature and Buddhism says life is in everything."

*"At least four of our members are fluent Māori speakers
and teachers and at least another 8 are learning the
language. So, culturally, Māori words, call to Māori
spirits of land, sea and forest and Māori myths and
legends are all incorporated into our 8 Druid ceremonies.
In Aotearoa New Zealand we have very different native
trees and while we honour the oak and other northern
hemisphere trees, our own native trees have greater
power and resonance. One of our members has created a
New Zealand tree Ogham. At the four directions we call in
kāhu, hawk of dawn for East, the pohutukawa tree with its
crimson flowers for North (yes, North is the strongest and
warmest light in NZ!); tuna (eel) or the Salmon of Wisdom
for West and Papatūānuku for South."*

*"Close to natural park spaces which I use for meditation
and ritual, lucky to have a garden enough to connect with
nature and plant/animals, cultural environment is a secular pluralist mainly Christian ethic of white colonial
immigrant European heritage overlaid on Aboriginal culture of 50-80 thousand year history. Makes me think
Aboriginal elders were probably the first druid archetypes. Affects my rituals in that I know I am on custodial
land. Availability of shared space, local park to perform
ceremony, availability of materials for the ceremony and
local symbols used (local animals for directions, inver-
sion of the directions and elements due to southern
hemisphere). Cultural heritage — difficult to explain,
dynamic tension between reliving old world traditions, or
adapting the old traditions to the new land and spirit."*

Finally, many Druids used only philosophical principles derived from
Druidry to inform the process of crafting entirely new rituals and cycles of
seasonal celebration from the particularities or their local, physical and cultural
environments. Rather than simply modifying the ritual forms and symbolisms
associated with traditional, Celtic holidays, these Druids focused on applying
the broader, meta-principles of Druidry to their local environments. They
studied local traditions and lore, and the ecology of their local environments.
They practiced nature connection, and built relationships with the local spirits
of place. They meditated on Druid elemental systems (e.g. air/fire/water/earth
or land/sea/sky), and on how those elements actually manifest in their local
landscapes and seasons. Then they crafted their rituals and celebrations, writing
localized liturgies to use in their practice. As Druids explained:

*"The Forest created me, named me. The land has shown
me dragons. The myths and all are nice, but the core of*

my personal practice is building and maintaining a connection to the land where I stand. Though, less misty-eyed and magical, I find there is a line to be walked."

"My practice is almost exclusively influenced by local culture and nature. Practice is irrelevant if not place-based. It's only religious fantasy otherwise."

"When we celebrate the Wheel of the Year it must always be what we are experiencing locally. There is no point in paying homage to something that is not happening in your own world."

"I'd rather work with a plant that I can have an actual personal relationship with rather than one I can only read about in a book."

"Many Druid rituals do not fit into my home environment of Subtropical rainforest in Australia. I am trying to reconcile this, and find my own path forward that is more in tune with the land I am living in. For example, the traditional Wheel of the Year is not relevant here. I am observing nature in my home town and creating one of my own."

The most vivid examples of this kind of deep, spiritual wildcrafting came from various regions of North America, Australia, New Zealand, and Brazil, for example:

"Even though I was drawn to Druidry because of its ties to my ancestral lands of Ireland and Wales, I have spent considerable time in my practice connecting to the land here [in the Pacific Northwest] *where I grew up. As part of my practice, I took a 9-month course in Ethnobotany to learn about the lore and plants in our area and I have taken classes to learn local native techniques in plant use, basketry, weaving, drum-making and honoring the stories of the land. We live in a truly beautiful place and that has inspired me to get outside and appreciate it more. I spent an entire year observing the plants around me and made a mandala each month with some of the surrounding flowers, leaves, and berries to get to know them better."*

"I have shifted the symbolism and meanings for the Wheel of the Year to reflect the monsoon seasons in the area. I'm working on shifting the offerings and symbols to local

organisms. Instead of having one growing season, we have multiple. I associate winter with lusher green plants that can't handle the summer heat. Reading about snowy and stripped landscapes in rituals doesn't make sense. So I'm trying to adjust the rituals. The solstices/equinoxes will remain steady in many ways, but the others I adjusted to monsoons and other regional effects."

"I live in the Northern Chihuahuan Desert. We get clumps of chaparral (creosote) bushes, we don't get groves of trees. In greeting and offering to the spirits of this land where I dwell, I address the river, the mountains, the underground bolsons where our water comes from, the desert per and in se, a local indigenous sacred area, and our regional flora and fauna."

"Our seasons are not based on light and temperature, but on rain, fog and drought. We have three main seasons here: Rain Season (FLOWERS! and lots of new green growth) from January through April; Fog Season, with a weekly cycle of dense fog and cold winds interspersed with warm sunshine, with slowing growth and gradual drying-out of the native flora, from 'May Grey' and 'June Gloom' through 'Foggust'; and then Fire Season, when the fog disperses, everything not irrigated withers and dies, and temperatures finally rise above 70 — but you still cannot open the windows because of drifting wildfire smoke. Since all agriculture in our hills must be irrigated, and the temperatures vary so little throughout the year, 'planting' and 'harvest' happen on an ongoing basis — potatoes and greens all year round, but never enough heat for a tomato. Given that reality, I have restructured my wheel of the year according to the Druid philosophical principles of Gwyar/Nwyfre/Calas. We bless seeds, plant, and celebrate the arrival of flowers, during Rain Season (I have since discovered that the Ohlone People who once lived here also celebrated Flower Season, up in these hills.). I do inner journeying while socked-in by the dense, chilly fogs of 'Summer'. We do a Fire Season ritual of singing down the rain, and rededicating ourselves to stewardship work for our other-than-human kin, during the time of death and dearth. We celebrate our Ancestors Day around the Autumnal Equinox, the driest and most fearsome time of the year. Yule is still a celebration of rebirth, with the return of the light, and hopefully the rain. It's is really all about our relationship to our land."

"The local Druids held a ritual to invite ancestral Matronae spirits from all participants to coalesce under a locally based epithet and be open to worship by anyone living in this region. We worship the Mothers of the Three Waters now. They're tied to the lands of the Potomac, Chesapeake, and Susquehanna."

"I adapt everything I do to western PA, which [...] means developing my own wheel of the year (so Imbolc for me is about the first flow of sap), working deeply with local trees, and the like. Culturally, my family is a big part Pennsylvania Dutch, which has its own magical tradition (Bracherei, also known as PowWow; this is also tied to the hex signs, etc). I've studied that and incorporated pieces of that into my practice, as I remember my grand-mothers practicing it."

"O ambiente natural e cultural sempre irá influenciar. Eu vivo no centro da América do Sul, um caldeirão cultural e um lugar onde muitos biomas se encontram. É um espaço lindo e cheio de diversidade. Muito. Inclusive percebo que o 'Ano Claro' e 'Ano Escuro' do calendário octuplo tem muita relação com a Chuva e a Seca.
[Translation:]
The natural and cultural environment will always influence. I live in the center of South America, a melting pot and a place where many biomes meet. It is a beautiful space full of diversity. A lot. I even realize that the 'Light Year' and 'Dark Year' of the eightfold calendar have a lot to do with Rain and Drought."

In the process of wildcrafting rituals and celebrations, many Druids turned to the lore of indigenous peoples, for wisdom and guidance on how best to connect with their local landscapes and spirits. However, most also do so with a keen awareness of and sensitivity to the risks of cultural appropriation. They worked to avoid appropriating elements of indigenous cultures, while also attempting to learn from the indigenous, "ancestors of place" for their regions. As Druids explained:

"Learning about native trees, shrubs, plants and wildlife and how they were viewed and used by the original tribes of the area, and using that information to tailor my own practice, while still being very mindful of avoiding cul-tural appropriations as well is a balancing act."

"There is a very solemn and heavy responsibility to recognize and honour the traditional owners of our land here in Australia, and to not co-opt any of their practices or spaces, without express permission. In recent years I've been presented with more and more opportunities to learn and help spread information about our indigenous cultures, and I hope to be invited on land walks and educational journeys with elders around my local area across the coming years. While nothing has ultimately impacted or influenced me directly, I believe that it will in time to come in such a way as I'll be more open to and aware of the spirits of place from an indigenous perspective, and could work more effectively from a truly Australian point-of-view rather than a Euro-centric one."

"My natural and cultural environment is a major factor in the form of my Druid rituals. When I first began, years ago, I wanted to include a few indigenous words, to include the first Nations, but academics insisted I had no right to do this and so I didn't. They speak to us in other ways however, in particular regarding where we conduct each ritual. The form of the landscape -- its hills & springs -- dictate where we conduct the 8 seasonal celebrations. I believe the Old Ones inspire us to discern the sacred geography/geometry of this place. And probably more than we are aware, influence the actual flow and detail of the ritual on the day. We acknowledge the traditional custodians at the start of our work. The natural environment has informed where we conduct the seasonal celebrations. In 2002, the place that was to be our sacred centre was revealed to us by a spirit-guide of that place. Since then we have celebrated the spring equinox to the east, Beltane to the north-east, summer solstice to the north, Lughnasadh to the north-west, autumn equinox to the west, Samhuin to the south-west, winter solstice to the south, and Imbolc to the south-east of that central site. Progressively, we have been shown/led to places with significant energetics. Two of these are aboriginal sacred sites and we do not conduct ritual at these, but nearby."

"With the rich native American culture in this area, I strive to be respectful of their beliefs and sensitive to the fact I'm living and practicing on stolen land."

"I think a lot, as an American, about the practice of Druidry. Obviously I'm native to North America, but the practice of indigenous North Americans is not something

I want to appropriate. But I'm not native to native Celtic lands. I'm not trying to reconstruct ancient Druidry (which I don't believe can actually be reconstructed truly). I'm not an ancient Celt. I'm a 21st century American. So what does my Druidry look like? For example, Imbolc really IS NOT the beginning of spring here in Massachusetts. It's still wicked cold and there is no hint of spring, as there might be in the British Isles because of the Gulf Stream. So how do I make Imbolc meaningful? Beltaine is not the beginning of summer for us. Etc. The stories of Celtic mythology are not the stories of my land. But the stories of my land are from a people's who culture I must be very careful not to appropriate. So I think about this a lot and am trying to work out these things. I think shamanic practices have helped me try to connect to the spirits of my land, but this is an ongoing question I'm walking with a lot."

In contrast to this struggle to avoid appropriation, Druids of mixed ancestry, and members of multicultural communities often discussed how they were attempting to create a multicultural form of Druidry, which integrated diverse cultural backgrounds into a single, coherent spirituality. Examples of such responses included:

"Regarding culture, I live in the melting pot that is the USA. Therefore, I feel justified in mixing cultural practices from various ancestors. They all exist within my blood together, so I don't see anything wrong with engaging in multiple practices or honoring gods from different ethnic groups in a single ritual."

"I live close to the Mexican border, and Samhain coincides closely with Dia de los Muertos. I tend to celebrate both. My fiance is of Mexican heritage and he enjoys celebrating it as well."

"The Māori cultural heritage is strong and very aligned with nature spiritualism. It is fully immersed in my / our ritual practice. The natural environment in New Zealand is awesome and very easily accessed to inspire my faith. For each celebration appropriate gifts and adornments are used to reflect the time of the year. A bi-cultural approach is always used to recognize the bi-cultural nature of New Zealand constitution."

"Being multicultural, I honor the wheel through several cultural traditions."

"Our neighbours are Cree and Metis. [...] As our rela-
tionships with our indigenous neighbours deepen, we are
growing more of a diverse cultural mix in the Wheel.
Paying attention to interfaith dynamics also influences
this."

Reinforcing Traditions

For 24% of Druids, who happen to live in the physical and cultural landscapes that gave birth to contemporary Druidry, connection with the natural environment often reinforces, and adds depth of meaning to the traditional ritual forms and celebrations. If done consciously and deliberately, this may still be a form of spiritual wildcrafting. However, it is not as readily apparent as wildcrafting done elsewhere because the resulting ritual forms and celebrations are nearly identical to those found in books.

Statistical analyses showed that Druids rooted in traditionally Celtic lands, especially those resident in the British Isles and Ireland, were much more likely to perceive a reinforcing influence of the land on tradition; while Druids of the Celtic Diaspora, especially those of North America and Oceania, were much less likely to experience a reinforcing influence.[13]

Examples of survey responses that clearly illustrate the prevalence of "wildcrafting modern Druidry in the traditional lands of the ancient Druids" include the following:

"My ancestry, birth and home is on the land of Great
Britain and its influence is in my very bones. I love the old
traditions - Morris Dancers, Wassailing, Harvest
Festivals, etc., and it was these very traditions that drew
me to Druidry. Culturally, I always seek out Morris
Dancers in the spring time to attend if possible, and will
always stop to watch and say a silent prayer to the season
if I happen upon a group. A drama group performs a free
street play celebrating traditional customs twice a year at
12th Night with wassailing and a Mummers Play, and
Harvest celebration in October which I always attend.
Bonfire Night/Guy Fawkes Night on 5th November
celebrates a political activist from 1605, but it replaced
the old Samhain celebrations so I always go to one near
me to enjoy the bonfire."

"Creation of spontaneous Irish language prayer to ances-
tral spirits and deities; use of local materia in offerings.
My celebration of cycle of year is more organically (or
less self-consciously) tied into wider and historically
deeper cultural celebration of these occasions"

"The natural environment especially trees, I use them as reference points in journeying and connect with them when I am among them. As I am British and living in Britain, the cultural environment as a Druid is everything. All rituals are influenced by my sense of the ancestors and of my total connection to the land here, as I am lucky to be living where some of my ancestors as far back as it is possible to live, have also lived. The Wheel of the Year is pretty much standard for us as we are in the northern hemisphere and are [part of a] grove with a rural setting, [and so are attuned] with the natural and agricultural cycles of the year."

"Both my natural and cultural environment have had great impact and influence on my rituals. Living on a small island, the principles of land and sea and sky are incredibly apparent and present. Culturally, many archetypes, the use of language and stories define my rituals both personally and as part of a larger group structure. Language is of particular importance. All of the names for the Wheel are taken from my culture with attributes and qualities for each found in the vernacular and written lore."

"I am a native Welsh speaker so will tend to greet the day in Welsh and have adapted some of my ritual words from Welsh sources. My current natural environment is the land where the Brigantes tribe once lived; it is full of natural springs, and the most prominent feature in the local landscape is known as the Bridestones, so I have rekindled my spiritual relationship with Bride. I like to study folklore as a way into a relationship with place, and try to incorporate folkloric practices wherever I happen to be living. When I lived in Cheshire, where there was lots of arable land, Lammas and the grain harvest was a more important seasonal event and celebration. Now I live in a steep, dark Pennine valley, observing the changes in the seasons is increasingly important to my mental health as I can tend to get S.A.D."

"The Scottish Highlands is a strong influence culturally. The natural landscape, heritage, stories and history are woven into my practice with Gaelic, spirits of place, ancestral tartan and tools and traditions and special festival days such as Burns Night and Culloden Anniversary. Scottish days of honouring as listed above relevant to spirits of place and ancestors."

"Als Kind war ich zu Maria Lichtmess Messen; das hat meine Assoziation von Imbolc mit Kerzenlicht geprägt. / Für mein Verständnis von Ostara waren unsere familiären Ostertraditionen prägend (Ich betrachte dieses Fest als Teil meiner Ostara-Feiern). / Für Beltane waren meine Assoziationen mit Walpurgisnacht prägend (ausgelassenes, nacktes um's Feuer tanzen, Hexensabbat). / Die Herbsttagundnachtgleiche assoziiere ich mit Erntedankfesten. / Jul ist natürlich von meinem Verständnis von Weihnachten geprägt, obschon ich beides als separate Fester feiere, gehört beides (inkl. der Adventszeit und insbesondere von Jul bis bis zum 6. Januar) zu den Rauhnächten.

[Translation:]

As a child I attended the Maria Lichtmess masses. This has shaped my association of Imbolc with candlelight / For my understanding of Ostara our family Easter traditions were formative (I consider this feast to be part of my Ostara celebrations). / For Beltane my associations with Walpurgis Night were formative (exuberant, naked dancing around the fire, witches' Sabbath). / I associate the autumn equinox with harvest festivals. / Jul is of course marked by my understanding of Christmas, although I celebrate both as separate celebrations, both (including the Advent season and especially from Jul until January 6th) belong to the Rauhnächten."

Even among Druids whose traditional practices are supported and reinforced by their physical and cultural environments, there seems to be an awareness that a true spiritual connection to land, sea, and sky is, and should rightly be, the driving force behind a Druid's practices — whatever form they may take in the end. Druids wrote, for example:

"I always adapt my practice to my surroundings. Also, the common European culture which I was born into and the traditions of which both modern Druidry and Witchcraft are built upon have a profound influence on my spiritual-ity as a whole. Without the influences of my cultural and natural surroundings I would have a totally different set of practices and understanding of spirituality than I have now. The festivals of the Wheel of the Year are strongly connected to the passing of the seasons in the temperate zone in which I live. Also, the form of celebration I use stems from an old pan-European and Celtic tradition. I think that if I had been living in a different climate zone surrounded by a different culture, my celebration of the festivals of the year would have been very different."

*"The traditions we follow [...] are drawn from the OBOD
curriculum as amended by our own piece of England."*

*"My natural environment influences my rituals because I
try to honour that which is there: the willow tree in the
garden, the local wild creatures, the river etc. Of course,
the weather has an influence on my rituals too. Living in
rainy UK, it can mean finding an alternative (indoor)
location or adjusting the ritual to not include things like
lighting fires. My cultural environment influences the
language of my rituals: I am a native English speaker, so
my rituals are in English rather than in a Celtic language.
The predominantly Christian cultural environment in
which I live influences where I do ritual, usually at home
in my back garden and never out in full public view where
people could harass or disrupt the ritual. I try to
celebrate based on natural signs like the first snowdrops,
hawthorn blossom, the wheat harvest or first frost. These
can vary year by year and come earlier or later than the
standard calendar date depending on the weather. I try to
adapt the Wheel of the Year to fit with what is going on
around me in nature."*

The two groups of Druids — those in the "wildcrafting" group and
those in the "reinforcing traditions" group — were almost entirely independent
of one another, with only one or two people falling partly into both categories.
Taken together, these groups account for 52% world Druids, with no notable
intergroup variations. While the end results of their nature connection activities
lead to somewhat dissimilar ritual forms and celebrations, the underlying,
philosophical approaches of the two groups are remarkably similar.

This raises a question: Is modern Druidry defined by a set of formal,
shared rituals and celebrations, or is it defined by the spiritual meta-practice
of connecting with and celebrating the land upon which one actually lives —
guided by a shared philosophical framework? It is a question worth pondering,
as it arises repeatedly when considering emergent themes like wildcrafting,
which might serve to unify what otherwise seems a disparate agglomeration
of localized traditions. We will see a similar pattern emerge when considering
the nature of Druid theologies, in *Chapter 5*, and the nature of Druid rituals
and celebrations, in *Chapters 6 & 7*, but more on this, to come.

Simplifying

The final impact of the physical environment on Druidry practices,
described by 15% of Druids, was simplification or elimination of formalities
within Druidry practice. The only intergroup variation was that North American

Druids were more likely to simplify their practices than other Druids[14], likely due to the safety and privacy issues discussed in *Chapter 3*.

For many Druids, this simply meant omitting formal ritual garb, ritual props and tools, and altars, or becoming more practical about if and when to use such things, for example:

> *"Well I can't see myself dressing in white robes where I live. [...] I do have attire I feel is more sensitive and calming for myself to wear. Simple gentle flowing clothing. Boots that can help protect me from rattlers when I'm out and about as there are a lot of them where I live. Safety is always an issues and some wildlife here is worth keeping a respectful distance from such as cougars and bears. When I am in my home or just outside, sometimes bare feet seem best."*

> *"Everyday practice is done in pajamas, most commonly. LOL. My natural environment has probably been the single biggest influence on the form of my Druid rituals. I grew up in rural and wild areas; my father worked for Yosemite National Park and I grew up going between the foothills of the San Bernardino Mountains (my mom) and the high Sierra Nevada Mountains (my dad). Both were outdoors people (met teaching outdoor science school) and I was raised as an animist and a strange kind of Christian who was told that my relationship with my personal god was to be found out in wilderness. My Druid ritual practice is centered around sitting/breathing meditation, movement meditation, contemplative prayer, nature mysticism, and seership/shamanic journey work. I have a lovely shrine room with altars, but all of my core practices are unscripted and require nothing but my body and breath. This was built, in part, because hiking into wilderness has been a core part of my practice and I don't want to pack a bunch of stuff in and back."*

> *"In my personal practice I am way more relaxed, unscripted and speak from my heart, responsive to nature's gifts in the moment. In my home garden environment, I can meditate with my tree or in some private outdoor spaces and create ritual there occasionally too. I can also create ritual indoors in a private space that has direct connection to a mostly private courtyard garden and bit of grass I have planted. I stand on that grass/earth most mornings to greet the day and the elements. I do a meditative walk by the sea that's close by every morning and greet the elements on the beach."*

"I do not tend to perform many formal rituals. That said, I have planted an Oak and Birch grove of trees in the woodland and am slowly adding plants and flowers to it to enhance the informal times I spend in contemplation there. Irrespective of where I am, I greet the sun most mornings with a prayer I wrote some years ago (an adaptation of someone else's) and take in some long slow breaths to start the day. A simple ritual maybe?"

"My rituals are quite sparse. Often they mostly involve finding the oldest, largest tree I can in a secluded part of the forest and meditating at its base. Occasionally I'll hold specific items for whatever I'm trying to achieve. [...] The biggest influence the natural environment [has] on my path is in Summer. Being in the Australian bush is such an overwhelming experience, it reminds me in many ways of the traditional use of sweat lodges for communing with spirits. It is hot. Oppressively hot. Very high humidity. And the cicadas are a constant, incredibly loud drone. A few hours in that changes your state of mind and I feel makes your mindset shift to sit somewhere between this world and the spirit world [...] thus making communication with the spirit world easier."

For others, *simplifying* meant focusing their full attention on making daily life a living prayer, or a moving meditation within the world, rather than focusing on a cycle of seasonal rituals, or on isolated sessions of "Druidry practice". For these Druids, ritual needed to be spontaneous, and responsive to Nature in the moment. It needed to be about developing a reciprocal relationship with the natural world, and not about ceremonial forms. The ways in which Druids accomplished this were many and varied, for example:

"My ritual is walking through the woods, attuning myself to the energies around me. I leave offerings at various places — the hollow of a tree trunk, a sunny rock, the seasonal streams during the spring thaw. I ask questions and open myself to receiving the answer as I follow the paths, whether it comes in the form of an animal or sudden realization as I look at hillside flowers. I don't follow the standard ritual format, as you can see. Living on 20 acres of forest, I can celebrate in the woods and soak up the local energies at these times."

"The decline in insects in my area has changed the energy dramatically. I can feel the energy of my environment strain under climate change. I have tried to do more healing work and work in permaculture gardening."

"[Thirty] *years ago, my spouse and I moved the old log home to this place, here where we live: a mix of old natural mixed forests, abandoned farmland (largely restored now), deep cedar swamps, and small limestone barrens, marshes and lakes. We set about applying our knowledge of natural ecosystems to planting native trees; setting stones for gardens, establishing a tall-grass prairie, and generally creating niches and habitats that blur the distinction between what is natural and what is cultural. This all started long before my interest or knowledge of things 'Druidry'— but much later, the significance and value of these places to my spiritual practice became apparent. [...] 'This place' now extends to the horizons around us, and beyond to the regional forests and abandoned farmlands and wetlands in which I work and Re-create. My suburban relatives do not understand why I have no interest in travel. The truth is I would much rather continue to get to know my own environment deeply (and it does take a life time or more of learning) than to know many environments only on the surface. The natural environment here is very much the spirit-source for much of the way I celebrate the turning of the seasons, and the inspiration for many of the poems which really chronicle the day, the place, the ritual."*

"*My work is focused on regenerative practices that seek to restore soil and trees in my immediate area (former cattle ranch). Using biodynamic practices and Druid meditation and energy work to directly engage with the immediacy of my environment.*"

"*Another core part of my practice that predated my Druid identity is working with horses. I've learned a ton from horse souls I've been blessed to work with, especially my own two boys, and consider horse training and dressage to be a form of moving meditation and shapeshifting.*"

"*My home is on 2.5 acres and adjacent to about 10 acres of woods. We have lived here for the last 4 years. I have enough room to plant a 60 ft diameter labyrinth garden. I have enough room to plant almost all the Ogham trees around my property. I don't have to drive somewhere to take a walk in the woods. Being able to do so much with plants has strongly influenced the path of my Druid practice away from the rituals and into the garden and interacting with trees. [...] I notice the changing of the seasons with much more detail now that I have a garden. I'm also pretty happy with low key celebrations.*"

*"Everything I do as a Druid is Druidry. And Druidry is
everything I do. I don't think a distinction between 'ritual'
and 'spiritual practice' and the everyday business of
living is in any way helpful. I have experiences that are
bounded by ritual time and space, but they are no more or
less important than other parts of my life. They are just
another part of the warp and weft of life itself. My
Druidry isn't a religion, or expressed only as ritual or
spiritual practice, and especially not a thing that I do in
robes on special occasions. In fact, I actively resist this
kind of expression of spiritual practice. I'm not interested
in fancy dress or amateur dramatics. If I wanted that, I'd
rejoin the church. Druidry only makes sense if it happens
in jeans and dirty boots, on walks in nature, standing on
the edge of the sea or in the heart of a city, following a
magpie with mud under my fingernails or dancing in a
nightclub pounded by music and bright lights. Druidry
makes sense when I'm taking environmental action,
caring for others, sharing wisdom, being inspired by
adventure. It happens at the edges of life and death,
between sleeping and waking, in dreams and nightmares,
yes, but it also happens eating dinner, watching TV, sitting
on a train or taking a shit. [Druidry is] a way of being in
the world."*

The Process of Becoming a Druid

Having considered each of the factors that influence Druids as they
craft their personal paths of Druidry, it is time to return to the question with
which we began this chapter: how does one become a Druid, circa 2020 c.e.?
As with so many things in Druidry, the answer is circular, and is largely dependent upon geography and social context.

Survey responses have clearly demonstrated that nature connection
is both the primary goal, and the primary source of inspiration, for nearly all
Druids, the world around. For nearly all Druids, this "connection with Nature"
also includes relationships with nature deities, and/or spirits-of-place. For
some, prior knowledge of the natural world and a predisposition toward nature
connection leads to a sense of homecoming upon the discovery of Druidry. It
is a spiritual path which validates these inclinations and habits, offers a sense
of community, and provides a ritual tradition that supports and encourages
this way of life. For those with prior knowledge of other Neopagan traditions,
or the myths and folk traditions of the Celts, Druidry may inspire a deeper
focus on nature observation and nature connection in the landscapes which
gave birth to those traditions.

No matter how one stumbles upon the path of Druidry, study seems to be the inevitable next step. For those fortunate enough to live in places where local Druid groups abound, face-to-face interactions with Druids and Druidry mentors may be highly influential. For most Druids, however, the lack of accessible, local Druid groups means that study takes the form of reading. Any combination of books on Druidry, or on books on historical, philosophical or scientific topics aligned with Druidry, or books of myths and legends from around the world, or curriculum materials from one or more Druid organizations may provide the fodder for this study. The selections are different for every Druid, but Druids share a habit of reading widely, in search of wisdom and new questions to ponder.

Reading among Druids rarely serves as a simple process of seeking ready answers to standard questions. It is rather a search for new ideas to explore, new experiences to try, and new seed topics for meditation. Druids may read about different ritual forms, or different ways of perceiving and interacting with nature, nature deities, and/or spirits of place, but then, they try things out to see what works in practice. Their individual experiences may lead to further readings and meditations, or to discussions with other Druids (face-to-face, or via internet forums), or to a shift within their personal Druidry practice, leading to an ever-deepening relationship with Nature.

To ask about the process of becoming a Druid — as if it were simply a matter of learning about, and then converting to a new and different set of beliefs — is to ask the wrong question. To become a Druid is to embark upon a process of endless becoming — a process of observing, studying, meditating, celebrating, and forging connections with the physical, spiritual, and divine essence of Nature.

CHAPTER 4 NOTES & REFERENCES

1 Regional variations in factors influencing Druids' spiritual paths (% of maximum possible influence):

British Isles & Ireland more influenced by —

Spirits	(79% vs. 71% of MPI) p=0.01
Curricula	(51% vs. 49% of MPI) p=0.00
Deities	(48% vs. 47% of MPI) p=0.00
Face-to-face	(54% vs. 40% of MPI) p=0.00
Ancestors-of-place	(56% vs. 34% of MPI) p=0.00
Druidry mentors	(38% vs. 32% of MPI) p=0.00

British Isles & Ireland less influenced by —

Druidry books	(56% vs. 57% of MPI) p=0.01
Other books	(51% vs. 52% of MPI) p=0.00
Internet forums	(43% vs. 46% of MPI) p=0.00
Dreams or past-life	(33% vs. 37% of MPI) p=0.00

Continental Europe more influenced by —

Curricula	(71% vs. 49% of MPI) p=0.00
Dreams or past-life	(44% vs. 37% of MPI) p=0.01
Druidry mentors	(38% vs. 32% of MPI) p=0.01

Continental Europe less influenced by —

Spirits	(63% vs. 71% of MPI) p=0.00
Deities	(46% vs. 47% of MPI) p=0.01
Internet forums	(45% vs. 46% of MPI) p=0.01
Ancestors-of-blood	(12% vs. 23% of MPI) p=0.00

North America more influenced by —

Spirits	(73% vs. 71% of MPI) p=0.00
Druidry books	(61% vs. 57% of MPI) p=0.00
Other books	(56% vs. 52% of MPI) p=0.00
Deities	(52% vs. 47% of MPI) p=0.00
Internet forums	(53% vs. 46% of MPI) p=0.00
Websites	(51% vs. 46% of MPI) p=0.00
Dreams or past-life	(40% vs. 37% of MPI) p=0.00
Druidry mentors	(33% vs. 32% of MPI) p=0.00
Ancestors-of-blood	(27% vs. 23% of MPI) p=0.00

North America less influenced by —

Curricula	(48% vs. 49% of MPI) p=0.00
Face-to-face	(34% vs. 40% of MPI) p=0.00
Ancestors-of-place	(30% vs. 34% of MPI) p=0.00

Oceania more influenced by —

Face-to-face	(57% vs. 40% of MPI) p=0.00
Dreams or past-life	(51% vs. 37% of MPI) p=0.00
Ancestors-of-place	(46% vs. 34% of MPI) p=0.00
Druidry mentors	(38% vs. 32% of MPI) p=0.01
Ancestors-of-blood	(28% vs. 23% of MPI) p=0.00

Oceania less influenced by —

Internet forums	(40% vs. 46% of MPI) p=0.01

2 Intergenerational variations in factors influencing Druids' spiritual paths (% of maximum possible influence by years of experience):

Emphasis on website resources —
1-10 years	(52% vs. 46% of MPI) p=0.00
10-20 years	(no significant difference)
20-30 years	(31% vs. 46% of MPI) p=0.00
30+ years	(26% vs. 46% of MPI) p=0.00

Emphasis on ancestors-of-blood —
1-10 years	(19% vs. 23% of MPI) p=0.00
10-20 years	(no significant difference)
20-30 years	(28% vs. 23% of MPI) p=0.00
30+ years	(51% vs. 23% of MPI) p=0.00

3 As described on the ADF web page: https://www.adf.org/ (as published on their web site, as of October 21, 2020)

4 Percent of maximum possible influence, ADF vs. non-ADF:
Nature	(82% vs. 92% of MPI) p=0.00
Deities	(68% vs. 45% of MPI) p=0.00
Internet forums	(59% vs. 45% of MPI) p=0.01
Face-to-face	(52% vs. 38% of MPI) p=0.01

5 Percent of maximum possible influence,n AODA vs. non-AODA:
Deities	(33% vs. 49% of MPI) p=0.00
Spirits-of-Place	(55% vs. 72% of MPI) p=0.00
Dreams and past-life	(22% vs. 38% of MPI) p=0.00
Face-to-face	(22% vs. 41% of MPI) p=0.01
Other books	(70% vs. 50% of MPI) p=0.00

6 Percent of maximum possible influence, OBOD vs. non-OBOD:
Curricula	(64% vs. 30% of MPI) p=0.00

7 Other, well-received, but less influential curricula included:
Templo de Avalon (Brasil) curriculum;
Reformed Druids of Gaia (RDG) publications;
Henge of Keltria publications
   (a formerly influential organization, officially dissolved in 2017);
Philip Carr-Gomm's *Lessons in Magic* course;
Green Mountain Druid Order curriculum;
Ordem Ramo de Carvalho (Brasil) curriculum;

Reformed Druids of North America (RDNA) publications;
Fellowship of Druidism of the LatterAge (FoDLA) curriculum
(an organization now apparently defunct);
The Druid College curriculum;
Clann Samaúma (Brasil) curriculum;
Albion Conclave curriculum.

8 Intergroup variations in the most influential types of books and media
(cited by: % of subgroup vs. % of Druids overall):

ADF: local myths	(13% vs. 28%) p=0.00
Celtic Diaspora: local myths	(16% vs. 28%) p=0.00
North America: local myths	(10% vs. 28%) p=0.00
Rooted in Celtic Lands: local myths	(57% vs. 28%) p=0.00
British Isles & Ireland: local myths	(70% vs. 28%) p=0.00
OBOD: local myths	(35% vs. 28%) p=0.00
BDO: local myths	(35% vs. 28%) p=0.00
TDN: local myths	(54% vs. 28%) p=0.00
OBOD: creative works	(32% vs. 26%) p=0.00
AODA: non-fiction books	(68% vs. 16%) p=0.00
AODA: spiritual books	(78% vs. 59%) p=0.01

9 Greer, John Michael. (2006). *The Druidry Handbook: Spiritual
Practice Rooted in the Living Earth.* San Francisco, California: Red
Wheel/Weiser LLC. p. 204.

10 Intergroup variations in the focus on nature connection
(% of subgroup vs. % of Druids overall):

Oceania	(93% vs. 76%) p=0.01

11 Cooper, Gordon. (2012). "Wild-crafting the Modern Druid."
— this article first appeared in OBOD's monthly, members-only
publication, *Touchstone,* and was later posted to the OBOD website:
https://druidry.org/resources/wild-crafting-the-modern-druid

12 Intergroup variations in wildcrafting Druidry practices
(% of subgroup vs. % of Druids overall):

Celtic Diaspora	(38% vs. 32%) p=0.00
AODA	(53% vs. 32%) p=0.01
Wet/Dry Climates	(56% vs. 32%) p=0.00
Oceania	(69% vs. 32%) p=0.00
Rooted in Celtic Lands	(17% vs. 32%) p=0.00
British Isles & Ireland	(8% vs. 32%) p=0.00

13 Intergroup variations in landscape reinforcing traditions
(% of subgroup vs. % of Druids overall):

Celtic Diaspora	(17% vs. 24%) p=0.00
North America	(19% vs. 24%) p=0.01
Oceania	(2% vs. 24%) p=0.00
Rooted in Celtic Lands	(42% vs. 24%) p=0.00
British Isles & Ireland	(50% vs. 24%) p=0.00

14 Intergroup variations in simplifying
(% of subgroup vs. % of Druids overall):

North America	(19% vs. 15%) p=0.01

CHAPTER 5:
THEMES & VARIATIONS IN DRUID THEOLOGY

What do modern-day Druids believe about the nature of the Divine? This is the first question likely to spring to mind when thinking about Druidry as a "new religious movement" — the broad, religious category into which most religious census databases place it. Responses to this seemingly simple question are complex, nuanced, and very difficult to categorize using standard theological labels.

Three questions on the *World Druidry Survey* probed into the nature of Druids' personal, theological beliefs. The first asked Druids whether they thought of Druidry as a religion, as a spiritual practice, as a philosophy, as a lifestyle choice, as a family tradition, as part of their cultural heritage, or as something else entirely. The second question asked Druids to classify their current, personal religious path or concept of divinity — whether monotheist, polytheist, pantheist, animist, agnostic, atheist, or something else. Finally, an open-ended questions asked:

> **Question:**
> *If you worship or venerate any specific god(s), or spirit(s)*
> *of nature or place, please describe them, and your*
> *experience of them. Who are they? What, if anything, do*
> *they represent to you? How did you first identify or meet*
> *them? Do you experience them as real, physical*
> *presences? as visions? voices? felt energies? Jungian*
> *archetypes? symbolic characters? something else*
> *entirely? Please explain.*

Due to the aforementioned aversion to using the word *religion*, only 45% of respondents considered Druidry to be their religion. The vast majority (89%) preferred to refer to Druidry as their "spiritual practice." Just over half of respondents considered Druidry to be a philosophy, or a way of life. These

I consider Druidry to be...

Response	%
A spiritual practice	89%
A philosophy	63%
A way of life	59%
My religion	45%
Part of my cultural heritage	41%
A family tradition	6%
My identity / inner calling	5%
A role in society	1%
An initiatory / mystery tradition	1%
A relationship with Nature	1%

*** Percentages are of all 725 Druids*

Varieties of Druid Theology

My current, personal religions path is...	%**
Animist	64%
"Soft" Polytheist	49%
Pantheist	37%
"Hard" Polytheist	15%
Monotheist	7%

*** Percentages are of the 659 Druids who reported having a theological framework within which they practiced their Druidry.*

responses further support the notion of Druidry as a "religious tradition" rather than a modern "religion." The complete set of responses, including all those identified by respondents, is presented in the table at left.

Druid Perceptions of the Divine

Popular notions of the religious beliefs of Druids tend to categorize all Druids as a subgroup of Pagans; but the term *Pagan* does not refer to a system of belief. It is, rather, a catch-all term referring to people following any one of a wide variety of nature-reverent religious traditions, all of which fall outside the perview of the Abrahamic religions. In this, it is akin to the term *Heathen*, which serves a similar purpose. The difference between the two terms is that *Pagan* tends to be used in reference to religions inspired by ancient Celtic cultures, while *Heathen* tends to be used in reference to religious traditions inspired by ancient Norse and Germanic cultures. The term *Pagan* was included in the *World Druidry Survey*, primarily to test the validity of this popular notion. As it turns out, only 63% of world Druids identify with either of the two general terms, *Pagan* or *Heathen*. Most of these individuals also identified with one or more other terms, which more precisely described their religious beliefs.

Seven percent of respondents reported being agnostic when it came to questions of theology. Two percent reported being confirmed atheists, with no theological leaning of any kind. The other 91% of Druids reported having a personal, theological belief system —

of one kind or another — related to their practice of Druidry. The most common varieties of Druid theology are listed in the table at left. A few Druids also used the *"Other (please specify):"* option to describe their personal religious path, writing in one or more of the following: Panentheist, Spiritist, Henotheist, Ietsist, Gnostic, Ancestral, Integral, Perennialist, Pluralist, Omnist, Monist, Wayist, and/or Unitarian Universalist. However, each of these was cited by fewer than 1% of respondents, and so cannot be considered patterns representative of more than a few specific individuals' beliefs.

Druidry's Animists

The majority of world Druids (64%) identified as animists[1], people who attribute "spirit" or "soul" not only to humans, but also to other-than-human elements of the natural world, such as animals, plants, trees, rocks, mountains, springs, storm clouds, celestial bodies, and so on. These Druids perceive the world as being richly populated by diverse spiritual beings with whom one might communicate, forge friendships, and engage in reciprocal relationships. Druids counted in this category checked the box for *animist*, and/or clearly described an animist perspective in their response to the open-ended question on theology. Examples of responses in this category included:

> *"My practice is mainly animistic. I am concerned with having respectful relationships with the others who people our world. I understand the gods as ancient beings of great power and wisdom, the rivers, the mountains, the forest, our father the sky and our Holy Mother Earth, all of these are living conscious beings. I do not generally understand the gods in anthropomorphic or supernatural-istic ways, but I do for example 'believe' in the green man as veriditas, the green spark, he is the ancestral, collective intelligence of the plant realm. I don't feel that it is helpful to try to pin down what exactly a god is, I prefer vagueness and ambiguity, everything is permeable. When I am encountering a god or spirit of a place it is felt bodily. Some gods can also be understood as archetypes, these might be said to be the gods that dwell within us, this makes them no less real."*

> *"I honour the spirits of the place I live. I will make offerings to the river I live near and greet it when I have to cross it. And I will anoint myself on my forehead/third eye with the water of a water body I am near, often result-ing in an energy exchange. I honour the trees that I sit beneath, usually offering some food and water in thanks for their shelter. These beings aren't anthropomorphic, but*

*me honouring the spirit of the actual river or tree in an
animistic way. I also greet any crows or ravens as they
pass. I often will speak with any other animals I
encounter."*

*"I venerate nature in all its glory: tiny weeds, huge trees,
birds, forests, rivers, stones, THE OCEAN. I wait. I listen.
I feel their presence, their energy. Occasionally I see
something out the comer of my eye, more often I feel or
hear a message. I have been walking in the bush (that's
what we call our forest) and clearly heard (in my head) a
tree or the bush call out my name. I stop and listen and
they have a message for me."*

*"I feel energies from older trees, more from oak and birch
than others. I feel like I can sense a voice when I sit for
periods of time with them, but more as an internal feeling
within myself than an actual embodied voice. My childhood home had a 70+ year old Oak tree that I would sit
under as I read books, napped or just relaxed. This was
the first tree I talked to. It was more like a friend to me
than humans could be. I felt like there was a true presence
within the tree, and have felt that in animals and plant life
over the years. I only recently re-embraced my desire to
build relationships with the natural world."*

*"During rituals, I address the Elements, the Ancestors,
and whoever will listen and that's usually the 'spirits' of
the immediate land around my property — animals and
plants as well as the rocks, weather, waterways, and land
itself. I give offerings — mostly food that the local critters
will eat — who is to say they are not the spirits? I find, as
I work with and venerate the local spirits, that I feel more
connected with my path and my spirituality. That my life
has become more balanced as I pay more attention to
what is around me."*

*"I am a Jew who doesn't believe in God (yes, it's
possible). I venerate nature because it sustains me, and I
am part of it. I don't call on specific deities, except maybe
Gaia, because Gaia represents all of nature. In the
Chalice Well Garden, Glastonbury, there are two ancient
Yew trees. As I walked around them, little faces appeared
in the bark. When I later tried to find those faces,
however, I couldn't. In my garden, I came to the
realization that I am not so much in charge, as I am part
of it. I have looked at my plants differently ever since. It's
a whole new regard for plants as fellow beings that I find*

hard to put into words. No, I don't apologize to the weeds for pulling them. In fact, I chide them for growing where they don't belong. I do thank the garden whenever I harvest food or flowers from it."

"Ich verehre keine bestimmte Gottheit, sondern eine universelle, männliche und weibliche Schöpfungskraft, mit der ich in Meditationen oder auch im Alltag häufig kommuniziere. Daneben kommuniziere ich mit allen möglichen Spirits in Bäumen, Pflanzen, Tieren, Bächen, Steinen, Wäldern, den vier Elementen, ganzen Landschaften oder des ganzen Planeten. Ich spüre und höre sie als eigenständige "Wesen", die auf ihre Weise genau so real sind wie wir in der physischen Welt. Bereits als Kind habe ich diese Spirits überall gesehen und mit ihnen geplaudert. Sie waren quasi meine Begleiter.
[Translation:]
I do not worship a particular deity, but a universal, masculine and feminine power of creation, with which I often communicate in meditations or in everyday life. I also communicate with all kinds of spirits in trees, plants, animals, streams, stones, forests, the four elements, whole landscapes or the whole planet. I feel and hear them as independent 'beings' who in their own way are just as real as we are in the physical world. Already as a child I saw these spirits everywhere and chatted with them. They were my companions."

"Bodies of water have always seemed animate and aware to me, all my life. When I look at a lake or river, I have the same sensation as when my eyes meet another human's eyes. I thought of them as playmates or friends when I was a child. Now, I think of them as holy beings that I wish to serve and protect. Not as Gods, but as divine spirits. I experience them as gendered. Lake Superior is female, the Mississippi River is male. I only learn the gender after I am very familiar with a body of water, though, after I have interacted with it for years. This has been true my whole life. Now, just the last couple of years after I became a practicing Druid, I am getting a related sensation from trees, but it is much harder to detect, more like sensing someone else's mood from their posture, without meeting their eyes."

"I [...] interact with assorted spirits of nature, but I see these less as deities, and more as honored, other-than-human Kin. Some (certain plants, birds, mammals, etc.) are like brothers and sisters to me, others (like certain

Redwoods and Mountains, the Summer Fog, or certain
winds) are more like great grandparents, much revered,
and excellent sources of day-to-day guidance. These I
tend to notice and converse with, in passing, on a day-to-
day basis. I also try to maintain a reciprocal relationship
with them, whereas I don't think there is much of anything
aside from songs of praise that I can offer to the gods. I
experience them primarily as felt energies, or voices that
are more 'in my head' than 'in my ears.' I suppose you
might call it a kind of clairsentience. I also occasionally
see auras around some plants and animals, and I notice
dramatic changes in those auras, when they occur."

Members of all Druidry groups were equally likely to identify as animists, with one exception: 86% of TDN members identified as animists, compared to 64% of the overall world population of Druids.[2]

About "Polytheism"

The term *polytheism* is generally used to refer to any system of belief characterized by the worship of a pantheon of gods and goddesses. However, there exist two important sub-categories of modern-day polytheism within Druidry, which represent significantly different theological perspectives: hard polytheists and soft polytheists.[3] Based upon several survey responses, it is clear that neither sub-group likes to be confused with the other. Therefore, the two subgroups — hard polytheists and soft polytheists — were coded, counted, and analyzed separately in this study.

Soft polytheists typically work with their pantheons in a symbolic manner. The various gods and goddesses of their pantheons may be seen as facets or faces of a single godhead, or as psychological archetypes that might have corollary deities in the pantheons of other cultures. As such, soft polytheists tend to assemble personal pantheons by selecting gods drawn from a variety of cultural traditions, basing those decisions upon the myths and images that most strongly speak to their personal spiritual needs, in the moment.

Hard polytheists are more literal about the gods they worship. They tend to worship a single, coherent pantheon of distinct, objectively real, divine beings, who are never seen as interchangeable with any other goddesses or gods.

Despite these differences, hard and soft polytheists tended to name similar sets of deities when describing their personal theological frames. A list of the most frequently mentioned deities can be found in the table at right; and a complete list of the gods, goddesses, and other divine beings mentioned in *World Druidry Survey* responses, along with a brief description of each, can be found in the *Glossary*. Deities revered by polytheist Druids fell into a few main categories, when sorted by their primary spheres of influence.

Nature deities of various kinds comprised the largest grouping of gods and goddesses, with 760 distinct citations within the survey responses. This included an assortment of deities associated with the sky, in general, or with specific elements of sky, such as the sun, moon, wind, rain, storms, lightning, thunder, dawn, dusk, and night. It also included deities associated with bodies of water, such as the ocean, the sea, rivers, lakes, and springs. Nature deities also included an assortment of Earth Mothers, and deities of specific places, mountains, plants, trees, woodlands, and groves. Finally, nature deities included gods and goddesses associated with wild animals, wild lands, and the overall wild power and fecundity of the natural world. The more popular deities of this category included Cernunnos, Gaia/Mother Earth, Danu, Manannán Mac Lir, Cailleach, Rhiannon/Rigatona, Thor, Artemis/ Diana, Father Sky, Bast, Epona, Pan, Papatūānuku, and Taranis.

The second-most popular set of deities, with 242 citations in all, were those deemed to be sources of artistic inspiration and craftsmanship, in fields such as writing, poetry, music, art, and crafts of all kinds. Brigid was, by far, the most frequently cited deity in this category, though her sphere of influence is far broader than poetry, arts, and crafts. Cerridwen and her cauldron of divine inspiration, or Awen, also ranked high on this list. Other deities in this category included Lugh/Lugus, and Athena (who, like Brigid, also had a broader sphere of influence than this category suggests).

Druidry's Most Influential Deities

Deity*	%**
Brigid	30%
Cernunnos	23%
Cerridwen	14%
Gaia / Mother Earth	11%
Morrigan	10%
Lugh / Lugus	8%
Odin / Woden	7%
Danu	6%
Manannán Mac Lir	6%
Dagda	5%
Cailleach	4%
Freya	4%
Elen of the Ways	3%
Hecate	3%
Rhiannon / Rigatona	3%
Thor	3%
Ganesha	2%
Gwyn ap Nudd	2%
Artemis / Diana	2%
Isis	2%
Loki	2%
Athena	1%
Blodeuwedd	1%
Father Sky	1%
Arianrhod	1%
Bast / Bastet	1%
Epona	1%
Hestia	1%
Pan	1%
Papatūānuku	1%
Persephone	1%
Taranis	1%

For deity descriptions see Glossary.
*** Percentages are of the 422 Druids who identified as polytheists.*

Deities of wisdom, law and justice accounted for 102 citations. Most popular among these deities were: Brigid, Odin/Woden, Dagda, Ganesha, and Athena.

Deities associated with forms of nurturance, including marriage, motherhood, childbirth, the healing arts, hearth, home, and hospitality accounted for 101 citations. The most popular deities in this category were Brigid, Isis, and Hestia.

Gods and goddesses of love, beauty, passion, compassion, festivity, fertility, and flowers were cited 96 times. The most common ones were Freya, Blodeuwedd, and Persephone.

Deities associated with fate, chance, circular time, and the endless cosmic cycles of birth, death, and renewal were cited 76 times. The most popular of these were the Morrigan, and Arianrhod.

Agriculture deities, particularly those related to the human acts of planting, plowing, harvesting, herding and animal husbandry, were cited 62 times in the survey data. The most popular god in this category was the Dagda.

Deities associated with liminal spaces, pathways, crossroads, and those who travel them were cited 33 times in the survey responses. Popular deities in this category included Elen of the Ways, and Hecate.

Gods and goddesses of underworlds, otherworlds, and other spiritual planes of existence were cited 22 times. The most popular among these was Gwyn ap Nudd.

Trickster gods and goddesses of chaos, disharmony, and various kinds of discomforting transformations were cited a total of 21 times. Most popular among these was Loki.

An additional set of revered beings, mentioned in 17 responses to the question on personal theology, were neither nature deities, nor deities of abstract spheres of influence, but rather, tribal gods, or legendary cultural leaders and heroes. As such, these spiritual beings fall somewhere between the realms of gods and ancestors, which will be further discussed later in this chapter, in *The Role of Ancestors in Druidry Practice*.

Druidry's Soft Polytheists

The second-most prevalent category of Druid theology was soft poly-theism, a theistic belief system held by 49% of survey respondents. Druids counted in this category checked the box for *polytheist*, and also described a soft polytheistic approach to worship. They may have done this by describing their relationship with deities as meditations on or visualizations of psychological archetypes, or as personifications of natural forces, or by indicating that they interacted with a variety of different gods, from different pantheons, at different times, or for different reasons. Examples of survey responses in this category included:

> *"I recognize my relationship to universal archetypes as if they are personalities I know. I accept that my perception of them changes regularly (as complexes in Jung's model), but I know they transcend an individual human's life and experience. Currently I feel strongly influenced by a character like Cerridwen, linking what I've read in the OBOD material to my own anima. I also recently experienced the unexpectedly clear imaginary presence of a protective she-bear (during 5 Rhythms dancing). These are therefore current examples of a goddess and a spirit animal guide who I honour and can connect to through meditation. I also recognize the significance and power of famous and unknown sites (e.g. Glastonbury Tor and an unremarkable local hill), but I don't think of these as having an anthropomorphic spirit. I may experience joy and awe in their natural energy unexpectedly or through deliberate meditative focus."*

> *"I have a relationship with the Hindu gods Ganesha and Kali. They called me rather than me seeking them out. I realize they are not actually Druid deities but they work for me. I have also had some experience with Odin and I have worked with Thor and even Loki a little but have not connected to the Norse goddesses as much. Once I decided to join Hearthstone, I really worked to work with the Norse gods and goddesses more since they are part of the family of gods within the European pagan religions. I am pretty sure neither Kali nor Ganesha are old enough to be part of the Vedic pantheon which is accepted in Hearthstone as an Indo-European culture. I am going to work with them until I am called by someone else. I do plan on studying different Indo-European cultures and working with different gods. I feel the gods [are] real in the sense humans have put much energy into their being, but I think they are more like archetypes than each one being an individual person. They are energy thought forms and by us working with them and worshipping them, we give them more power and energy. I have a hard time explaining what I believe they are but I do believe in Ganesha as a person and at the same time, I do not believe there is an elephant headed man dancing in the heavens, if that makes any sense."*

"Auf schamanischen Reisen bin ich Isis, Morrigan und Aphrodite begegnet, welche mich bei unterschiedlichen Themen unterstützen. Ihnen sowie Bastet und Freya stehe ich daher und wegen der Themen und Energien die sie für mich ausstrahlen und verkörpern am nächsten. Ich nehme Gottheiten als Personen wahr, jedoch sind sie für mich Ausdruck bestimmter Energieformen (Liebe, Schutz, Mut, Sanftheit, etc.) einer Allumfassenden Energie, die für mich jedoch nicht greifbar ist, weshalb dieses Allumfassende sich in bestimmte Energieformen - Gottheiten - "teilt", um greifbarer zu werden
[Translation:]
On shamanic journeys I met Isis, Morrigan and Aphrodite, who support me with different topics. Therefore I am closest to them as well as to Bastet and Freya because of the themes and energies they radiate and embody for me. I perceive deities as persons, but for me they are expressions of certain forms of energy (love, protection, courage, gentleness, etc.) of an all-encompassing energy that is not tangible for me, which is why this all-encompassing energy 'divides' into certain forms of energy - deities - in order to become more tangible."

"When I first started, I could feel the presence of Cernunnos and Cerridwen when I went on walks in the evening. Then, because I am one who serves others to the extreme, Xipe Totec, Our Lord the Flayed one came into my life, and requested my adherence. Lately, Tonantzin/ Coatlicue has been appearing in my life, in statues and illustrations, usually manifesting as the 'Our Lady of Guadalupe' archetype. And I seem to be attracted to sky gods, after practicing the ADO Triskele ritual and serving as the sky point. Beli Mawr, Quetzalcoatl-Ehecatl and Sköll."

"Nature, including the universe as a whole, is what I consider 'God/dess'. The planet Earth I view as a Goddess who may have many names depending on the culture, and she is the main entity I pray to when I pray. I occasionally pray to Cerridwen and Brighid, and vener- ate Cernunnos and Lugh. Cerridwen is the goddess of inspiration, and Brighid the goddess of healing. To me, Cernunnos and Lugh represent a sort of Enkidu/ Gilgamesh polarity, with Cernunnos being a god of shamans and wilderness and Lugh being a god of civilization and knowledge. I believe that everyone has a spirit animal, or 'familiar' - I have had two so far in my

*life, and they have probably played the largest role in my
spiritual path than any other deity. I have more of a
reverence for deity, not a direct worship, and I focus my
practice more on spirits of the elements, plants, or
animals."*

*"I have worked with many of the Brythonic
Gods/Goddesses including, but not exclusively;
Cerridwen, Arthur, Tegid, Taliesin (as the narrative
spirit), Manawyddan, Llyr, Gogyrwen. Gwyn ap Nudd,
Spirits of place and nature (particularly woods, trees and
stone circles) I do not 'see' with my material eyes but
sense them as internal images, feelings, internal narrative, or energy sensations. I see the whole Universe as
mind/consciousness therefore I can be in [a] relationship
[with] any other 'person' be it seen as a living creature or
considered by most an inanimate object such as a rock or
stream. I also see the gods has having an aspect of
Jungian archetypes, but through apotheosis they also
have a degree of autonomy. I also see some of the ancient
deities as primordial aspects and forces of creation that
are still at work within our universe to this day and can
be accessed through ritual and meditation."*

*"I have an affiliation with Cernunnos that was possibly
born, in part, from my own conflicted struggles at a time
when I was torn between competing allegiances. I not
only hunted what I loved, I was also responsible then for
scrutinizing the demanding task of managing and conserving hunted populations of deer, elk, moose —
balancing ecology with competing interests of hunters,
governments, and animal rights activists. Planning what
number of adult and young animals of each sex could be
'sustainably harvested,' and then seeing it out, was a dark
responsibility, but one based ultimately on a love and
understanding of Nature. That is hard for people to
understand. Cernunnos, however, would be completely
comfortable with the challenges and seeming contradic-
tions, the interplay between life and death, love and loss,
men & Nature, all that. Perhaps Cernunnos is just a
Jungian archetype to me — I don't know. I do not worship
Cernunnos, but I do let him in (or out) when I write. And
scribbling poetry about Love, Nature, [and] our responsibility to Nature (and the perils of ignoring Her) is a
significant part of my spiritual practice."*

Members of all Druidry groups were equally likely to identify as soft polytheists, with one notable exception: 73% of ADF members identified as soft polytheists (compared to 49% for the overall world population of Druids).[4]

Cultural sources for deities referenced by soft-polytheistic Druids were many and varied. Religious traditions and mythological sources from which Druids derived their personal, polytheistic pantheons included: Christian/Biblical stories, Arthurian legends, Fantasy novels, and the ancient myths and legends of African-matrix religions, the Basque Country, China, Cornwall, Egypt, England, Gaul, Germany, Greece, India, Ireland, Italy, Japan, Judaism, Latvia, Mexico (Aztec), the Middle East, New Zealand, Nigeria, North American First Nations (Hopi, Inuit), Polynesia, proto-Indo-European traditions, Rome, Russia, Scandinavia, Scotland, Tibet, and Wales. The most common type of pantheon was a cultural mélange of polytheistic traditions, influenced by personal spiritual needs, and mystical experiences.

Druidry's Pantheists

Thirty-seven percent of Druids identified as pantheists, people who believe that God is the universe, and the universe is God.[5] For pantheists, all of Nature is, in essence, a single, divine consciousness, and so divinity can be perceived in all things. Druids counted in this category checked the box for *pantheist*, or clearly described a pantheistic system of belief in their comments on theology. Examples of responses in this category included:

> *"I venerate Nature. [It] isn't just the trees, the animals, the water, etc. It's the sun, the moon, the stars, the whole Universe. We are a very tiny part of it, and it is a big part of us. Nature is divine. Nature is whole. Nature IS."*

> *"I believe in a divine monad and that the earth & cosmos are animate or biospiritual (almost Taoist) in nature."*

> *"I do not worship anything but I do venerate nature. I perceive Great Spirit to be all the energy in the Universe, all is part of it, so vast and immense. I believe specific deities are a way for humans to interact and comprehend particular aspects of it. I get a sense / feeling, like an unspoken whisper which I believe is the spirit in me connecting my body and consciousness to source."*

> *"I now feel the Divine as an Energy who binds the Universe, which is part of each of us and connects all living beings together. I would call it 'God' or 'Great Spirit,' not in the sense of Monotheism but closer to Pantheism."*

"Ik ervaar de energie van de Great Spirit wanneer ik mij daarop focus of met rituelen bezig ben, in de natuur ben of in gedachten bezig met de Great Spirit. Ik zie (en voel) dit als een alles overkoepelende energie (die je ook godheid zou kunnen noemen) waarvan wij allemaal onderdeel zijn. Al zo lang ik mij herinneren kan, geloof ik in reïncarnatie. Wanneer ons fysieke lichaam sterft, gaat ons stukje energie of onderdeel van de Great Spirit weer terug naar het grote geheel. Ik geloof dat we daarom ook zo graag 'bij een groep horen'. Om weer één te zijn met het grote geheel. Als kind had ik een petrischaaltje met een bol kwik (gekregen van mijn vader nadat een koortsthermometer was stuk gevallen). Als je dat schudde, lieten vele kleine bolletjes de grote bol kwik los. Als je even wachtte, versmolten al die kleine bolletjes weer met elkaar. Zo zie ik ook onze energie, als kleine bolletjes die uiteindelijk allemaal weer deel zullen uitmaken van het grote geheel (tot het moment waarop we weer reïncarneren en een tijdelijk thuis vinden in een nieuwe fysieke gedaante). Deze energie is voor mij voelbaar (hoe dichterbij je een andere persoon komt, hoe sterker het gevoel wordt) en voelbaar als Great Spirit. Ook is het voor mij zichtbaar, als energieveld om mensen, bomen, planten en dieren en heeft het ook kleuren.

[Translation:]

I experience the energy of the Great Spirit when I focus on it or am busy with rituals, am in nature or have the Great Spirit in mind. I see (and feel) this as an all-embracing energy (which you could also call deity) of which we are all part. For as long as I can remember, I have believed in reincarnation. When our physical body dies, our piece of energy or part of the Great Spirit goes back to the big picture. I believe that's why we like to 'belong to a group' so much. To be one with the big picture again. As a child I had a petri dish with a ball of mercury (given to me by my father after a fever thermometer had fallen apart). When you shook that, many small balls let go of the big ball of mercury. If you waited a while, all those little balls melted together again. That's how I see our energy, as small balls that will eventually all be part of the big picture again (until we reincarnate again and find a temporary home in a new physical form). This energy can be felt by me (the closer you get to another person, the stronger the feeling becomes) and can be felt as Great Spirit. It is also visible to me, as an energy field around people, trees, plants and animals and it also has colours."

> *"I would not say I worship any Gods or Goddesses but I would say that sometimes I am touched by the concepts of the Morrigan or Pan. I experience them as personalities during meditation but as energies, thoughts and feelings in the imminent world. It is my belief that during meditation the mind works in metaphors and that the concepts of the Morrigan and Pan stand for my relationships with certain energies at work within physical reality. It is my belief that in the final analysis everything is one, there is just the Universe and the Universe is divine, we are all part of the universe, mushrooms as it were on the fungus that is divinity and as such we are all divine or carry divinity within us."*

> *"As a Pantheist, I see the divine in people and nature, though people and trees seem to have more concentration of the divine in them. I also feel energy from the earth itself when I focus on it. It is very real. I can also feel some people I know even when they are at a great distance through our connection in the divine."*

There were no statistically significant differences between Druidry groups, in the proportion of members who identified as pantheists.

Druidry's Hard Polytheists

Hard polytheistic beliefs were reported by 15% of survey respondents. Druids counted in this category checked the box for *polytheist*, and also clearly described a hard polytheistic approach to worship, with a single, culturally consistent pantheon, and interactions that addressed deities as objectively real, individual, divine beings, as opposed to interchangeable symbols or archetypes — as discussed in *About "Polytheism"*, earlier, in this chapter. Descriptions of hard polytheistic practices and beliefs included:

> *"My patron deity is Mercury, specifically the Gaulish Mercury whose companion is Rosmerta and whose holy places include the Puy de Dôme in Auvergne. I have been a devotee of Mercury ever since I encountered his stories as a child. Other deities I have known have usually been introduced to me through him, or by virtue of his pre-eminence over Gaul. I can feel his numen (his 'energy') more or less at all times; I consider my own genius to be an emanation of his numen. I am also a regular worshipper of Cernunnos, Rosmerta, Apollo Grannus, Ðirona, Lenus Mars, Ancamna, Jupiter Optimus Maximus, Juno Regina, Jupiter Optimus Maximus*

Dolichenus, Isis, the divine Faustina Augusta, Diana, Silvanus, Hercules Saxsanus, Epona, Ritona, and other deities."

"My primary deity relationship is with Brighid, of whom I am a devotee. [...] I felt that She exemplified many of the virtues and skills that underlie therapy and the values I have in this life. So I celebrated Imbolc to Her in 2018 as essentially an atheist. And She showed up in my mind, pushing for an oath and for me to do Her work in the Worlds. I got skittish, so I said I would take a year and a day to figure all this out. Since then I have felt Her, although I don't hear specific words in another voice or even my own voice, I get knowledge I shouldn't have that checks out and messages for others that are somehow exactly what they needed in that moment and fire in the head moments of poetry. [...] I think there are some serious issues with the mono-myth perspective that ignore the very real differences across these stories and cultures, especially what they mean within their cultural context, that are often ignored by Jungians. At this point, although I often have doubts and feel like maybe I'm going insane, I'm a hard polytheist. I don't believe that there are any omnipotent, omniscient divinities (certainly not any that are omni-benevolent) but rather that gods are different from us, although apotheosis was certainly apparently possible at some time in the past. I work with other deities and energies in group ritual and do hope to build relationships with other deities but Brighid is my Lady."

"I consider the Gods and other spiritual beings to be real and to have their own agency. I do not consider them archetypes. I am a devotee of Gwyn ap Nudd and Elen of the Pathways. I am not clairvoyant or clairaudient, I experience the Gods and spirits through feelings and energies. I first experienced Gwyn as Cernunnos when I began learning about him. I am still not sure if they are the same entity. After visiting Glastonbury it became clear to me that Gwyn is who I was dealing with. Elen I found much later, in the last 5-7 years I guess. Once I found out about her, I rejoiced as I had been wanting to connect to a Goddess, but never really found one that seemed to fit. I should mention that I am also a member of The Daughters of the Flame, and have tending flame for Brigid for many years. I did this in the name of my Goddess daughter for along time, but had not really connected to Brigid as I lean more toward Welsh spirituality than Irish. Only in the

*past five or so years have I begun to realize that Brigid is
likely the same entity as Brigantia and have been
honoring her in that capacity since."*

*"Norse deities, land and house wights. They are felt
entities and are most definitely not archetypes but
independent sentient beings. Celebrate reconstructed
Norse Heathen feast days honouring the gods with a
kindred of Heathens. Developing devotion to Celtic
deities in OBOD practices."*

*"Manannán mac Lir (patron deity), Brigid, Ogmios,
Nehalennia, the Cailleach, Baba Yaga, the Matronae,
Garanus Crane, the domovoi (house spirits) of my dwell-
ing, spirit of the Honey Locust. I conceive of these spirits
— and all gods and spirits — as true, distinct entities. I'm
a fairly hard polytheist, though I also allow for the fact
that, for example, there's an obvious connection between
Ogmios and Ireland's Ogma, or that Brigid/ Brigit/ Brìde
seems to be essentially the same figure across cultures.
Most of them I've met through either introduction in rituals that I attended/supported or through specific trance
journeys wherein I felt it was important (or just interesting) to seek them out. I tend to interact with spirits most
strongly in trance, and there I feel them as strong physical, visible presences. I don't hear distinct words through
my vision-ears, but I do receive definite clear verbal
messages from the gods. The nature spirits (Garanus,
Honey Locust, the domovoi) tend to be non-verbal, but
their intents are nevertheless clear. All the spirits are real
entities with existences separate from my own conception
of them, and desires and actions independent of my
perception of them, though obviously my understanding is
mediated through my own understanding."*

There were no statistically significant differences between Druidry
groups, in the proportion of members who identified as hard polytheists.

Cultural sources for deities worshipped by hard polytheists were less
diverse than those cited by soft polytheists. The pantheons of hard polytheist
Druids included: "Celtic" gods and goddesses, "the Pagan God and Goddess,"
as well as deities specific to Gaulish, Irish, Welsh, Greek, Roman, Vedic,
Norse, Egyptian, Maori/Polynesian, and Germanic traditions. The specific
gods and goddesses mentioned, within each of these traditions, were similar
to those mentioned by soft polytheists, as discussed earlier.

Druidry's Monotheists

The last significant category of theological belief, reported by 7% of respondents, was monotheism — a belief in one, and only one god. However, many Druids who reported being Christian monotheists also noted that their beliefs were Trinitarian — a position that places their theological beliefs somewhat closer to monism.[6] Several Druids also reported working with Christian Saints and Archangels, whom they saw as more approachable than the Christian God, himself. From an external point of view, this type of belief may seem closer to soft polytheism, however these Christian Druids still self-identified as monotheists.

Monotheistic Druids did not always provide detailed descriptions of their beliefs, however, some did, and frequently described elements of animism or pantheism blended with their monotheistic beliefs. Several monotheistic Druids also expressed an openness to learning about other gods, whilst maintaining a basically monotheistic, or trinitarian approach. Examples of responses in this category — beginning with the most traditionally Christian variety, and ending with more blended versions — included:

> *"My understanding of God is entirely in line with the traditional orthodox teachings of the Christian church, as would be expressed in the Nicene Creed, Chalcedonian Definition, Athanasian Creed, etc. With that, I believe that God is One, eternally existent in three modes of being, Father, Son, and Holy Spirit. I believe that Father, Son, and Holy Spirit are three persons of one substantial essence (not three gods, but one God). I recognize Jesus Christ as the perfect union between God and humanity, through whom relationship with the Father is established. My own spiritual journey began at the age of 13 when I prayed with my older brother to begin a relationship with God through faith in Christ. I did not expect anything to happen, but immediately burst into tears, feeling an overwhelming sense of peace and joy wash over me. This experience not only led me to a deep personal faith, but also to pursue vocational ministry as a pastor. I cannot say that I have heard God speak to me audibly or through any kind of visions, but I do sense many times that I am being led or convicted by God in my personal dealings, relationships, etc. I understand the different elements to be flavors, so to speak, of the energies that suffuse the world. In this sense, energies of fire or water or air or earth are of the same energetic stuff, but are not all alike. I see this to be metaphorically related to God's own identity--while I acknowledge one God and am a monotheist, God's nature is expressed in a Trinitarian fashion,*

*through three different, but not separate, persons. I see
the elements to be likewise 'one in substance,' but air is
not fire, neither air nor fire are earth, and water is
different still. With my own orthodox theological
convictions concerning God and the way we are to relate
to him, I also do not feel in any way comfortable seeking
connections with other spiritual powers or angels. While I
certainly believe that angels exist and may even be
present with us in times and places, I believe that God
should be approached directly. As such, each of the
invocations I make, for example, when calling the
elements are different Hebrew God names, and, when I
invoke Spirit Within, it is in the name of Yehoshua (Jesus
in Hebrew) who is the incarnate God in flesh."*

*"I have a belief in one creator God who manifests
through Nature. I also venerate Christ as druid and
Brigid as the female aspect of divinity. I experience them
in meditation both as figures and voices. I also encounter
Brigid at a local well, where she seems to dwell."*

*"I worship the One Universal Spirit God Jah as expressed
in the three persons of the trinity. I believe the Holy Spirit
is female. God's Spirit permeates all of physical nature
and creation 'swims' in God as a fish swims in water.
God's Spirit also inhabits special 'thin places' in a more
intense and powerful manner. All of nature is alive and
infused with this Spirit, including trees and even rocks.
Trees have communicated with me and shared their love
and wisdom. I have seen the winged-creatures and heard
them singing in the forest-I am not sure what to call them
— Angels, Fairies, or Bird People. I do not seek to speak
to those who have passed over but at times they visit me."*

There were no statistically significant differences between Druidry
groups, in the proportion of members who identified as monotheists.

Complex and Evolving Beliefs

In both the *Varieties of Druid Theology* table on page 114, and the
ensuing discussions of the five most prevalent varieties of Druid theology, it
is notable that the sum of the responses is greater than the total number of
survey respondents. This is because the majority (52%) of world Druids listed
more than one category of religious belief system as being relevant to their
Druidic paths.

In describing their personal theologies, 35% of Druids indicated that the reason for their multiple-listing was that their personal beliefs were forever evolving, as they studied and learned, and developed as Druids. The stories they submitted, describing their personal spiritual journeys, illustrated this point beautifully. Druids wrote, for example:

"This is a tricky one for me. A few years ago I would have been talking in terms of archetypes but now I am moving towards a hard polytheism, and still not quite sure how this fits into my wider world view. At the moment it is more a subjunctive approach, behaving 'as if' the gods are real and seeing where that leads me. I am drawn, particularly, to Brigid, Rigatona, Manawethan, Loki, Woden, Maponos and Shiva/Parvati (yes, I know!)"

"My first non-Catholic spiritual experience was with a 'crow that flew through my closed bedroom window and spoke directly to my mind' (as I wrote when I was quite young). I believed the crow to be my spirit guide or animal totem, and to this day Crow or Raven is still my symbolic spirit animal, though my view on such manifes-tations of spirit have evolved since. The form that Deity took for me first, once my path moved away from the Catholic dogma of my school and family, was as cross-pantheon human-formed Goddess and God figures that gave the names Aradia and Pan [...] and so I took it on faith that this was who they were. As I grew in both age and evolving understanding of my spirituality, I came to believe that the faces and names presented to me by 'Pan' and 'Aradia' were just archetypal representations that I would be able to understand and relate to, until such time as I was able to evolve my thinking. Probably a decade in, in my mid-teens, I began to view deity less as having any-thing to do with humanity and more to do with existence on a cosmic scale. The human avatars that spirit / deity takes is for our limited worldview and capability to under-stand, to process, and so looking beyond that surface I began to believe that the names and faces of deity the world over were all simply facets and aspects of a singular energy. Today, I don't view such energy as a 'conscious' entity in the traditional sense of the word, nor as an 'entity' at all, but rather a force that permeates and resides within all things at the micro and macrocosmic level. To use a pop culture reference, The Force from Star Wars is a living energy that surrounds, penetrates, and binds all things together. It has no will, no agenda,

nothing that we can quantify or categorize within the scope of our understanding. One of man's greatest failings when it comes to relating to spirit is to try to anthropomorphize deity to fit within a construct made of human emotions and limitations. The movements of deity or spirit or existence are beyond us to grasp, and the acceptance of this is freeing to the point that one can truly exist in the moment and just appreciate and honour the fact we are here and alive and gifted with this experience. As to the early manifestations, they never appeared as physical beings to me but always as visions with voices. I could see them in waking hours or during meditation, and my practices being mostly energy-based definitely involved the sensation of 'presence' - not like a ghost, but just as a 'knowing' that the feeling or sensation of the atmosphere contained more that just oneself."

"Venus and the moon were my first concepts of deity, as a vaguely Pagan teenager, long before I'd heard of the existence of Druidry specifically. I'd been wishing on the evening star since a young child, since my parents first read me the nursery rhyme, 'Star light, star bright/ First star I see tonight/ I wish I may I wish I might/ Have the wish I wish tonight'. This became something of a daily ritual for me. As a teen this slowly turned into prayer, and then expanded to include the moon. I would go for long walks in the moonlight and talk to her comforting face. [...] My animist beliefs also connect me to the ancestors of mine who were animist in their own ways, and to other animist peoples around the world. Forging connections with my ancestors is very important to me, so I seek to know the gods that my ancestors may have venerated, or lived in relationship with. That has led me to explore a few gods of the British Isles such as Briga, Brigantia, Andraste, Babd, Macha, Nemain, Grian, Manannán Mac Lir, and the Cailleach, and also an ancient Basque goddess named Mari. My relationships with them are, so far, more archetypal, or symbolic, and lack the immediacy of my relationships with the spirits of place, trees, rocks etc, that I previously described... but it's early days yet."

"This is an area that I am still growing in. I come from a Christian background however I broke away from the practice because of its dogmatic scripture and preaching. Therefore the concept of deities and spirits is something I am trying to keep an open mind towards. I have since learned a meditation from my teacher to help connect me to my inner sacred grove. The more I practiced this, the

more vivid the experiences and visions became. During my first Samhain ritual I felt a connection to the state of my recently deceased grandmother and friend, and whether or not they would find peace. At the following winter solstice ritual I experienced a feeling of the land waking up. These feelings just came to me whilst I was tuned in during the meditative state we were trying to achieve, and I could simply just comprehend their meanings without effort of deciphering. Since then I have learned and attempted self-readings of tarot, and I treated my spreads with the same respect and space as I would a Druidic gathering or ritual. For the three spreads I read for myself, the cards were correct for my current situation each time as well as my past. I interpret these experiences as myself being able to connect to some spiritual force either within or outside of me, and that it is helping to grant me more vision beyond that of rational or logical means. Overall, these connections and experiences are helping me to connect to a greater universal power, I believe, and encourage my understanding of divine forces. This, however, is a microscopic piece of a long learning process."

"Before Druidry awareness I related to 'Life Spirit' through all living beings and nature - and was carefully gender neutral. I still do in many ways, relating more to Nwyfre in this way. Now I also relate in a more person- alized way also with my personal Earth Goddess — who I connect to with various names; Papatūānuku (Māori name for Mother Earth) & Gaia among others. Cerridwen, Brigid & Quan Yin are also important Goddesses to me. Initially in relating to them I thought of them more as Jungian archetypes, but now that view is shifting a little as I experience them so personally and as clear personalities. That is why I checked the concept of Divinity is still evolving. These Goddesses I first met through our women's Full Moon circle. Then later as I studied Druidry some were in the stories and teachings. I now often experience them as visions, felt energies and voices — Goddesses I can seek guidance from. Whether it is my own inner voice of wisdom I hear or Goddesses, it does not matter to me. I have also been surprised by some spirit guides who have been amazingly vivid and particu- lar when evoked for ritual or through meditations during gwersi practicums and rituals. Their unexpected instant presences have taken me by surprise and so in those times I have experienced them as distinct visions or presence that indeed does seem very real on an inner plane. I

*certainly acknowledge the Spirit of a very special
Pohutukawa tree that I have developed a special
relationship with here at my home. Here I physically
experience the tree's energy. Sometimes I sense a tree
spirit being also — more of a vision and feeling as
distinct from the direct energy of the tree."*

The other 17% who used multiple categories to describe their personal religious path did so not out of confusion about their own beliefs, but because the complexity of their personal belief system did not lend itself to such over-simplified categorization. They might be agnostic on certain points of belief, but for the most part, respondents did not see this ambiguity as a problem, because they did not feel that one's beliefs about the gods mattered nearly as much as the relationship one cultivated with them, and with the natural world. Examples of their stories included:

*"I believe several things at once, on different levels. I see
the whole of creation, the Earth, the Universe and
Multiverses as, at one level, one consciousness, let's call
Her the 'Goddess of All'. She's like a background heart-
beat to everything else. Then I believe in the female and
male energies of creativity and I think of them as The
Goddess, and God. I pray to them and worship them
generically. As part of them I pray and worship specific
manifestations of them: specific goddesses and gods that
have been singled out by humans over time, usually for
specific purposes. Since I dedicated myself to Paganism, I
have been guided, in visualizations, by the Goddess
Brighid, The Antlered God and the God Ganesh in
particular. For Wiccan coven purposes and now for
Bardic purposes I am also building a stronger relationship with Cerridwen and a number of other deities. What
are they? That's a tricky one. On one level I know they are
anthropomorphic images that I and many others before
me have used to embody certain concepts about life, to
help me think things through and concentrate my mind to
get things done, but I talk to them, with reverence, every
day so part of my mind accepts them as 'real'. There is a
part of me that thinks they are actual evolved beings, but
this final stage I cannot prove and have no control over. I
choose to think it is a possibility. The same as the
Christian concept of having to make a 'leap of faith'. I
have a very special relationship with the 'spirit' of the
land in which I have chosen to live: Devon, UK. Every
morning as I greet the world about me I visualize growing
roots down into the soil and 'experience' the earth, the*

rocks and the waters below my feet. I have felt a growing bond of love between us since practicing this and receive healing and revitalizing energies in return."

"Most of the gods and goddesses I worship are from the Irish pantheon, and most are part of the Tuatha Dé Danann. I have inner spirit guides, power animals, and totem animals. I also have known of and interacted with fairies since I was about 3 or 4 years old. When I was choosing my patron gods and goddesses, they came to me and claimed me. I have a special relationship with all of these, including some ancient ancestors, as well as recent ancestors, who guide me and are with me. Since I believe in the Oneness of all, I believe they are independent beings in their own right, and yet part of the Oneness, and therefore, ALSO symbolic, archetypal, and part of me as well as part of all."

"I venerate several deities including Hu, Danu, Celi, Niwalen, Belenos, Sul, Esus, and Cerridwen, each associated with a particular holy day as taught in 'The Druidry Handbook'. I also venerate Dyéus Pter (from proto-Indo European pantheon), Brighid, Cernunnos, and Lugh. I often address the deities collectively as the Holy Ones, Sacred Ones, the Divine, or High Gods. I do not view the gods as personal beings but as spiritual forces or entities associated with aspects of Nature, the universe, or social concepts such as hearth, home, clan, etc. As I am a pantheist, I also believe that all things (nature, spirits, gods, humanity, etc). are deeply interconnected and come from a unified Divine source that is impersonal and formless. All things are part of one great cosmic order that has been called Logos, Asha, or Dao in different religions and philosophies. Ultimately, all worship goes to the Divine Source, order, or Spirit of All. I think of the deities as emanations or manifestations of the Universal Spirit (Divine Source). I try to stay mindful of sacredness during prayers, meditation, and daily life. I once experienced a vision of a goddess or spirit in early January 2018 without specifically invoking a deity, but do not know the name of the being. It was a short, wonderful, loving encounter but I was not sure what to make of it. In general, I do not have visions or hear from the deities as voices. I sometimes feel a presence or energies during ritual and meditation, and on two occasions felt in touch with the cosmic order."

"I believe Deity is all things and more, every possible combination at the same time — one god, many gods, psychological archetypes, individual entities, new, old, real or just stories, simply names ... all the ways gods are perceived by human beings are the ways I believe they exist. I've had experiences with different deities in different ways and acknowledge the experiences of others. I experience them usually as feelings, symbols and they appear in dream forms and visions in deep meditation."

"I sometimes have conflicting decisions on what I think is 'divine' or if I'm truly 'polytheist'. I feel that the Earth is alive and is our Goddess — And I think anything made of this Earth is divine as it carries a part of that ever evolving and transcending earth-spirit. From biological life to rock, water, fire, etc. I think that we are all connected as Earth-beings and cannot thrive properly without each other. I sometimes call parts of this divinity by names of Celtic gods, as a way [of possibly tapping into them] more intimately than [I would to] a certain aspect of the natural world. For example, if I'm drawing on the divinity of the forest, I may call it by the name Cernunnos as an all encompassing being. I may call to the thunderstorm as Taranis or just personalize the storm as if it's a living force of its own. Sacred Earth as the ultimate divinity."

Whether simple or complex, static or evolving, Druid perceptions of the divine — however conceived — describe only one end of a spectrum of spiritual beings with whom Druids develop relationships, as a part of their Druidry practice. Some Druids also work with a variety of legendary kings, queens, and tribal demi-gods, who are often considered mythic "ancestors", and many make it a point to honor their beloved and honored dead — that is, real, human ancestors of blood, spirit, or place.

The Role of Ancestors in Druidry Practice

Many, though not all, modern Druids involve ancestors of various kinds in their Druidry practice. This most frequently involves *ancestors-of-blood*, ranging from beloved, recently-deceased family members to ancient members of their family lineages traced through genealogical research. Ancestors-of-blood are honored by 51% of survey respondents. The second-most commonly honored type of ancestors are *ancestors-of-spirit*, including beloved dead who were not blood relatives, including loved ones, honored teachers and mentors, founders of spiritual traditions, or other inspirational role-models from the past. Ancestors-of-spirit are honored by 42% of survey respondents. The final category of ancestors honored by Druids are *ancestors-of-place*, meaning the individuals, or peoples, who once walked the lands which modern Druids now inhabit, and who cared for that land in earlier times. Ancestors-of-place were honored by 32% of world Druids. To more fully understand the nature of this reverence for ancestors, and how it was manifest in Druidry practice, an open-ended question asked:

> **Question:**
> *Which ancestors (if any) do you venerate within your Druidry practice? Ancestors of blood? of spirit? of place? Are they ancestors, in a general sense, or specific individuals? Please describe the role that ancestors play within your practice, and the manner in which you typically interact with them. (Please write "none" if this does not apply to you. Feel free to add additional pages, as needed.)*

In response to this question, 77% of Druids reported that they did honor ancestors, of one kind or another, in some manner — though the manner was often quite informal. There were several statistically significant intergroup variations, in both the overall prevalence of ancestor veneration, and the types of ancestors most frequently venerated by members of different Druidry groups.[7] ADF members were more likely than members of other groups to acknowledge ancestors-of-blood and ancestors-of-spirit; and they were less likely to report no role for ancestors in their Druidry practice. OBOD members and TDN members were both more likely to acknowledge ancestors-of-place than other Druid subgroups.

When describing the nature of their relationships with the various ancestral groups, many Druids explicitly stated that *veneration* was far too strong a word, for the simple kinds of honoring and remembrance they engaged in. They wrote, for example:

> *"I'm not sure if this counts as veneration, but I honor my ancestors through family history and genealogy, working to find their names and share the stories of their lives, or as much as I can find out about them. I honor my ancestors more generally and more inclusively at Samhain."*

> *"Not so much. I love my ancestors; I will toss goodwill up now and again — ask them for guidance in life if they were more experienced with something I'm facing. But aside from pictures around the house, I'm not sure you could call it veneration."*

"I often bring to mind specific deceased individuals who were close to me in a respectful way (venerate seems too strong), including my parents and grandparents. I acknowledge their huge influence on me, and I aspire to feel them standing at my shoulder, lending their support. I feel a similar relationship to influential teachers and mentors who may still be alive but who I am no longer in touch with. I connect to these remembered people in meditation and at the Samhain ritual specifically. I'm also sometimes aware of a link to those who historically celebrated at sacred sites (as ancestors of place and spirit) and feel a continuity in our practices, but this is weaker."

"I would not really use the word venerate. I connect with ancestors of blood, and ancestors of my spiritual path and spirits of place. I connect with ancestors of blood and my spiritual path during meditation and ritual. I talk to them and in doing so I clarify my own thoughts, feelings and beliefs. I connect with spirit of place in a more immediate way, I feel it, immerse myself in it and become one with it. I believe that all is connected and therefore I am one and part of spirit of place wherever I am."

"Compte tenu du destin des êtres après leurs désincarnations (sont-ils réincarnés, entre deux mondes ou dans l'Autre-Monde ?) je ne pratique aucun culte des ancêtres. Les ancêtres ne sont pas par ailleurs sacrés. Pourquoi rendre culte à des personnes, qui plus est désincarnées, alors que c'est aux Divinités que l'on doit rendre culte ? Je leur rends juste hommage et respect par le souvenir et la mémoire, à la fête de la Désincarnation. Par contre je suis en contact et œuvre avec des 'ancêtres' liés à ma prêtrise et qui n'ont pas passé les Grandes Portes menant vers l'Autre-Monde. Il s'agit d'une relation pour faire progresser et réémerger la prêtrise du Cornu.
[Translation:]
Considering the fate of beings after their disincarnations (are they reincarnated, between two worlds or in the Other World?) I do not practice any ancestor worship. Ancestors are not sacred. Why worship people, especially disembodied people, when it is to the Divinities that we must worship? I just pay them homage and respect through remembrance and memory, on the feast of Disincarnation. On the other hand, I am in contact and work with 'ancestors' linked to my priesthood who have not passed through the Great Gates leading to the Other World. It is a relationship to advance and re-emerge the Cornu priesthood."

For the most part, Druids reported simply honoring the memory of their ancestors, acknowledging them in passing, or at the start of rituals, and offering simple words of gratitude for the fact that their lives had enabled modern Druids to become the people who they were today. For these Druids (51% of survey respondents), this relationship was not considered a form of ancestor worship, but rather a demonstration of respect for the lives of those who had come and gone before them. It was a way to feel connected to the past and the future, a way to feel connected to the landscapes of their heritage, or the landscapes upon which they currently lived. Honoring the ancestors was also a way to feel validated while pursuing spiritual traditions and social roles that are not generally celebrated by mainstream culture. Examples of survey responses that described ancestral relations in these terms included:

> *"I find that as I get older, there are more and more of the people I love who are dead. Frankly, I miss them and find it nice to be able to bring them to mind — what is so lovely is that I can hear their voices — their replies, their thoughts — probably a process of knowing how they would have reacted to various things that happen/might be done, etc."*

> *"I work with my grandfather, who was a Cheyenne-Arapaho Holy man. He fulfils the Spirit of Spirit, Blood and Place. He speaks to me through my DNA. He is a part of me, but also he is his own person. Our people are a part of this land and always speak to me through the wind, the water, the sky and the earth."*

> *"I venerate the line of mothers that eventually dissolves into an all-mother. One of my primary practices is domestic art, the art of making a home, which is highly personal, cultural, and feminine. I count this as ancestor veneration because I am deliberately shedding the consumer-capitalist model of life, so I am reaching backward in time through my own mother and grandmother to pre-industrial mothers who are ideas rather than specific people."*

> *"I have ancestors from western Ireland stretching back very far, and direct ancestors from a Scottish highland clan. They help me feel connected to the land even though I no longer live there. Several of my ancestors were also musicians, and taught their children music, who taught theirs, etc. both sides of my family still highly value traditional music and have learned songs taught by our grandparents, etc."*

"I venerate my ancestors because they are the ones who have enabled me to be who and where I am today. I see their struggles, their defeats and their victories and I am trying to make them proud of me, and feel like their lives were not in vain. I see them — they were not invisible. I keep their belongings and images with me. Even the ones where they tried to look Caucasian (the Native American side of the family) by using white powder. I remember them."

"The ancient Celts. That is 71% of my DNA, but no known, specific individual ancestors. I also find myself sending mental apologies to the Ojibwe and Dakota ancestors of the land where I live, though I don't really think apologizing in my head is the same as veneration."

"Ancestors of my land, both known and unknown. Ancestors of my spiritual path who have been influential in my journey, i.e. Iolo Morganwg, Ross Nichols, etc. I honour them and give gratitude for their influence in building up this tradition."

For 23% of world Druids, ancestor worship was a more formalized part of their Druidry practice. These Druids described practices such as maintaining an altar or shrine dedicated to their ancestors, praying and making offerings to their ancestors, petitioning ancestors for guidance, and aid in earthly undertakings, and simply undertaking shamanic journeys, to spend time in their presence, and learn whatever might come from the experience. Examples of this type of response included:

"All of the above, ancestors of blood, spirit & place as well as ancestors of tradition, those who have kindred ideas, ancestors of past and future. Ancestors from before we were human, before bacteria, before the earth. I feel them with me when I need strength. I speak to them in ritual. I offer them food. I offer them my work. I ask them for guidance and protection for myself and my children in the form of prayer."

"Ancestors play an important role - I honour ancestors of blood and place. Ancestors of spirit are linked in when I do shamanic style journeying. Once a month, I light a candle in front of photos of my blood ancestors and create an altar to them on Samhain. Ancestors of place and spirit tend to appear as guides during vision work - shamanic journeying or guided meditation."

"I am deeply connected to my ancestors in all three senses and I spend a lot of my ritual time trying to connect to them, both to give thanks and to ask for guidance and strength. In times of trouble, I visualise a vast ancestral army behind me, giving me their strength. My altar often includes photographs of my ancestors and symbols connected with them. My female line, I visualise as Welsh dragons and to show my respect for both my English and Welsh ancestry, I made a banner that has a red dragon and a white one, clasping hands."

"I regularly give offerings to the ancestors of blood, spirit and land. I honor the river of my bloodline that flows to me from those who have come before me, and that same river flows on through my son and into those who will come after me. I honor those of spirit, from whom I try to reconstruct a practice that they would recognize and that they may help to guide me in developing my practice. I honor those of the land I live in, who had lived in the area I live in, farmed it, knew it's spirits and ways for thousands of years before my city was raised and I came to live here."

"Ancestors of Blood, Spirit and Place. Some specific ancestors, my foster parents. My great-grandfather, my grandmother. I light candles, burn incense, have an honor shelf for their pictures. Ask them to watch over me and my family, ask for guidance and advice. I've told a couple that I'm OK now and its OK if they need to walk on ahead. I've asked forgiveness of ancestors of place for things done in the past."

Concurrently Practiced Religions & Spiritual Paths

Path*	%**
Buddhism	24%
Christianity	20%
Shamanistic Traditions	17%
Witchcraft	17%
Wicca	12%
Northern Traditions	10%
Hinduism	7%
Native American Traditions	6%
Unitarian Universalism	6%
Magickal Traditions	4%
Taoism	4%
Polytheistic Reconstructionism	4%
Yoga	4%
Goddess Traditions	3%
Quakerism	3%
Reiki	2%
Faerie	1%
New Age Beliefs	1%
Judaism	1%
Shinto	1%
Polynesian / Māori traditions	1%
Anthrosophy	0.5%
Umbanda / African-matrix religions	0.5%
Western Mystery Traditions	0.5%
Islam / Sufism	0.5%

See Glossary for Path descriptions.

**Percentages are of the 335 Druids with multiple, concurrent paths.*

Religions and Spiritual Traditions Practiced with Druidry

Druidry was the sole religious or spiritual path for a majority (54%) of world Druids; the rest reported that they practiced Druidry concurrently with one or more other religious traditions. The most commonly mentioned religious traditions practiced with Druidry (each cited by at least two Druids) are listed in the table, at left. Concurrent practice of at least some elements of other major world religions, such as Christianity, Islam, Buddhism, Hinduism, and Judaism, was mentioned by 53% of Druids pursuing multiple, simultaneous paths; but nearly all (96%) Druids pursuing multiple paths also practiced some other, lesser-known spiritual tradition(s) along with their Druidry. For readers unfamiliar with these traditions, I have provided brief descriptions of each in the *Glossary*. There were no statistically significant differences between any major Druidry subgroups, in the prevalence of concurrent spiritual practices.

Aside from simply naming the other religious and spiritual traditions they practiced, 244 Druids also described the specific ways in which those concurrent practices were combined. Nearly all of these Druids — 93% of them — described an ongoing process of seeking wisdom from multiple sources, and then consciously working to integrate useful aspects of each tradition into a new, and highly personalized spiritual or religious path. Examples of their responses included the following:

"Difficult to say because my path is one. But I use el-ements I learned from other traditions. So for example I use gestures, visualizations and meditation techniques I learned from my Yoga teacher, and irregularly, I do some Asanas in the morning. My most used meditation pose I learned from Zen, the Zazen pose. I use Christian songs and prayers for two reasons: [firstly,] I know them from childhood on and some of them are very dear to me; [and secondly,] I don't know any Pagan prayers or songs that are so strong to me as the traditional Christian ones. Every now and then I visit churches for silent prayers, but usually not for service. There are a lot of churches that I experience as strong spiritual places; and there I feel the Mother of the Mountain, Mother Mary and the Mother of the Dead to be one. Here the Christian and the Pagan seasonal festivals are one, or at least very similar."

"Ásatrú, eklektisches Hexentum, Chaos Magic. Es gibt Aspekte meiner Praxis, die sich eindeutig einer Tradition zuordnen lassen - insbesondere wo ich mit anderen Menschen zusammen feiere (einer OBOD-beeinflussten Druidengruppe und einer Ásatrú-Gruppe). Diese zuordnbaren Aspekte sind durch andere Traditionen bere-ichert und beeinflusst; z.B. hat meine bardische Auseinandersetzung mit Poesie zu poetischen Beiträgen in unserer Ásatrú-Gruppe geführt oder mein Wissen um die germanische Mythologie hat mir das Erkennen von Paralellen in der keltischen Mythologie erleichtert. Meine persönliche Praxis ist sehr eklektisch. Ich mische wild.
[Translation:]
Ásatrú, eclectic Witchcraft, Chaos Magic. There are aspects of my practice that clearly belong to a tradition, especially where I celebrate with other people (an OBOD-influenced Druid group and an Ásatrú group). These assignable aspects are enriched and influenced by other traditions; e.g. my bardic engagement with poetry has led to poetic contributions in our Ásatrú group or my knowledge of Germanic mythology has made it easier for me to recognize parallels in Celtic mythology. My personal practice is very eclectic. I mix wildly."

"I retain some elements of Gardnerian practice in my private ritual, particularly the four classical elements (and their symbolism), the use of energy manipulation (circles, shields/wards, banishment, and empowerment/ enchantment of objects), and the idea of 'awakening' or making contact with innate spirits of natural or crafted objects. For example, I have a ritual staff which is carved,

painted, wrapped, awakened, enchanted, etc. specifically to assist with spellwork and travel. Druidry tends to deemphasize such spellwork and tool collection, in my current experience. Druidry's influences upon my prior tradition include the following: 1) Inspiration/Awen - I hadn't dwelt much on the concept of a divine inspirational force before coming to Druidry, but since that time, it has become a growing concept and element of my practice. 2) Fire, Well, and Tree - I like the Hallows (per ADF terminology) as primal symbols of elemental forces. Three-fold symmetry works better than four in many cases, particularly with the Fire and Water as endpoints with Life or Matter as a joining center. These concepts are used because of their enduring productivity in ritual, and it should have been no surprise these elements proved useful when incorporated into my personal practice. My working altar now features a candle in the South for combined Fire/Fire, a chalice in the West for Water/Well, a Tree or Stone (the Omphalos, in Hellenic tradition) in the North, and a bell or other sound-maker for Inspiration/ Air. 3) Ancestors - I hadn't given much space or thought to Ancestor worship before starting with ADF, but once introduced, it made sense as a missing element. In a practical sense, we ought to give respect to those who came before, if we want the same regard when we are done living. As integration, I attend public rites and private Sixth Night rites in ADF's Core Order style, but privately practice in Core Order, Wiccan-like home tradition, or a blend of the two, as the purpose demands. My devotions to Hermes are done in a more Hellenic style, not traditionally Druidic, but learned through my study in ADF."

"I try to follow Sufism in the most liberal way that I can. I don't want to upset the family. Meditation is a central part of Sufism as well. There are daily prayers and above all what is called dhikr. This means 'remembrance' and is a time to reflect through chanting. My way in Sufism chants 'Allah' the exact same way that Druidry chants 'Awen'. In a grove gathering, I also enter into the circle by holding my hands out to the sky and say silently 'Bismillah ar-Rahman ar-Raheem' with the most liberal intention I can get in Islam. I am not sure that there are any other Muslims with the same attitude as I have."

"Buddhism. I still meditate, but with Druidry I've added chanting and a more active form of meditation with visualization, path working, and connecting with places."

"Shinto (certain aspects - such as a belief in nature spirits or kami), Buddhism (ancestor 'worship'). Shintoism is polytheist and connects us all to nature. The spirits, gods or kami, reside in us as well as the features of nature. The notion of respecting nature and being a part of nature makes these aspects of Shintoism very compatible with modern Druidry. The belief in working with and respecting ancestors in Japanese Buddhism also is very compatible with modern Druidry. Both are organized religions dictating a set way to perform rituals in which passive participants largely sit quietly while a priest intones prayer. I think the overall movement in paganism and modern Druidry is involved ritual and involved prayer. That is - a priest or priests may lead a ceremony, but all members are active. This is what I personally prefer, and my own inclination in Druidry at the moment is largely solitary practice."

"I'm a baptized Christian active in a social-justice [and] *environmentally caring inner city and have not felt the need to renounce this. I have a theology degree and a fascination with the world faith traditions. I don't feel Druidry is exclusive. I feel it can bridge different paths and draw people together as a wisdom tradition — intermingling of stories, shared love of & care for earth, sanctity of life, I've written books encouraging Christians to be more in relationship with the natural world."*

For others who blended spiritual traditions, the process of integration was so effortless, and so organic, that they had difficulty deciding where one tradition ended and another began. These Druids typically saw all spiritual paths as having some useful perspectives and techniques which might contribute to their personal process of spiritual formation. They wrote, for example:

"[I previously studied] *Taoism, Buddhism, Christianity, Wicca/Witchcraft. Currently exploring Christian Mysticism, 'A Course in Miracles', and Vedic influences. I work with what seems to resonate with my soul. I don't worry about putting things in boxes. All paths up the mountain lead to the same summit."*

"I attend Mass most Sundays. I have found many parallels with Catholicism and Druidry. Mother Earth has many of the same qualities as Mary. The saints are similar to the Jungian archetypes seen within Druidry too."

"Sou Bruxo tradicional italiano, além de ter sido criado dentro do catolicismo e ter flertado por muitos anos com a umbanda. Tudo faz parte do um só.
[Translation:]
I am a traditional Italian witch, besides having been raised within Catholicism and having flirted for many years with the Umbanda. It's all part of the one."

"I never named what I did before, other than earth spiritual like. I also am native American (50%) and that was influential growing up. Native American practice is about the earth so that is similar, possibly more shamanic."

"Shamanic practices — is that 'in addition' or part of Druidry? I don't know how to answer that. There is no separation between the two for me."

"I suppose my experience in [Buddhist] *meditation and ritual has given me a good grounding in these aspects of Druidry. Many pujas (Buddhist ritual) I have done have Druidic elements and visa versa. Lightbody meditations similar across both practices as well as ethical frameworks for how I live my life."*

"I am an attending Quaker. The essence of worship within the Quaker tradition is 'waiting on God' and listening in silence. The special energy of a 'gathered silent meeting' is a very special energy that leaves space for the divine to show themselves in whatever form is most appropriate to the situation. I draw on silence and non judgement from the Quaker tradition. I am a Pilgrim who walks to connect with the divine, I have walked the Camino de Santiago as a seeker, not as a Catholic. I regularly grace the paths I walk with the description 'Pilgrimage'. For me to pilgrim is to walk with the awareness of the divine and of the sacred nature of the earth being walked. Pilgrimage is not unique to any particular spiritual tradition and is one of the few practices which crosses many, maybe most, different religious boundaries including Christian, Hindu, Muslim, Pagan and Shinto."

Only ten percent of the Druids who followed multiple, concurrent religious traditions practiced those religious traditions separately, keeping each tradition in its own context, for example:

"Vajriana Buddhism, to a lesser extent. They're mostly separate and in totally different domains. Druidry is the divinity of the earth and the other is the structure/path and its clearing for the purification/strengthening of spirit from life to life."

"Tradições afrodescendentes. Não faço hibridismo. Cada qual no seu contexto. Como era a prática da religião na antiguidade.
[Translation:]
Afro-descendant Traditions. I don't do hybridity. Each one in its own context. As was the practice of religion in antiquity."

"Christian, Kabbalah, Magic, Reiki. In my morning prayer and meditation session, I work from various sources. At other times, I usually compartmentalize one system at a time."

Five percent of Druids said they occasionally worked with groups from other traditions, simply because they wanted to be part of a spiritual community; but their private, personal Druidry practice did not include those traditions, for example:

"I study Wicca and Norse spirituality, but the former is more for the company than anything else. I got lonely and needed the fellowship of likeminded people. The latter aligns closely with many core principles that I believe in: Family, kinship, friendship, integrity, community, locality, generosity, courage, conservative values such as self-reliance and family first, etc. That said, I'm not affiliated with any group or creed."

"I attend services at my local UU fellowship as a way to commune with others who share similar values, even if their beliefs and practices are different from my own. I also occasionally join with other UU pagans both at my own church and another UU congregation in the area that has a CUUPs chapter."

Two percent of Druids said that they participated in other traditions in order to learn more about themselves, and their own beliefs, by seeing them through the eyes of others. They did not actually blend their religious practices, as one Druid explained:

"I have an interest in the teachings of Buddha and the Shamanic practices of various peoples. The other spiritual traditions which I follow don't have an effect on the way I physically practice Druidry so much as in the way I think about the Druidry which I practice. I believe they help to expand and deepen my understanding of Druidic teachings."

Spiritual Wildcrafting as a Form of Devotion

As evident in so many of the anecdotes in the previous section, rather than seeming worried by the lack of constancy or coherence in their religious practices and theological beliefs, Druids tend to see complexity and fluidity of belief as a natural part of the human condition — either as an opportunity for meditation and continued exploration and study, or as an inevitable artifact of the limited human psychological faculty striving to make sense of and forge connections with the eternal Divine. It is in the ongoing process of striving, studying, exploring, experiencing, and building personal relationships with the Divine — rather than in the details of any particular system of belief — that Druids seem to find their meaning.

While some saw themselves as either practicing Druidry alongside other concurrent traditions, or blending multiple traditions, others saw Druidry, itself, as a spiritual path defined by plurality and evolution. To them, the whole point of being a Druid was to seek wisdom, inspiration, and spiritual and ritual techniques from a variety of sources, grounded in a variety of world cultures and natural environments; and then to wildcraft a deeply personal, ever-evolving religious path from those findings. They wrote, for example:

"Druidismo Moderno é uma espiritualidade plural e sempre está crescendo como uma árvore, dando novos brotos, sugando novos nutrientes da terra, florescendo com novas perspectivas. Não é uma religião estática. [...] Outras tradições podem nos responder as lacunas que nos dão dor de cabeça.
[Translation:]
Modern Druidism is a plural spirituality and is always growing like a tree, giving new shoots, sucking new nutrients from the earth, blooming with new perspectives. It is not a static religion. [...] Other traditions can respond to the gaps that give us a headache."

"I can't really understand the question. I'm a Druid, which means to me that I incorporate ideas from many traditions based on my study of nature. Many things in the

coursework, I just don't believe in, others I do. I look out-
side the Druidry literature to support my spiritual goals."

"I see Druidry as a lens and a frame that helps me seek
knowledge. It doesn't appear to have all the answers or
want exclusivity as such. I've been Pagan for a little over
a year and I'm still reading widely as I seek to study
Druidry more deeply."

In this sense, it is not only one's spiritual journey toward Druidry, but also one's continuing spiritual journey within Druidry that is the key to understanding Druidry as a religious tradition.

Cultivating Relationships with the Divine

While the survey responses described many diverse systems of theo-logical belief, they also contained an emergent theme, which served to unify those seemingly disparate responses. Although many Druids simply listed the spiritual beings (deities / nature spirits / spirits of place) who played a significant role in their personal practices, the majority (67% of respondents) also discussed the ways in which they perceived those spiritual beings, the nature of their interactions with those beings, and the reasons for their interactions. Of the 482 Druids who provided this level of detail, 80% wrote that their relationships with spiritual beings were neither a matter of simple worship, nor a matter of obedience to rules, but rather a deliberate process of cultivating reciprocal, working relationships with them.

This theme was evident in survey responses from animists, hard and soft polytheists, pantheists, and monotheists, alike. Druids described developing relationships with deities of various pantheons, with nature spirits and spirits of place, with elemental forces of nature, plants, animals, rivers, oceans, rocks and mountains, sun, moon, and stars, and even with symbolic powers attributed to the four directions. For some, perceptions of those spiritual beings were cultivated through meditation, trance, visualizations, or shamanic journeying. For others, simply walking in nature, while maintaining full sensory and spiritual awareness, was enough to allow for spontaneous connection and communication to occur, either through clairvoyant, clairaudient or clairsentient experiences, or through signs and portents in the natural environment, which were later interpreted through meditation. Survey responses describing this type of relationship-building, in the context of each type of theological belief system, included the following:

"My relationship with my gods is informed by the
Northern tradition. I am not a supplicant, in need of their
mercy, asking for them to fix my life or to save me. I stand

confident in their presence and call on them to witness me. I do not expect them to be all-knowing or all-power-ful, or even to be particularly interested in me. They have strengths and weaknesses too. They are deliciously flawed. But they are my allies. I devote my rituals to them, and my declarations of where I am going, what I am doing and who I am."

"I see the God/desses as being the accessible view of the vast creative energies of regeneration through which the universe evolves. I experience them with inner sight and each has specific qualities, gifts and restrictions. [...] I also see every aspect of nature as sentient and enspirited and communicate with my local flora, fauna and water sources. This is a case of slowing down, being quiet and listening for inner impressions which are often ratified on the physical plane."

"As a child I talked to the trees, and never really stopped. [...] I still talk to trees, to the moon, to Venus, to rivers and rocks, to 'the spirits of place'. I like to believe that my attempts to communicate with non-human beings are a worthwhile endeavour. [...] They make me feel at home in the world, and give me a way of integrating the rare strange times when I have 'heard' voices, or felt spoken to/communicated with by non-human beings. They give me a sense of companionship and belonging when I'm in places where there are no other humans - a feeling that is very precious to me, and good for my mental health!"

"I have had several experiences throughout my life that made me feel very connected to something larger, with synchronicities that couldn't seem to have been happen-stance. I don't spend a lot of time or energy on specific deities, but I do feel a spiritual connection to something greater. I feel very close and connected to nature, the plants, the flora, fauna and the elements. I think that seeing our connection to nature and the Earth as divine and sacred is important, and that it is the lack of this sacred connection which continues to inflict damage and cause environmental devastation."

"When I was five, I first heard about Jesus, but no one in my family could tell me anything about him. So I learned to read to learn more and read the children's Bible. After that, I knew that my way was in the teachings of Jesus. [...] At the same time, I was always very connected to the world around me. Even as a child, my mother and great-

grandmother taught me a lot about the plant world. So I knew early on which plants I can eat, which [I cannot eat], which can heal, and where and when to find them. Our kitchen was always full of herbal bouquets. I had a special relationship with the plants and trees in my life. I even talked to them. There were a few years when I stopped listening and lost my grip. But [then] this stag came into my life. Yes, really a stag! Not physically, but only in meditation and then it was like an ongoing audio-visual contact in visions and dreams. Which arises again and again. He led me to the spring that filled my life with strength. He showed and explained things to me. He stood behind me and [...] gave me strength. Once we even merged. He never said that he is a deity, but he is my friend and I feel that I can trust him, and what he said helped me. And he gave me access to an inner peace."

In discussing the nature of their developing relationships with divine, and other spiritual beings, Druids mention, again and again, that the nature of their interactions is not the formal "worship" of the mainstream Abrahamic religions, but more of a respectful, two-way, working relationship.

At times, Druids described their relationships in terms of showing neighborly respect, for example:

"I venerate all nature. I have a specific relationship to the land which I belong. My first experience with this was the woods I played in when I grew up. I specifically remember feeling respectful of them, even then when I respected very little. When I was mad I would go into the woods and I would not even lash out at the trees physically for fear of hurting them. I've always felt the land as energies. Sometimes on hikes certain trees will have a strong physi-cal presence. I believe every being has a unique life-force and the land is alive and there are spirits of different lands but I also currently identify as an agnostic-atheist."

"While there have been several encounters with spirit entities over the years, we have always treated each other as fellow travellers on this planet. While these encounters have always been originated by others, worship has never been asked or demanded. Mutual respect has been the order of the day."

"I respect spirits of trees and landscape as they make themselves known to me through energetic sensations, warmths, 'force-fields,' etc, feelings of welcome, or of 'go no further'. I try not to project deity ideas onto

*environments but to be open to whatever might be there,
my own being communicating respect, non-harming and
an openness to positive connection."*

*"Almost every time I've been into the bush, particularly
on my own I've felt an overwhelming presence, of
multiple spirits. They feel to be ancestral protectors of the
land, and just observing what I'm doing. I've never had
any direct contact with them, but often leave offerings."*

*"My Druidry is entirely about developing and deepening
my relationship with The Land. My relationship with the
Land involves a state of heightened awareness and
sensitivity to the 'mood' and 'energy' of places. It is a
bi-directional exchange, not merely exhaltation or
worship. I derived inspiration, health and rejuvenation
from wild places."*

At other times, they spoke of budding friendships, focused on companionship, conversation, and a growing sense of comfort and ease while in the familiar presence of those other spiritual others, for example:

*"My experience of the deities have been through trees and
animals. Occasionally spirit of place - specifically rivers
and mountains. They represent life and the methods of
living. And I do experience them as real physical
presences, as they exist with me in the moments just as
happening across a friend in a coffee shop or market."*

*"I guess my conversations with my goddess is something
like a telephone call with a friend in a different country.
But she does not say much — I do most of the talking!"*

*"There is also the Badger, who is a close friend and soul-
mate. He appeared to me first in a dream, who became a
poem, then a book, and in the process of writing the book
we became well acquainted. He is what you might call a
power animal, a fylgja or a spiritual companion. He is
clearly not the spirit of all badgers, but very much an
individual Badger. He is also a creature of the in-between,
something of an emissary between humanity and the rest
of nature."*

*"Spirit of Willow Lake (a nearby lake to my home that has
called me to walk its banks and share sacred space),
Arabia Mountain and its numerous spirits and voices from
the wilderness that surrounds it... I'm also friends with*

*many trees and seem to connect quickly and easily with
animals. And, I work a lot with stones found in natural
environments."*

*"As an animist, all natural features be they rock or tree,
stream or herb, have a spirit and an awareness. As such, I
tend to greet many things I pass in a day — yes, I am one
that 'high-fives' trees, and stoops to compliment wild
flowers on their beauty."*

Some described the relationship in terms of kinship — complete with the
sense of loyal support, and occasional irritation — as one might expect of
close family members, for example:

*"I've worked with other beings — demi-gods/divinities,
perhaps. They are brothers and sisters on the path; more
powerful than our human forms — wiser. I believe they
are of alternate/parallel realities or worlds — worlds that
we will also go to."*

*"In the forest the trees reach out as family members —
generations of sisters/brothers/aunts/uncles although I
don't worship them."*

*"I have a spirit of my home, who I just call 'The House
Deity'. It is represented by a Papua New Guinean carved
mask hanging on the wall. He is a reminder of the need to
keep order in my home, both literally and metaphorically,
and will make his displeasure known if I don't. I first got
the carving as a souvenir without thinking about its
significance, but as my spiritual awareness grew, he came
to be a representation of the spirit of my home."*

*"It may sound an odd thing to say, but while I look at
Manannán as a Father, the Tuatha do feel like they are my
extended Spirit Family."*

*"I also have had very close, familial relationships with
spirits of place, nature and forest spirits for my entire life.
Each one or group has a slightly different way that they
would like me to honor them. Almost all of the ways I
honor gods or spirits are based on conversations I have
had with them to find out what they would like."*

Many Druids also described the divine, and other spiritual beings in their lives,
as advisors, teachers, mentors, and guides, who offer counsel, answer questions,
and assist Druids in their efforts to become wiser and more skillful at a wide

range of activities, both in their personal lives, and at work. Examples of responses in this category included:

> *"Vereren is voor mij niet het juiste woord en aanbidden ook niet. het is leren, hulp vragen of bedanken of samenwerken om iets te bereiken. Ik heb contact met natuurspirits of goden, die kan ik soms zien of horen. Ik voel de aanwezigheid.*
> [Translation:]
> *For me, veneration is neither the right word nor worship. It is learning, asking for help or thanking or working together to achieve something. I have contact with nature spirits or gods, whom I can sometimes see or hear. I feel the presence."*

> *"Cougar is my heart-most guide, though I did offend her by not listening to her and spent a long time making it up to her for that grave mistake. Coyote is more of an advisor, both in sincerity and in sarcasm, and not unlike a peanut gallery will sometimes pop in with commentary, asked-for or not. I speak to many others - Crow, his cousin Raven, Rabbit, Fox, Rat, his little brother Mouse, Rattlesnake, House Cat, Wolf, Bear, Elk, and countless more - as I need guidance and opinions. They each have their own voice, their own advice. It's impossible to properly describe how I experience them without sounding insane. Voices in my head? Impressions? Sensations in the air that you can feel but not see?"*

> *"Mir ist die Große Göttin als Mutter Erde heilig. Ich sehe sie in allem, das mich umgibt, in Bäume, Steinen, Tieren, Wäldern, Felsen, den Elementen und dem Boden, der mich trägt. Ein Funke von ihr ist in allem Leben. Sie vereint für mich alle Göttinnen in sich, bzw. alle Göttinen wie Aphrodite, Demeter oder Holla sind ein Aspekt von ihr. Sie ist das weibliche Prinzip. Natürlich gibt es auch das männliche Prinzip, einen Gott, der alle Götter in sich vereint, aber zu ihm fehlt mir ein wenig der Zugang. Ich spüre die Anwesenheit der Göttin, wenn ich draußen bin, mal als Energie des Ortes, mal in einem Baum, den ich berühre, mal in Tieren, die mir begegnen und mal im Wind, der mir ins Gesicht weht. Manchmal beschäftigt mich ein Thema und ich gehe damit hinaus und wende mich an sie. Und während ich draußen bin, kommt mit plötzlich ein neuer Gedanke, ein Impuls der vorher nicht da war oder ich bin auf einmal inspiriert, wie ich etwas angehen will. Das kommt für mich von Ihr.*

[Translation:]
*The Great Goddess is sacred to me as Mother Earth. I see
her in everything that surrounds me, in trees, stones,
animals, forests, rocks, the elements and the ground that
carries me. A spark from her is in all life. For me she
unites all goddesses in herself, or all goddesses like
Aphrodite, Demeter or Holla are an aspect of her. She is
the female principle. Of course there is also the male
principle, a God who unites all gods in himself, but I lack
a little access to him. I feel the presence of the goddess
when I am outside, sometimes as the energy of the place,
sometimes in a tree that I touch, sometimes in animals
that I meet and sometimes in the wind that blows in my
face. Sometimes I am occupied with a theme and I go out
with it and turn to it. And while I'm outside, suddenly a
new thought comes along, an impulse that wasn't there
before or I'm suddenly inspired how I want to approach
something. That comes to me from her."*

"The Moon Goddess and The God. To me they represent
lasting presences of the divine inherent in nature, which
can be experienced in the Wheel of the Year, and the
course of life. Their guidance becomes visible to me in
visions, as warning — when I am endangered somehow —
or as a supportive voice — giving me the opportunity to
reflect on my choices of e.g. action/behaviour — and in a
shift of energy. I don't remember a time without them."

"I generally meet deities because they have contacted me
via synchronistic messages. Then I reach out to them in
meditation and speak with them there. I do visualization
meditations in which the spirits interact with me through
vision, sound and direct knowledge (as in a dream). My
experience of these spirits is quite complex. Odin, for
example, has given me stories and visions for about ten
years, and I have learned a lot about his relationship with
Loki, the concept of gender, and how to be a better father
and how to perform better at work."

Some also described their working-relationships as those of collaborators and
co-creators, with each contributing knowledge, resources, strengths, and skills,
to achieve a mutual goal. Examples of this type of response included:

"Brigid is the goddess who helps me daily in my work as
a Nurse. I feel her power in my hands, guiding my
practice."

"When I plant my garden I always speak with Ranginui and Papatūānuku to ask them help me look after their children. Our vegetable garden was blessed by four Druids in a ceremony before we first planted anything."

"I have a strong connection to the deer as a spirit animal and she is always in my bardic grove when I meditate before studying my Druidry course material. She is also there whenever I embark on a shamanic journey. I feel a strong connection to the spirit of deer and feel it when I am in the woods (I feel like a deer!). The only deity I have so far encountered is Elen of the Ways, whose statue spoke to me in a shop in Glastonbury: I bought it and have been learning about her since. I have looked to hear and asked her guidance but not seen her in a vision as such. She appeared in a meditation where I was asking for artistic inspiration and I took the message to paint a reindeer (which I did). The artwork has generated a lot more interest than my usual work: people seemed to connect with the piece — one person even thought the reindeer looked like me!"

"I do not 'worship' in a traditional sense. I like to use the words 'work with,' 'align,' and 'celebrate'. For example, I work with, as a friend, the local water Taniwha (dragon?). I celebrate the weather. I try to align myself with that 'something more' to co-create a better way forward."

"I venerate and serve the spirits of nature — animals, plants, and places — not only through my spiritual work but also through my professional work as an ethnoecologist. In my experience, rocks give me 'energies' as communications (not emotional feelings, but a sort of shift in my body's mood and energy). Animals and plants give me visual messages and sometimes 'knowings.' Animals seem to be more visual than plants for me. Places give me 'knowings' and feelings/energy. I also honor the gods in the Celtic pantheon (plus Durga, who is just too much in my life to leave out). The gods, to me, are associated with visions and messages/knowings that are usually more verbal."

Finally, two Druids spoke of their relationship with their gods and spiritual companions as others might speak of a love affair:

*"I have a budding relationship with the spirit of a
particular tree close to where I live. I took particular
notice of this tree on one of my regular walks in the area,
and we have had a coy, flirting relationship since that
time. She reminds me of the sensuality in nature."*

*"I worship a Creator God, Ogma, and Goddess, the
White Tara. They are life and breath to me, my main
guides and teachers, my best friends and lifelong
partners, the Ones I serve in all I do. I love Them more
than anything and feel filled with Their love on the inside
in every moment. It is a mystical marriage."*

As was true of the theological beliefs held by Druids, there is also substantial diversity in the nature of the relationships that Druids forge with spiritual beings, be they deities, spirits of nature or place, legendary tribal leaders, or revered ancestors of blood, spirit, and place. The common theme that emerges repeatedly in Druid descriptions of their relationships with the divine is the concern for developing webs of reverent, reciprocal relationships with others, and using those relationships for inspiration, encouragement, and support whilst striving to become ever wiser, more honorable, and more skillful in their personal journeys through life.

CHAPTER 5 NOTES & REFERENCES

1 Harvey, G. (2017). *Animism: Respecting the Living World (2nd Ed.).* London: C. Hurst & Co. Ltd.

2 Intergroup variations in identity with animism:
    TDN members much more likely (86% vs. 64%) p=0.01

3 Kraemer, C. H. (2012). *Seeking the Mystery: An Introduction to Pagan Theologies.* Englewood, Colorado: Patheos Press. pg. 26-38

4 Intergroup variations in identification with soft polytheism:
    ADF members much more likely (73% vs. 49%) p=0.00

5 Harrison, P. (2013). *Elements of Pantheism: A Spirituality of Nature and the Universe (3rd Ed.).* Shaftesbury, Dorset: Element Books.

6 Kraemer, C. H. (2012). *Seeking the Mystery: An Introduction to Pagan Theologies.* Englewood, Colorado: Patheos Press. pg. 28-29

7 Intergroup variations in ancestor veneration:
    ADF: ancestors-of-blood more likely   (72% vs. 51%) p=0.00
    ADF: ancestors-of-spirit more likely   (66% vs. 42%) p=0.00
    ADF: no ancestor veneration less likely   (6% vs. 23%) p=0.01
    OBOD: ancestors-of-place more likely (36% vs. 32%) p=0.01
    TDN: ancestors-of-place more likely   (68% vs. 32%) p=0.00

CHAPTER 6:
DRUID RITUAL & DEVOTIONAL PRACTICES

Having addressed the questions of *whom* Druids worship, and *why*, we now turn our attention to the question of *how* Druids worship. What are the core elements of religious ritual and devotional practice in contemporary world Druidry?

The word *ritual* is nearly as difficult to define as the word *Druid*. Religious scholars have defined *ritual* in a variety of ways.[1] Some have argued for limiting the use of the word *ritual* to describing only formal, ceremonial activities performed in social groups. Others allow for the possibility that any human activity might have ritual aspects associated with it, depending upon the context and the intention behind the activity. In her book, *Ritual Theory, Ritual Practice*[2], Catherine Bell proposes that, rather than speaking of *ritual* as a noun, we might more profitably speak of the process of *ritualization* — any strategic, culturally-embedded action that serves to distinguish sacred activity from the mundane, whether practiced within a group, or alone. By way of example, Bell describes elements of Zen Buddhist monastic life[3], in which the simple act of eating breakfast becomes a ritualized, spiritual act because of the mindful attitude that is cultivated and maintained throughout the meal. Given the wide variety of activities — group and solitary, formal and informal — that contemporary Druids consider to be a part of their spiritual lives, it seems best to approach the discussion of *Druid Ritual and Devotional Practices* from the broader perspective of ritualized activity.

In popular media (as verified by a Google search), "Druid rituals" typically involve large circles of white-robed people, with flowers, banners, staffs, swords, and assorted offerings for ancestors or gods, gathered at some public monument. Even scholars of modern Paganism represent contemporary Druids in this fashion.[4] This is frequently done with unsupported assertions, or extrapolations based upon very limited data, such as a single photograph of a public, Druid ritual at Stonehenge.

In contrast to this popular imagery, the *World Druidry Survey* data indicate that elaborate, public group ritual in formal garb represents only a very small portion of the ritual and devotional practices of contemporary world Druids. As we will see, most world Druids rarely, if ever, engage in rituals involving more than one Druid. Most never participate in any type of public ritual. Only half of world Druids ever wear ceremonial garb, of any color, in their ritual practice. This begs the question: what kinds of ritual and devotional practices *do* most Druids perform?

Since ritual plays such an important role in most world religions, questions pertaining to ritual practices within Druidry comprised a large portion of the *World Druidry Survey*. Questions explored the types and frequency of common ritual practices, the types of sacred objects (if any) used in ritual, the types of common ritual locations, and the types of social groups (if any) in which Druids conducted their rituals. A second set of questions explored the ritualized, everyday activities that contemporary Druids performed as part of their regular, spiritual practice.

In the remainder of this chapter, I present the overall results for each of these topics, and discuss all statistically significant results for intergroup comparisons based on: Druid age; years of experience practicing Druidry; Druidry group membership; level of personal connection (if any) to traditionally Celtic lands and culture; residence in light/temperature driven biomes versus residence in water/moisture driven biomes (see page 26); and region of residence (British Isles & Ireland / continental Europe / Oceania / North America). In the interest of readability, I have chosen to discuss these results in plain language, using simple graphics. The detailed numeric results for all analyses can be found in the chapter endnotes.

Common Ritual Practices Among Druids

The most common ritual practices among Druids are reported in the chart on the facing page, ranked in descending order of prevalence among Druids (based on a weighted average of reported frequency). The frequency with which Druids practice each ritual act is illustrated by the shading, ranging from black for daily practices, to pale grey for ritual practices performed only a few times each year. *Daily* practices also include practices for which Druids reported striving for a daily practice, but managing only several times per week. *A Few Times Per Year* indicates practices that are associated only with annual gatherings, or with one or more Wheel-of-the-Year celebrations, which will be further discussed in *Chapter 7*. Discussion of these practices will follow, in the order listed in the chart. The overall percentage of Druids who engaged in each practice will at times appear out of sequence. This is because, for the sake of discussion, daily and weekly practices were given more weight than those performed only few times each year.

Common Ritual Practices among Druids

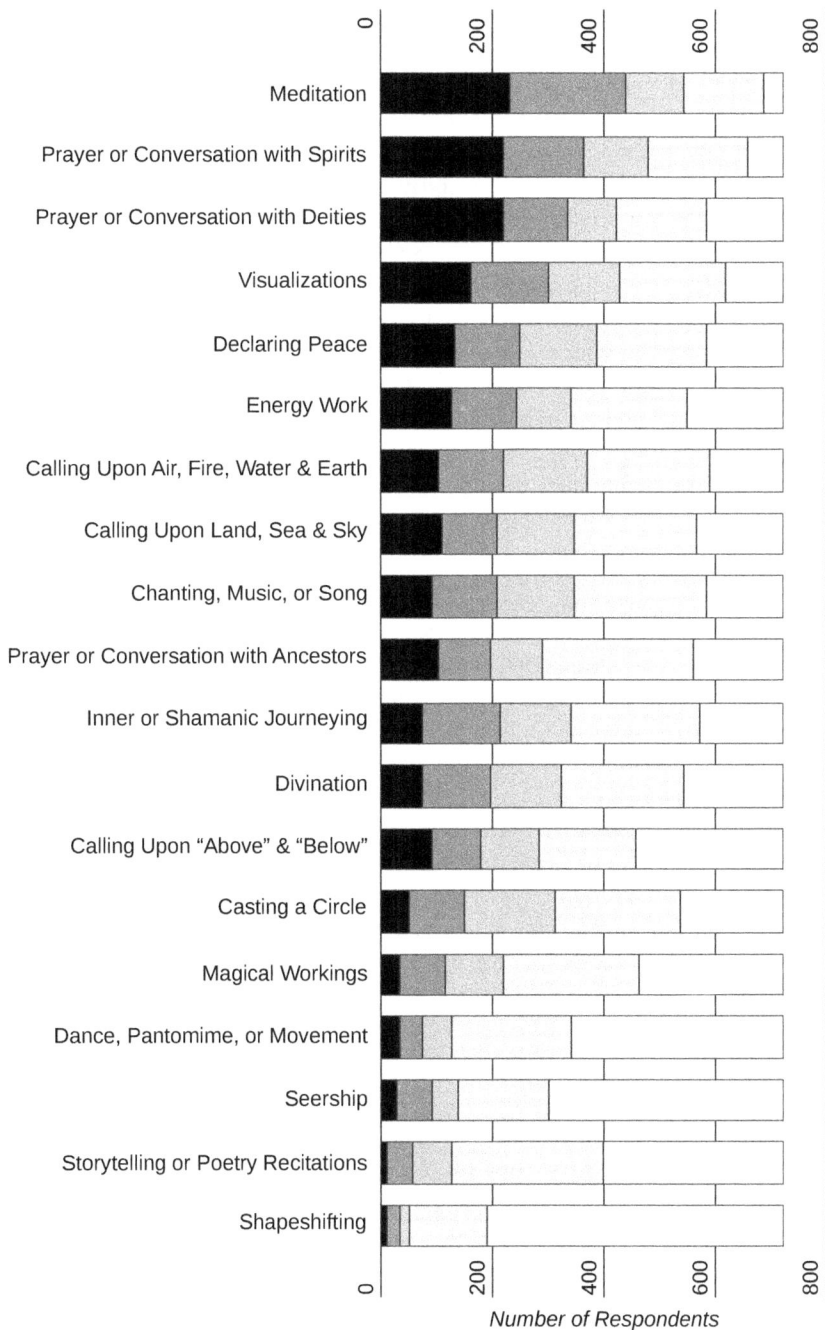

Number of Respondents

Legend: ■ Daily ▓ Weekly ▒ Monthly □ A Few Times/Year □ Never

Meditation

Nearly all Druids (95%) practice some form of meditation as part of their regular Druidry practice. The types of meditation practice vary, but the cultivation of a calm, focused mind capable of controlled attention and deep concentration is at the heart of all of these practices. As discussed earlier[5], for some Druids this meditation practice is a continuation of a prior meditation practice developed within another spiritual tradition — such as Zazen, or the mindfulness, loving-kindness, or insight meditation practices of other Buddhist-Druids. For Contemplative Druids, it might be a form of receptive meditation, in which one extends the senses to become more fully aware of and connected to an element of the natural world.[6] For others, discursive meditation is the preferred mode, in which a seed topic or theme drawn from Druid lore or other reading material is slowly and deliberately explored and examined through a formal process of internal dialogue.[7] In all cases, meditation practice allows Druids to become less reactive, and better able to exercise wisdom when dealing with turmoil in the inner or outer worlds. There were no significant intergroup variations in the prevalence of meditation practice among Druids.

Prayers or Conversations with Nature Spirits or Deities

Nearly all Druids (94%) regularly interact with nature spirits, and/or deity or deities (depending upon personal theology), through conversation, or prayer, or by an alternate mode of interaction, as previously discussed in *Chapter 5: Cultivating Relationships with the Divine*. Considered separately, 91% of Druids interact with nature spirits, and 81% do so with deities, but there is significant overlap between the groups, and the work of developing reverent, reciprocal, working relationships with nature spirits and/or deities is common to both groups. There were no significant intergroup variations in the prevalence of prayer, conversation, or other forms of personal interaction with nature spirits or spirits of place. However, members of ADF are much more likely than other Druids to have a regular practice of interacting with deities.[8]

Visualizations

Most Druids (85%) use visualizations as part of their regular Druidry practice. For some, this involves calling to mind — in rich, multisensory detail — sacred, inner landscapes in which one might meet and converse with inner, spiritual guides. For others, visualizations might take the form of things such as: colored streams of energy; or spiritually symbolic animals such as hawks, deer, salmon, and bears; or spiritually symbolic trees such as birch, oak, and yew; or other symbols and elements of spiritual practice. These visualizations may serve a number of purposes, for example: as a focus for mediation, for magical workings or energy work, or as a ritual entry-way into the world of spirit, for inner or shamanic journeying. The only significant intergroup variation in the practice of visualization[9] is that OBOD members are more likely than others to regularly practice visualizations.

Declarations of Peace

Most contemporary Druids (81%) include a declaration of peace as part of their regular, ritual practice. In formal group rituals, this may involve partially unsheathing, and then resheathing a sword while declaring peaceful intentions to each of the four cardinal directions. In the more informal rituals of many solitary Druids, it may take the form of a raised hand in gesture of peace, or a prayer for peace, or a simple act of meditation, in which a deep sense of peace is cultivated within, and then radiated outward, through the web of life. Two intergroup variations were statistically significant for this ritual practice.[10] Members of OBOD were more likely to include declarations of peace as part of their regular practice, while ADF members were much less likely to do so.

Energy Work

Most world Druids (76%) engage in energy work as a part of their regular Druidry practice. In Druidry, *energy work* describes either a process of connecting with nature, and absorbing energy from that connection, or of applying energy thus derived to soothe, strengthen, encourage, heal, or otherwise transform oneself, or others — of human, or other-than-human kind. Druids may draw in solar energy from the heavens, or telluric energy from deep within the Earth, or *nwyfre* (life-force energy) from trees, stones, or waterways. They may draw in energy from any of the Four Elements, or the Three Realms. They may apply this energy to help heal people, plants, or animals, or to make amends and work to heal the land, sea, and sky in areas where human activities have caused harm to the natural environment. As with most other ritual acts in Druidry, the specific details and interpretations may vary, but the general concepts and practices are shared. There were no significant intergroup variations in the prevalence of energy work in Druidry.

Calling Upon the Four Elements: Air, Fire, Water, and Earth

A key part of ritual practice for most contemporary Druids (82%) is to call upon the four elements: Air, Fire, Water, and Earth. In Druidry, these elements are not considered physical components of matter, but rather, spiritual aspects of the living world. Each of the elements is associated with a variety of thematically related concepts, symbols, and/or powers, such as: a cardinal direction; a time of day or year; a cognitive, emotional, or spiritual skill; or a symbolic plant or animal. Many correspondences are held in common among Druids, for example: Air is traditionally associated with clarity of thought, vision, and communication; Fire is associated with qualities such as strength, passion, and will power; Water relates to emotions, intuition, and wisdom; and Earth is associated with qualities such as stability, security, and perseverance. Other correspondences may be discovered by Druids, individually, through a process of spiritual wildcrafting (as described in *Chapter 4)*, and meditation. The resulting correspondences hold deep, personal meaning for the Druid, and may vary from those traditionally used by contemporary Druids in Britain. However, the act of calling upon the elements, and the reason for calling upon them are shared: it is a way of calling to oneself, and cultivating within oneself, specific qualities and powers of spirit, which correspond to the specific elements called. The only two significant intergroup variations for this practice[11] were that OBOD members were more likely to invoke air, fire, water, and earth, while ADF members were much less likely to do so.

Calling Upon the Three Realms: Land, Sea, and Sky

Most Druids (78%) will also call upon Land, Sea, and Sky as a part of their regular Druidry practice. Land, Sea, and Sky — also referred to as the *Three Realms* — is another framework for perceiving and interacting with the natural and spiritual worlds. For some Druids, calling upon the *Three Realms* is simply a matter of connecting with and calling to mind the physical realms of land (islands, continents, soils, mountains, etc.), sea (seas, oceans, rivers, waterways, wells, etc.), and sky (air, wind, sun, stars, etc.), upon which all living beings depend for their lives. For others, the *Three Realms* refers to three spiritual worlds, correlating to the mundane world (Land), the spirit world (Sea), and the world of the deities (Sky). For still others, Land, Sea, and Sky are thought of as a system of symbols related to the three elements of the Druid Revival, *Calas, Gwyar,* and *Nwyfre* — roughly corresponding to the qualities of solidity, fluidity, and life-force.[12] Despite the differences in how individual Druids may interpret the *Three Realms,* calling upon Land, Sea, and Sky is still a common ritual practice among Druids. The only significant intergroup variation in this area[13] was that AODA members were much less likely to call upon the Three Realms than others.

Chanting, Music & Song

Musical expression, in various forms, is a part of the regular ritual practice (or ritualized activities) of 81% of Druids. This may include something as simple as chanting the Awen, or singing songs or hymns, or playing a musical instrument during ritual. At the other extreme, a (very) few survey respondents reported working to develop and publicly perform a full repertoire of narrative songs celebrating the history, mythology, and beauty of their land, as one Druid described:

> "*I sing narrative songs that attempt to tell the stories of the land and the people who have lived on it. I get out to sing 'in public' at least a couple of times a week and try to cycle through my repertoire, (keeping lists to prevent me from repeating myself too much). In common with traditional bards, I have a repertoire of about 300 songs/tales committed to memory of which, for example, I sang 234 different ones in 2018. I do this partly to keep the songs themselves alive (they are only alive when actually being sung from memory) and partly because I feel it is my calling to share these songs and the stories within them. Sometimes doing so gives me the opportunity to pass on some of my love of Nature and some of the history, folklore and mythology of these Isles.*"

Only two significant intergroup variations were evident in the data on chanting, music, and song in Druidry[14]: AODA members were much less likely to engage in musical practice, while OBOD members were more likely to do so.

Prayers or Conversations with Ancestors

Prayers, conversations, or other interactions with ancestors — of blood, of spirit, or of place (as discussed in *Chapter 5: The Role of Ancestors in Druidry Practice*), form a regular part of Druidry practice for 77% of world Druids. Only one significant intergroup variation was evident in this data[15]: ADF members were much more likely than other Druids to include ancestors in their practice.

Inner or Shamanic Journeying

Spiritual journeys through visualized, inner landscapes, or shamanic journeys into other, "nonordinary realms of existence",[16] to meet with spiritual guides, to gather knowledge, and to acquire power for later use, are part of regular Druidry practice for 79% of world Druids. The knowledge and power derived from such journeying is generally used to help oneself, or others in the community, with things such as healing, divination, or spiritual formation. The only significant intergroup variation for inner or shamanic journeying[17] was that OBOD Druids were more likely to engage in journeying on a regular basis.

Divination

The practice of divination in Druidry, that is, the practice of reading portents of the future, or signs which reveal the deeper truths of things, or the best way to move forward in a challenging situation — is most commonly performed using tools such as the ogham, runes or tarot cards. Overall, 75% of Druids perform some kind of divination as a regular part of their Druidry practice. The only significant intergroup variation was that ADF members are much more likely than other Druids to have a regular divination practice.[18]

Calling Upon the Two Powers: "Above" and "Below"

Just over half (63%) of Druids call upon the Two Powers, or *Above* and *Below*, as part of their regular Druidry practice. In Druidry, *Above* refers to solar energy radiating down from the heavens, while *Below* refers to telluric energy emanating from deep within the Earth.[19] These two powers can also be thought of as the Ouranos/Gaia or Father Sky/Mother Earth pairings. The only significant intergroup variation for this data[20] was that AODA members are much more likely than other Druids to call upon *Above* and *Below* as part of their regular practice.

Casting a Ritual Circle

As members of a religious tradition that maintains no permanent, consecrated spaces in which to perform rituals, most Druids (74%) will at least at times cast a circle within which to perform their ritual activities. This may involve walking the perimeter of a ritual space, and marking its edges energetically, or placing markers such as flowers or seashells or candles or stones around the perimeter. Druids participating in a group ritual will often stand in a circle, at the outer edge of that ritual space, facing inward, while the main ritual activities play out in the center. Upon completion of the ritual, the circle will then be ritually "opened," or dissolved.

Several significant intergroup variations were notable for ritual circle casting.[21] Druids born and bred in traditional Celtic lands, or resident in continental European countries were more likely to cast a circle as part of their regular ritual practice. Druids of the Celtic diaspora, particularly those in North

America, were less likely to do so. ADF Druids were much less likely to ever cast a circle, and OBOD Druids were much more likely to do so.

Those who did not cast circles as part of their ritual practice often explicitly stated that they felt the practice was neither necessary nor appropriate for Druids celebrating out-of-doors, as one Druid explained:

> *"In Nature, I do not cast a circle or call the elements. The elements are all around me and it doesn't feel right to create a separation from Nature, then call them in."*

Magical Workings

Just over half (63%) of Druids engage in some kind of magical work as part of their regular Druidry practice. This may involve ceremonially imbuing ritual tools or talismans with special energies. It may involve cultivating various energies within oneself, which can be directed either inward, to affect change in oneself or in one's life experience, or outward, for purposes such as: protecting and healing the environment, people, or sprits of place; or achieving better success at work; or achieving greater harmony in one's relationships; and so on. The specific forms of magic used vary with the Druid. Some practice formal systems of Ceremonial or Ritual Magic, involving colors, symbols, and ritual tools such as candles, wands, and cauldrons. Others work with simple, Natural or Kitchen Magic, using herbs and simple charms, based on old folk customs. The only significant intergroup variation was that ADF members were much more likely than others to engage in magical workings.[22]

Dance, Pantomime, or Other Movement

Just under half (47%) of all Druids include dance, pantomimes, or other forms of ritual movement as a part of their regular Druidry practice. Examples of ritual movement reported by survey respondents included: ritual gestures, tai-chi, yoga, eurhythmics, and ritualized re-enactments of mythic battles and other tales. There were no significant intergroup variations in the prevalence of dance, pantomime, or movement in Druidry practice.

Seership

A significant minority of Druids (41%) include seership as a part of their regular Druidry practice. Seership is similar to divination in purpose, but rather than relying on interpreting patterns divination tools (such as ogham, runes, or tarot cards), seership focuses more on cultivating the trance-like states of mind in which clairvoyant, clairaudient, or clairsentient experiences are more likely, revealing information about distant, past, or future realities.

There was a significant trend in the data, correlating seership practice with level of experience in Druidry.[23] The percentage of Druids who practiced seership increased from 33% for novice Druids to 73% for those with more than 30 years of experience. Since there were no significant intergroup variations in seership corresponding with age of Druid, this trend indicates that seership may become more important as a Druid gains in knowledge and skill.

Storytelling or Poetry Recitations

Just over half (55%) of Druids include storytelling or poetry recitations as part of their regular Druidry practice. Spoken-word performance of poems thematically related to a ritual (often composed for the occasion), or the retelling of a pertinent story or myth, are a key part of the Bardic tradition of Druidry. However, the skill and confidence needed for public performance of a story or poem require time to develop. As a result, these activities tend to be reserved for major seasonal celebrations, or eisteddfodau. The only significant intergroup difference was that AODA members are much less likely than others to include storytelling or poetry recitations as part of their regular practice.[24]

Shapeshifting

A significant minority of Druids (27%) include shapeshifting as part of their regular Druidry practice — a practice that involves transforming one's consciousness in order to perceive, comprehend, and behave like a specific animal, plant, or other object.[25] Two statistically significant variations were evident in the survey data on shapeshifting.[26] Firstly, OBOD members are more likely than others to practice shapeshifting. Secondly, there is a trend in the data, correlating shapeshifting practice with level of experience, ranging from 21% of novice Druids to 48% of those with more than 30 years of experience with Druidry. Since there are no statistically significant differences corresponded with age, this trend indicates that shapeshifting may become more important as one gains in knowledge and skill as a Druid.

Sacred Objects in Druid Ritual & Celebration

The physical trappings associated with a religious tradition are often the first things that people point out when trying to describe that tradition. In Druidry, most of the stereotypical Druidic trappings — the long, white robes, the oak trees and stone circles — do apply to some Druids, at least some of the time, but the prevalence of these things among contemporary Druids, and the frequency of their use are somewhat different than typically assumed.

The most commonly used sacred objects in Druidry are listed in the chart, below, in descending order of prevalence among Druids. The frequency with which Druids use each type of sacred object is illustrated by the shading, as it was for the common ritual practices, discussed earlier.

Altars and Shrines

The most commonly used sacred object among Druids is a personal altar or shrine. Most Druids (83%) maintain at least one personal altar. Many Druids report having several, placed in various locations about their homes, offices, and/or gardens. In addition to reporting the simple fact of having or using an altar, and the frequency with which it was used, 155 respondents submitted photographs of their altars (see page 170 for examples),[27] which

Sacred Objects Used in Druid Ritual & Celebration

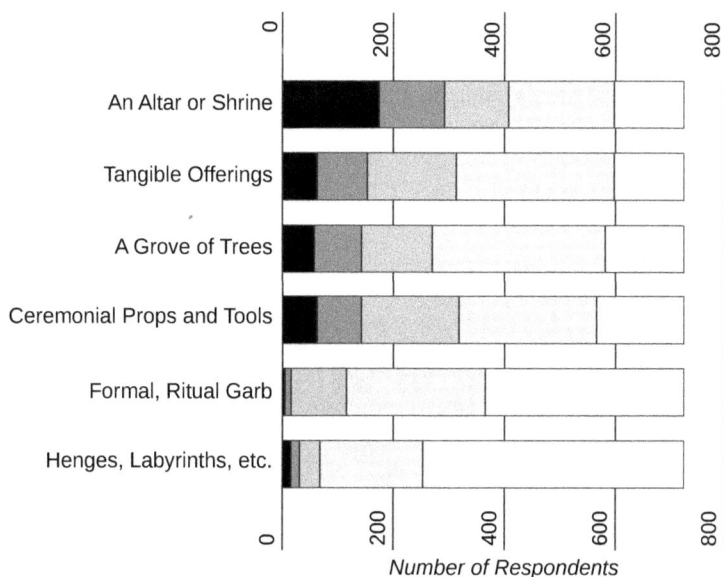

Number of Respondents

Legend: ■ Daily ▨ Weekly ▢ Monthly ☐ A Few Times/Year ☐ Never

offer further insight into the nature of Druid altars, and the elements which they tend to have in common.

Druid altars range from discreet arrangements of collected, natural objects (e.g. stones, shells, feathers, and herbs), to elaborate, working altars with all the accoutrements required for divination, magical work, and making ritual offerings. Druid altars include things such as: statues or images of one or more deities, nature spirits, and/or ancestors; a religious symbol such as the Awen or a pentacle; ritual items, such as colored candles or other objects representing the Four Elements or the Three Realms; plates, chalices, or other vessels used for offerings; and magical or ritual tools such as wands, swords, Ogham staves, runes, cauldrons, or drums. Oftentimes, Druid altars and shrines are decorated with objects that represent the theme of a particular festival or seasonal celebration. The only significant intergroup variation was that members of ADF are more likely to perform their rituals using an altar.[28]

Examples of Druid Altars & Shrines

Offerings for Deities, Spirits, and Ancestors

Making offerings of various kinds to deities, ancestors, spirits of place, or other spiritual beings — such as the *Outdwellers* of the ADF tradition — is part of regular Druidry practice for 82% or world Druids. According to survey responses, offerings are most often made in a spirit of praise, gratitude, and reciprocity, rather than in supplication. Offerings may be as simple as a pinch of wildflower seed, a scattering of flowers, or a plate of food set out for the ancestors. Some Druids also offer libations of things like milk, mead, wine, ale, or water. Contrary to the imagery portrayed in modern fiction and video media, contemporary Druids never engage in blood sacrifice, of any kind. The only significant intergroup variation is that members of ADF are more likely than other Druids to make regular offerings to their deities.[29]

A Grove of Trees

Druids really do love trees. As it turns out, the stereotypical image of Druids performing rituals in a grove of trees is one of the few that actually hold true for the vast majority of contemporary Druids. Overall, 81% of world Druids do, at least occasionally, perform rituals in the company of trees, at times assembling simple altars on the ground, in the grass, or among the fallen leaves of the forest floor. There were no statistically significant variations in the data for rituals in groves of trees.

Ceremonial Props and Tools

A majority (78%) of world Druids use one or more ceremonial or magical props or tools as part of their regular Druidry practice. These tools might include things like: colored candles or other objects representing the Four Elements or the Three Realms; magical or ritual tools such as wands (for directing energy), swords (for ritual declarations of peace), Ogham staves, runes, or tarot or oracle cards (for divination), cauldrons (for containing water, fire, incense, or salt), and musical instruments or drums (to aid in shamanic journeying). The only statistically significant variation was that OBOD members were more likely than others to use ritual props or tools in their practice.[30]

Formal, Ritual Garb

Half (50%) of world Druids wear formal, ritual garb — of some kind — as part of their regular Druidry practice. Mostly, this is reserved for monthly or major seasonal celebrations, though a few Druids reported wearing formal garb as part of their weekly devotional practice. In addition to reporting the frequency with which formal ritual garb was worn, 106 survey respondents submitted photographs of their garb, examples of which can be seen, at right.[31] Analysis of the photos shows that 60% of ritual-garb-wearing Druids do, in fact, wear white robes (meaning that 30% of modern Druids dress in a manner consistent with popular imagery). One-third of these wear colored cloaks or tabards over their white robes, which tend to be deeply hued, single-tone garments, with colors that vary widely, including various shades of green, brown, black, blue, purple, red, and grey. The other 40% of the ritual garb photos show Druids in everyday clothes or wearing mainstream, semi-formal wear, with the addition of a stole, a piece of ritual jewelry, or a sprig of a seasonally relevant herbs or flowers, or occasionally, a ceremonial headdress, such as a wreath of leaves and flowers, or stag's antlers.

There is only one statistically significant intergroup variation in the prevalence of formal ritual garb in Druid ritual practice: Druids in North America are far less likely than other Druids to wear any kind of formal, ritual garb.[32] This is consistent with the safety and privacy concerns reported by American Druids (see *Chapter 3*).

Varieties of Druid Ritual Garb

Henges, Labyrinths, and other Ceremonial Structures

The image of Druids conducting rituals at Stonehenge has become something of a cliché; but, despite the popularity of the image, the majority of world Druids have never done so. In fact, only 35% of world Druids report having conducted or participated in any rituals involving a henge, labyrinth, or any other ceremonial structure.

As would be expected, there were several statistically significant variations for this practice.[33] Druids resident in traditionally Celtic lands — especially the Druids of the British Isles and Ireland — were more likely to perform rituals within a henge, labyrinth, or other ceremonial structure than Druids who lived elsewhere in the world, especially those in North America. Members of BDO and TDN were also more likely than members of other Druid groups to do so.

Interestingly, the habit of performing rituals in a circle of standing stones is not limited to Druids who live near neolithic monuments. The power of circles and standing stones is such that a number of Druids who live elsewhere in the world have constructed their own stone circles for ritual use. Ten Druids submitted photographs of ritual stone circles they had constructed locally[34] (see examples, depicted on page 174).

Despite this enthusiasm, there is also evidence in the data that the importance of stone circles, labyrinths, and other ceremonial structures is fading with time. There was a significant trend in the survey data in which older Druids are more likely (61%) to perform rituals using ceremonial structures, while younger Druids are much less likely (10%) to do so.

Places of Druid Ritual & Celebration

Aside from the physical trappings of a religious tradition, the most photogenic sites of group ritual celebration are generally assumed to be the center of spiritual life for the tradition. Druidry has no cathedrals, mosques, or temples to serve as regular places of worship. Even Stonehenge, which is by far the most popular site to be photographed with Druids in mid-ritual, turns out to be far less important to world Druidry, overall, than is popularly believed. So, what are the most common sites of Druid ritual and celebration?

The single most common location for Druid ritual, cited by 92% of world Druids, is indoors, at home, or at the home of a friend — frequently at a home altar or shrine. The second most common ritual location for Druids (cited by 90% of survey respondents) is outdoors, in a garden or wild space, with as much privacy as can be reasonably managed. Variations in the type of private(ish) outdoor spaces used correlated with ease of personal access to private gardens and wild spaces, with preference given to more private locations.

Stone Circles Built by Contemporary Druids

For most, this was a private garden or wild space; for others, it was a semi-private garden or wild space that might be shared with neighbors or overlooked by passers-by; and occasionally, Druids celebrated in secluded areas of public parks or wild lands. There were no statistically significant, intergroup variations in the prevalence of indoor or outdoor rituals, provided that they could be performed with at least some measure of privacy.

Less than half (48%) of world Druids have ever participated in rituals performed "in the eye of the sun," that is, in any location in which they might be readily observed by members of the general public. This includes any of the following: public garden or wild spaces viewable by the general public (32% of Druids); rented, indoor spaces such as wedding venues or conference centers (26% of Druids); or public monuments, such as Stonehenge, Avebury, the Ring of Brodgar, the ancient redwoods of Humboldt Redwoods State Park, or any other popular tourist destination (18% of Druids). These types of public ritual locations were used almost exclusively for special occasions, or as part of major seasonal celebrations.

There were a number of statistically significant variations, when it came to the subgroups of Druids who were most open to performing rituals

Places of Druid Ritual & Celebration

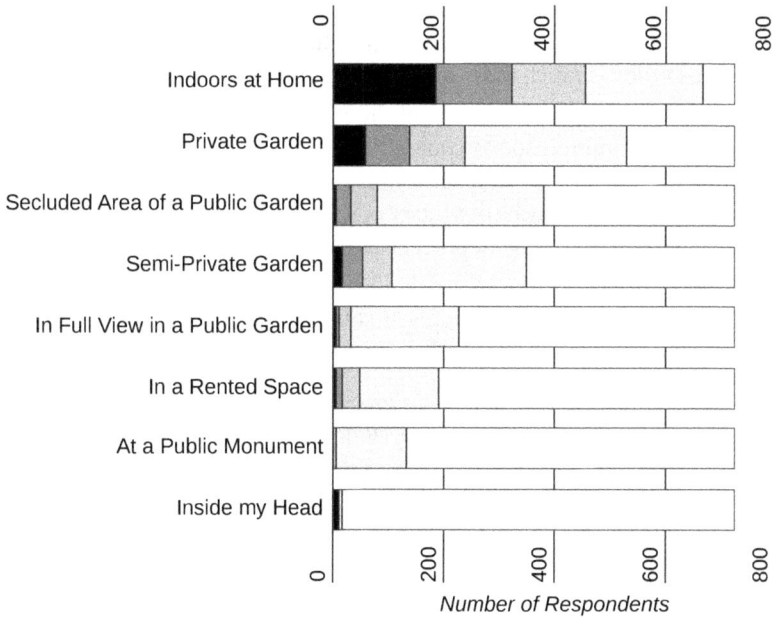

Number of Respondents

Legend: ■ Daily   ▨ Weekly   ▤ Monthly   ▢ A Few Times/Year   ▢ Never

in publicly viewable locations.[35] Members of ADF, BDO, and TDN were more likely to participate in rituals held in public locations, as were Druids born, raised, and resident in traditionally Celtic lands — particularly those in the British Isles and Ireland. AODA members were significantly less likely to do so. In addition, there was a trend in the data, correlating participation in public rituals with years of experience in Druidry. Less experienced Druids were less likely to participate in rituals held in public locations, while those with more experience were more likely to do so.

Finally, two percent of Druids reported that the majority of their daily and weekly practices took place inside their heads, in visualized inner groves, rather than at any particular location in the outer world. This corresponded with situations in which respondents reported feeling particularly at risk in their communities, due to anti-Pagan sentiments.

Social Contexts for Druid Ritual & Celebration

Religions, and religious traditions, are often described in terms of community cohesion — as sets of beliefs and practices which help to bind communities of people together.[36] In the case of contemporary Druidry, it seems that the cohesive power of the religious tradition is most commonly applied to the relationships between a Druid and his or her deities, and other-than-human kin — the plants, animals, nature spirits, and spirits of place which inhabit a Druid's physical neighborhood. In many cases, the companionship of other Druids is much more difficult to come by.

According to the results of the *World Druidry Survey*, solitude is by far the most common social context in which Druidry is practiced. Solitary practice was cited by 92% of survey respondents. There were two significant variations in the prevalence of solitary practice[37]: Druids residing in traditionally Celtic lands are less likely to practice alone; and Druids of the Celtic diaspora are more likely to do so.

For a few Druids, the idea of solitary practice was inconceivable due to the orthodoxy of their particular Druidic tradition, as one Druid explained:

> *"In my/our practice we follow what we consider to be the 'Primordial Tradition' of Druidry, following the Galician line (not so well known abroad). Thus, we may represent a quite 'orthodox' approach to Druidry, where 'solitary Druids' are not normally accepted and where direct social/community involvement is paramount."*

However, this perspective was reported by only very small minority of contemporary world Druids. Rituals performed as part of a Druid group, or as a part of a group of other, like-minded Pagans, were reported by just

65% of world Druids. Although a few Druids explicitly stated that they preferred solitary ritual practice to group practice[38], the key determining factor, in most cases, was ease of access (or lack thereof) to local Druidry groups.

Many Druids expressed frustration at their inability to locate other Druids within a reasonable commute from their homes. For example, in the final survey question — which prompted respondents to add anything they felt was important about their Druidry practice, which had not yet been explicitly addressed — respondents wrote things such as:

> *"I lived in Seattle for 7 years and I really miss the vibrant Druid community up there. Where I live now there are a lot of other pagan friendly folk, but they are not quite my tribe. I have been working in the past year to really be ok with being a solitary practitioner now and hoping that in the future I can connect back up with more Druids who want to be part of a practicing community."*

> *"Although I am a solitary Druid, I have little choice, as Australia is such a large country, and I am finding even locating others in my area very difficult!"*

Social Contexts for Druid Rituals & Celebrations

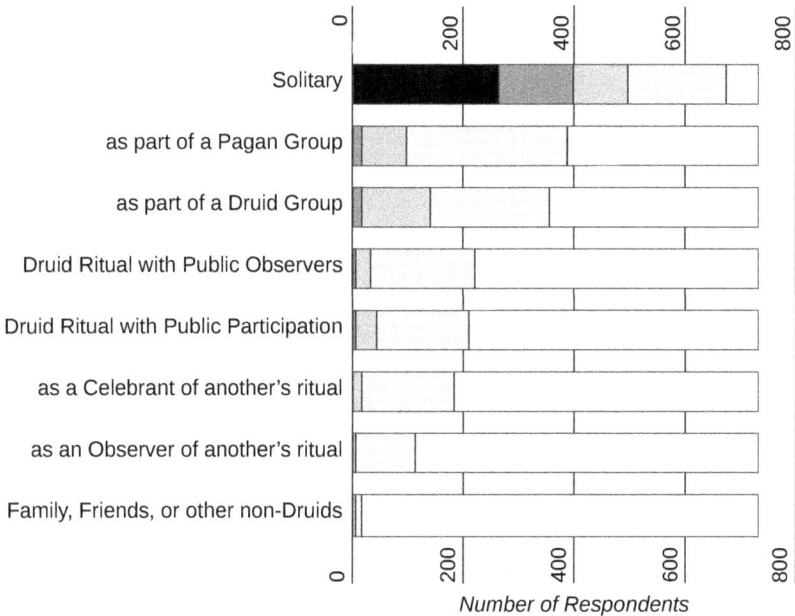

Number of Respondents

Legend: ■ Daily ▨ Weekly ▢ Monthly ▢ A Few Times/Year ▢ Never

"When I first joined OBOD I couldn't find any other practicing Druids within 300 miles. After a few months I've found 5. It makes me feel a little lonely that there are so few of us but I'm very hopeful that this spiritual path will gather more people and we will grow."

Clearly, for Druids who are not part of a large Druidry organization, with a strong, local presence (and for this, ADF and OBOD are the only plausible options), ritual is limited to solitary practice, or to work within a mixed Pagan group, which is unlikely to feel like a true, spiritual home.

Even for Druids who are able to connect with other Druids locally, group ritual practice tends to be reserved for special occasions like full-moon rituals, new-moon rituals, or major seasonal celebrations.

There were several significant variations in the prevalence of group ritual among Druids.[39] ADF members, and OBOD members based in Britain, where the geographical density of Druids per square mile is much higher, were much more likely to participate in Druid group rituals. AODA members, North American Druids, and Druids with fewer than 10 years experience were significantly less likely to work in any kind of group, while Druids with more than ten years experience were much more likely to have found or established a Druid group with which to perform rituals.

Rituals open to, and encouraging public viewing or participation, such as those described by the two Druid respondents cited in *Chapter 3*,[40] are a part of the regular ritual practice of only 37% of world Druids. As with all other group rituals, the practice was largely reserved for monthly, or major seasonal celebrations. The only significant intergroup variation was that ADF members were much more likely to participate in public rituals.[41] There is also a slight trend in the data correlating years of experience in Druidry with higher prevalence of participation in public rituals: Druids with 1-10 years of experience are less likely to participate in public rituals, while Druids with 10-20 years experience were more likely to do so.

Other, less common social contexts for Druid ritual included: hand-fastings, coming-of-age celebrations, or other rituals in which the Druid served as a celebrant for others (25% of Druids); rituals attended as a non-participant observer (15% of Druids); and private rituals attended by non-Pagan family and friends (2% of Druids). All of these were limited to special occasions, or major seasonal celebrations. There were two statistically significant variations in these less-common social contexts for Druid ritual.[42] One was that ADF members are much more likely to engage in ritual both in the role of celebrant and in the role of non-participant observer. The other was a trend in the data, correlating celebrancy practice with years of experience. Less experienced Druids were less likely to serve as celebrants; and those with more experience were more likely to do so.

Sacred Activities in Everyday Life

As we have seen, ritual practices among modern Druids range from highly formal, large-group public ceremonies, with ritual garb, props, and tools, to simple, informal ritualized actions performed by solitary Druids in silence. Farther along this continuum lie a variety of everyday activities that non-Druids might consider to be mere hobbies or entertainments, but which Druids consider to be integral parts of their spiritual or religious identity.

To identify the most commonly practiced sacred activities in everyday life, the *World Druidry Survey* included several pages of check-box items, clustered into the broad categories of *Nature-Related Activities, Artistic Activities, Educational & Activist Activities, Spiritual Leadership Activities,* and *Areas of Personal Study or Academic Research*. Druids were also prompted to write in any other everyday activities which they felt were an integral part of their Druidry practice.

The resulting data-set contained descriptions of hundreds of specific activities — far too many to make sense of, individually. Therefore, using cluster analysis techniques[43], I grouped the individual items based on thematic similarity, and similarity of response distribution. Chi-squared tests for intergroup variations were then performed for each cluster, and those results were sorted into seven major categories of activity, for discussion (see table, below).

Nature Connection & Environmental Stewardship

The most common types of sacred activity, in the everyday life of contemporary Druids, are nature connection and environmental stewardship. Nearly all world Druids (89%) perform at least one of these, and the vast majority of Druids do both types of work, which are seen as sacred duties. As

Sacred Activities in Everyday Life

Type of Activity	% of Druids
Nature Connection & Environmental Stewardship	89%
Creative & Artistic Work	80%
Ongoing Studies in Spiritual Philosophy	80%
Cultural Studies & Preservation Work	76%
Environmental & Social Justice Activism	63%
Healing Work	58%
Education & Spiritual Leadership	48%

such, there are no statistically significant intergroup variations for these two types of activity.

Nature connection practices are performed by 86% of world Druids, with no significant variations between any survey respondent subgroups. These practices include things like engaging in receptive meditation in nature, and working to develop keener sensory awareness — with all five senses — so as to better and more easily perceive subtle details of the natural world. Nature connection also includes communing and communicating (listening, speaking, singing, etc.) with plants, trees, animals, and various spirits of nature or place, interpreting bird and animal language, interpreting plant and tree language, and reading the weather in the wind and clouds. This also typically includes the simple act of walking the land, an activity that, by itself, was cited by 76% of Druids. Although this category also included things like hiking, rambling, mountain climbing, wildland camping, or outdoor swimming, the point of these activities for Druids was not to conquer nature or collect impressive photographs, but to cultivate deep, personal relationships with the landscapes, seascapes, and skyscapes of home, or of lands abroad, when traveling.

Environmental stewardship activities are regularly performed by 85% of world Druids, with no statistically significant variations between any survey respondent subgroups. This includes activities as simple as planting trees and native plants, to those as complex as restoring native ecosystems, gardening to provide wildlife habitat, forestry, wood-lot management, wildfire prevention, and fire-fighting. Druids also reported performing environmental stewardship activities such as hunting (practiced as a devotional form of wildlife population management), and installing solar power or wind power systems, or other green/sustainable energy sources to protect the environment from damage by burning fossil fuels. The focus of this type of everyday sacred activity is the care, protection, and healing of land, sea, and sky, by way of physical activities grounded in science.

The most commonly cited subcategory of environmental stewardship work is a process of changing personal habits to live more lightly upon the Earth. This is a sacred activity regularly performed by 66% of world Druids. It involves making one or more specific, carefully weighed choices about how to live one's daily life, in a manner that lessens the negative impact of one's life upon the environment. Such decisions might include any of the following: eating vegan or vegetarian foods; reducing, reusing, and/or recycling rubbish; growing one's own food; composting; conserving energy; conserving water; reducing consumption of unnecessary "stuff"; using less plastic; seeking ways to reduce one's carbon footprint while traveling; reducing the use of toxic chemical detergents, cleaning supplies, fertilizers, and pesticides; and so on. It also includes cultivating a habit of mind, which constantly seeks new ways to change habits for the further benefit of Mother Earth.

Another commonly cited subcategory of environmental stewardship is gardening or farming, to benefit humankind. More than half (56%) of world Druids do some kind of gardening — with their own, personal hands in the soil — rather than simply enjoying gardens that are planted and tended by others. This includes things such as: growing flowers and a few tomatoes in pots on the patio; designing, planting, and tending ornamental flower gardens; keeping kitchen gardens; full-scale organic farming and orcharding; or planting and tending permaculture food forests. Several Druids also reported raising, breeding, and caring for flocks of sheep and goats, stables of horses, or other domesticated animals. The only statistically significant, intergroup variation in the gardening/farming subcategory of environmental stewardship is that ADF members are much less likely than other Druids to engage in gardening or farming activities.[44]

In order to succeed at any of the above mentioned activities, many Druids often also engage in continuing studies in topics in the sciences such as botany, ecology, zoology, and various Earth sciences (soil science, hydrology, meteorology, global climate change, etc.). In addition, Druids reported participating in a variety of nature conservation research initiatives, including tracking and recording the migrations of wild life, and gathering water quality data for local waterways.

Creative & Artistic Work

Channeling the flow of divine inspiration (which Druids call *Awen*, or in Ireland, *Imbas)*, to create original works of writing, music, or other art forms, is a key element of Druidry practice for 80% of world Druids. For 64% of Druids, the practice is incorporated as a formal part of ritual; for others, it qualifies as a sacred activity in everyday life. In either case, the number of Druids who engage in creative and artistic works as part of their spiritual path is consistent across all respondent subgroups, with no statistically significant variations. However, the specific types of artistry practiced do vary widely.

Writing original works of poetry, fiction, or creative nonfiction, as well as activities like designing original board games, blogging, or journaling in preparation for such writing, comprise the most common category of artistic activity, practiced by 52% of world Druids. These writings are often inspired by nature, by myths and legends, or by personal interactions with deities, ancestors, or spirits of place.

Inspired craftsmanship of hand-made, functional works of beauty, is another common category of artistic endeavor pursued by 43% of world Druids. The kinds of arts and crafts created by Druids varied widely. Examples of their work included: sheep-to-shawl fiber work; forest-to-finish woodcraft; garden design; sewing, knitting, crochet, and embroidery; silversmithing and other metal-work; leather working; lapidary; wood carving, turning, and joinery; and soap and candle making.

Brewing & other culinary arts were forms of artistry mentioned by 37% of world Druids. This subcategory of artistic endeavor includes wildcrafting foods — foraging nuts, berries, and edible weeds, and preparing them as food — for example, making acorn flour, manzanita jelly, or homemade vinegars and breads. It includes home brewing, mead and wine making. It also includes ritual acts conducted during harvest and food preparation, which turn the work into a devotional practice, imbuing the food with healing energies, or magical powers, or making them seasonally and culturally relevant to specific Druidic seasonal feasts.

The practice of fine arts — the creation of artistic works with the sole purpose of communicating meaning or emotion without the use of verbal language — is a regular spiritual practice for 35% of world Druids. This may include things like nature photography, drawing, painting, or sculpture.

Musical performance, including both public performance, and the act of singing or playing an instrument for private, personal enjoyment, or with small groups of family and friends, was an artistic activity reported by 25% of world Druids. The related creative arts of music composition and song writing are practiced by 16% of Druids.

Ongoing Studies in Spiritual Philosophy

Ongoing studies in spiritual philosophy is a regular part of everyday life for 80% of world Druids. The specific books read and topics studied vary greatly (see *Chapter 4*), but the habit of ongoing study was consistent across all respondent subgroups, with no statistically significant variations.

Druid philosophy was the most popular subcategory of ongoing study, pursued by 65% of Druids, with no significant intergroup variations. This might include the study Druidic conceptions of things such as: the nature of the human soul; or the structure of the multiverse; or the metaphorical, meta-physical, or magical implications of the Four Elements, the Three Realms, or the three Druid Elements, *Calas, Gwyar,* and *Nwyfre*; or the symbolism of the stations of the Wheel of the Year; or meditations upon Druidic ethics, or upon wisdom triads. It may also involve meditations on the Awen (the most common religious symbol of Druidry, representing the flow of divine inspiration, also know as Imbas, in Ireland):

The second most popular subcategory of study was tree lore, and in particular, the lore associated with the Ogham — an ancient, Irish alphabet, which many modern Druids use as a tool for divination. Each letter, or *few*, of the Ogham alphabet is associated with a particular tree, as well as with a variety of other symbolic and magical correspondences, identified through study and meditation. The Ogham is a topic of ongoing study for 42% of world Druids.

One-third (33%) of world Druids study other world religions as part of their ongoing spiritual studies, consistent with the Druidic habit of seeking wisdom wherever it may be found. For this subcategory of study there were a few statistically significant, intergroup variations: ADF Druids and North American Druids were both more likely to study other religions, while Druids in Oceania were less likely to do so.[45]

A minority of world Druids also focused on other areas of spiritual and philosophical study, including: animal lore (32%); elements of esotericism (26%); star lore and astrology (24%); and alternate forms of divination, such as runes, and tarot (1%). The only statistically significant variation in these areas was that AODA members were much more likely than other Druids to study elements of esotericism as part of their Druidry.[46]

Cultural Studies & Preservation Work

Ongoing studies pertaining to human cultural traditions, including readings and research in fields such as history, archaeology, traditional myths, legends, and lore, and the linguistic studies required to translate and interpret them, was an activity regularly pursued by 76% of world Druids. There were no statistically significant intergroup variations for this general category of study, although there were a few variations apparent in the details.

Studies pertaining to the history and sociology of Druids and Druidry was an activity reported by 59% of world Druids, with only one statistically significant variation[47]: Druids in Oceania are much less likely to study the history of Druids and Druidry.

The study of world myths and legends was part of everyday life for 54% of Druids. This included things like reading and meditating upon a myth's symbolism and interpretations, or comparing different versions or translations of a traditional tale. Much of this activity focused on Celtic lore, but for Druids residing outside of traditionally Celtic lands, this also included researching local myths and legends related to the landscape, seascape, and skyscape, and indigenous flora and fauna, and peoples of their region.

The study and preservation of endangered linguistic and cultural traditions was a category of activity pursued by 51% of world Druids. This includes things like learning to speak, read, and write in endangered languages such as Welsh, Cornish, or Te Reo Māori, or learning about, and attempting to revive and preserve dying cultural traditions and celebrations, and so on. When sorted by linguistic and cultural milieu, 39% of Druids focused their cultural study and preservation work on Celtic traditions; 26% focused on languages and traditions indigenous to the land where they lived; and 22% studied languages and cultures of other parts of the world. At this level of detail, a few significant, intergroup variations emerged[48]: North American Druids, and Druids of the Celtic Diaspora were more likely than other Druids to study both Celtic cultural traditions, and cultural traditions from other parts of the world; Druids from Oceania and those with no hereditary ties to Celtic culture were much less likely to study Celtic language or culture.

Environmental & Social Justice Activism

The general category of environmental and social justice activism includes a range of activities calling on the aid of other humans and other-than-human beings, in support or defense of the environment, of other people, or of political causes such as the protection of and access to public monuments and cultural heritage sites. For some Druids (55%) this primarily involved prayer or magical workings; for other Druids (34%), this work relied upon the more mundane acts of writing letters, filing law suits, organizing and/or participating in demonstrations, or serving on advisory boards. There was some overlap between these two groups, and so overall, environmental and social justice activism activities were part of everyday life for 63% of world Druids, with a few notable intergroup variations[49]: Druids with fewer than 10 years of experience were significantly less likely to engage in magic or prayer in support of their causes, and were also less likely to engage in social justice activism of any kind. Members of OBOD were significantly more likely to perform all manner of activist activities, in support of the environment.

Other activist activities, which were written in by survey respondents included donating money to environmental causes, animal rights activism, and regular prayer and magical workings to protect home and family, crops and livestock. A few Druids also mentioned engaging in reconciliation work with the indigenous peoples of their region.

Healing Work

Healing work, of various kinds, is part of everyday life for 58% of world Druids. The most commonly cited healing practice among Druids was herbalism — including the study of the herb lore required for the practice — which is part of everyday life for 56% of world Druids. Allopathic medical practices, such as mainstream medicine or psychiatric work, were mentioned by 16% of Druids. A small minority of Druids (1%) listed an assortment of other, alternative healing modalities, such as reiki, crystals, homeopathic remedies, ecotherapy, aromatherapy, animal-assisted therapy, and the like. Some Druids also reported creating medicinal foods and medicines from wild-sourced herbs and plants. There were no statistically significant, intergroup variations in the prevalence of any form of healing work.

Education & Spiritual Leadership

A rather broad range of activities fell into the general category of education and spiritual leadership within Druidry — a regular part of everyday life as a Druid for 48% of survey respondents. The educational activities in this category included things such as: non-fiction writing about Druidry, or related activities; public speaking and/or teaching classes and workshops about Druidic or Pagan topics (in contexts ranging from Pagan and Druid gatherings, to early childhood education, to university courses); mentoring new Druids on a one-on-one basis, either privately, or through a Druidry group's official mentoring program; and managing or producing informational websites, blogs, or podcasts about Druidry. The spiritual leadership activities in this category included things like: organizing and/or leading group rituals; writing liturgy; organizing Druid groups and gatherings; providing celebrancy services; representing Druidry in interfaith groups; and creating new monuments or sacred spaces for Druidry (such as the new stone circles, discussed earlier in this chapter.

Two significant intergroup variations were evident in the prevalence of educational and spiritual leadership activities.[50] First, members of ADF were much more likely than other Druids to perform educational and spiritual leadership activities. There was also a strong trend in the data, as would be expected, correlating educational and spiritual leadership activity with years of experience in Druidry.

Universal Themes in Druid Ritual & Devotional Practice

While no specific element of formal ritual is practiced by all world Druids, there are five universal themes, or general categories of ritual activity, which are performed by nearly all world Druids, with no significant intergroup variations. These are:

1. a regular meditation and/or visualization practice
   (96% of world Druids)

2. a regular practice of prayer, conversation, or other relationship-building activity with spirits of place, nature spirits, and/or nature deities
   (94% of world Druids)

3. a regular practice of one or more extra-sensory methods of seeking wisdom, aid, and guidance from the world of spirit, such as divination, seership, inner or shamanic journeying, or shapeshifting
   (90% of world Druids)

4. using a nature-based, spiritual and energetic framework, such as the Four Elements or the Three Realms, to lend structure to formal and informal rituals
   (90% of world Druids)

5. a regular practice of nature connection and environmental stewardship work
   (89% of world Druids)

It is important to bear in mind that this relatively short list of near-universal practices does not limit the range of ritual and devotional practices that individual Druids, or localized groups of Druids, see as essential to their personal or local group practice. There was a second cluster of ritual practices that were also very popular among Druids. However, a significantly smaller number of Druids engaged in each of these second-tier activities, and there were also significant intergroup variations in the prevalence of each of them — variations which did not exist for the five, above-mentioned, universal themes. This second cluster of common ritual practices included:

- maintaining one or more altars or shrines (83%);
- making offerings to deities, and nature spirits (82%);
- chanting, music, and song (81%);
- declaring peace to all living beings (81%);
- seeking out the company of trees (81%);

- engaging in creative & artistic works (80%);
- ongoing studies in spiritual philosophy (80%);
- using ceremonial props and tools (78%);
- honoring ancestors (77%);
- energy work (76%);
- circle casting (76%); and
- cultural & linguistic studies and preservation work (74%).

Beyond this, there are no doubt many other devotional practices which individual Druids consider important, especially considering the Druidic tendency to seek wisdom wherever it may be found, and to integrate practices that best serve one's personal spiritual development. However, when considering Druidry as a global spiritual movement, the five universal themes in Druid ritual and devotional practice may be considered the key factors that serve to identify world Druids as members of a cohesive religious tradition.

CHAPTER 6 NOTES & REFERENCES

1 Bell, Catherine. (1992). *Ritual Theory, Ritual Practice*. New York, NY: Oxford University Press. pg. 69-74

2 ibid

3 Bell, Catherine. (1997). *Ritual: Perspectives and Dimensions*. New York, NY: Oxford University Press. pg. 151

4 Druid rituals are described in this manner by:
    Harvey, Graham. (2011). *Contemporary Paganism: Religions of the Earth from Druids and Witches to Heathens and Ecofeminists (2nd Ed.)*. New York, NY: New York University Press. pg. 19
with one citation, referencing a single photograph found in:
    Ellis, Peter B. (1994). *The Druids*. London: Constable and Co. Ltd. pg. 129
This vision of Druid ritual is also asserted, with no references to any form of data, whatsoever, in:
    Davy, Barbara Jane. (2007). *Introduction to Pagan Studies*. Lanham, MD: Altamira Press. pg. 158

5 See *Chapter 5: Themes & Variations in Druid Theology*, pg. 142-149

6 Nichol, James. (2014). *Contemplative Druidry: People, Practice, and Potential*. CreateSpace Independent Publishing Platform. pg. 85-92

7 Greer, John Michael. (2006). *The Druidry Handbook: Spiritual Practice Rooted in the Living Earth*. San Francisco, CA: Red Wheel/Weiser LLC. pg. 204

8 Intergroup variations in Prayer and Conversation with Deities:
    ADF: much more likely   (98% vs. 81%) p=0.00

9 Intergroup variations in Visualizations:
    OBOD: more likely   (90% vs. 85%) p=0.00

10 Intergroup variations in Ritual Declarations of Peace:
    ADF: much less likely   (60% vs. 81%) p=0.00
    OBOD: more likely   (89% vs. 81%) p=0.00

11 Intergroup variations in Calling Upon Air/Fire/Water/Earth:
    ADF: much less likely   (56% vs. 82%) p=0.00
    OBOD: more likely   (90% vs. 82%) p=0.00

12 Greer, John Michael. (2006). *The Druidry Handbook: Spiritual Practice Rooted in the Living Earth*. San Francisco, CA: Red Wheel/Weiser LLC. pg. 59-63

13 Intergroup variations in Calling Upon Land, Sea, and Sky:
    AODA: much less likely   (57% vs. 78%) p=0.00

14 Intergroup variations in Ritual Chanting, Music, and Song:
    AODA: much less likely   (64% vs. 81%) p=0.00
    OBOD: more likely   (85% vs. 81%) p=0.00

15 Intergroup variations in Prayers or Conversations
   with Ancestors:
    ADF: much more likely   (94% vs. 77%) p=0.00

16 Cowan, Tom. (1993). *Fire in the Head: Shamanism and the Celtic Spirit*. New York, NY: Harper Collins Publishers. pg. 3

17 Intergroup variations in Inner or Shamanic Journeying:
    OBOD: more likely   (85% vs. 79%) p=0.00

18 Intergroup variations in Divination Practice:
    ADF: much more likely   (89% vs. 75%) p=0.00

19 Greer, John Michael. (2006). *The Druidry Handbook: Spiritual Practice Rooted in the Living Earth*. San Francisco, CA: Red Wheel/Weiser LLC. pg. 70-72

20 Intergroup variations in Calling Upon Above and Below:
    AODA: much more likely   (82% vs. 63%) p=0.00

21 Intergroup variations in Casting a Ritual Circle:
    ADF: much less likely   (41% vs. 74%) p=0.00
    OBOD: more likely   (85% vs. 74%) p=0.00
    Rooted in Celtic Lands: more likely (84% vs. 74%) p=0.00
    Continental Europe: more likely   (89% vs. 74%) p=0.00
    Celtic Diaspora: less likely   (71% vs. 74%) p=0.01
    North America: more likely   (68% vs. 74%) p=0.00

22 Intergroup variations in Magical Workings:
    ADF: much more likely   (85% vs. 63%) p=0.00

23 Intergroup variations in Seership:
    Practicing 1-10 yrs: less likely   (33% vs. 41%) p=0.00
    Practicing 20-30 yrs: more likely (64% vs. 41%) p=0.00
    Practicing 30+ yrs: more likely (73% vs. 41%) p=0.00

24 Intergroup variations in Storytelling or Poetry Recitation:
    AODA: much less likely   (32% vs. 55%) p=0.00

25 Cowan, Tom. (1993). *Fire in the Head: Shamanism and the Celtic Spirit*. New York, NY: Harper Collins Publishers. pg. 28-48

26 Intergroup variations in Shapeshifting:
    OBOD: more likely   (32% vs. 27%) p=0.00
    Practicing 1-10 yrs: less likely   (21% vs. 27%) p=0.00
    Practicing 30+ yrs: more likely (48% vs. 27%) p=0.00

27 Photo credits for photos of Druid altars (pg. 170):
    Top photo: used with permission from
        Bea Lehmann
    Middle photo: used with permission from
        Athena Grey
    Bottom photo: used with permission from
        Nathan Large

28 Intergroup variations in Use of Altars & Shrines:
    ADF: more likely   (95% vs. 83%) p=0.01

29 Intergroup variations in Making Offerings:
    ADF: more likely   (96% vs. 82%) p=0.00

30 Intergroup variations in the Use of Ceremonial Props & Tools:
    OBOD: more likely   (83% vs. 78%) p=0.00

31 Photo credits for photos of Druids in ritual garb (pg. 172):
    Top photo: used with permission from
        Sarah Meister
    Middle photo: used with permission from
        Rev. Wm. E. Ashton, ADF
    Bottom photo: used with permission from Malcolm Brown,
        Peaceful Earth Druid Grove on the Isle of Wight, England

32 Intergroup variations in the Use of Formal, Ritual Garb:
    North Americans: less likely   (45% vs. 50%) p=0.01

33 Intergroup variations in the Use of Henges, Labyrinths, etc.:
    BDO: much more likely   (58% vs. 35%) p=0.01
    TDN: much more likely   (68% vs. 35%) p=0.00
    Rooted in Celtic Lands/British Isles & Ireland:
        more likely   (51% vs. 35%) p=0.00
    Celtic Diaspora: less likely   (31% vs. 35%) p=0.00
    North Americans: less likely   (27% vs. 35%) p=0.00
    Born before 1950: more likely   (61% vs. 35%) p=0.00
    Born 1951-1960: more likely   (47% vs. 35%) p=0.01
    Born after 1990: less likely   (10% vs. 35%) p=0.00

34 Photo credits for stone circles constructed by modern Druids
    (pg. 174):
    Top photo: used with permission from
        The Rising Stones Institute
    Middle photo: used with permission from
        The Circle of the Six-Fold Path Druid Grove of Oklahoma.
    Bottom photo: used with permission from
        Patrick Ford, author of "Stone Journals:
        Journeys to the Mysterious Standing Stones of Europe."

35 Intergroup Variations in Rituals in the "Eye of the Sun":
    ADF: more likely   (66% vs. 48%) p=0.00
    BDO: much more likely   (73% vs. 48%) p=0.01
    TDN: much more likely   (79% vs. 48%) p=0.00
    AODA: much less likely   (25% vs. 48%) p=0.00
    Rooted in Celtic Lands: more likely (57% vs. 48%) p=0.01
    British Isles & Ireland: more likely (61% vs. 48%) p=0.00
    Practicing 1-10 yrs: less likely   (42% vs. 48%) p=0.00
    Practicing 10-20 yrs: more likely (61% vs. 48%) p=0.00

36 See quotation in *Chapter 1*, pg. 2, referenced from:
    Bettis, J.D. (1975). *Phenomenology of Religion*. London: SCM,
    pg. 170

37 Intergroup variations in Solitary Ritual Practice:
    Rooted in Celtic Lands: less likely (87% vs. 92%) p=0.01
    Celtic Diaspora: more likely   (94% vs. 92%) p=0.01

38 See *Chapter 3*, pg. 29-30

39 Intergroup variations in Group Ritual Practice:
    ADF: Druid group more likely   (67% vs. 49%) p=0.00
    OBOD: Druid group more likely   (54% vs. 49%) p=0.00
    Practicing 10+ yrs: Druid group more likely
                                (64% vs. 49%) p=0.00
    AODA: any group less likely   (41% vs. 65%) p=0.00
    N. America: any group less likely (60% vs. 65%) p=0.01
    Practicing 1-10 yrs: any group less likely
                                (59% vs. 65%) p=0.00

40 See survey respondent quotations in *Chapter 3*, pg. 25

41 Intergroup variations in Public Ritual Practice:
    ADF: much more likely   (60% vs. 37%) p=0.00
    Practicing 1-10 yrs: less likely   (32% vs. 37%) p=0.00
    Practicing 10-20 yrs: more likely (49% vs. 37%) p=0.01

42 Intergroup variations in Celebrancy and Observer Status:
    ADF: celebrancy more likely   (44% vs. 25%) p=0.00
    ADF: observer status more likely (31% vs. 15%) p=0.00
    Practicing 1-10 yrs: less likely   (16% vs. 25%) p=0.00
    Practicing 10-20 yrs: more likely (38% vs. 25%) p=0.00
    Practicing 20-30 yrs: more likely (45% vs. 25%) p=0.00
    Practicing 30+ yrs: more likely   (50% vs. 25%) p=0.00

43 See discussion of cluster analysis in *Chapter 2*, pg. 21-22

44 Intergroup variations in Gardening:
    ADF: less likely   (38% vs. 56%) p=0.00

45 Intergroup variations in Studies of World Religions:
    ADF: more likely   (54% vs. 33%) p=0.00
    North Americans: more likely   (37% vs. 33%) p=0.01
    Oceania: less likely   (14% vs. 33%) p=0.00

46 Intergroup variations in Studies in Esotericism:
    AODA: much more likely   (52% vs. 26%) p=0.00

47 Intergroup variations in Studies of the History of Druids:
    Oceania: much less likely   (39% vs. 59%) p=0.00

48 Intergroup variations in Studies of Linguistic & Cultural Traditions:
    Oceania: Celtic less likely   (18% vs. 39%) p=0.00
    N. America: Celtic more likely   (44% vs. 39%) p=0.00
    N. America: 'Other' cultures more likely
                       (26% vs. 22%) p=0.01
    Celtic Diaspora: Celtic more likely (43% vs. 39%) p=0.01
    Celtic Diaspora: 'Other' cultures more likely
                       (26% vs. 22%) p=0.01
    No Ties to Celtic culture: Celtic studies much less likely
                       (19% vs. 39%) p=0.00

49 Intergroup variations in Environmental & Social Justice Activism:
    OBOD: magic, prayer, and activism for the environment
      more likely   (62% vs. 56%) p=0.00
    Practicing 1-10 yrs: magic & prayer for any cause less likely
                       (50% vs. 55%) p=0.01
    Practicing 1-10 yrs: magic, prayer, and activism for people
      less likely   (43% vs. 48%) p=0.00

50 Intergroup variations in Education & Spiritual Leadership:
    ADF: much more likely   (65% vs. 48%) p=0.01
    Practicing 1-10 yrs: less likely   (39% vs. 48%) p=0.00
    Practicing 10-20 yrs: more likely (62% vs. 48%) p=0.00
    Practicing 20+ yrs: more likely   (73% vs. 48%) p=0.00

CHAPTER 7:
DRUID FESTIVALS & CELEBRATIONS

At last, we come to the most colorful, and outwardly visible aspect of the modern, religious tradition that is Druidry: the festivals and celebrations which mark the passage of time through the Druid year. Modern Druids perceive time as a cyclical, rather than linear, construct — a sacred *Wheel of the Year*, with each season ever flowing into the next, in an endless circle. While there is significant diversity in the number, timing, and symbolism attributed to the various festivals celebrated by each individual Druid, the *Wheel of the Year* serves as a universal framework for contemplating, discussing, and celebrating the ever-changing seasons of Nature.

According to the traditions of Neopaganism in general, and Druidry in specific[1], the *Wheel of the Year* is usually portrayed as a wheel with eight spokes, spaced evenly throughout the year (see illustration, page 194). One set of crossing spokes points to the solstices and equinoxes of the solar year; a second set of crossing spokes points to the *cross-quarter celebrations*, also known as the *fire festivals*. The fire festivals coincide with key moments in the agricultural year, as manifest in and around the isles of Britain and Ireland.

According to the results of the *World Druidry Survey*, 47% of world Druids celebrate all eight of these festivals, in some form, every year; 26% celebrate a subset of them, focusing on the festivals which are most meaningful in their local environments; and the remaining 27% do not celebrate any of the festivals, but focus instead on daily or weekly rituals of nature connection and devotion. The percentage of world Druids who celebrate each festival[2] varies between 54% (Lughnasadh) and 68% (Winter Solstice). Solar festivals are more popular than fire festivals, with the exception of Samhain, which is more popular than the Autumnal Equinox, though not nearly as popular as the Winter Solstice.

Among the Druids who celebrate one or more festivals of the Wheel of the Year, there is significant variation in the level of formality used in the

The Traditional Druid "Wheel of the Year"

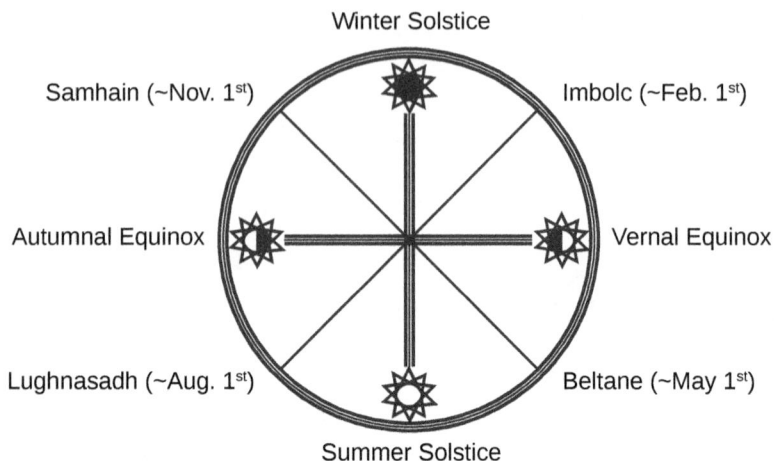

Winter Solstice

Samhain (~Nov. 1st)

Imbolc (~Feb. 1st)

Autumnal Equinox

Vernal Equinox

Lughnasadh (~Aug. 1st)

Beltane (~May 1st)

Summer Solstice

celebrations. This is partly due a preference for simplicity in solitary devotional practice,[3] and in part, it is due to the lack of a local religious community with which to celebrate.[4] Large group rituals are by necessity more complex, and are often at least partially scripted, so that all participants — many of whom have never or only rarely engaged in ritual practice with other Druids — will know who is to do what, and when, within the ceremony. Solitary Druids may also perform elaborate, ceremonial rituals, alone, but survey data show that, much more frequently, they keep their celebrations simple.

The most common form of solitary seasonal celebration was a simple nature ramble with a bit of meditation thrown in, or a seasonal meditation, as Druids described:

> *"At each festival I take a walk outside with my Rowan staff and take in the weather, how the day feels, and find a spot to sit and watch the world go quietly by. I also reflect on the festival and what it means."*

> *"I briefly meditated during the solstices and equinoxes, but that is about all. As far as spiritual meaning, I considered the place of humanity in nature and how the natural world rules over all of us."*

> *"I generally take a nature walk on these days, to observe the season and the natural world at this point in the cycle. The wheel represents the natural progression of all things — new to old, birth to death, naive to wise, fortune to misfortune, or vise versa, etc."*

In formal Druid group ritual, the seasonal celebrations will generally involve a fixed ceremonial framework, with a central activity that varies with the season. The components of the ceremonial framework, and the sequence in which the events transpire will vary from group to group, however, most of the formal rituals described by survey respondents shared many similar characteristics.

Seasonal ceremonies typically begin with casting a circle (though circles are not cast in ADF rituals) around a central altar decorated for the season. The altar will contain objects to be used in the ceremony, such as tools for divination, offerings for god(s), ancestors, or nature spirits, or tools for magical workings, or other symbolic elements, as described in *Chapter 6: Altars and Shrines*. Next, Druids generally acknowledge, call upon, or invite into the circle the powers of the Four Elements, or the Three Realms. This is often followed by a declaration of peace to the four directions. Finally, Druids welcome local nature spirits, ancestors, and/or god(s) and/or goddess(es), as appropriate to the season and the theological beliefs of participating Druids.

The central, seasonal activities are performed next. These might include ritual retellings or re-enactments of seasonal tales, poetry recitations, musical performances, meditations, divination, magical workings, journeying, making offerings, or performing any of the other ritual practices described in *Chapter 6*. Whatever the specific central activity, it is likely to be thematically related to the spiritual metaphors represented by the season, as will be further discussed, later in this chapter.

Once the seasonal activities are completed, any attending gods, spirits, or ancestors will be thanked, and the circle dissolved.

Examples of survey responses describing the general format of formal, Druid group rituals included the following:

> "*Festivals* [are celebrated] *with bathing, incense, candles, rituals (casting a circle, honouring/inviting/welcoming the elements (air, fire, water, earth, spirit, void), spirits (trees, plants, animals, stones, sprites, ancestors), Goddess and God, dancing, celebrating the seasonal changes, giving thanks and saying my goodbyes. Symbols representing the elements: air - incense* [or] *feathers; fire - candles* [or an] *open fire; water -* [a] *bowl of water* [or a] *tub of water; earth - stones, gems,* [or] *earth; spirit - poems; void -* [the] *space in between the others.*"

> "*We always have a ritual with a central fire, a short drama telling the story of the festival, song, dance and an eisteddfod. We meditate on the meanings* [of] *the time — new beginnings, growth, energy, fruitfulness, ripening and harvest, declining and hibernating.*"

"Usually I go to my stone circle and open the circle and the quarters and then I honour the deities, spirits of the particular festival and show gratitude for what has happened during the year, or plant seeds for the future or ask for help in making some project come to fruition. It depends. Quite often I will make a medicine wheel to honour my power animals and allies, or plant spirits. I pour a libation on the ground and leave a piece of bread and honey or scatter bird seed."

"We celebrate outside and then come inside to eat a potluck dinner and for bardic merriment (or just to visit). [...] We have usually 7-10 participants for the ritual. We have 4 flat-top boulders that serve as directional altars and they all get filled with that element's representation: water and sea shells on the west stone for water; pine cones, salt, flowers on the north stone for earth; incense on the east altar for air along with a vertical stretch of cloth on a pole with slits that hold feathers- it's a Native American thing that one of our members (who is of Native American descent) introduced, and a wind chime; and red pepper flakes, a shed stag antler, and lantern on the south altar for fire. We also have a festival altar that travels around the circle and placed at the festival's place."

"We celebrate indoors, in a beautiful Unitarian Universalist chapel during the colder months and out-doors at different private properties or parks in the warmer months. We use the Core Order of Ritual[5] per ADF. The Deity of the Day can be from different Indo-European cultures though often of Celtic or Norse derivation. We start by welcoming all who have come to the rite with a brief explanation that the circle is not closed in ADF rites and that you may come and go at will. That you may participate in any part of the rite or bless-ings that you like, as ADF has a defined series of steps but not a defined set of beliefs. That you are not required to participate and may step back at anytime, especially if you do not wish to receive the blessing. Then the altar is decorated for the season, indoors lots of candles, out-doors a central fire. We have beautiful liturgy much of which is written by our Senior Druid [...]. We go through the Core Order of Ritual usually with a short meditation on the Two Powers and honor the season and Deity of the rite with words and offerings of food, herbs, oil to the fire, or slips of paper with written prayers. We may have a craft or a story told during the ritual. An omen is always

taken. The blessing is shared as a sprinkling of water by feather, or as a handful of grain to take home, or as hot chocolate sipped together. And our group loves to bring food. Most events include a potluck afterward and money collected for a local charity."

Depending upon the past ritual experiences, personal preferences, and Druidry group affiliations of the participants, Druids may also tailor their rituals to be a mélange of several different ritual traditions, for example:

"I celebrated pretty much all of the holidays, usually, this meant doing Wiccan ceremonies with my wife, but I did a couple of ADF-style rituals by myself. I write the liturgy for our combined rituals and use a lot of language from both Wicca and AODA Druidry. I synthesize the two and strive for a balance between Witchcraft and Druidry."

"As a Prison Pagan Chaplain, I celebrated the full Wheel of the Year and led the ceremonies for Yule 2017 to Samhain 2018. As you will appreciate due to security restrictions we have to do the best we can with a minimal of props. Although the Pagan Group was mixed I still conducted each ceremony with the Druid blessings and Opening/Closing ritual, including AWENS and giving Peace to the Quarters. As standard within the ritual itself, I always left the central portion open to the participants to do their own personalised contribution as we had Pagans of all traditions participating."

"I also lead a local group in a 'summit of the Gods' format (i.e., if you are there, your Gods are there, so invite them) using the ADF ritual format for each High Day. Occasionally, I will use the Welsh names for Samhain (Calan Gaeaf) or Beltainne (Calan Haf), but as most folks are unaware of these terms, the Irish/Wiccan is used more often."

In whatever manner a Druid chooses to celebrate the seasonal festivals, the central themes of those celebrations are likely to echo the natural cycles of life, death, and seasonal rebirth, which are evident in the natural world. The natural cycles which define the themes of the "Traditional" Druid Wheel of the Year are those of Britain — birthplace of the modern Druidic tradition. However, this is not the only Wheel celebrated. We will therefore make two journeys through the Wheel of the Year, the first to illustrate the originating tradition, and the second to explore the many ways in which the Druids of the world "wildcraft" their celebrations, grounding them in the local landscape.

The Traditional Druid "Wheel of the Year"

The most popular seasonal festival among world Druids is the Winter Solstice, that moment of time when the Sun is reborn into waxing luminous power, with its promise of hope and new life to come. It is therefore with this festival that we begin our discussion of the traditional, Druid Wheel of the Year.

Winter Solstice

In the natural world, the Winter Solstice is the time of the longest night and the shortest day. Celebrated at the moment when daylight hours begin to grow longer, instead of shorter, with each passing day; it is a celebration of the rebirth of the Sun. The spiritual symbolisms attributed to the Winter Solstice include the cultivation of light in the darkness, the kindling of hope, and the reawakening dreams and desires for the future. Druids also wrote of death and rebirth, reincarnation, and the "season of heart". The Winter Solstice is celebrated by 68% of world Druids, along with a constellation of other mid-winter holidays, which might include Saturnalia, Advent, Christmas, Mother's Night, or Twelfth Night, depending on the Druid.

Common ritual activities associated with the Winter Solstice include symbolic acts of cultivating light in the darkness, such as holding all-night vigils with bonfires, burning Yule logs, or lighting lots of candles. Druids also acknowledge the rebirth of the Sun by staying awake to witness the sunset and/or sunrise bounding the longest night of the year. For a significant number of Druids, this involves attending the Solstice festivities at Stonehenge.

Ritual acts of kindling hope and joy include things like putting out winter food for the birds and animals, and wassailing the orchards, singing to bring the fruit trees health and prosperity in the coming year. For many, the Winter Solstice involves decorating the house with evergreens, wreaths, Yule trees, and ornaments; giving gifts and sending greeting cards; and offering hospitality, including hosting feasts with free-flowing mead, mulled wine, or mulled cider. In this aspect, the celebrations may seem quite similar to the secular Christmas and New Year's celebrations of mainstream culture.

Druid celebrations of the Winter Solstice will also include quieter ritual acts such as reflecting on the past year's accomplishments, and making plans for the new year; performing divination rituals, and blessing altar tools for use in the coming year.

A wide variety of deities and mythical figures are associated with the midwinter festival. Most commonly, these figures are symbols of returning light and hope, including: the Welsh divine youth, Mabon; the Irish god of youth and beauty, Angus Óg; and the legendary king, Arthur, symbolic Sun

King of Britain, reborn at the moment of the winter solstice, or the Celtic sun god, Belenos. Many Druids also wrote of the great battle between the Oak King (personification of waxing light), who wrests control of the year from the Holly King (personification of waning light) at the winter solstice. For Christian Druids, hope returns with the birth of Jesus Christ.

Other common (though not universal) midwinter themes celebrated by Druids at this time include honoring the Cailleach, the Celtic goddess of winter weather, and the trio of Celtic mother goddesses known as the Matronae. Heathen-Druids celebrate Norse gods related to the Yuletide tradition, including the Aesir, Baldur, and Odin. Others acknowledge Kore (a.k.a. Persephone), the goddess of vegetation, resting deep in the Underworld at this time of year; and in Wales, several Druids mentioned participating in a wassailing tradition involving the skeletal horse goddess, Mari Llwyd.

Aside from these, a number of other gods are honored at the winter solstice — gods which are personally meaningful to the individual Druids, but not necessarily symbolic of this particular time of year. These included Larouco, Lleu Llew Griffiths, Brigid, Anu, Dagda, Cernunnos, and Mother Earth (see *Glossary* for descriptions).

Survey responses describing Druids' Winter Solstice celebrations, and the meanings which they attributed to their midwinter festivities, included:

"I reflect on how we are celebrating the return of the light and that it shows that even in the darkest of times there is always hope and light. I take with me a food offering for the animals nearby, something seasonal like fruit and nuts. At home I light a candle and read through my favourite ritual for that festival."

"I set up a Winter altar with a russet cloth with crows on it, and a dark green felt cloth over that. I had images of the Oak King and Holly King (the one doing battle and dominating the other as the darkest day is passed), a candle to represent the fading light of the year. I watched the dawn come up the morning after."

"I absolutely love the winter solstice, and bringing a tree into my home to decorate with symbolic ornaments (animals, gnomes, mushrooms, stars, etc.), the mid-winter feasting, gift-giving, and symbolism of light and warmth in the darkness."

"This time for me means a time of welcoming back the sun, rebirth and awakening to my inner light, igniting my dreams and desires for the year ahead."

> *"An assortment of little rituals, with a theme of cultivat-*
> *ing light in the darkness (literal, and metaphorical). We*
> *light the Yule tree, host a Yuletide Revels, wassail the*
> *orchard, exchange gifts to bring joy to humans and*
> *scatter wildflower seeds to bring joy to the wild. We*
> *dream up, and commit to writing (in an altar prayer box),*
> *our plans and dreams for the forthcoming year."*

Imbolc

The agricultural festival of Imbolc is most often associated with the blossoming of the first flowers of the year — snowdrops — and with the birth of new lambs. Depending upon location, Druids also mentioned the start of the maple sap runs (in New England and Canada), the strengthening sunlight and hope of spring-to-come, or the actual arrival of spring in warmer climes. The spiritual symbolism for this festival focuses on spiritual renewal, on the contemplation of and preparation for new beginnings, nurturing one's inner child, kindling creative fire, and finding inspiration for new works. Imbolc is traditionally celebrated at the beginning of February, and is observed by 56% of world Druids.

Common ritual activities for this festival focus on Druids' relationships with their lands and gardens, as the chill and darkness of winter recedes. Druids wrote about planning and preparing for planting season; blessing their garden tools; wassailing the orchards; pruning and clearing deadwood from gardens; and blessing and sowing seeds (both physical, and spiritual). Where the blessings of Nature are already becoming ready for early harvest, Druids also engage in activities such as maple sugaring, drinking new milk, and eating the first spring greens.

In addition to these nature-related activities, many Druids see Imbolc as a time for celebrating their relationship with the Celtic goddess, Brigid, who is known as a goddess of hearth and home, healing, and crafts, as well as being a patron deity of bards (among other things). These Druids perform ritual activities such as: lighting candles in her honor; making Brigid's crosses; making offerings of milk, honey, or grain; spring cleaning; healing work; and working on handicrafts.

Aside from Brigid, several other deities are celebrated at Imbolc. For Druids in regions still gripped by winter, the Cailleach is particularly relevant. For those in warmer climes, where the world is already coming alive with new growth, a celebration of the return of Persephone/Kore is more appropriate. In New Zealand, Druids honor Hine-Ahu-One, the first mother, and Mahuika, the fire god. Several Druids also celebrate the life of Arthur, as a child.

When asked to describe the ways in which they celebrated Imbolc, and the meanings which they attributed to this agricultural festival, Druids wrote in their survey responses:

> *"I spent the day thinking about new beginnings and what ideas I wanted to 'plant' in order to nurture them in the coming year to fruition. I spent time in the garden centre enjoying the spring flowers on sale and visited a small wood in town and enjoyed the company of the trees and birds. Well, the blackbirds and Robin — not the Ring-necked parakeets, they're too aggressive! In the evening I dedicated my altar to the Goddess Brighid. I had a green cloth, a shallow ceramic blue tray with a central candle and 8 tea lights floating around it in a pool of water. I had objects associated with Brighid around the outside: a piece of shaped iron (for her forge work and being a fire Goddess), a Brighid's Eye that looks like the sun because I was celebrating stirring of the Goddess in the Earth for the very beginning of Spring; I had some wool because it is also the time of the first lambing (in - milk = Imelc); I had Berkano and Kano rune staves representing the Goddess and her Bardic connections - her communica-tion/ story-telling skills; I had some milk in a chalice, a Brighid Cross representing the sun again, a hare which is one of her sacred animals; a blooming snowdrop in a pot representing the beginning of Spring, and a Brighid Doll. In visualisation I spent time in my Sacred Space with my Inner Child as Imbolc is associated with the God/Arthur as a young child."*

> *"With the first faint stirrings of Spring, we celebrate the festival of Imbolc. The fire of spring which had apparently lain dormant in the earth shows us that it has merely been gestating in the earth — the first [green] shoots and the appearance of the snowdrop herald the Spring that is to come — one that will occur not only in the outer world of nature, but also, hopefully, within our hearts. Though we never (almost never) get snow here in Wellington. This festival is an opportunity for us all to reflect on our relationships with the divine feminine, and to be aware of how masculine and feminine is balanced (or not), within us, and within our society."*

> *"Imbolc carries the symbolism of nurturing the green shoots of our plans and hopes, and last year I was involved in writing and carrying out the ritual, which*

focused on the transformative power of Fire to help us bring change into our lives. This year, we were guided in a visualisation involving symbols of purification, awakening and thawing, in which we identified something in our lives that we wished to thaw or release, while holding a birch twig. We then invoked our circle outside around a fire, and after one member spoke for Bridget, we threw our twigs into the fire while naming what we were thawing/releasing. I've also attended some one-day women's retreats, run by Druids but open to anyone, which incorporate ritual and other elements of Druidry. For example, the Imbolc retreat, as well as opening the circle, involved a talk about Bridget and a visualisation of both her and the Cailleach. There was also drumming and chanting, and we made a Bridie doll incorporating a small bundle of herbs chosen to represent energies we wished to invoke such as protection, healing or clarity."

"I baked a sun/fire associated elemental cake (e.g. using cloves, cinnamon, nutmeg, allspice, etc.) with attention to the early arrival of spring (e.g. using seeds; homemade butter), and a milk based drink to commemorate the traditional association of Imbolc with the availability of new milk (it was a lavender milk tea). We also made St. Brigid's crosses from palm fronds and discussed the themes of emerging light, what that means for us personally, what that means in terms of Christian symbolism, and what we want to focus on growing in our own lives. [...] Imbolc corresponds to Candlemas, when Jesus is presented in the Temple — the light who is growing and becoming stronger."

"Although it is still winter and will be for another month or more, by now I generally see at least some crocus and daffodil leaves poking up, and the witch hazel is blooming. The theme is pruning unproductive growth from not only trees and shrubs, but from my life as well, since it's still too cold to do much else. Within the grove I awaken my amaryllis bulbs with a blessing, which is symbolic of the (slow!) awakening of growth outside. During the next several weeks I complete winter pruning and garden planning and begin to start vegetable, flower, and herb seeds on the glassed-in front porch."

Vernal Equinox

In nature, the Vernal Equinox is the moment when light triumphs over darkness, as day is finally longer than night. It is also traditionally the first day of spring, and marks the death of winter. Symbols in nature include new green growth, hatching eggs, breeding rabbits, and an abundance of flowers. Druids wrote of watching for the first fawns to be born, for lambs in the fields, for birch trees leafing out, daffodils blooming, and lots and lots of mud. Spiritually, Vernal Equinox symbolizes balance, rising energy, optimism, inspiration, creativity, fertility, and a time for new growth. The Vernal Equinox is celebrated by 59% of world Druids.

The most common ritual activities associated with this festival focused on caring for awaking gardens, and celebrating the start of a new season of growth — both physically and spiritually. Examples of garden-related rituals included: blessing gardens, seeds, garden tools, and water sources; blessing trees just awakening from their winter dormancies; preparing soil for planting, sowing seeds, and planting out crops; and beginning active care of the garden. For the majority of Druids, these were literal tasks as well as spiritual. Many Druids also spoke of planting spiritual "seeds" by taking the first active steps in implementing projects that had been conceived and planned at Imbolc. Also mentioned several times were spring-cleaning rituals, and the Ostara traditions of engaging in family fun with children, including cook-outs, sing-alongs, egg hunts, and flower crowns.

A variety of deities and mythological beings are associated with the Vernal Equinox. These include Cerridwen, with her simmering cauldron of inspiration, and the sun god, Belenos, whose power has finally overcome the darkness of winter. More common yet are deities associated with youth, beauty, flowers, fertility, herbs, and the vibrant, green-growing earth, such as Mother Earth, Brigantia, Anu, Nemetona, Kore, Airmid, Cernunnos, Mabon, Angus Óg & Caer Ibormeith, and Yggdrasil, the sacred tree of life.

When asked to describe the ways in which they celebrated the Vernal Equinox, and the meanings which they attributed to this festival, Druids wrote for example:

> *"Frühlingstagundnachtgleiche - Die Saat keimt, wir feiern das Erwachen der Natur, lassen aber auch die Saat unserer Projekte und Ziele für dieses Jahr keimen*
> [Translation:]
> *Spring equinox - The seeds germinate, we celebrate the awakening of nature, but we also germinate the seeds of our projects and goals for this year."*

"Alban Eiler, within a day or two of the spring equinox. The daffodils are blooming and spring has arrived; it's a little too early for gardening outside, however, so this celebration focuses on my deep gratitude for the end of winter and the greening of the land and on the soon to be started garden. After the ritual I change my daily prayer altar to its spring colors, and I might prick-out seedlings or start seeds on the glassed-in porch. During the next several weeks I begin planting cool-season crops in the garden."

"Alban Eilir: growth spurt, fertility, new life emerging. A balance of light and dark. A deep sense of Awen and the trinity of the Goddess. Planting of seeds for harvest in Summer and Autumn. Preparation of my garden."

"Open Gorsedd ritual and private Grove ritual, celebrating the coming of spring, crops being sown or beginning to grow, new life, lambs in the fields. the warming of the earth and the promise of summer."

"On the spring equinox, I had a quiet day of mediation on the life of a sapling, growing and spreading into the world. In a celebration of life, I greeted the sunrise, decorated the shrine with plants and porcelain rabbits, and dined on boiled eggs."

Beltane

The fire festival of Beltane is marked in the natural world of Britain and Ireland by the flowering of hawthorns and apple trees, and with a festive celebration of fertility as the world rapidly re-greens. The spiritual symbolism of this festival traditionally relates to vibrant new growth, life, love, and passion. Many Druids also write of Beltane as a liminal time in which the veil between the mundane world and the world of spirit is thin, allowing for visits with the Faerie folk and ancestors. Beltane is celebrated by 57% of world Druids, and traditionally takes place at the beginning of May.

Common ritual activities associated with Beltane tend to focus on revelry and merriment celebrating the unbidden blessings and fertility of nature, through celebratory feasts (including eating spring greens), drumming and other music-making, dancing (especially Morris dances, and dancing around Maypoles), handfastings, cook-outs and camp-outs with bonfires and fire-jumping. For many Druids, this is also a time for interactions with the world of spirit, by visiting with Faerie folk, or performing divinations. Other ritual activities focus on the care of other-than-human living beings, with blessings on the land for the healthy growth of fields and gardens, blessings of cattle, and sheep-and-wool festivals.

The deities and mythological beings most frequently associated with Beltane include the sun god Belenos, the antlered god of nature, Cernunnos, the woodland goddess, Flidais, and the goddess of magical herbs and healing, Airmid.

When asked to describe how they celebrated Beltane, and the meanings which they attributed to this festival, Druids wrote, for example:

> *"Beltane — private grove ritual but also the start of the Morris season so a weekend of dance, music and waking the Jack in the Green at dawn on May Day morning. The trees are suddenly in full leaf and there is that restless need for change."*

> *"Calan Mai - 1st May. Celebration of the full awakening of Spring and the palpable fertility that can be sensed all around one in nature. I decorate the Altar with May flowers, Hawthorn, as each flowers anther is shaped like a small pink heart, representative of love. This is a time when the God and Goddess can be felt when out in the natural environment."*

> *"I return to Padstow in Cornwall for May Day celebrations where the Obby 'Oss gallop free for a day of music, song and revelry. It embodies and celebrates the fertility of the land - the town is decorated with oak branches, the bunting flags are hung, and everyone dresses up in white and red, or white and blue. It either 'Oss catches a girl/woman for a dance they will fall pregnant within the year (my ex-wife was caught by both the blue and red 'Oss, and we had twins born 14 months later!!)"*

> *"Fertility, fecundity — not only physically and sexually, but also in terms of the flowering of creativity and productivity. The beginning of the light half of the year."*

> *"Self-designed ritual. Includes a Maypole ritual where each ribbon represents blessings for self, family, spiritual community, and the world respectively. As I wind the ribbons around the pole I meditate on my wishes for each of these entities. I also have 4 candles on my seasonal altar. I light one at each phase of the moon until they are all finally lit at the Summer Solstice."*

Summer Solstice

Summer Solstice marks the longest day, and shortest night of the year. It marks a shift from the waxing power to the waning power of sunlight. The signs and portents that Druids look for in nature at this time include growing beans, squash, and corn, ripening berries, abundant flowers, herb and fish harvests, and lots and lots of people outside, celebrating Summer. The spiritual symbolisms attributed to this time include celebrating the warmth and power of the sun at its peak; a celebration of the element *fire* (both in nature, and metaphorically, such as in the phrases *fire in the head* — referring to inspiration, or *fire in the heart* — referring to passionate emotions, etc.), beginning to harvest the fruits of one's labors; and withdrawing inward to rest from the heat. The Summer Solstice is celebrated by 61% of world Druids.

Common ritual activities at this time include celebrating the longest day of the year with feasts, bonfires, cook-outs and picnics, hikes to watch the sunset or sunrise, and participation in the festivities at Stonehenge. Druids also re-enact the battle between the Oak King and Holly King at this time, and exchange citrines (a golden-yellow, crystalline mineral), as a symbol of the peak power of the Sun. Others recall the blessings of shade in the blistering sunshine. More mundane ritual acts performed at this time include assisting elements of the natural world that are stressed out by heat, by mulching plants and setting out water for wild animals, before retreating indoors to rest and avoid the summer heat.

The deities and mythological beings most frequently associated with the Summer Solstice include a variety of sky and sun god/desses, such as the Polynesian/Māori gods Ranginui and Tamanuiterā, Belenos, and Baldur. Also popular at this time are deities associated with love and fertility, such as Aine and Freyr. Some Druids also honor gods which are personally meaningful, or traditionally honored at Midsummer, but not necessarily symbolic of the time of year. These include Lugh, Manannán Mac Lir, and Airmid.

When asked to describe how they celebrated the Summer Solstice, and the meanings which they attributed to this midsummer festival, Druids wrote survey responses including the following:

> *"Sommersonnenwende - der Eichenkönig übergibt seine Krone dem Stechpalmenkönig, der uns in die dunkle Zeit führt, Höhepunkt des Lichtes, größte Macht der Sonne, Belenos übergibt sein Zepter an Lugh.*
> [Translation:]
> *Summer solstice - the Oak King hands over his crown to the Holly King, who leads us into the dark time, highlight of light, greatest power of the sun, Belenos hands over his sceptre to Lugh."*

"Midsummer, I tend to celebrate the first sign of the return of darkness. As I am somewhat prone to burnout as an Aries, I find it important to have this yearly reminder that even the sun has her limits, and will have to stop growing brighter at some point."

"Summer Solstice (Alban Heruin). I always put a bottle of water out in the Sun on this day as to absorb the brightest light of the year, then I give a libation of this water at the winter solstice that is supposed to represent balance of the light with the dark. I use the summer solstice water throughout the rest of the year for ritual cleansings and other purposes."

"I celebrated summer solstice by being outside with my partner until sunset with a picnic and some wine and toasting the day."

"Summer Solstice — We honor Manannán mac Lir. Given the many waters around us, including the St. Lawrence River that connects to the Atlantic Ocean, we feel very connected to him as a grove. We 'pay the rent' with offerings of yellow flowers and reeds. In my household, I also honor Airmid and work with herbs in my garden. My family usually goes strawberry picking around this time."

Lughnasadh

The agricultural festival of Lughnasadh celebrates the beginning of the grain harvest, and the blueberry, blackberry, and apple harvests of Europe. It may also mark the start of the vegetable harvest, depending upon one's local climate. The spiritual symbolism of Lughnasadh generally relates to the year's harvest of personal accomplishments. It is a time to share with one's community the harvested wealth of food produce, completed works, and polished skills. It is also a time of thanksgiving, and for recognizing the need for times of sacrifice in life. Traditionally celebrated at the beginning of August, Lughnasadh is observed by 54% of world Druids.

The most common ritual activities at Lughnasadh involve celebrating, processing, and eating the year's harvest, by baking bread, making cornhusk dollies, and processing foods for winter storage. This includes canning and preserving, making jams, and pressing and bottling ciders. In addition, Druids celebrate the spiritual "harvest" of the fruits of their labors. They share food with neighbors, and offer up their newly developed skills for the benefit of community. Several Druids also compete in Summer or Highland Games.

The deities and mythological beings associated with Lughnasadh are limited to Lugh, for whom the holiday is named, and his mother, Tailtiu.

When asked to describe how they celebrated Lughnasadh, and the meanings attributed to this agricultural festival, Druids wrote, for example:

> *"Lammas. The beginning of autumn. I bake bread and give thanks to the nature spirits for the harvest they have provided."*

> *"The first harvest, sacred to Lugh and his mother, Tailtiu. Further celebration of community, with specific focus of the importance of 'sharing the wealth' that we may provide for all, as Tailtiu gave of herself to provide for her people."*

> *"Lughnasadh (a bread, berry and cider-making kitchen feast for the harvest)."*

> *"Lughnasadh: time for a cattle raid! We meet with other clans and have competitions in athletics, dance, recitation, composition. Great fun. Usually have a weekend campout. We celebrate grain as Lugh and Tailtiu's gift."*

> *"Calan Awst around 2nd August. A celebration of the first harvest where we celebrate and enjoy the fruits of our labours. It's a time to rejoice in the knowledge that we will be safe through the dark winter to come as the Sun has provided our sustenance that will get us through the dark times. It's a time to reflect on what we have achieved through the year and how these achievements will sustain us through the coming dark times, both materialistically, i.e. food etc, but also psychologically and within the context of our community. It's a time for the community to gather in celebration. My altar uses harvest fruits such as wheat sheaves etc."*

Autumnal Equinox

The Autumnal Equinox is another time of balance between light and dark, as the sun's power wanes at the approach of winter. At this time of year, in the isles of Britain and Ireland, trees are laden with ripe fruit and nuts, colored leaves begin falling from trees, and apples, acorns, and chestnuts are ripe for picking. The spiritual symbolism of this time of year involves expressing gratitude for the second/fruit harvest, and for the "harvest" of achievements from one's work. It involves transferring focus from outer to inner activity, and honoring the need for rest, as the time of death and dying approaches. The Autumnal Equinox is celebrated by 58% of world Druids.

Ritual activities for this festival focus on the work of the harvest, acts of charity, and giving thanks for nature's bounty. Druids wrote of harvesting crops of vegetables, nuts, and fruit, making ciders and jams, and canning foods, and then preparing the garden for winter, and sowing winter cover-crops. Druids also participate in rituals of gratitude, making offerings to deities and nature spirits, to share the bounty with other-than-human beings, and making donations to charities, to share the bounty with other humans. This is also a time to host thanksgiving feasts.

The deities and mythological beings most commonly associated with the Autumnal Equinox include Gaia the Earth Mother, the agricultural goddess, Demeter, and Demeter's daughter, Persephone, departing for her six-month stay in Hades. In New Zealand, Druids honor Hine-Raumati, the Summer Maid, who hands over control of the year to Hine-Takurua, the Winter Maid, at the moment of the Equinox. They also honor Pani-tinaku, the mother of the kūmara (sweet potato), harvested at this time. Druids following Northern Traditions honor Njordh, the Norse god of the harvest, and Idunna, who guards the golden apples of eternal life. In addition to these, a number of Druids honor gods which are personally meaningful, though not necessarily symbolic of the time of year. These include Eriu, Nerthus, and Belenos.

When asked to describe how they celebrated the Autumnal Equinox, and the meanings which they attributed to this harvest festival, Druids wrote things like the following:

> "A time of balance when day and night are equal. A quiet time to reflect on what has been achieved, and how the seeds of these achievements will gestate over the winter, [to be] ready to germinate in the spring. A time for reflection and planning. For my altar I use objects representative of balance, dark and light, scales etc. plus seeds such as acorns and horse-chestnuts that I have collected."

> "My grove typically honors the Earth Mother on this day. We give thanks to the harvest. It's our Thanksgiving. We give offerings and reflect on how we can better care for and live with the land. My family picks apples."

> "I celebrated the Autumn equinox with my local Pagan group in a woodland ritual. We talked of the significance of leaves falling from trees — letting go — getting ready to retreat for winter. Turn inwards."

"Alban Elfed: ik voer het ritueel iets anders uit, omdat de kastanjes willen meedoen. Van te voren roepen de kastanjes mij als het tijd is om kastanjes te rapen. Soms is het eigenlijk nog te vroeg, maar ze leiden me altijd naar een plek waar ik kastanjes kan vinden. Ik zoek er zoveel mogelijk. Elke kastanje staat voor iets waar ik dankbaar voor ben. Bij het ritueel zijn ze verspreid over de windrichtingen. Verder voer ik het ritueel uit zoals in het boekje staat. Dankbaarheid is het thema van dit feest. Daarnaast ben ik naar de gathering van NL druiden in de ommuurde tuin in Renkum geweest. Daar staat het delen van de oogst centraal. Er was een give-away en een ritueel met een oogstbuideltje dat in het vuur werd geofferd. Het gezellig samen zijn en het delen van informatie en van eten is voor mij ook een belangrijk onderdeel.
[Translation:]
Alban Elfed: I perform the ritual a little differently, because the chestnuts want to participate. In advance the chestnuts call me when it's time to pick up the chestnuts. Sometimes it's too early, but they always lead me to a place where I can find chestnuts. I look for as many as possible. Every chestnut represents something for which I am grateful. During the ritual they are scattered in the directions of the wind. I also perform the ritual as stated in the booklet. Gratitude is the theme of this feast. I also went to the gathering of NL druids in the walled garden in Renkum. The focus there is on sharing the harvest. There was a give-away and a ritual with a harvest pouch that was sacrificed in the fire. Being together and sharing information and food is also an important part for me."

"Balance between light a dark. Pick rest of apples, store or bake and freeze pies. Pick more hedgerow fruits and make preserves. Dig over garden and allow it to rest."

Samhain

The final festival in the Druid Wheel of the Year is Samhain, which is traditionally celebrated on November 1st, about the time of the first hard frost, and the final harvest of the year. It marks the start of the dead, winter season, and is most frequently symbolized by fallen leaves, jack-o-lanterns, apples, pomegranates, and pumpkins. As a liminal time between life and death in the natural world, Druids also see it as a time when the veil between the worlds of the living and spirit is thin, and conducive to visits with ancestors of spirit, blood, and place. Spiritual symbolisms attributed to Samhain include ideas of death and rebirth (both of the year, and of things within oneself), of letting go of that which no longer serves, and of beginning to incubate plans for the new year. Samhain is observed by 62% of world Druids.

The most popular ritual activities for Samhain include honoring and making offerings to ancestors and deceased loved ones, and retelling stories from family histories. For many Druids, this is also a time to engage in inner or shamanic journeying, and to perform divinations, prior to formulating resolutions for changes in the year to come. Folk traditions at this time include pre-winter housecleaning, harvest celebrations, bonfires and burning wickermen, costume parties, trick-or-treating, and awakening the skeletal horse goddess, Mari Llwyd, for the forthcoming wassailing season.

The deities and mythological beings honored at Samhain tend to be associated with otherworlds, underworlds, winter, death, and wisdom. Those most frequently mentioned in the survey included: the Cailleach, Cerridwen, Hecate, Morrigan, Hades, and Yggdrasil. In addition, ancestral gods such as the Dagda, and Donn are often honored. Finally, Cernunnos is honored by some, and petitioned for protection and success in winter hunts.

When asked to describe the ways in which they celebrated Samhain, and the meanings which they attributed to this fire festival, Druids wrote:

"Samhain. This is an important time in which I contemplate death. I focus on accepting my own mortality and realizing that we must make the most of the time that we have. Recently I have discovered the Cailleach on Samhain, who I have begun developing a love for. She is so old, and she has seen so many mortals pass, that she knows all our problems and reminds us that it shall pass."

"Calan Gaeaf - I fold Halloween into the tradition, candy for the neighborhood kids, a plate for my ancestors, and an offering to the small gods and animals in my woods (I should mention this offering is usually offered when I celebrate any holiday, but has a special significance for me on Calan Gaeaf). I try to also incorporate special rituals for Cernunnos at this time, for a peaceful and easy winter, for protection against the growing darkness, and for the honor, mercy, and success of hunters."

"Samhain is our Celebration of Remembrance for the dead. We do a dumb supper, make food offerings and whiskey offerings to the dead and the ancestors, create a shrine of mementos in their honour. We do otherworldly journeying and divination, as well as renewal of contracts or vows. Deities invoked and honoured are Morrigan, and Donn."

"O principal tema desse festival é o agradecimento, a honra e a conexão com nossos ancestrais, desde os entes queridos que não estão mais entre nós, até aqueles que não sabemos mais os nomes, inclusive os deuses. É o momento em que o Outro Mundo fica mais acessível, a fronteira entre os mundos fica pouco definida e a data é propícia para se comunicar com os espíritos em busca de inspiração, cura e bênçãos. Bom momento para oráculos. Sobretudo, é hora de honrar os mortos e agradecer aos ancestrais pelo dom mais precioso que nos deram, nossas vidas. Podemos materializar esse agradecimento através de oferendas que são queimadas nas chamas da fogueira ritual ou revendo velhos álbuns de família, desenhando nossa árvore genealógica, convidando os mais velhos da família a contar histórias de suas vidas. É costume se deixar acesa uma vela numa das janelas da casa para mostrar aos ancestrais que eles são bem vindos. Ritual introspectivo, silencioso, respeitoso, celebrado à noite.
[Translation:]
The main theme of this festival is gratitude, honor and connection with our ancestors, from the loved ones who are no longer with us, to those [for whom we] no longer know the names, including the gods. It is the moment when the Other World becomes more accessible, the boundary between the worlds is little defined and the date is favorable to communicate with the spirits in search of inspiration, healing and blessings. Good time for oracles. Above all, it is time to honor the dead and thank the ancestors for the most precious gift they have given us, our lives. We can materialize this gratitude through offerings that are burned in the flames of the ritual bonfire or by reviewing old family albums, drawing our family tree, inviting the elders of the family to tell stories of their lives. It is customary to leave a candle lit in one of the windows of the house to show the ancestors that they are welcome. Ritual introspective, silent, respectful, celebrated at night."

"Samhain - We honor the Ancestors of blood, heart, and place. We give them offerings of their favorite foods (if none are known, we give culturally traditional foods or drink). We clean the home and welcome their visit. We carve pumpkins and turnips, and we light them to scare away the more dangerous spirits wandering around. We take our daughter trick-or-treating, and we also hand candy out to visitors, in the spirit of hospitality."

Seasonal Festivals in a Globalizing Tradition

The trouble with this traditional Wheel of the Year is that, as Druidry spreads to distant countries and cultures, the agricultural symbolism of the wheel often loses its relevance. For a few Druids (~1%), adherence to tradition mattered more than connection to the land, sea, and sky of the region in which they lived. Their survey responses indicated that they were both deeply aware that the seasons where they lived were nothing like those of the British Isles and Ireland, and also deeply committed to maintaining traditions as described in the textual references which they had studied. As one Druid explained:

> *"Donde vivo hay un clima templado, pero la temporada de lluvia se da en verano, no en primavera o en otoño. El invierno es frio o templado, bastante seco y no nieva. Aunque los huracanes no nos afectan de forma directa, lo hacen de manera indirecta, con lluvias y fuertes vientos. Antes de vivir aqui viví en paises donde las estaciones estaban en sintonia con los climas de Irlanda/ Inglaterra/ Francia. Celebré las ocho festividades de la Rueda del Año. [...] Cuando el clima de donde vivo no acompaña al que nuestroa antepasados celtas vivian en la misma festividad trato de recordar las sensaciones vividas en la misma epoca del año en los paises donde vivi con anterioridad y los significados de la estacion.*
> [Translation:]
> *Where I live there is a temperate climate, but the rainy season is in summer, not spring or autumn. The winter is cold or mild, quite dry and does not snow. Although hurricanes do not affect us directly, they do so indirectly, with rain and strong winds. Before living here I lived in countries where the seasons were in tune with the Irish/English /French climates. I celebrated the eight festivities of the Wheel of the Year. [...] When the climate where I live does not correspond to the one that our Celtic ancestors lived in for the same festivity, I try to remember the sensations of the same time of the year in the countries where I lived before, and the meanings of the season [there]."*

However, this was far from the norm.

As we saw repeatedly in *Chapters 5 & 6*, Druidry is, first and foremost, a religious tradition of nature connection. As a result, local variations in the Wheel of the Year turn out to be quite common. Some variations involve shifts in the timing of festivals throughout the year, or the inclusion of local folk customs concurrent with the festival. In many cases, variations in the locally manifest cycles of Nature lead to entirely new interpretations of the spiritual meanings attributed to each festival in the Wheel of the Year.

Traditionally, Samhain (around the time of the first hard frost in England) marks the death of the old year, and the start of the new. However, in climates where there is never a killing frost, and seasonal cycles are driven by moisture, rather than by warmth and light, a solstice or equinox is typically used as the start of the year. The choice is most commonly based upon the timing of an obvious symbol of returning life, such as the first rains of the year in a wet/dry climate, the first growing light after the Winter Solstice in light/dark climates; or the first sprout of green after "mud-and-stick" season (a fifth season described by several Druids as falling between the frozen winter and the greening of spring).

Variations in festival timing are derived from a focus on Nature, rather than on calendar dates. Some Druids calculate the eight festival dates astronomically, by the timing of solar transits, or by the location of particular constellations, or to align with a particular phase of the moon, for example:

> *"I celebrate all my Holy days on their astrological dates, which often differ from the traditional dates, so they are different every year."*

> *"I use natural signs especially astronomical alignment for picking the exact days of celebrations. For example Samhain falls on 15 degrees of Scorpio."*

> *"Die Sonnenwenden und Tagundnachtgleichen feiere ich an den entsprechenden Tagen, dagegen richte ich mich bei Samhuinn (Neumond), Imbolc (wachsende Mondsichel), Beltaine (Vollmond) und Lughnasad (abnehmende Mondsichel) nach dem Mondstand.*
> [Translation:]
> *I celebrate the solstices and equinoxes on the respective days, but I turn to the moon's position at Samhuinn (new moon), Imbolc (growing moon crescent), Beltaine (full moon), and Lughnasad (waning moon crescent)."*

Some Druids, in the southern hemisphere, shift their festival dates six months, to align with the southern seasons (Winter in June; Summer in December) — as one respondent from New Zealand explained:

> *"In the Grove Of the Summer Stars, we celebrate all of the seasons in the eight-fold year. We do adjust the dates for the southern hemisphere, and for us, sunwise is anti-clockwise. Which is opposite to Northern Hemisphere practice."*

And many Druids celebrate seasonal changes or seasonal "firsts", rather than traditional calendar dates, as they explained:

"I also celebrate weather-related firsts. By that I mean the First Thunder of Spring, First Buds, First Mud (after frozen ground), First Turn of the leaves, First Frost, First Snow... that sort of thing. I don't think my symbolism is particularly novel - growth, change, letting go... birth, death, rebirth at various levels... I'm kind of a bog-standard Neopagan there."

"Gwyl Braint (approx 2 - 15 February), marked by the flooding of the River Braint."

"I do celebrate the 8 main wheel of the year events, but prefer to live and work more closely attuned to my immediate environment. For example, I had a small thanksgiving ceremony for Lughnasadh on the actual date, but my real harvest only occurred at the end of March as I gathered in the last of my tomatoes, beans and pumpkins. I had an impromptu thanksgiving ceremony in my vegetable garden. I celebrate on my own as there are no groves anywhere near where I live. I follow the OBOD formula and include my own meditations and prayers that are relevant to the time and place."

"Temperate, warm summers, cool autumns, cold but rarely freezing for long, winters, early springs. The signals in nature are extremely varied, for instance my stagshorn sumac starts to change its leaves in August, whereas it is November before the liquidamber strachifolia does so - by then the first early daffodils are out in favoured places so one part of my garden can be in the next-but-one (or last-but-one) season to another part. It is all a flow with individuals responding to their experience of weather patterns. I tend to observe the changing of the seasons and energies rather than having a particular celebration of any. Of course I am delighted it is the solstice today so we can start 'looking forward' but this is a manufactured concept imposed on a natural cycle, nature depends upon the weather cycles which are different every year and changing constantly although everything responds in its own particular way to the shortening and lengthening of days, ourselves no less than any other being although so many humans appear unaware of it or fail to acknowledge it."

*"Less so particular days like Beltane, but more marking
of seasonal changes - time of snowdrops, time of bluebells, etc. Also birds - time when the lapwings return to
the moors is a particular one."*

In many cases, simply changing the timing of celebrations proves inadequate. When either the physical or cultural environment in which a Druid practices is sufficiently different from the lands in which the modern traditions of Druidry were born, Druids report adding, subtracting, or entirely reinterpreting the celebrations of their Wheels of the Year, deriving their holidays entirely from their relationship with and connection to Nature.

Celebrating Cycles of Life, in Nature

The majority of world Druids (76%) use the concept of the Wheel of the Year as a gentle, cyclical reminder to get outside and connect with nature. It is only this act of nature connection that brings real meaning to the festivals of their Wheels of the Year, however formally or informally they choose to celebrate them — as one English Druid concisely explained:

*"I am not sure if the festivals have specific spiritual
meaning to me. Rather, they mark the passage of time
through the seasons and through life. They are how I
connect with the Natural World and recognise I am a part
of it. I am a part of the spirituality that is Nature."*

The act of nature connection either reinforces and enriches the symbolism of the traditional Wheel of the Year, or encourages wildcrafting of observances, rituals, and celebrations, as discussed in depth, in *Chapter 4: The Role of Geography in the Evolution of Druidry*. If we use the term *wildcrafting* to denote both ritual wildcrafting in foreign (i.e. non-British/Irish) ecologies, and the process of observing and verifying the extent to which Druid ritual and festival traditions are *reinforced* by the local ecologies of the traditional lands of the ancient Celts, then survey data indicate that 52% of world Druids wildcraft their Wheel of the Year celebrations.

For Druids resident in the British Isles and Ireland, where the traditions of modern Druidry were originally developed, this wildcrafting often takes the form of more deeply connecting with physical landmarks (hills, wells, standing stones, or henges with long tradition), or the physical manifestation of the traditional seasons, which are actually a living part of these lands. Wildcrafting here is also supported by local cultural traditions and festivals, which similarly derive from the local landscape, as Druids described:

"Midwinter and midsummer with OBOD in open ritual. Midsummer on top of Glastonbury Tor and Midwinter in Chalice Well gardens honouring the trees and mistletoe. Yule celebrated in local woodlands honouring the mistletoe and the trees and sending love and healing throughout the world by sending the properties of the mistletoe into the rivers and into the seas. Yule celebrated in the garden here by burning last year's mistletoe and corn gleanings, The ashes are then returned to the earth so the cycle continues."

"I tend to celebrate the traditional Wheel of the Year, as it was developed here in the UK and matches the climate pretty well (although climate change is making some festivals like Imbolc come earlier than the 'calendar date'). I celebrated the following holidays: Imbolc, when the first snowdrops appear; Spring Equinox; Beltane, when the hawthorn is in blossom; Summer Solstice; Lammas , when the wheat is being harvested; Autumn Equinox ; Samhain, when the first frost appears; Winter Solstice/Yule. For each of these I did a solitary Druid ritual except Lammas where I was at a Pagan camp and did a group ritual. I also tend to cook seasonal food and make time to go walking and observe what nature is doing around me. Where possible, I try to celebrate by natural signs [and] not [by] calendar dates. The holidays for me represent the cycle of nature, and by celebrating them I am bringing myself into greater attunement with nature."

"Well... West coast of Ireland, what to say more?... Wet, windy and misty most of the year. A perfect atmosphere to connect to the true Celtic spirit and to the magic of the elements. We live on a peninsula which contains 4,000 standing stones, forts and mounds. It is a fabulous ground for the revival and practice of the old ways. The land is very powerful and its beauty breathtaking. We live in total tuning with Nature. For instance, we celebrate Bealtaine when the Hawthorns blossom, the Winter Solstice when the sun rolls down the hill and sets between a row of standing stones on a particular hill, or Imbolc when snow drops and lambs make their appearance."

"[I] try to go along with as many local folk customs as possible, such as the Pace Egg in spring and the Rushbearing in summer. These holidays are primarily observing seasonal changes in the natural environment of my home, which I find helps me to live in a healthier rhythm with the changing length of the day."

For Druids resident in other countries and cultures of the world, these reinforcing cultural and ecological elements are absent. The cognitive dissonance caused by the mismatch between local geography and tradition encourages Druids to wildcraft their rituals from the local landscape. Druids generally begin this process by studying the local climate and seasons, for example:

> *"The wheel is focused on the traditional 4 seasons, which don't match with my climate [in the Sonoran Desert]. I've slowly been trying to develop my own wheel, with celebrations tied to my work in the garden and landscape and recognizing the changes that [I see] throughout the year."*

> *"While we don't have any Māori members of our Grove, at least four of our members are fluent Māori speakers and teachers and at least another 8 are learning the language. So, culturally, Māori words, calls to Māori spirits of land, sea and forest, and Māori myths and legends are all incorporated into our 8 Druid ceremonies."*

> *"In Aotearoa New Zealand we have very different native trees and while we honour the oak and other northern hemisphere trees, our own native trees have greater power and resonance. One of our members has created a New Zealand tree Ogham."*

> *"Australia - Mediterranean climate. This makes the onset of winter like spring, when flowers occur and things become green. Wheat is planted and grows over winter... very different. Kenya - "spring" is in the wet seasons, of which there are two. in both cases the seasons are driven by rain, not sun. that is the biggest difference to Europe. [I celebrate the 8 festivals], but reversed for southern hemisphere and acknowledgement of the local processes at the time."*

> *"As an initial step toward a local spiritual meaning for the holidays, I foraged a wild plant from my suburban yard to use as my offering and to represent life at that time of year.*

While the surface features of these wildcrafted celebrations may vary, it is interesting to note that the spiritual and philosophical framework that supports them is still closely tied to the Celtic Druidry tradition. This is seen in the ritual framework, and in the kinds of spiritual metaphors that Druids read in the natural world around them, as they explained:

"I always recognise the solstices and equinoxes using those names. And will often see there being a summer / spring / winter / autumn quarter. I do recognise the times of Samhain and Beltaine for their more esoteric meanings. Symbols I attach to all these tend to natural movements within my environment, so natural patterns of flora and fauna."

"Even though we are northern, temperate, and not a desert, we are still very different from the environments and nature cycles that gave rise to the traditional Celtic Wheel of the Year. We are not even truly 'Mediterranean' here, as our weather never gets warm enough. And so I rewrote our Wheel of the Year, and created new symbols and celebrations, in accordance with the actual seasons where we live. For example, we do not remember ancestors at Samhain time, because that is when our first rains arrive, and it is a time of joyous rebirth; we have our ancestors' celebration at the autumnal equinox, which is our peak fire season, the time of greatest death and dearth. We celebrate First Flowers around Imbolc time — when the first native shrubs are in peak blossom. By Ostara time, peak flower season is nearly over, though we do have a huge influx of brush rabbit babies at that time, so we celebrate Ostara rather more like Beltane. By Beltane time, our spring warmth has disappeared beneath the icy summer fog bank, and we celebrate a time of turning inward to meditate and do inner journeying work, until the heat returns (with the fires) in August. While others are turning inward, at the winter solstice, we are donning gortex to race outdoors and begin our native garden plantings for the year. So, we do observe most of the traditional symbolisms of the Druid wheel of the year, but in a different order, and at very different times of year."

"I [...] interpret the seasonal shifts in my own manner. I usually observe each event with a fire outdoors, meditation and divination, and food offerings. I observe the seasonal shifts as metaphors for internal emotional or spiritual changes."

By regularly connecting with the natural world, at least eight times, throughout the year, Druids become deeply familiar with their land, sea, and skyscapes, noting the patterns of the seasons passing. For some, the point of the Wheel of the Year is simply to observe nature, celebrate the seasons, meditate upon the spiritual metaphors evident in those seasons, and offer praise and gratitude to Nature. Druids wrote, for example:

"The wheel of the year goes on around me and I live it quietly. I do not specifically celebrate them, I just note them as they go by."

"Give thanks all year to The Universe / Collective Unconscious / God(dess) for the remarkable seasons and the different aspects that we can experience. For nature in all of her amazing splendour. For the magic all around each and every day if we just take time to look, feel, and hear."

"I did have a special meditation and coffee and a sweet treat, fruit based pie generally, and sit outside on the first day of each season. Summer was at the beach with iced coffee and coldcuts. I say thank you to the ocean and the sky and the winds, the sun and the moon and then usually walk barefoot into the water or around the woods for a time."

For other Druids, the point of the exercise is to attune the activities of one's life to the natural cycles of nature, using natural metaphors observed in the land, sea, and sky as a guide to spiritual life, thus improving one's ability to grow and thrive, in harmony with the natural world. Survey responses of this type included the following:

"I often find that spontaneous informal rituals, usually going outdoors and noting some sign of the season, is more meaningful to me than following a script. The meaning or intention is to draw myself into harmony with the cycles of the natural world."

"I acknowledge the changing of the seasons by changing my lifestyle to suit. Winter I rest or repair hedges and trees as sap is down. Spring I become more active fitness wise, Summer I work long and hard. Autumn I recuperate and repair my self."

"I have specific rituals (adapted from the AODA curriculum) that I perform for each holiday, and I change my altar with the changing seasons. I also see the seasonal holidays as being symbolic of the year of my life, with corresponding activities and practices that help me to stay spiritually connected to the seasons. I see it like breathing in and out through the year."

"Samhain gaf me de kans om nare ervaringen af te schudden, Yule en Imbolc on herboren te worden, Ostara om 3 wensen te zaaien, Beltane om door magie de liefde tot mij te brengen, Litha om het geluk en het leven te vieren en Lughnasadh en Mabon om de rijke oogst, zowel letterlijk als figuurlijk, te vieren en de goden als dank bijvoet en wijn te offeren.
[Translation:]
Samhain gave me the opportunity to shake off unpleasant experiences, Yule and Imbolc to be reborn, Ostara to sow 3 wishes, Beltane to bring love to me through magic, Litha to celebrate happiness and life and Lughnasadh and Mabon to celebrate the rich harvest, both literally and figuratively, and to sacrifice to the gods, as a thank you, a bit of food and wine."

"Through the cycle and seasons we talk about life, death, hope, letting go, waiting for the new. The fact that seasons of growth and of dying back are part of life, reflecting on what this might mean in our lives. We talk about hope that is unseen, as we go into winter it seems that all is dead but we are sure that the light will return and with it new life. At times we connect this to death and resurrection themes in the Christian story, also the Yule/Christmas connection is powerful as the return of light to the physical world is aligned with the coming of Christ. Thankfulness is a constant theme, and connection to God as we connect to the natural world. Also trust, that what we can see isn't the whole reality, trusting God to bring new life when the time is right for it."

Frequently, this act of spiritual nature connection also involves a habit of detailed seasonal observations. When asked to describe their local climate and seasons, 11% of Druids merely named their locations, and 57% offered very general descriptions, such as the following:

"Aqui considera-se duas estações: o período de chuvas (de setembro à março) e o período de seca (de abril à outubro). Os sinais da natureza são claros: as chuvas torrenciais do verão e a seca prolongada do inverno.
[Translation:]
Here two seasons are considered: the rainy season (September to March) and the dry season (April to October). The signs of nature are clear: the torrential rains of summer and the prolonged drought of winter."

"California. Short wet winter. Then long hot spring into very hot dry summer for most of the year."

"Classic British seasons of Winter (nothing much grows, cold, snow, ice, rain), Spring (cold - growing warmer, wet, new growth, many births), Summer (varies, some warm dry days, some cool and wet, occasional heatwaves - maturing growth), Autumn formerly known in UK as 'Harvest' (warm, growing cooler, dry days becoming wetter - field crops brought in, orchards picked)."

"I live in a humid subtropical climate. ~3.5 months winter, ~2.5 months spring, ~3.5 months summer, ~2.5 months fall. Winter - starvation of wildlife and decay, spring - return of soft green life and birds, summer - busy movement of wildlife, fall - harvest of all kinds."

"Maritime climate with mild summers and winters."

However, for 32% of Druids, the descriptions of local seasons and environments contained a level of detail that could not have been realized without years of careful observation and study. These Druids kept diaries chronicling their nature observations; they logged seasonal observations in spreadsheets; and they wrote poems, odes to the changing seasons, and the natural world around them. Their survey responses demonstrated indepth knowledge of seasonal weather patterns, prevalent wind directions, endemic plant and animal species, and the timing of specific animal migrations. They wrote of the precise timing of changes in the colors, smells, qualities of light and humidity, and so many other fine details of the normal seasons for their areas, as well as the specific ways in which those seasons were shifting and changing as a result of global climate change.

This kind of detailed response was common among Druids of the British Isles and Ireland, the seasons of which were the original inspiration for the Neopagan Wheel of the Year, for example:

"4 distinct seasons. Spring (late March to early June): Wildflowers such as primroses and bluebells flower, buds swell, leaves burst, dawn chorus of bird song, daylight lengthens, swallows arrive back from Africa, cuckoos too, insects such as butterflies and bees reappear. I could go on! Summer (June to early September-ish): Hopefully warm sunny weather, trees, shrubs, flowers in full bloom and leaf, long daylight hours, young birds fledge, young mammals appear, (farm and wild). Apples, plums, etc., start to ripen. Autumn/Fall (Mid Sept to Late November): Daylight shortens, temperature falls, summer visitor birds depart, deciduous trees' and shrubs' leaves turn yellow, then brown, and start to fall, the first frosts come. Gales commonly recommence, with heavy rain. Winter (Late

November to late March): Long nights, short daylight hours, sun low in sky, winter visitor birds such as red-wings and fieldfares arrive from colder climes, holly and ivy more visible in the hedges and woods. Bird feeders need replenishing more often. Hens stop laying eggs or lay irregularly, turbulent weather with storms of wind, rain, sometimes snow, often heavy frosts but mild spells too. First snowdrops appear around early January and honeysuckle shows its tiny new leaves, a promise of spring to come."

"Torbay, Devon, UK. Four seasons but tending to be earlier with spring and warmer winters than my native South East of England. Devon is a large county with two coast lines, being affected by coastal mists. Inland they might be a-blaze with sunshine but on the coast here we're living in a cloud. Today it was sunny in Paignton but I could see a brownish mist in the bay between us and Torquay. Being in the west of England it tends to be very wet compared to the East. I moved here in mid March, early spring and the flowers were definitely further ahead here than back East. The central part of the county is high: Dartmoor. The bogs can be treacherous and people lose their lives in them. The only snow I saw when I lived in Exeter in the 1990s was on the rooves of cars that had come down off the moors. We never got it further down towards the coast. Having said that it snowed heavily in Exeter this year. Torbay and the surrounding countryside is interesting in that you have agricultural and grazing land a mile inland, with all the wild flowers and deciduous trees you expect to see in the English countryside: oak, alder, holly, hawthorn etc, and then you have the urban coastal strip where the remnants of a flourishing 19th and 20th century tourist trade has left a legacy of mature, or in many cases, elderly more exotic palms, fancy evergreen oaks, cedars and a lot of Scots Pine. I haven't been observing for long here so I can't really comment on the length of the seasons but only these general thoughts. My memories of my time here in the 90s was of a LOT of rain and as a result the greenery was intense and vibrant compared with the savannah of the Kent coast. Devon was all lush green grass while 'home' was dry brown pastures. Birdlife here seems more varied. I even saw a song thrush the other week which I haven't seen in Kent in decades. Sadly the Herring Gulls, Wood Pigeons and Ring-necked Parakeets seemed to be driving everything else out back in the East."

"Local climate is a prevailing north westerly wind which comes off the Atlantic. I'm on the north coast of Scotland. The seasons are quite distinct, winter here can be bleak and long with gales and wet, the sun sets midwinter at about 4.30pm and rises about 8.45am. By contrast, [at] midsummer the sun hardly sets, it gets dusk about midnight and becomes light about 2am the sun rises about 4.30am. The seasons of winter last from November 'til April, spring from April 'till June, summer from June 'til September, and autumn from September 'till November. For me, spring is when the curlews return to nest in the fields and the geese migrate to their summer nesting grounds, summer is when the first swallow returns, autumn is when the geese fly back and winter is when nothing does anything much, but when the buttercups finally stop flowering (could be December sometimes)."

This level of detail in nature observations was also prevalent among Druids of northern, continental Europe, eastern Canada, and the northeastern portions of the United States, all of which have similar climates and seasonal cycles to Britain. Druids from these areas wrote, for example:

"Denmark is situated in the temperate zone. We have four seasons which last approximately 3 months each. Spring (March, April, May): rainy and windy. If there has been any snow during the winter, the rest will melt during March at the latest, but there can still be frosty mornings. It is said that spring arrives when the leaves of the beech tree (the national tree of Denmark) unfold. The ground is covered with erantis, crocus, snowdrops, daffodils, anemones and wild garlic. The smell of manure being strewn on the fields [is] in the air. [There are the] yellow rape fields, the songs of the lark and the cuckoo, the sowing of seeds, [and] the taste of new potatoes. Summer (June, July, August): usually not hotter than 25-30 degrees Celcius (although it has been increasingly hot during the last couple of years) and very rainy (especially in June). [This is the season of] golden corn fields, shadowy and cool woods of beech and oak, the smell of wild flowers, the song of the blackbird, lying on the beach with an ice cream, the taste of strawberries, and bright nights. Autumn (September, October, November): the light is drawing in. [This is the season of] morning fogs and the smell of the first frost touching the leaves, red and golden coloured forests, windy and rainy [weather], the smell of wet leaves, the taste of mushrooms, candle light and warm cocoa, lying in fresh straw in the middle of a newly

harvested field, the sound of migrating geese, [and] *pumpkin carving. Winter (December, January, February): usually very rainy (sometimes with a bit of occasional snow) and stormy.* [This is the season of] *naked hedges and the silhouettes of trees against a lead-colored sky, feeding birds, walking across muddy fields, sea foam covering the beaches (where it's pretty hard to stand up because of the fierce western wind), winter sun, the feeling of hibernation,* [and] *the smell of pine trees and wet moss."*

"Winter [in Canada] *goes from October to April. We feel climate change here. December, January and February used to be quite cold here between -20°C & -30°C. Now, -16°C is cold and we get 7°C in the middle of January. The Mountain Pine beetle is having a devastating effect on the pine trees here because it no longer gets cold enough to slow them down. Spring arrives usually mid April, but for me it's not official until I see and hear a Robin. Things don't green up until mid May. The Waxwings arrive and eat all the rowan berries in the trees in front of my place — it's a sight and a half to see 100+ birds in 3 trees. June is the beginning of summer. Here we notice climate change too. We used to get weeks at a time of 30°C, now were lucky to get a few days all summer that hot. Summer here brings out the urban rabbits, and their babies — which bring out the coyotes. It's odd and sad to see a coyote running across a major parking lot, kilometers away from any green space. The end of summer is my favorite time, I love going for drives in the country and seeing canola field after canola field, the brightness of the yellow against the green is awesome! Fall arrives about mid September. The leaves start turning yellow, By October, the leaves are red, the bunnies are white, and by Samhain there is usually snow. We go from not being able to see Orion in the sky to seeing him most of the winter."*

"We have four seasons. Winter (Nov-March) begins with the first snowfall, early snows are gentle and fluffy. Midwinter is bitter cold, snow is light but hard, biting wind, always dark (the average work-day is longer than the sun is up). We have one freak thaw, usually in early February. Late-winter then begins, snow gets very wet and heavy. Sugar season begins; the maple trees wake up and the sap starts to run (this lasts 3-8 weeks). Ice dams form on all the houses. Spring (Apr-May) begins when the sun starts to feel warm again in late March. Everyone gets a

sunburn on their face while still wearing coats outside.
Snowmelt floods the streets, streams, and rivers (some-
times disastrously). Canada geese pass by on their way
North. Ramps, squill, and crocuses start to poke up before
the snow is gone. Robins, herons, sparrows return. Trees
flower and leaf out; bees wake up. Major thunderstorms
begin. Summer (June-Aug) begins when the trees set fruit
(mulberries and cherries especially). Grass bolts. Most
vegetable gardens are planted in late May/early June. Air
becomes very humid and hot during the day. Mosquitos
and butterflies outside; fruit flies and moths inside. Lakes
are warm enough for swimming. Fall (Sept-Oct) begins
when the tops of the sugar maples turn orange. Possums
start to hang around the house at dusk. Squirrels bury
walnuts all over the neighborhood. Most vegetable
gardens produce harvest late Aug. and Sept. Days stay
hot, but night gets suddenly cold. Crows begin to gather
and roost together (we have something called the
'Minneapolis Mega-murder' of thousands of crows).
Canada geese pass by on their way south."

One might expect Druids living in places with climates and seasons very different from those of Britain to rely on books, rather than observations of the natural world, in order to maintain a heart-felt connection to a cycle of seasonal festivals and celebrations derived from a foreign land. However, the opposite turned out to be true.

World Druidry Survey data showed that Druids from climates different from Britain's are significantly *more* likely (58-59% compared to 32% for Druids overall) than other Druids to include detailed, seasonal, nature observations as a key component of their Druidry practice.[6] In addition, the level of detail and specificity reflected in their descriptions of the local environment was much higher than that of other Druids' descriptions. This was particularly true of Druids residing in Oceania, and in climates driven by wet/dry seasonal cycles. Examples of landscape descriptions from Druids in non-traditional biomes and climatic zones included the following:

"This is the Pacific Northwest Coast of North America in
the era of growing climate change. I live on a hill above a
river valley that is approximately 50 miles north by north-
west from the river's source on a 14,000+ foot high
volcano named Takopid (She Who Gives Us the Water)
and also named Mt. Rainier in the center of a National
Park. I am also approximately 12 miles from the Wulge,
or Puget Sound on the Salish Sea. I am within sight of the
Sound to the west, and also of the Olympic mountains to

*the west over the Sound, and the Cascade mountains to
the east, northeast and southeast of me.*

*My home region is dominated by weather patterns
driven eastward off the Pacific Ocean, and around the
Olympic Mountains to the Southeast of me up the
Chehalis River Valley to the southern Puget Sound, and to
the Northwest of me through the Straits of Juan de Fuca
to the northern Puget Sound. Frequently these wind
driven weather patterns converge on the Sound somewhere before rising up over the Cascades, and they drop
an annual rainfall average of 35 inches on my home and
keeps the temperatures mild and moderate.*

*Occasionally the Pacific weather sweeps into the
continent far to the north of us and we get weather patterns that throw overland winds that blow down the Puget
Sound lowlands out of Canada. This air is much dryer
than the air that blows in off the oceans, and we get hotter
or colder temperatures*

*Our annual rainfall is not diminishing too much at
this point in global warming, but the seasonal schedule is
changing noticeably. Our usual pattern is cool wet late
winters and springs that gradually yield to dryer warmer
summers followed by gradually cooling wetter falls and
early winters. Around mid-winter, in January or February
we usually get a few weeks of cold dry weather that marks
the end of the old cycle and the beginning of the next.
What is changing now days is the timing of these weather
shifts, and the dryer summers are becoming longer and
dryer each year, while the wet seasons are shorter and
just slightly less wet. The mid-winter dry spell is also
shortening. Winter temperatures during the wet seasons
are also warmer and snowfall is diminishing in the mountains. As a result of these longer dry spells there is greater
glacial melting on our big mountain in the longer
summers as well, and coupled with the warmer winters,
the glaciers are shrinking.*

*The traditional plant ecology on the Puget Sound
was a mixed deciduous/conifer temperate forest of firs,
hemlock, and cedar mixed in with alder, sour cherry,
large leaf maples, and dogwood. There were also large
stretches of glacial till grass prairies in the south Sound
spotted with oak trees. But a hundred years of commercial
forestry has largely replaced the wide native mixed forests
with single species forests of second and third growth
furs, and smaller segregated stands of alders and maples,
and mixed fur, hemlock, and cedar. As forestry practices
segregated the trees the whole nature of our forests were
subject to environmental stresses everywhere, as were the*

*pressures of clearing the land for more and more human
use and the introduction of non-native species. Right now,
many plants that are not drought tolerant are suffering
through the longer warmer summers, while other plants
that are more drought tolerant are thriving. This effects
animal life as well in thousands of ways. So everything is
changing."*

*"New Zealand has a temperate climate so the seasons are
not clearly defined. We have also been known to experience four seasons in one day. Summer is heralded by the
flowering of the Pohutukawa tree and the song of the
cicada. It is a time to gather honey and cut the hay. Late
summer brings the first harvest of corn and wild black-
berries, as the godwits prepare to fly north. Vineyards
[are] covered [with] grape vines, ready for vintage.
Autumn is a time to harvest the kūmara and corn, as the
evenings close in when daylight saving ends.Through the
Winter we rest, celebrating the rise of Matariki (Pleiades)
and the Māori New Year with feasting, mulled wine.
Spring is the time to plant the kūmara for the following
year, the song of the long-tailed cuckoo can be heard as
the shining cuckoo returns from Hawaiki, along with the
godwits from Alaska. The kowhai tree is in flower, the
whitebait are running."*

*"According to the local Noongar people [of Australia], we
have six [seasons]. Birak (Dec-Jan): hot and dry, the blue
tongue goannas come out of hibernation and Jarrah often
flowers. Bunuru (Feb-Mar): Warm to hot, Marri tree
flowers, Zamia palms begin to fruit. Djeran (Apr-May):
Ant season, cooler and pleasant but often no rains yet,
sheoaks flower, bankisas blossom. Makuru (June-July):
First rains, cold and wet, Acacias bloom, grass grows.
Djilba (Aug-Sep): Growing season, weather changeable,
wildflowers begin to proliferate in the bush, Magpies
begin to swoop. Kambarang (Oct-Nov): Wildflower
season, warming, rains drying up, Christmas trees
(Nuyutsia) flower, as do the red and green kangaroo
paws."*

*"Summer here [Salish-Kootenai Nation, Montana, USA]
is sunny, dry, almost without rain, horses run through the
pastures nearby, plants grow quickly and then stop all
summer, soaking up the sun but surviving without rain. A
day starts around 4 AM, the sun sets at 10 PM. We head
into fire season in August and September, and the sky can
be choked with smoke, the animals grow restless, anxiety*

deepens if the drought continues, but it seems to be a natural cycle in this ecosystem, worsening with climate change. Fall brings the hungry bears which eat the apples off our tree, the chokecherry along the river, deer's fur thickens, and this year's young turkeys congregate, move in gangs of adolescents through the woods. Then comes an overcast winter, with snow and deep cold in January and February, though the days begin to lengthen after Imbolc. Soon after the snow melts, green leaves show up on Aspen and Dogwood, elderberry, rowan, and June berry burgeon, the birds return, the bear awakens, and it's time to stay away from the deepest forests and the hungriest animals. Next the deer drop fawn, we see them tottering around, the wild turkey are followed by their brood."

"We have five [seasons] *in the Sonoran Desert. The additional season being foresummer drought in May and June is exceedingly hot and dry but the saguaros bloom. Then summer comes with the Summer Monsoons (Las Aguas) and explosive thunderstorms and haboobs. Some wildflowers bloom with the temporary water almost like a second spring. When the dryness returns and the air begins to cool, fall is in season, and the backyard begins to grow. The Winter Monsoon brings gentle rains (Equipatas), and our garden flourishes. Spring warms up the desert again gradually and palo verdes and wild-flowers bloom."*

In addition to simply paying closer attention to what is going on in the natural world, Druids who focus on detailed nature observations are also significantly more likely to celebrate all eight festivals of the Wheel of the Year. In fact, the habits of detailed nature observation, and wildcrafting seasonal rituals were the two most important factors in predicting a Druid's likelihood of celebrating the festivals. These two habits were more influential than Druidry group membership, or even the habit of spiritual nature connection, as evident in the following, statistically significant, intergroup variations in the likelihood of Druids celebrating all eight festivals[7]:

- 47% of Druids, overall;
- 53% of OBOD members;
- 55% of Druids focused on spiritual nature connection;
- 60% of Druids focused on detailed nature observations;
- 62% of Druids focused on wildcrafting/reinforcing their rituals and seasonal celebrations, through observation

These numbers suggest that nature observation, nature connection, and spiritual wildcrafting — all of which serve to deepen a Druid's personal relationship with the land, sea, and sky of the place in which he or she happens to live — are the most important factors encouraging Druids to regularly celebrate the festivals of the Wheel of the Year. This raises the question: if Druid Wheels of the Year are wildcrafted, in what ways, if any, do the resulting festivals correspond to those of the traditional, Celtic Wheel of the Year? In what ways do they differ?

As noted earlier[8], 52% of world Druids wildcraft their Wheels of the Year, to some extent, but for those in northern and western Europe, this act of wildcrafting generally reinforces traditions, or results in only minor shifts in timing. What happens when wildcrafting takes place farther afield?

Druidry's Wildcrafted Wheels of the Year

Variations in local ecology, culture, social customs, myths and lore can all play a role in wildcrafted Wheels of the Year. However, nearly all Druids still rely upon the idea of a cycle of eight festivals, spaced 6 or 7 weeks apart, throughout the year — even if not all are celebrated. The aspects of the seasonal celebrations most likely to change are the signs of the passing seasons in nature, and in some cases, the spiritual symbolism associated with those signs. In addition, non-traditional social and cultural contexts often lead to blended traditions incorporating elements from each participating tradition.

To illustrate the ways in which such variations are manifest abroad, let us take one more journey through the Wheel of the Year, again beginning with the winter solstice.

Winter Solstice Traditions wildcrafted from the local environment:

As a solar festival marking the return of light in the darkest time of the year, the Winter Solstice generally maintains its symbolic meaning, when celebrated in other localities. However, the celebrations are often adapted and blended with other cultural traditions, such as with the reinterpretation of tales, or the inclusion of Northern feasting rituals, as shown in the following quotes:

> *"Yule (Winter Solstice) - Dec 21 - Celebrated in Grove*
> *tradition as the Norse Yule, including a Sumbel to honor*
> *the gods with boasting, toasts, and oath-making. We like*
> *to fill the longest night with drink, song, laughter, and*
> *good company."*

"Alban Arthuan, within a day or two of the Winter Solstice. This celebration marks the beginning of the new year for me, and it incorporates adapted imagery from my favorite Christmas carol, which I change to three wise Druids bringing gifts of knowledge, power, and peace to the newly born Child-year. I meditate on the new life being born as a tiny spark within deep winter; even though spring is still far off, and in fact the deepest cold is still to come, the new year is born as the day slowly lengthens and the sun's power slowly increases. After the ritual I change my daily prayer altar to its winter color. During the next several weeks, I complete my goals for the year and my analysis of the garden results from the previous year, and I begin planning the next garden and doing winter pruning."

In southern locations, Druids focus more keenly on the astronomical events associated with the time of year, rather than on Yuletide or Christmas traditions, which are offset by six months from the celebration of the Winter Solstice, as Druids explained:

"Yule is [...] in the height of summer, so activities that I traditionally associate with [it] aren't appropriate. So I made it an astronomical event - this is where the orbit is, this is the continuation of the cycle."

"Midwinter/Alban Arthan - 21/22 June We welcomed the birth of the boy child (The Mabon).We also celebrated Matariki, the Māori name for the constellation Pleiades, and the turning point of the year."

In locations that differ not merely by hemisphere, but also by the ecological cycles, and seasonal markers, the emphasis may be on rains and harvests, rather than on the cycles of light and dark, for example:

"Season of Heart (Winter Solstice, end of June) New Moon, time to seek shelter again, it's cold, windy and raining too much to be outside, a time of harvest and hearth, to stand by and to celebrate around the fire, and also to journey inward, to seek the inner light that shines a path through the darkness, of breathing in. A time to re-strict one's diet, and direct attention inward."

Imbolc Traditions wildcrafted from the local environment:

Imbolc, which is traditionally marked by the birth of lambs and the first appearance of flowers amidst melting snow and frosty soil, is the first festival to show significant variations in both seasonal markers and symbolic meaning. This diversity is due to variations in both the duration and the intensity of "winter" as a season of frozen dormancy.

Where the winter weather is more extreme and longer lasting, Imbolc is a meaningless date in the midst of the hard freeze. In these cases, Druids focus more on the mythology surrounding Brigid, the traditional patron deity of the holiday, for example:

> *"I feel very detached from Oimelc here in Minnesota. [...]
> Nothing grows amid a dead frozen world, blanketed under
> two feet of snow. I associate Oimelc more with crafts and
> hobbies. My Grove has scheduled a robe-making party,
> and I will bring my sewing machine and other supplies to
> participate. We will have an outdoor ritual, using organic
> heavy cream as the sacramental Waters-of-Sleep in a
> stoneware goblet. Sometimes we will celebrate outside of
> a tropical conservatory in Saint Paul with a short ritual,
> then go in to warm up among the jungle plants. Plus,
> admission is free which is nice."*

For Druids in slightly warmer locations, where lambs and snowdrops might be absent, but other herbs and flowers are sprouting, the symbolism of "earliest signs of spring" may still hold, but the specific plants and animals noted will vary with the region, for example:

> *"Prayer addressed to Yggdrasil Tree of Life. Offering of
> Creeping Charlie, the only green edible herb available in
> my yard in deep winter. Ceremonially eaten in gratitude
> for the gifts of the land after essence of the offering ac-
> cepted."*

> *"Imbolc is my favorite as spring is returning, but in my
> area there are no sheep, so I tend to time this celebration
> to three things that first emerge here: ryegrass, daffodils,
> and sofwood blossoms."*

For Druids in warmer locations, where the world never freezes, and where cycles in nature are driven primarily by seasons of rain and drought, the focus will often shift to celebrations of the arrival of monsoon rains, and the purification and revival of the land, which follows. It might also shift to the planting of crops in newly rain-drenched land — a type of celebration that is more traditionally reserved for the Vernal Equinox or even Beltane, in colder climes. Examples of such responses included:

> *"I'm making adjustments as needed. For Imbolc I plan to shift to a focus on the winter monsoon and link that to purification, light, and water."*

> *"First Flowers: We walk the land, greeting and celebrating the beginning of peak Flower Season. Then we prepare and plant out our farm beds with seeds for the first crop of the new year, and perform ritual blessings for the wildlife gardens and food-growing beds. The theme is nurturing and encouraging new life."*

Vernal Equinox Traditions wildcrafted from the local environment:

Celebrations of the Vernal Equinox also change due to variations in winter's severity and duration. In far northern climes, where variations in day length are at their most extreme, the symbolism of the vernal equinox, when daytime finally overtakes nighttime in duration, is a powerful cause for celebration, as is the desire to see an end to winter — as evident in these responses:

> *"Ostara (Spring Equinox) - We honored Old Man Winter, in his many forms (including the Germanic Wodan), thanking him for his time and asking him to withdraw his power. As noted above, winter lasts a long time here, so by April, we are more than ready to be done. This year, we decided to be polite about revoking his welcome."*

> "[In Sweden,] *Spring is celebrated with making a huge bonfire and singing, from sunset and into the night. Prior to the Spring equinox, we bring birch branches into the house and decorate them with coloured feathers."*

In areas ruled by wet/dry seasonal cycles, the Vernal Equinox is sometimes seen as a shift from the cool, rainy season, to the hot, dry season. It can also be seen as a time for feasting and a celebration of warmth and fertility, similar to Beltane celebrations elsewhere, for example:

> *"Spring Equinox — Balance* [of] *fire/water, earth/air, internal/external. Moving more definitively into fire season from water season. Feeling the growing excitement and preparation for the garden. Usually just spend the day in the garden and meditating."*

"Arapyaú ('New Year' - Spring Equinox, end of September) Crescent/First Quarter Moon, time to celebrate new cycles, beginnings and ends, end of the rainy and cold season and start of the dry and hot one, a time of activity, of pruning and active care, of breathing out and going outside. A time to feast and celebrate!"

"We celebrate peak flower season, bunny-breeding season, and the season of swimmable waters with a beach picnic at which we weave flower wreaths to distribute to random passers-by. We also color eggs, and give chocolate bunnies out to the kids. The theme is recognizing and celebrating unbidden blessings sent by the gods. It is our equivalent of the traditional Beltane — by which time, for us, warm weather and flower season is over."

Blending the traditions of the Vernal Equinox with other family and local cultural traditions leads to yet other kinds of celebration, for example:

"Alban Eilir ('Light of the Earth'), at the Point of Balance between Imbolc and Beltane — as it is at the point of balance between day and night — is a time for festivity and celebration for it marks the beginning of a new phase, the beginning of the triumph of light. In ancient Māori society, the rising of the star Aotahi (Canopus) announced the arrival of Spring, together with the flowering of kowhai, rangiora and kotukutuku, the plants of the fourth lunar month spanning September and October. The flowering of the kowhai signified the fish are getting fat and a sign for kūmara planting to begin."

"Easter this year was celebrated with my immediate family - all my children and grandchildren together for the first time in a long time. We played games, sang songs around the fire-pit while toasting marshmallows, We made family memories."

Beltane Traditions wildcrafted from the local environment:

The focus on fertility and fecundity at Beltane is celebrated around the world, though wildcrafted celebrations may involve myths derived from different cultures, or natural symbols taken from different ecologies, such as those described by Druids from New Zealand:

"At Beltane Papatuanuku (Earth Mother) dresses the land in green. Tane Mahuta - god of the forest and the 'great fertiliser'— answers her call."

"To the Māori, this was Whiringanuku, the fifth month, when ka whakaniho nga mea katoa o te whenua i konei ('all things now put forth fresh growth'). A good flowering of ti kouka (cabbage tree) is said to be a sign that a long, fine summer will follow. Beltane is the third of the Spring celebrations in the Druid tradition. The invigorating energies of spring growth are flowing at their strongest through the earth, and indeed through us too."

In other cases, the personal/social context was the main influencing factor, requiring the fertility theme of Beltane to be reinterpreted so that all Druids would feel welcomed and included, even if their personal lives did not conform to traditional, gender-binary norms, as two Druids explained:

"Beltane. This is a very important holiday because it symbolizes complementary forces coming together to form a complete being. For me it is about self-acceptance. As a gay person this has been one of my major challenges."

"Beltane has always been a complicated one for me, because of the sexual symbolism associated with it. As an asexual, I do not engage in sexual activities, and so I mostly focus on the miracle of the creation of new life in nature, as well as making it an exercise in stepping out of my comfort zone, and learning about those things that lie outside of my own experience."

Wildcrafted Beltane celebrations often also include activities that help Druids connect with local Faerie Folk, or spirits of place, for example:

"At Beltain my pagan friends and I often have a fire, and I like to take an evening walk on Beltain-eve in hopes of glimpsing the parts of the woods that blur with Faerie, if nothing else, it feels auspicious to have this walk yearly."

"May day is dancing and visiting The Good Folks to leave gifts of thanks and dressing wells."

Finally, Beltane may be altogether reinterpreted in regions where the seasons are either much slower or much quicker to reach their peak levels of spring warmth and fertility. Around the first of May in some places, the ground and ice-filled rivers are only beginning to thaw, and so the focus in not on peak fertility, but rather, on the first signs of spring, and spring planting, for example:

"This is late spring, around the time when I plant the frost-sensitive plants and seeds for corn, beans, and squash and when the year's first fruits, strawberries, are being harvested. This is also a time of colorful spring flowers. Because this is smack in the middle of planting season, I include a growth blessing for all the plants in my yard as part of the ritual. After the ritual, I may plant seeds or seedlings as appropriate."

"Beltane is about the action of planting. It is usually at the beginning of May that the ground is ready to be worked. I clean my home and outside areas and plant my gardens. I also change the decorations on my altar again and set up a mini maypole."

"Beltane usually involves some sort of baptism in the ice cold river. [It] is celebrated when the apples blossom."

In warmer areas, Beltane marks the end of the first season of warmth and growth, and is a time of harvest celebration, for example:

"First Fog (around May 1): We visit the beach once more for a picnic, to greet the first Great Fog Bank of Summer (and to say farewell to the warm waters of the Pacific, as the weather turns cold again). We celebrate the arrival of the salad fairies, as our first harvest of the year begins."

"Beltane, Mayday. Spring rolls over into Summer, first harvest is in. Party time. Big feast, dance the maypole."

Summer Solstice Traditions wildcrafted from the local environment:

Opposite the Winter Solstice on the Wheel of the Year, the Summer Solstice traditionally focuses on the longest day, the midpoint of the year, and the time of the Sun's peak power, as it transitions from waxing to waning power. For those Druids who live in far northern regions, this is the moment of peak warmth and fertility, and the celebration may be like a later Beltane, as described by a Druid from Sweden:

"Midsummer. You dance - often there are at least 2-3 circles around a pole that is very phallic and dressed in flowers and leaves. Dance until you are tired, then have a dish made with seafood or fish of some kind. Dessert is fresh berries - and a lot of drinks... At night, maidens and bachelors pick 7, 9 or 11 different kind of flowers (it varies what people want but it is always an odd number),

*lay them under their pillow, and if they are lucky, they will
see their future spouse in a dream."*

For other Druids, whose physical and cultural environments differ
from the traditional, the symbolic meaning may be maintained while using
localized mythologies, and signs and portents in nature, for example:

*"Summer Solstice honours Ranginui (Sky Father) and
Tamanuiterā (Sun King). A world peace-working at this
time of greatest light is led by the children bearing
candles (the Sacred Flame)."*

*"Summer Solstice, the longest day, arrives as the year is
coming to an end and the summer holiday season about to
begin. Although this is when the sun's light reaches its
maximum, it is but the threshold of summer. The crimson
flowers of the pohutukawa fringe the coastline, dancing
against the blue sea. The essential feature of this festival
is the recognition that we are at the mid-point of the year,
the turning or balance point between the waxing powers
of spring and early summer and the waning powers of late
summer and autumn. It is therefore an ideal time to work
on the qualities of integration and balance."*

*"Alban Heruin, within a day or two of the Summer
Solstice. At this time my favorite flower, purple cone-
flower, is blooming, and it is featured on the altar and in
the meditation theme as I find deep physical and spiritual
meaning in it. I mark the brightness, freshness, and glory
of early summer blooms and the ongoing harvest of cool
season crops while remembering the winter before and the
winter to come, realizing that I depend entirely on the
Powers of Nature for my sustenance and my life. After the
ritual I change my daily prayer altar to its summer colors,
and I might harvest herbs if the weather is favorable."*

Finally, for Druids in warmer, moisture-driven climes, the Summer
Solstice focuses on the transition from cooler, wetter seasons to hot and dry
seasons that are often fraught with severe storms and natural disasters, such
as hurricanes and wildfires. In these areas, Summer Solstice celebrations often
include concrete preparations, meditations, and prayers for protection from
the dangers of the incoming season. Examples of such responses included:

*"Inner journeying and meditation retreat, in the cold,
grey midsummer weather. It is a time of rest immediately
following the first harvest. Upon our return, we sow our*

*second crop for the year, and then begin preparations for
the impending fire season (pruning deadwood from
drought-dormant shrubs and trees, cutting back dry
grasses, etc.)"*

*"I celebrate the sun at its height and the energies of joy
and manifestation; I also often ask for protection from
drought and hurricanes and flooding associated with this
time of year."*

*"Season of Light (Summer Solstice, end of December)
Full Moon, time to seek shelter, noon is too hot to be outside, a good time to plan, to preserve things from the heat,
to mulch and seek continuity, to fast (we eat less when it's
too hot), of breathing in and going inside. A time to fast
and reflect."*

Lughnasadh Traditions wildcrafted from the local environment:

As the first of the traditional harvest festivals, Lughnasadh typically
focuses on the grain harvest. While harvest may still be the theme in other
parts of the world, the nature of the harvest will often vary, for example:

*"Lughnasadh is celebrated when fireweed blooms and the
blueberry harvest begins. At Lughnasadh we have a
special community garden party."*

*"Lughnasad, around August 1. This is the first of the
year's major harvest festivals, as the tomato harvest is at
its peak at this time and many other vegetables and fruits
have been or are being harvested. It is also the time when
I need to prepare space to accept seeds for autumn greens
and roots when the weather is right; even though summer
is still near its peak and there are several more weeks of it
left, autumn is close enough to shift into making preparations for it. My celebration focuses on gratitude for the
harvest already received and on the work to manifest
harvests for the remainder of the gardening season. It is
also time to remind myself that even as summer ages and
winter comes into sight, spring will come again. After the
ritual, I gather the day's harvest."*

In many of the warmer, wet-dry climes, the essential nature of this
holiday changes, since the natural world may be between harvests, in a lean
time, or even in a dying time, rather than a time of harvest bounty. Examples
of such responses included the following:

"The theme of this season is the ageing of the year as the Earth Mother becomes the Crone and the warrior Sun King Lugh is soon to be felled. At this season we are faced with divergent meanings, depending on which cultural tradition we look at. In the European grain cycle of wheat and barley, it is the beginning of harvest, and the first loaves of bread are offered to the Great Mother. In the Māori cycle of the kūmara, [the sweet potato] is not yet harvested; in fact - far from being a time of plenty - it is te waru patote, the lean month, when the staple crop is at its scarcest."

"First Fires. Our most solemn observance of the year, in which we meditate upon the time of death, dearth, and fire that is before us. Our rituals at this time are more mundane than symbolic. We refresh and restock all emergency supplies, pre-pack our bug-out bags for the fire season, review all emergency preparedness procedures, and set out water and food for the wildlife, to help comfort them through the dying time. The timing of this festival coincides with the first day of really hot weather — after the summer fogs fade — which may be before or after August 1. With luck, we get all this done before the wildfires actually arrive."

"Lughnasadh — small private ritual or meditation, indoors, in the air conditioning and away from mosquitoes and ticks and the various deadly diseases they carry around here."

Autumnal Equinox Traditions wildcrafted from the local environment:

The Autumnal Equinox, which is traditionally the time of the fruit harvest in Europe, may celebrate an alternate-crop harvest in other climes, such as in New Zealand:

"The Autumn Equinox represents a time of reflection and contemplation of how the balance of light and dark tips at equinox and, as we now enter the dying time of the year, the mysteries of life and death. This is when we make the transition from outer to inner, from above to below. At harvest, European and Māori symbolism is similar. The rua, or underground kūmara pit, is a symbol that parallels the European imagery of the return of the seed to the earth. The stories of Persephone, Pani, and the Mabon all follow this theme."

> *"Autumn equinox - This was when the kūmara was har-*
> *vested in NZ. We celebrate harvest and abundance."*

It may also be a time of planting in some regions, as the warm/dry season yields to the cooler, wet season, as in Brazil:

> *"Araymã ("Old Year" - Fall Equinox, end of March)*
> *Waning/Last Quarter Moon, time to prepare, to care for*
> *the health of the house, if a nose or roof is dripping, end*
> *of the dry and hot season and start of the rainy and cold*
> *one, also a time of activity, this time to plant seed and*
> *sapling on the ground, waiting for the rains to come, of*
> *breathing out and going outside. We plant the corn at this*
> *time, so it can be ready for the St. John festivities in June.*
> *Another time to feast!"*

In yet other places, the Autumnal Equinox is a time of death and dearth, reserved for reverent communion with ancestors, as described by this Druid in California:

> *"At this time of year, when wildfires and smoke blanket*
> *our landscape, the animals are dying of thirst and hunger,*
> *and all native plants are drought dormant, we observe our*
> *equivalent to the traditional 'Samhain'. As a dinner-time*
> *ritual, the family lists the names of all our beloved dead*
> *on the dining room blackboard, toasts their memory, and*
> *tells stories about their lives, recalling all that we have*
> *learned and gained from the roles they once played in our*
> *lives."*

Samhain Traditions wildcrafted from the local environment:

While some Druids connect with ancestors of blood, place, and spirit earlier in the year, most do so as part of their Samhain celebrations. In wild-crafted traditions, this often focuses more clearly on ancestors of place, for example:

> *"We invite the Ancestors to our Circle. We welcome the*
> *spirits of those who migrated from the Savannah, and all*
> *the subsequent migrations undertaken that brought us to*
> *be living in this blessed land of Aotearoa."*

> *"This is a festival of the ancestors. Remembering our*
> *loved ones who have passed. 25 April is a national*
> *holiday in New Zealand, ANZAC day. It remembers the*
> *war dead."*

For Druids in regions where growing seasons are longer, this is often the time of the final harvest, a time for thanksgiving, and harvest celebrations, as several Druids described:

"First Rain (usually around Nov 1, but with climate change, the date has been moving later and later, each year): We stop everything to go outside and dance and sing to welcome the first measureable rains of the year — a joyous moment of rebirth, as the danger of fire season is finally over. Then, we quickly harvest our final crops for the year (squash, beans, and corn, firethorn berries and acorns), before the rain has a chance to spread mold. We hold our Thanksgiving Feast at this time, celebrating not only the bounty harvested from our family's farm, but also the safe harbor the rain brings to all those who survived the year's wildfires. As a dinner-time ritual on this day, we list on the dining room blackboard all the tangible results that we have harvested from our efforts and activities throughout the year: crops harvested, achievements at work (or school), new skills mastered, crafts projects completed, etc."

"Samhain: end of April (always held in the evening and inside). In the Māori calendar, Haratua (Samhain) is the time when crops are stored in pits, labours are over and when the emphasis now shifts into the bush, the domain of Tane, as a food source. The kiore (rat) is traditionally important at this time as it grows fat in the late autumn and winter when feed is plentiful."

"This is near the end of the gardening year, for the first autumn frost generally occurs within two weeks either side of this date, and winter resident birds like juncos and white-throated sparrows have arrived. I meditate on the harvest, not just the garden harvest but [the symbolic harvest of] what I have learned and accomplished during the past year. I spend the time between this date and the winter solstice calculating garden yields, writing down my accomplishments for the past year, and beginning to consider what I want to accomplish in the following year."

Additional Druid Celebrations

In addition to these variations on the eight festivals of the Wheel of the Year, a few dozen Druids also mentioned regularly celebrating lunar cycles, such as the new moons or full moons of the year. Some also celebrated holidays of personal significance, or of importance within other religious or cultural communities to which they happened to belong. Examples of such responses included the following:

> "We further observe a lunar cycle of celebrations on the sixth night of the new moon. These are monthly celebrations named after the months of the Coligny Calendar, each of which has a designated Gaulish deity, and many of which have designated practices, e.g., the (re)blessing of border stones under the auspices of Sucellos at Rivros in January, the blessing of homes under the auspices of Brigando (=Brigid) at Anagantios in February, the (re)blessing of travel amulets under the auspices of Nehelennia at Simivisonnios in June."

> "I also celebrate the full moon, new moon and the start of each month with a short meditation, prayer and intention."

> "Family Day, celebrating the adoption of our son, with ritual re-tellings of the story of his discovery and adoption — a kind of future-generations celebration, to balance out the past-generations' focus of Ancestors Day."

> "Hen Galan (old New year), [Jan 13th,] with the making of a Calennig, a talisman for good fortune made with an apple, cloves and greenery. This is also the final outing for our Mari Lwyd, skeletal horse Goddess."

> "Added are Burns Night in January, and Hogmanay, the anniversary of [the] Glencoe massacre in February, and the anniversary [of the] Culloden battle in April."

> "Alfarblot - sacrifice of turkey to the land spirits, harvest of the Kindred garden, followed by giant feast/BBQ with friends the next day."

> "Easter, the most important Christian festival."

Universal Themes in Druid Festivals & Celebrations

Despite the many ways in which Druid seasonal celebrations vary around the world, there is still a common thematic core that unifies Druidry's Wheels of the Year: the celebration of physical and spiritual gifts bestowed by the living Earth, at the moments when Nature first heralds their arrival. These gifts may arrive at different times in different regions, and the sequence and frequency of these gifts may also vary, but the nature of the gifts, and the reverence for their perceived sources is shared.

Druids celebrate moments in which hope is rekindled. That may be the moment when the waning sunlight of autumn changes to waxing light at midwinter. It may be the time of the first thaw, or the first flower pushing up in spring. It may be the time of first rain after a drought, or the return of life-giving monsoon rains. Whatever form the metaphor of hope takes in the natural world, Druids perceive it as a sign to be inspired, to reawaken to new possibilities, and to work to cultivate their inner spark of light.

Druids celebrate times of planting, be it of crops in the field or projects of the hands and heart. They bless their seeds, and tools, and soils (both the physical and metaphorical). They prune and clear away the dead-wood, plant their seeds, and cultivate their projects and plantings, to bring their harvests home.

Druids celebrate moments when the Earth offers up an abundance of unbidden blessings. This typically occurs when a perfect combination of sunlight, moisture, and warmth causes the world to explode in glorious, flowering, fertility. At such times, the presence of beneficient nature deities and spirits of place become palpably real for Druids, and indeed, the entire world of faerie seems to open its doors to friendly visitors.

Druids celebrate a multitude of harvests: vegetables, fruits, and grains from the garden, and fruits of creative, personal projects. They share the bounty of their harvests with acts of charity to their wider communities, of both of human, and other-than-human kinds.

Druids reverently observe the moments when the living Earth is dying, or falling dormant for a season. This may happen at the first hard frost, or at the start of a wildfire season. At such times, Druids honor those who have lived, and died, and gone before, for their roles in connecting the past with the future, for the lasting fruits of their labors in life, and for the wisdom they may yet have to convey.

Druids observe and respond to the moments when Nature dictates a time of rest and retreat, withdrawing from the outer world, for a fallow time of reflection and rejuvenation.

The specific moments of celebration are generally based upon careful observations of the natural world, and a process of forging deep, personal relationships with nature. Rather than celebrating a symbolic cycle of theoretical seasons, the majority of world Druids connect with their local, natural environments first, and wildcraft their celebrations, adapting them to fit the realities of their local, physical and cultural environments.

CHAPTER 7 NOTES & REFERENCES

1 Theoretical discussions and descriptions of the "traditional" Druid Wheel of the Year can be found in:

Billington, Penny. (2011). *The Path of Druidry: Walking the Ancient Green Way.* Woodbury, MN: Llewellyn Publications. pg. 81-86

Greer, John Michael. (2006). *The Druidry Handbook: Spiritual Practice Rooted in the Living Earth.* San Francisco, CA: Red Wheel/Weiser LLC. pg. 74-83

Harvey, Graham. (2001). *Contemporary Paganism (2nd Ed.).* New York, NY: New York University Press. pg. 1-14

2 Percent of world Druids celebrating:

Winter Solstice:	68%
Imbolc:	56%
Vernal Equinox:	59%
Beltane:	57%
Summer Solstice:	61%
Lughnasadh:	54%
Autumnal Equinox:	58%
Samhain:	62%

3 See *A Preference for Solitude,* in *Chapter 3,* on pg. 31

4 See *Social Contexts for Druid Rituals & Celebrations,* in *Chapter 6,* on pg. 178

5 The *ADF Core Order of Ritual* can be found at: https://www.adf.org/rituals/explanations/core-order.html

6 Intergroup Variations in Detailed Seasonal/Nature Observations:
Oceania: much more likely   (58% vs. 32%) p=0.00
Wet/Dry Climates: much more likely (59% vs. 32%) p=0.01

7 Intergroup Variations in Likelihood of Celebrating All 8 Festivals:
OBOD members: more likely
                              (53% vs. 47%) p=0.01
Druids focused on Nature Connection: more likely
                              (55% vs. 47%) p=0.00
Druids focused on Detailed Nature Observation: much more likely
                              (60% vs. 47%) p=0.00
Druids focused on Wildcrafting: much more likely
                              (62% vs. 47%) p=0.00

8 See *Chapter 4,* page 104.

CHAPTER 8:
DRUIDRY'S SPIRITUAL COMMON CORE

This journey of exploration, immersed in the sea of stories and lived experiences of the many, diverse Druids of the world, is now at its end. It began with a series of perennial questions, repeatedly asked by Druids the world over, but never definitively answered, until now:

- What do modern-day Druids believe?
- What are their religious and spiritual practices?
- How do their beliefs and practices vary over time, and over distance?
- What, if anything, do the Druids of the world hold in common?

In the past, responses to these questions have of necessity taken the form of educated guesses based on limited data, often biased by ease-of-contact, and Druidry group affiliation. The responses may have been well intentioned, and based on goodly consideration of the content of an assortment of how-to books and curriculum materials, but they could not speak to the day-to-day realities, religious beliefs and manifest spiritual practices of the world population of practicing Druids.

The *World Druidry Survey* was the first, large-scale global effort to collect, interpret, and learn from the stories of all the practicing Druids of the world. The questionnaire included 189 items, organized into 42 sets of questions, including 18 open-ended/essay questions, probing into the details of: Druids' physical, social, and cultural environments; their social and cultural identities; their theological beliefs, ritual practices, and celebrated holidays; and the factors which had influenced their development as Druids. It was offered in multiple formats, and in multiple languages, to facilitate global participation. The resulting data set was highly representative of the world population of

Druids, along lines of age, gender, ethnic identity, level of experience with Druidry, and Druidry group membership, if any. It included responses from practicing Druids in 34 nations, on six continents. Completed surveys were returned by 725 individuals, representing 147 Druidry groups from all over the world, as well as 131 unaffiliated, solitary practitioners. The survey responses included both vast quantities of numeric data and thousands of pages of rich, narrative data, allowing for the use of robust, mixed-methods analysis tools to paint a vivid picture of the modern religious tradition that is World Druidry.

While all conclusions drawn from this data set are strongly supported by the data, it is important to bear in mind that any universal or near-universal themes which emerged are statistical norms for the group, on average. They are not necessarily accurate descriptors of any one particular Druid, or local sub-group of Druids. Nor should they be taken as such. This study has revealed a spiritual common core for World Druidry, but it has also revealed intergroup variations which should be neither overlooked nor discounted. I will therefore begin this final chapter with a summary of the more prominent variations to be found in World Druidry.

Druidry Variations due to Druid Group Membership

The public websites, books, and curriculum materials produced by some of the larger, international Druid groups present significantly different approaches to Druidry. These materials have, to some extent, influenced the developing spiritual practices of between 57% and 88% of each group's members, depending upon the group. However, 25% of world Druids belong to multiple groups, making it unclear which curriculum, if any, takes precedence within their personal practices. Also, nearly all world Druids reported being much more strongly influenced by a variety of other factors than they were by the curriculum materials from the Druid group(s) to which they belonged. As a result, the impacts of Druid group membership on the Druidry practices of any individual Druid would likely be limited. Indeed, survey results show that there are more similarities than differences in the ways that most Druids actually practice their Druidry. The most pronounced variations in Druidry practice were seen among members of ADF, the AODA, and the OBOD. Only minor variations were evident in the responses from members of the BDO and TDN, and were primarily related to their focus on Druidry in Britain.

Ár nDraíocht Féin (ADF)

Consistent with ADF's official position as being a *"Pagan church based on ancient Indo-European traditions,"* ADF members do, on average, place more emphasis on prayer and formal ritual interactions with deities, and with ancestors of blood and spirit (though not with ancestors of place). They also much more frequently identify as soft polytheists, as opposed to other theological systems of belief. During their rituals, whether in solitary practice or as part of a group, ADF members are more likely than other Druids to make use of an elaborate altar, to make offerings to deities, to practice divination, and to engage in magical workings. Their rituals are much less likely to involve circle casting, the four elements, or formal declarations of peace.

In terms of ongoing spiritual development, ADF members are more likely than other Druids to follow a formal program of study pertaining to one or more ancient, Indo-European religious traditions. As members of a Pagan church, they are also more likely to train for celebrancy, and formal spiritual leadership roles such as writing liturgy, and organizing public group rituals.

In daily life, ADF members place less emphasis on nature observation, nature connection, and gardening. They also place less emphasis on local myths and legends, focusing instead on ancient Indo-European traditions.

Ancient Order of Druids in America (AODA)

Members of the AODA tend to place more emphasis than other Druids on the study and practice of elements of esotericism, especially those of the Hermetic Tradition. As a result, the spiritual development of AODA members tends to rely more heavily on the study of books philosophically aligned with Druidry, while not being written about Druidry, per se. AODA members are more likely than others to study works of esotericism, as well as non-fiction works of science, ecology, and ecological philosophy.

In ritual, members of the AODA place more emphasis than other Druids on the two powers "Spirit Above" and "Spirit Below." However, this is not in lieu of the four elements, but in addition to them, as part of a complex energetic ritual called the *Sphere of Protection*. AODA rituals tend to be solitary, and place much less emphasis on music, poetry, storytelling, or other performing arts. They are also much less likely to work with the three realms.

Finally, members of the AODA are somewhat more likely than members of other Druid groups to engage in spiritual wildcrafting, adapting their rituals and seasonal celebrations to the land, sea, and skyscapes in which they live.

Order of Bards, Ovates, and Druids (OBOD)

Members of the OBOD are much more likely than other Druids to rely exclusively on the curriculum materials provided by their Order for their spiritual development. Other sources of inspiration include studies of local myths and legends, and works of art, music, poetry, and fiction.

In ritual, OBOD members are somewhat more likely to emphasize group rituals, casting circles, calling the four elements, declaring peace, using ceremonial props and tools, and performing music. They are also more likely to honor ancestors of place in their rituals, and to practice visualizations, shapeshifting, and journeying through inner landscapes.

In daily life, OBOD members are more likely than others to engage in environmental activism work.

British Druid Order (BDO)

Members of the BDO are much more likely than members of other Druid groups to use henges, labyrinths, or other ceremonial structures in their ritual practice, and to seek inspiration for their practice in localized myths and legends. They are also much more likely to perform their rituals in groups, in public, in the "eye of the sun." Aside from these minor variations, the beliefs and practices of BDO members are more likely to align with the norms of World Druidry.

The Druid Network

TDN Druids are also more likely to use formal ritual structures such as henges and labyrinths, and to seek inspiration from studying local myths and legends. They are also more likely to identify as animists, and to honor ancestors-of-place in their practice.

Other Possible Druidry Variations

Not all Druidry groups represented in the World Druidry Survey had a sufficient number of respondents to allow for a valid statistical analysis of intergroup variations. Only the five, above-mentioned international groups had the necessary numbers. However, there were suggestions in the data that other intergroup variations might exist. For example, members of a few of the smaller, more localized groups of Druids mentioned historical authenticity as an important part of their local group practice. A few others indicated that within their tradition, Druidry could not be practiced outside the context of a Druidic community. However, historical authenticity and community practice are not significant global themes. While these practices and perspectives are clearly important to a few individuals, and might be indicative of local group norms, it is impossible to either confirm or deny whether these assertions hold true for all, or even most, members of those smaller, local Druid groups.

Druidry Variations due to Geographical Location

Contemporary Druidry was born in Britain, in lands that once were the home of a variety of ancient Celtic cultures. Since then, the religious tradition has spread throughout the world, growing and changing while taking root in other physical and cultural environments. Survey data have shown that both the cultural context and the physical environment in which Druidry is practiced have profound effects on the nature of Druidry practice. In some places this reinforced the British traditions, and in other places it led those same traditions to be reinterpreted, revised, or completely reinvented.

The British Isles and Ireland

Most Druidry curriculum materials emphasize the myths, lore, cultural traditions, landscape features, and seasonal cycles of the British Isles and Ireland. It is therefore unsurprising that Druidry curricula are more influential in the practices of Druids who live in those areas — where the lore of the landscape is also the lived reality.

Druids in Britain and Ireland also live in much closer proximity to one another, allowing for these traditions to be further reinforced via face-to-face interactions with mentors and other Druids. The density of Druids per square mile in Britain and Ireland is ten times greater than in North America, and 100 times greater than in Oceania.[1] This proximity really does make a difference. The survey data show that Druids in the British Isles and Ireland do in fact rely less upon books and internet resources, and more upon face-to-face interactions, when developing their personal paths of Druidry.

In this region, Druids are more likely to be influenced by Celtic deities, nature spirits, and ancestors-of-place, which also tend to reinforce, and to be reinforced by the local traditions and lore. They are less likely to be influenced by dreams or past-life memories.

Ritual practices in the British Isles and Ireland are more likely to em-phasize public group ritual, the use of henges, labyrinths, or other ceremonial structures, circle casting, and the use of local languages, myths and legends, both in formal Druid rituals, and through participation in local folk-festivals and holiday traditions. Druidry in Britain and Ireland is, first and foremost, a religious tradition wildcrafted from the regional land, sea, and skyscapes, which gave rise to the founding traditions of Druidry.

Continental Europe

Druids in continental European nations are not nearly as numerous, and are more widely dispersed than Druids in Britain; however, the majority of them live the northern regions of Europe, where the climates, ecologies, and weather patterns share much with those of Britain. These regions of Europe are primarily characterized by human-crafted farming and grazing lands, or temperate deciduous forests. As such, the seasonal folk-traditions of continental Europe frequently parallel those of Britain.

Druids on the continent will wildcraft their Druidry to some extent, blending local folk-customs with Druidic traditions; however, the seasonal cycles and symbols of Druidry adequately describe their lived experience of the land. Therefore, Druids of continental Europe are more likely to adhere to the forms and practices suggested in curriculum materials when crafting their personal paths of Druidry. They are also more likely to rely on input from Druidry mentors.

Being culturally distinct from the Druids of Britain, continental European Druids are less likely to be influenced by ancestors-of-blood. They are also less likely to be inspired by deities and nature spirits, and more likely to find inspiration in their dreams and past life memories.

North America

North American Druids are much more varied, both in terms of lived experience, and in terms of Druidry practice. This is in part due to the vast geographical area over which they are spread, in part due to a culture of violent, religious intolerance (in the United States), and in part due to the many diverse biomes that North American Druids inhabit.

Having a Druid population density of about one-tenth that of Britain and Ireland, North American Druids are much more likely to have a solitary practice, as face-to-face interactions with other Druids are impractical, if not impossible for many people. As a result, group ritual practices are much less common. Privacy and safety concerns are also much more prevalent in North America, which reinforces this tendency toward simpler, solitary ritual practice. There is less emphasis among the Druids of North America on circle casting, ritual garb, and the use of ceremonial structures. A greater emphasis is placed on contemplative practices, and private ritual, rather than on formal ceremony.

The biomes inhabited by North American Druids also play a significant role in shaping Druidic practices. While many in the northeastern parts of the United States, and the eastern parts of Canada do reside in temperate deciduous forests like those in Europe, their winters are much colder and longer, leading many to adjust the seasonal calendar, by varying the symbols or the dates. However, many North American Druids also live in biomes very different from those of Europe, in deserts, savannas and prairies, coniferous forests, temperate rain forests, chaparral, and tundra. In such places, the traditional Druid wheel of the year, the Druidic plant and animal lore, and the Druidic signs and symbols of nature simply do not apply. As a result, North American Druids are less likely to be influenced by curriculum materials in their practice, and more likely to seek inspiration and guidance from all manner of books and internet resources, deities, nature spirits, ancestors-of-place, local cultural and folk-traditions, and other world religions.

While seeking more broadly for locally relevant elements, symbols, and patterns to apply in their personal Druidry practice, North American Druids are also much *more* likely than other Druids (even those in Britain and Ireland) to study Celtic cultural traditions and lore. From these studies, some North American Druids draw the precise forms of their Druidry. Others focus in on the philosophical principles represented in the Celtic traditions — which allowed traditional Druidry practices to be wildcrafted from the landscapes of the British Isles and Ireland. They then apply those philosophical principles to the task of wildcrafting their Druidry from the landscapes of North America. For example, a Druid might consider the cyclical power of the four elements (air, fire, water, and earth), to determine which ones best correspond with which of their local seasons. A North American Druid might then design a new seasonal ritual, using the local correspondences as their ritual framework, rather than the correspondences used in Britain. In doing so, North American Druids are more likely to rely on input and guidance from Druidry mentors, as opposed to specific curriculum content.

North American Druids are also more likely to be inspired by dreams, past-life memories, and ancestors-of-blood.

Oceania

The average population density of Druids in Oceania is one-tenth that of North America. However, residents of Australia and New Zealand tend to cluster in smaller, more densely populated regions of their national landscapes. This means that, while isolated Druids in Oceania may be much more isolated, there are also clusters of Druids, allowing for group practice. As a result, Druids in Oceania are, on average, more likely to be influenced by face-to-face interactions with mentors and Druids, and less so by internet resources.

The biomes inhabited by the Druids of Oceania are many and varied, including tropical rain forests, tropical deciduous forests, temperate mixed forests, deserts, savannahs, and scrubland. Unlike North America, they have no temperate deciduous forests of the type found in Europe. As a result, Druids in Oceania are more likely to spend time making detailed observations of their local landscapes, and focusing on nature connection. They are also more likely to wildcraft their Druidry, learning about local landscapes from indigenous peoples, and incorporating local cultural and linguistic traditions which might help them forge deeper connections with the local land. Druids in Oceania are also more likely to honor ancestors-of-place in their practice, in recognition of the source of that borrowed wisdom. While there are still Druids in Oceania who keep to traditional, Celtic Druidic practices, most Druids in this region are less likely to study Celtic cultural traditions and lore, and less likely to study other world religions.

As with North American Druids, Druids in Oceania are more likely to find inspiration in dreams, past-life memories, and ancestors-of-blood.

Global Ecologies Driven by Wet/Dry Seasonal Variations

The practice of spiritual wildcrafting in Druidry is even more clearly demonstrated when one considers, as a group, all Druids the world around who happen to live in biomes driven by wet/dry seasonal cycles, rather than the light/dark and hot/cold cycles typical of northern Europe. In this grouping, we find the Druids of the North American arid Southwest, the Mediterranean West Coast, the subtropical South, and the temperate rain-forested Pacific Northwest. This group also includes Druids of New Zealand and Australia, as well as Druids from the Brazilian rainforest, the African savannah, the Caribbean Isles, and the monsoon-driven climate of the Indian subcontinent.

When Druids from all of these non-traditional Druid landscapes are considered together, we saw even more emphasis on detailed observations of local landscapes and seasonal markers, more focus on nature connection in practice, and more focus on spiritual wildcrafting of rituals, in order to fully understand and celebrate the natural cycles of life, death, and rebirth found in the flora and fauna of the local landscapes.

How Druidry Traditions Have Evolved Over Time

In the decades since Druidry first began to rapidly gain popularity as a "new religious movement," in the early 1990s, the core beliefs and ritual practices of contemporary world Druids have remained relatively constant. Only three intergenerational changes were evident in the survey data — changes made apparent by variations due to the timing of when respondents first identified as Druids, but not related in any way to the age of the Druids in question. These intergenerational changes do not necessarily represent a change in the values of Druids with long years of experience with Druidry in Britain, but more likely represent a shift in the proportion of Druids, due to an increase in the total number of extant Druids, including those newer to Druidry, who are learning and practicing in different geographical and cultural contexts.

The first of the intergenerational differences was a gradual lessening of emphasis on blood ancestry, and Celtic cultural heritage in Druidry. The second was a lessening emphasis on elaborate group rituals performed at public monuments such as henges, labyrinths, or other ceremonial structures local to the British Isles and Ireland. Finally, there has been an increase in the use of the internet as a resource for novices wishing to learn the fundamentals of Druidry, and as a tool for practitioners wishing to build and maintain relationships with other Druids, when face-to-face interactions are impossible. All of these changes are consistent with what would be expected of a globalizing religious tradition taking root in diverse countries and cultures.

Druidry's Spiritual Common Core, circa 2020 c.e.

In our journey through the results of the World Druidry Survey, we have seen that Druidry can indeed be defined as a religious tradition, in the manner described by J.D. Bettis[2]. While Druidry is religious in nature, it is neither the theological beliefs, nor the symbols and surface features of ritual which form the common core. It is the deeper, shared spiritual meta-practices of Druidry which form the "cultural tradition that provides the fundamental means of individual and social identification." Druidry's common core is manifest in the ways that Druids connect with and build relationships with nature. It is manifest in the relationships they forge with the divine, with ancestors, and with other spiritual beings. It is manifest in the lifestyle habit of continually seeking and integrating new wisdom, from many diverse sources and spiritual traditions. And it is manifest in the ways that Druids interact with themselves, and with other human beings, in the process. All of these manifestations are united under the theme of honorable relationship.

Druids overwhelmingly find their spiritual inspiration from a deeply felt and tangibly experienced connection with the natural world. It is not merely inspired by an idealized dream of the natural world, adored from a distance. Druidry is, in practice, deeply influenced by the concrete details of the specific physical and cultural environments in which a Druid resides. Druidry is about spiritual journeys, but it is equally about muddy clothing, midge bites, and hands in the dirt, as stewards of the land. Druidry is based upon a real, tangible, and ever-deepening relationship with the land, sea, and skyscapes of the place in which a Druid lives. As with any truly honorable relationship, this means respecting the other-than-human beings of a region, and striving to form a truly reciprocal relationship with them — giving back as much as we receive. This principle is manifest in the nearly universal devotional practice of environmental stewardship work among Druids.[3] This type of sacred activity in everyday life included works as varied as learning to interpret the language of animals, planting trees, organic farming, ecosystem restoration projects, wildland fire management, installing solar and wind-power systems, and changing one's personal lifestyle habits to minimize one's carbon footprint, or other negative environmental impacts.

The seasonal festivals celebrated by Druids also derive from their relationships with the land.[4] All over the world, Druids celebrate a cycle of seasonal celebrations, acknowledging the physical and spiritual gifts bestowed by the living Earth, with each passing season. The timing and themes of each celebration may vary with the climate and ecology of the local landscape, but the themes of the celebrations are universal. Druids celebrate cycles of light, moisture, warmth, and fertility. They celebrate hope, and the germination of seeds, both physical and metaphorical. They celebrate the delights of vigorous growing seasons, flowers, fruits, and harvests. They acknowledge quiet times of decline and death, as symbols of the need for spiritual rest, a time to withdraw and gather inner strength, to fuel a future season of growth. Druids acknowledge and honor these cycles both as those of the natural world in which they reside, and as those of the spiritual world, which resides within.

After connection with the natural world, the most important influence and source of inspiration for a Druid is his or her personal relationship with the divine. (Only for ADF Druids is this order reversed.) Druid relationships with the divine are neither based upon remote adoration and obedience to the divine, nor upon supplication in exchange for divine gifts. Instead, Druids tend to engage in an ongoing process of respectful, two-way communication, with regular expressions of gratitude, and an earnest effort at reciprocation. Druids also role-model off of divine example, either as set forth in myths and legends, or as instructed via personal conversations with the divine, or by way of metaphors observed in Nature, and interpreted though meditation.

Druidry does not have rules, or even norms, pertaining to a Druid's beliefs about the nature of deity. In fact, the range of theological beliefs represented within the world Druid population is astonishingly large.[5] However, there is a common core to Druidry when one considers the ways in which Druids interact with whichever deities, or spiritual beings they revere. Whether an individual Druid believes that Nature *is* deity, or that elements of nature are enspirited by deities, or whether nature is the artistic creation of a more distant, creator-deity, there is still a perceived obligation to build and maintain honorable, respectful, and reciprocal relationships with those divine beings.[6] The goal is to become ever wiser, more honorable, and more skillful in life, through active collaboration with those beings, for the benefit of all living beings — of both human and other-than-human kind.

The Druidic religious tradition, or *"style of life"* is also defined by an ongoing process of seeking wisdom, wherever it may be found, unconstrained by the content of purely "Druidic" curricula, writings, and lore. Druids read in topics as diverse as history and archaeology, world myths and legends, earth sciences and life sciences, ecological philosophy, psychology, and other world religions and cultural traditions — all with an eye toward uncovering new ideas to explore, experiences to try, and seed topics for meditation. They read to learn about different forms of ritual, or different ways of perceiving and interacting with nature, nature spirits and deities, and even about their own cultural biases, traditions, and norms.[7] As part of this process of seeking wisdom, many Druids also honor and acknowledge ancestors of blood, spirit, or place, for their role in helping Druids to become who they are, and providing a wisdom heritage to help light their way forward.[8]

Devotional practices universal among Druids[9] work to support this search for wisdom, or to facilitate the process of building and maintaining honorable relationships with denizens of the natural and spiritual worlds. The first category of universal Druidic devotional practices comprise methods for developing skill at focusing and directing one's attention and energy, either cognitively, or emotionally, or spiritually. This may include a meditation or visualization practice, or the practice of one or more extra-sensory methods of seeking wisdom, such as divination, seership, journeying or shapeshifting. It might also include using a nature-based spiritual and energetic framework, like the four elements or the three realms, to structure formal and informal rituals. The second category of universal Druidic devotional practices comprise methods of forming and maintaining relationships. These include maintaining a regular practice of prayer, conversation, or other relationship-building activity with spirits of place, nature spirits, or deities, and regularly engaging in nature connection and environmental stewardship work, to build one's relationship with the land.

In the final analysis, Druidry is a religious tradition characterized by an ongoing process of building honorable relationships. Druids build honorable relationships within themselves, by acknowledging who they truly are, and who they might become, through effort. The practice of Druidry is in large part a practice of endless becoming, developing the skills and acquiring the wisdom needed to live in honorable relationship with all others. The goal is to honor, respect, and nurture all other living beings — Druids, humans of other spiritual paths, deities, spirits of nature and place, the flora and fauna that people our lands, the rich living soils, the mountains and streams — all things engaged in Nature's endless cycles of birth, growth, transformation, decline, death, repose, and rebirth. So, what does it mean to be a Druid, circa 2020 c.e.? I leave the answer to that, as is proper, to the words of three Druids:

> *"Love for the land and the nature in which you live, that deep connection to the Earth, that is Druidry."*

> *"The gods and spirits call who they will. Druidry as a set of practices and devotions is open to any and all."*

> *"Ultimately, my Druidry is about a connection to the land, and being a steward of that land, and finding allies in all the spirits which inhabit it."*

CHAPTER 8 NOTES & REFERENCES

1 Druid density calculations, based on Druid population estimates, as calculated in *Appendix B*, divided by the geographical area (in square miles) of the countries included in the region:

British Isles & Ireland:
(4,528 Druids) / (128,555 sq. mi.) = 0.04 Druids per sq. mi.

North America:
(53,564 Druids) / (7,651,842 sq. mi.) = 0.007 Druids per sq. mi.

Oceania:
(1,207 Druids) / (3,073,407 sq. mi.) = 0.0004 Druids per sq. mi.

2 See quote from J.D. Bettis, page 2.

3 To revisit these points, see *Chapter 6*, pages 179-181.

4 To revisit these points, see *Chapter 7*, pages 242-243.

5 To revisit these points, see *Chapter 5*, pages 114-136.

6 To revisit these points, see *Chapter 5*, pages 149-157.

7 To revisit these points, see *Chapter 4*, pages 80-83.

8 To revisit these points, see *Chapter 5*, pages 137-141.

9 To revisit these points, see *Chapter 6*, pages 186-187.

AFTERWORD

The *World Druidry Survey Project* has been an arduous, three-year journey for me. When I first set out to ask the Druids of the world about their spiritual beliefs and practices, I expected no more than perhaps 60 responses, and fervently hoped that I might get as many as 100 responses to such a lengthy questionnaire. If I was really lucky, I might receive 10-12 responses from each of a few different countries, to allow for at least some analysis of international variations. I was fairly certain I would gather sufficient data to write the proposed Mt. Haemus paper, but I never dreamed it would amount to more than a little, academic side-project. Much to my surprise and delight, over 1000 people either requested links to the Survey-Monkey form, or downloaded copies of a PDF questionnaire. A total of 725 people completed it, and they wrote reams of material, leading to an incredibly rich, diverse, and detailed set of stories, which it has been my privilege and delight to explore. My little side-project had mushroomed into a potentially major work of scholarship. It was daunting; but once I calculated the number of hours the Druids of the world had devoted to their responses, I realized I owed it to them to conduct a thorough analysis of the entire data-set, and to present the full findings of that analysis, using as many of their own words as possible.

While I enjoyed the privilege of being able to read all the stories first, this project has never been about me, or my personal opinions about Druidry. I am but a messenger for the Druids of the world, bringing to light for the first time in history a complete picture how contemporary World Druidry has grown and evolved as it spread and took root in so many countries and cultures of the world. This book is about the Druids of the world, from their perspective, and in their own words.

As I reflect upon both the universal themes that define World Druidry as a coherent religious tradition, and the diverse practices that are both widely practiced and widely accepted by those Druids who do not practice them —

I find myself in awe of the inclusiveness of this religious tradition, its wonderous diversity, and its willingness to learn from all cultures and religious traditions, while still maintaining a distinct common core. I feel humbled, and honored to count myself as one among this group of inspiring people.

Many of the findings of the *World Druidry Survey* were surprising to me, given the common assertions that are made about the nature of contemporary Druidry (e.g. largely male, white robed, and performing public rituals at Stonehenge). I realize now that, lacking the resource of a large, and truly representative data-set, those common assertions must have been based upon interviews and interactions with Druids who were contacted through public groups and gatherings. The Druids who made those assertions may have been entirely accurate in their representations of the beliefs and practices of the subset of Druids they happen to have met at those gatherings. However, given the high proportion of practicing Druids who have never attended a public gathering, they could not help but miss the mark. Their reports, while valid, represent the beliefs and practices of only a small minority of the world's Druids — those who feel comfortable practicing and celebrating their Druidry in the eye of the Sun.

I will never again underestimate the need for all the members of a new religious movement to tell their stories to a sympathetic audience. Nor will I underestimate their desire to understand themselves, and the others of their religious tradition.

Given the studious nature of most Druids, it should have come as no surprise to me that the survey instrument, itself, was taken as an opportunity for self-reflection and learning. However, it was a complete surprise to me when fifteen participants wrote to thank me for the incentive they felt was created by the survey, for them to reflect upon their Druidry paths and progress. Their email messages included the following:

> *"Thank you for this rare opportunity to reflect upon my own spiritual journey. It was a deep dive indeed — at times personally unsettling — for it has been filled for as long as I can remember with mysteries and truths I cannot explain even to myself. Though I have attempted in the survey to answer the questions about the environments, and people, and resources that may have influenced my own spiritual journey, I feel that many of my long responses are still inadequate. (It is our language that is limiting, perhaps.)"*

> *"Taking this survey made me feel incredibly validated — that so many of my experiences were answers on a survey made me feel like they are valid experiences. Thank you for that. Thank you for your work."*

"Larisa, this questionnaire is huge! I think I never looked so much in detail and in depth upon what I did and what influenced me, etc., in the past decades. Thank you for giving me that opportunity! I think it will take me a bit of time to complete it, but my answer will come."

"[The survey] has sparked me on to doing some more with the Druidry, as your questions provoke options in me that I had not seen. Thanks for the asking. I am going to now create an excel spreadsheet to observe the seasonal changes that I am noticing as I progress through the wheel of the year."

"I'm in the process of taking the survey myself, which as someone else mentioned on the Forum, is an occasion for a thoughtful assessment of my Druid path and thus a valuable experience for me. I'll be very interested in your Mt. Haemus publication once it's available."

"I have received the link [...] and am looking forward to the reflective process completing this survey will be. Thanks for all your thoughtful work that's gone into it. It's really helpful to have the PDF version to get an overview. [...] What a wonderful opportunity to reflect on my evolving journey."

"Thank you for a wonderful questionnaire which has helped me reflect more profoundly on my journey with Druidry so far and cleared my mind about my future progress. Bright blessings!"

Since it seems that the survey form itself may be of some ongoing value for self-study, outside of any continuing research, I have decided to make the survey form freely available to any who might wish to use it as a learning tool. The English survey form is reproduced in *Appendix A*, in a condensed format, but the full-sized, complete PDF form, in all six languages, is now available for free download on the website: https://www.worlddruidry.com.

I invite any other scholars with an interest in this field of enquiry to continue the research that I have begun. This might involve using the survey instrument to supplement the current data-set by gathering additional data from areas that I was unable to reach. It might also involve expanding upon this work by continuing the scholarly exploration of World Druidry as it continues to grow and evolve as a nature-based religious tradition of the future.

APPENDIX A: THE SURVEY INSTRUMENT

Welcome to the World Druidry Survey!

About the Project

The World Druidry Survey explores the ways in which Druidry, as a globalizing path of nature spirituality, is evolving both in the traditional lands of the ancient Druids, and elsewhere, as it spreads and takes root in other countries and cultures of the world. As we, the practicing Druids of the world, learn and grow and develop our personal paths of Druidry, what do we continue to hold in common? In what ways do our practices and beliefs diversify? What, if anything, forms the spiritual, common core of contemporary World Druidry? Your experiences and perspective as a practicing Druid are important to this work. Thank you for your willingness to share your story!

About the Questionnaire

In responding to this survey, you confirm that you are over 18 years of age, that you are a practicing Druid, and that you voluntarily consent to participate in this research. The survey contains 42 questions, 30 of which are simple, short-answer format questions, and 12 of which are more open-ended, requiring a bit more thought and reflection. If you require more space for your responses than this form allows, please feel free to add pages, as needed — just be sure to note the question number for each of your responses!

Once you have completed the survey, you may scan and email your completed form (along with any additional pages or attachments) to:
      <World Druidry Survey email address>

Or, you may return it via postal mail to:

<World Druidry Survey postal address>

If you decide you would prefer to enter your responses via the SurveyMonkey web interface, email me at <World Druidry Survey email address> to request a personalized link to the web-survey form.

As you respond to the survey questions, please bear in mind: we all have beautiful memories of things we once could do, but can no longer achieve, and things we aspire to achieve, but have not as yet accomplished. In order for the results of this study to provide an accurate picture of World Druidry as it exists in the world at this moment in history, it is important that when you answer the questions, you describe only your beliefs and practices as they are currently manifested. Remember: all responses will be analyzed and reported anonymously. No one will be judging you.

May your journey into memory bless you with its richness;
May Awen flow for you, as you formulate your responses!

Yours, under the California Coast Live Oaks,
Larisa A. White, M.S.Ed., Ph.D.

A Bit About Your Physical and Cultural Environments

1. Which of the following best describes your personal connection (if any) to the traditional lands of the ancient Druids of Europe? (check one)

   ☐ Born in, raised in, and currently live in one.

   ☐ Raised in one, but currently live elsewhere.

   ☐ My family heritage derives from one, but I was raised elsewhere; I lived in one or more of them as an adult.

   ☐ My family heritage derives from one, and I have visited one or more of them, but have never lived there.

   ☐ My family heritage derives from one, but I have never lived in one, and I have never visited one.

   ☐ No genealogical ties to any traditional land of ancient Druids, but I have spent time living in one or more of them.

   ☐ No genealogical ties to any traditional land of ancient Druids, but I have visited one or more of them.

   ☐ No genealogical ties to any traditional land of ancient Druids, and have never visited.

2. Which nation or set of nations forms your personal, cultural identity? (This may be your nationality, or the nation(s) of your ancestry. In the case of adult third-culture-kids, it may also include childhood host-nations, or simply your identity as a third-culture-kid.)

   _____

3. In which nation do you currently live? _____

4. Which of the following best describes the environment in which you currently live? (Check all that apply.)

   ☐ Tropical Forest   ☐ Swamps/Wetlands

   ☐ Temperate Forest   ☐ Mountains/Highlands

   ☐ Boreal Forest   ☐ Agricultural/Cropland

   ☐ Scrubland   ☐ Agricultural/Grazing land

   ☐ Savannah/Grassland   ☐ Urban landscape

   ☐ Desert   ☐ Suburban landscape

   ☐ Tundra   ☐ Rural landscape

   ☐ Maritime/Coastal   ☐ Other (please specify):

                                 _____

5. Which of the following best describes your primary place of residence? (Check all that apply.)

☐ A home with access to a private wild space or garden.

☐ A home with access to a semi-private wild space or garden (shared or in public view).

☐ A home with access to only a public park or public garden.

☐ A home with no convenient access to any wild space or garden.

6. What is/are the most prevalent religion(s) practiced in the region where you live?

7. To what extent (if any) do privacy or safety considerations currently influence your Druidry practice(s)?

Not an Influence		Minor Influence		Major Influence
○	○	○	○	○

8. What (if anything) causes privacy or safety in your Druidry practice to be a matter of concern for you? (Please write "n/a" if this does not apply to you. Feel free to add additional pages, as needed.)

9. Which of the following best describes the people (if any) with whom you currently share your personal living space? (Check all that apply.)

☐ Adults who share my religious/spiritual beliefs and practices.

☐ Adults who are accepting and respectful of my religious/spiritual beliefs and practices, but do not share them.

☐ Adults who tolerate my religious/spiritual beliefs and practices, with some sense of forbearance or trepidation.

☐ Adults who are unaccepting and disrespectful of my religious/ spiritual beliefs and practices (or would be, if they knew).

☐ Children/adolescents of adults tolerant of Druidry.

☐ Children/adolescents of adults intolerant of Druidry.

☐ None of the above; I live alone.

10. In what ways (if any) has the presence of children or other non-Druids in your personal living space influenced the ways in which you practice your Druidry? (Please write "none" if this does not apply to you. Feel free to add additional pages, as needed.)

11. In which decade were you born? (check one)

☐ 1940 or earlier   ☐ 1941-1950
☐ 1951-1960   ☐ 1961-1970
☐ 1971-1980   ☐ 1981-1990
☐ After 1990

12. With which gender do you identify? (check one)

☐ Female   ☐ Male   ☐ Other (please specify): _____

Factors Influencing Your Personal Path of Druidry

13. To what extent (if any) has each of the following inspired you, or helped you shape and define your personal path of Druidry?

	Not an Influence		Minor Influence		Major Influence
Face-to-face interactions with Druids	○	○	○	○	○
Internet-based interactions with Druids	○	○	○	○	○
Inspiration from Nature	○	○	○	○	○
Inspiration from Deities	○	○	○	○	○
Inspiration from Spirits of Nature or Place	○	○	○	○	○
Dreams and/or past-life memories	○	○	○	○	○
Ancestral traditions of places I've lived	○	○	○	○	○
Ancestral traditions of my family	○	○	○	○	○
Teaching order curricula	○	○	○	○	○
Druidry mentors or tutors	○	○	○	○	○
Books on Druidry	○	○	○	○	○
Books philosophically aligned with Druidry	○	○	○	○	○
Websites, podcasts, or other periodicals related to Druidry	○	○	○	○	○
Other (please specify, below:	○	○	○	○	○

14. Which specific books, media, or online resources (on Druidry or on other, related topics), or teaching order curriculum materials (if any) have been most influential and inspirational to you, as you crafted your personal path of Druidry? (Please write "none" if this does not apply to you. Feel free to add additional pages, as needed.)

15. Which specific myths, legends, or traditional tales — of any world culture — (if any) have been most influential and inspirational to you, as you crafted your personal path of Druidry? (Please write "none" if this does not apply to you. Feel free to add additional pages, as needed.)

16. Please list any Druidry groups/organizations (if any) in which you are currently an active member. (Please use full names of listed groups or organizations; write "none" if this does not apply.)

17. For how long have you had an interest in Druidry? (check one)

☐ less than 1 year ☐ 1-2 years

☐ 2-5 years ☐ 5-10 years

☐ 10-20 years ☐ 20-30 years

☐ 30-40 years ☐ 40+ years

18. For how long do you consider yourself to have been a practicing Druid? (check one)

☐ less than 1 year ☐ 1-2 years

☐ 2-5 years ☐ 5-10 years

☐ 10-20 years ☐ 20-30 years

☐ 30-40 years ☐ 40+ years

19. How important are Celtic language, culture, and/or traditions to your personal path of Druidry?

Not Important		Moderately Important		Essential
○	○	○	○	○

A Bit About Your Religious Beliefs

20. Which of the following terms most accurately describe(s) your current, personal religious path, or concept of divinity? (Check all that apply.)

☐ Monotheist ☐ Humanist
☐ Polytheist ☐ Atheist
☐ Pantheist ☐ My concept of divinity
☐ Animist   is still evolving.
☐ Pagan ☐ Other (please specify):
☐ Agnostic

_____

21. If you worship or venerate any specific god(s), or spirit(s) of nature or place, please describe them, and your experience of them. Who are they? What, if anything, do they represent to you? How did you first identify or meet them? Do you experience them as real, physical presences? visions? voices? felt energies? Jungian archetypes? symbolic characters? something else entirely? Please explain. (Please write "none" if this does not apply to you. Feel free to add additional pages, as needed.)

22. Which ancestors (if any) do you venerate within your Druidry practice? Ancestors of blood? of spirit? of place? Are they ancestors, in a general sense, or specific individuals? Please describe the role that ancestors play within your practice, and the manner in which you typically interact with them. (Please write "none" if this does not apply to you. Feel free to add additional pages, as needed.)

23. Do you consider your Druidry practice to be... (Check all that apply.)

☐ Your religion ☐ A lifestyle choice
☐ A spiritual practice ☐ A family tradition
☐ A philosophy ☐ Part of your cultural heritage
☐ Other (please specify):

_____

24. What religious/spiritual tradition(s) (if any) did you follow before coming to Druidry? (Please write "none" if this does not apply to you.)

25. What other religious/spiritual tradition(s) (if any) do you currently follow, in addition to Druidry? (Please write "none" if this does not apply to you.)

26. If you currently follow other religious/spiritual tradition(s), in addition to your Druidry, in what ways (if any) do you combine your religious/spiritual traditions and practices? (Please write "none" if this does not apply to you. Feel free to add additional pages, as needed.)

A Bit About Your Approach to Ritual and Spiritual Practices

27. In the past year, approximately how frequently did you engage in Druid rituals (formal or informal, group or solitary) or spiritual practices, in each of the following types of location?

	Never	A Few Times	Monthly	Weekly	Daily
Indoors, at home or at a friend's home	○	○	○	○	○
In a borrowed or rented indoor space	○	○	○	○	○
In a private garden or wild space	○	○	○	○	○
In a semi-private garden or wild space	○	○	○	○	○
In a secluded area of a public garden or wild space	○	○	○	○	○
In full view, in a public garden or wild space	○	○	○	○	○
At a public monument	○	○	○	○	○
Other (please specify, below):	○	○	○	○	○

28. In the past year, approximately how frequently did you engage in Druid rituals (formal or informal) or spiritual practices, in each of the following types of gathering?

	Never	A Few Times	Monthly	Weekly	Daily
As a solitary Druid	○	○	○	○	○
With a group of Druids	○	○	○	○	○
With a mixed group of pagans, or other pagan-friendly folk	○	○	○	○	○
In a gathering open to observation by the general public	○	○	○	○	○
In a gathering open to participation by the general public	○	○	○	○	○
As a celebrant for another's rite	○	○	○	○	○
As an observer of another group	○	○	○	○	○
Other (please specify, below):	○	○	○	○	○

29. In the past year, approximately how frequently did your personal spiritual practices or rituals (formal or informal) involve each of the following types of activity?

	Never	A Few Times	Monthly	Weekly	Daily
Invoking or evoking air / fire / water / earth	○	○	○	○	○
Invoking or evoking land / sea / sky	○	○	○	○	○
Invoking or evoking above / below	○	○	○	○	○
Declaring Peace	○	○	○	○	○
Casting a circle	○	○	○	○	○
Prayers or conversations with deities	○	○	○	○	○
Prayers or conversations with spirits of nature or place	○	○	○	○	○
Prayers or conversations with ancestors	○	○	○	○	○
Chanting, music, or song	○	○	○	○	○
Dance, pantomime, or movement	○	○	○	○	○
Storytelling	○	○	○	○	○
Meditation	○	○	○	○	○
Divination	○	○	○	○	○
Seership	○	○	○	○	○
Shapeshifting	○	○	○	○	○
Inner journeys	○	○	○	○	○
Energy workings	○	○	○	○	○
Magical workings	○	○	○	○	○
Visualizations	○	○	○	○	○
Other (please specify, below):	○	○	○	○	○

30. In the past year, approximately how frequently did your rituals (formal or informal) or spiritual practices involve each of the following tangible objects?

	Never	A Few Times	Monthly	Weekly	Daily
A grove of trees	○	○	○	○	○
An altar or shrine	○	○	○	○	○
A henge, labyrinth, or other formal structure	○	○	○	○	○
Formal, ritual garb	○	○	○	○	○
Tangible offerings for deities, nature spirits, or ancestors	○	○	○	○	○
Magical or ceremonial props or tools	○	○	○	○	○
The creation of tangible works of artistic expression	○	○	○	○	○
Other (please specify, below):	○	○	○	○	○

31. If you are able, please share a photo of a typical ritual space/altar set-up that you used for your personal Druidry practice, during this past year. (Send as a jpg/jpeg file, attached to your emailed survey, or if mailing, please be sure to send only copies — I will not be able to return them to you.)

32. If you are able, please share a photo of the typical clothing or ritual garb that you wore for your personal Druidry practice, during this past year. (Send as a jpg/jpeg file, attached to your emailed survey, or if mailing, please be sure to send only copies — I will not be able to return them to you.)

33. In what ways (if any) has your natural or cultural environment influenced the form of your Druid rituals? (Please write "none" if this does not apply to you. Feel free to add additional pages, as needed.)

34. Please describe your local climate and seasons. What are your seasons like? How many do you have? How long do they last? What are the signs and signals in nature, which you associate with each of the local seasons? (Feel free to add additional pages, as needed.)

35. In the past year, did you celebrate a Druid "Wheel of the Year" in some form? If so, please name and describe the holidays that you celebrated. When did they occur? What did you do to celebrate them? What spiritual meanings or symbolisms (if any) did you attribute to each of your holidays? (Feel free to add additional pages, as needed.)

36. In what ways (if any) has your natural or cultural environment influenced the way in which you celebrated your Wheel of the Year? (Please write "none" if this does not apply to you. Feel free to add additional pages, as needed.)

A Bit About Your Daily Life as a Druid

37. In the past year, which of the following practical, nature-related activities (if any) were a regular part of your life as a Druid? (Check all that apply.)

    ☐ Nature awareness practices
    ☐ Hiking/rambling/walking the land
    ☐ Environmental stewardship activities (wild space clean-ups, tree planting, creating wildlife habitat, etc.)
    ☐ Gardening/growing food to benefit humans
    ☐ Changing lifestyle habits to live in harmony with nature
    ☐ Allopathic healing work
    ☐ Herbalism
    ☐ None of the above
    ☐ Other(s) (please specify): _____

38. In the past year, which of the following artistic activities (if any) were a regular part of your life as a Druid? (Check all that apply.)

    ☐ Music composition/song-writing
    ☐ Music performance
    ☐ Creative writing (poetry/fiction/myth/etc.)
    ☐ Storytelling/poetry recitations
    ☐ Acting/role-playing
    ☐ Dance/movement/pantomime
    ☐ Fine arts (painting/photography/sculpture/etc.)
    ☐ Arts & Crafts (woodworking/fiber-arts/etc.)
    ☐ Brewing or other culinary arts
    ☐ None of the above
    ☐ Other(s) (please specify): _____

39. In the past year, which of the following public education or activist activities (if any) were a regular part of your life as a Druid? (Check all that apply.)

☐ Persuasive, motivational, or informational writing (blogs, articles, etc.)

☐ Persuasive, motivational, or informational speaking

☐ Environmental activism activities (letter writing, legal actions, demonstrations, etc.)

☐ Cultural heritage activism activities (letter writing, legal actions, demonstrations, etc.)

☐ Linguistic or cultural preservation activities (Celtic)

☐ Linguistic or cultural preservation activities (indigenous to the land on which you live)

☐ Linguistic or cultural preservation activities (other cultures)

☐ Magical/ritual activities to protect or heal the land/sea/sky

☐ Magical/ritual activities to protect or heal people(s)

☐ Magical/ritual activities to influence social/ political initiatives

☐ None of the above

☐ Other(s) (please specify): _____

40. In the past year, which of the following spiritual leadership activities (if any) were a regular part of your life as a Druid? (Check all that apply.)

☐ Peacemaking work

☐ Celebrancy work

☐ Teaching courses/workshops on Druidry topics

☐ Mentoring students of Druidry

☐ Organizing Druidry groups or gatherings

☐ Writing liturgy or designing rituals

☐ Organizing or leading rituals

☐ Creating new monuments or semi-permanent sacred spaces for Druidry

☐ None of the above

☐ Other(s) (please specify): _____

41. In the past year, which of the following areas of personal study or academic research (if any) were a regular part of your life as a Druid? (Check all that apply.)

☐ Earth Sciences (geology, meteorology, hydrology, etc.)

☐ Ecology/ecosystems

☐ Botany/Plant science

☐ Zoology/Animal science

☐ Global Climate Change

☐ Astronomy

☐ Archaeology

☐ Linguistic or cultural traditions (indigenous to the land on which you live)

☐ Linguistic or cultural traditions (Celtic)

☐ Linguistic or cultural traditions (other cultures)

☐ History or sociology of Druidry/Druidism

☐ Studies in Druid philosophy and/or spirituality

☐ Comparative religious studies

☐ Study of one or more forms of Esotericism

☐ World myths and legends

☐ Ogham/Tree lore

☐ Animal lore

☐ Astrology/Star lore

☐ Herb lore

☐ None of the above

☐ Other(s) (please specify): _____

42. If there is anything else you feel is important to add or elaborate upon, regarding your personal beliefs and practices of Druidry, and how they relate to the physical and cultural environment in which you practice, please feel free to add it here, and add additional pages, as needed.

You have arrived at the end of the World Druidry Survey.
Thank you so much for sharing your story!

Please take a moment before you leave to consider:
Do you know any other practicing Druids,
who might not yet be aware that this study is ongoing?
If so, would you please tell them about this survey,
and encourage them to participate as well?

They can access the web-survey directly, or download printable survey
forms, at: <World Druidry Survey website>

Many thanks!

APPENDIX B: DRUID POPULATION ESTIMATES

Anecdotal evidence suggests that the number of people, around the world, who consider themselves to be Druids in a spiritual or religious sense has been growing steadily since the late 1980s and early 1990s, following the rebirth of the Order of Bards, Ovates, and Druids under the direction of Philip Carr-Gomm, the founding of Ár nDraíocht Féin by Isaac Bonewits, and the posthumous publication of the writings of Ross Nichols' in *The Book of Druidry.*[1] However, obtaining an accurate, current count of world Druids is not possible. In part, this is because new religious movements tend to be overlooked or miscounted by census takers, whose forms do not yet include the appropriate categories. In such cases, disparate new religions are typically lumped together in an aggregate category such as "none of the above" or "other". Moreover, modern Druids face a second problem, described by Miranda Aldhouse-Green in her book, *Caesar's Druids*[2]:

> *"Modern followers of 'new religious movements' such as Wicca, Druidry and Odinism are often — in my view unacceptably — ridiculed as espousing wacky cults that are a blend of cobbled history and 1960s' hippy culture. Surely, the only 'crime' of which modern Druids are guilty is that of using an ancient name to identify themselves. Most modern Druids are highly intelligent thinkers who are fully aware of who they are and who they are not. They do not deserve or merit scathing dismissal for their genuine belief-systems."*

Though not entirely inaccurate, her assessment of the problem turns out to be a gross understatement. Aside from fears of mere "scathing dismissal," fears of verbal harassment, social persecution, and bodily violence at the hands of misinformed and fearful outsiders are also quite common among the world's practicing Druids.[3] Concerns such as these would inevitably lead to under-reporting by Druids, when asked. Practitioners would rather remain quiet, allowing others to simply assume that they are members of a more prevalent religion. Evidence of this behavior can be seen in many of the World Druidry Survey responses to questions pertaining to privacy and safety, for example:

> *"Where I live, there is a general lack of awareness and understanding of religious paths other than Christian, so I stay mostly quiet about my practice. People just assume I'm Christian, too."*

In light of this, we must assume that any government census figures, or figures based upon surveys conducted by researchers outside of the Pagan community will likely underrepresent the current population of Druids. However, it is still worth considering what figures we may.

The Census Data

Before delving into the numbers, it is worth noting that the available census data is neither as relevant nor as consistent as one might like, being nearly ten years out of date, and often containing only vaguely "Druid-like" statistics, rather than having precise counts of Druids. Also, census data is collected in different years, in different countries. At the time of the survey, some countries were beginning to release a new round of census data, however, the publicly searchable databases were still only populated with broad, summary data, and did not yet offer the level of detail needed for this study. So, working with what we have, we must rely on rough, back-of-the-envelope style calculations, in our search for evidence of biases in the World Druidry dataset.

According to the 2011 U.K. census results[4], 4,189 people in England and Wales identified as Druids. Given that many Druids report following other spiritual paths in addition to Druidry,[5] it is also worth noting that the overall number of people falling into all "Druid-like" religious categories (Druid, Animist, Heathen, New Age, Pagan, Pantheist, Shaman, Wiccan, Witchcraft, and Occult), totaled 80,416 people.

In Scotland, the 2011 census[6] counted 245 people as Druids. The number of people falling into all Druidry-like religious categories (the same list as for England and Wales, with the additional category of Reconstructionist), combined, totaled 5,327 people.

The 2011 census for the Republic of Ireland[7] did not include a detailed breakdown of Pagan religions. The only category that may have included Druids was "Pagan/Pantheist". The 2011 census results identified 1,883 people in this category. By 2016, that number had risen to 2,645.

The United States Census Bureau does not ask questions about religion, so as to uphold the traditional separation of church and state. In order to fill that data gap, the American Religious Identification Survey (ARIS) project was created, to track changes in America's religious geography over time. The ARIS 2001 report[8] contained data pertaining specifically to Druids, New Agers, Wiccans, and Pagans, as individual groups. In the 2008 report, those groups were aggregated, along with several unrelated religions, in a group called, "New Religious Movements & Other Religions."[9] The earlier dataset estimates an American Druid population of 33,000, and if all the above-mentioned, Druid-like religions were counted together, the number would be 375,000 people. The more recent dataset shows a growth trend in the NRM & Others category, from 1,770,000 people in 2001 to 2,804,000 people in 2008. To generate a very rough estimate of the number of Druids in America in 2008, one might apply a similar rate of growth (58.4% growth) to the Druid number, resulting in an estimated 2008 U.S. Druid population of 52,000 people, and an estimated 2008 population of Druid-like people calculated at roughly 594,000. This was, unfortunately, the most recent data available for the United States, as of the time of this writing.

According to the 2011 Canadian National Household Survey[10], 130,835 people self-identified as "Other Religions" and within that group, there were several subgroups that fell into the "Druid-like" categories used for the U.K., Scotland, and Ireland (specifically: New Age, New Thought, Wiccan, Other Pagan, and Pantheist), although no census category explicitly referred to Druids. If numbers for these "Druid-like" categories were combined, the result is a 2011 population of Druid-like people, calculated at 31,285.

In the 2011 census for Australia[11], 32,083 people identified as Pagan in very broad terms (a census category which also included "Druid" as well as the other "Druid-like" categories: Animism, Nature Religions, Druidism, Paganism, Pantheism, and Wiccan/Witchcraft). The number of Australians reporting specifically as Druids in 2011 census was 1042.

Statistics New Zealand's 2013 census data[12] shows 165 people in the "Druid" category. If all "Druid-like" categories were counted together (New Age, Nature Based Religions, Animist, Druid, Pantheist, and Wicca), this would yield a total of 7,572 people.

The Central Agency for Statistics in the Netherlands[13] provides religious affiliation data for Roman Catholic, Reformed, Dutch Reformed, Islam, Hindu, Buddhist, Jew and "other denomination". No categories exist for any other form of religious belief or practice. It is therefore impossible to determine whether or not there exists any kind of geographical distribution bias within the World Druidry Survey data from the Netherlands.

In Germany, the 2011 census results[14] provided detailed religion data only for populations of various forms of Christianity, and Judaism. All other religious beliefs were lumped into either the "Others" category, or a category labeled, "Not a member of a public-law religious society." It is therefore impossible to determine whether or not there exists any kind of geographical distribution bias within the World Druidry Survey data from Germany.

In Brazil, the census data for 2010 is similarly vague.[15] Although the census did have categories for various indigenous and Afro-Brazilian syncretic religions, the only category that might possibly apply to Druids would be "Tradições Esotéricas" or "Esoteric Traditions" — which could include religions as diverse as Druidry or Shintoism. Therefore, it is not possible to use this data to assess possible biases within World Druidry Survey data for Brazil.

I did not seek out religious census data for countries other than those listed above because no other country had a sufficiently large survey response rate to make any valid statistical analyses possible, in any case.

With all of the census data that was available at the time of the *World Druidry Survey* now in hand, we can begin to assess the survey response rates for each of the English-speaking countries. Only some of the available census figures referred to Druids as a distinct religious category. In Ireland and Canada, Druids were lumped together with an assortment of other religious paths such as Witchcraft and Wicca, Heathenism, Paganism, Animism, Pantheism, New Age beliefs, and the like. However, if we consider the ratios of Druids to Druid-like people within the census data for the other English-speaking nations, we can calculate an estimate of the number of Druids likely to have been living in Ireland and Canada at the time of the survey.

The ratio of the estimated number of Druids in each country to the estimated number of Druid-like people in each country is shown in the table below. For example, if we take the 4189 Druids from the England/Wales census, and divide that by the 80,416 Druid-like people from the same census,

Census Data on Druids

Census	Est. # Druids	Est. # Druid-like	Ratio
United States	52,000	594,000	0.09
England / Wales	4,189	80,416	0.05
Scotland	245	5,327	0.05
Canada	?	31,285	?
Australia	1,042	32,083	0.03
New Zealand	165	7,572	0.02
Ireland	?	1,883	?

Survey Response Rates by Nation

Census	Est. # Druids	# Suveys	Response Rate
United States	52,000	358	0.69%
British Isles	4,434	137	3.09%
Canada	1,564	44	2.81%
Australia	1,042	42	4.03%
New Zealand	165	24	14.55%
Ireland	94	11	11.70%

we obtain a ratio of 0.05. If we now calculate an average Druid-to-Druid-like ratio for all of the English-speaking countries (giving an equal weight to each of the five national cultures represented by actual census data), we obtain a figure of (0.09 + 0.05 + 0.05 + 0.03 + 0.02)/5 = 0.05.

Applying that 0.05 average ratio to the Druid-like census figures for Ireland and Canada, we can calculate an estimated population of Druids for those countries, thus: 0.05 x 31,285 = 1564 Druids for Canada; and 0.05 x 1883 = 94 Druids for Ireland. It is important to bear in mind that these are only rough estimates, and likely to be under-counting the actual Druid population in these countries. However, the way in which these figures have been calculated means that they will be proportionally undercounting, in the same way that the census figure have under-counted Druids in the other countries, allowing for a fair comparison.

Using these rough estimates of the number of practicing Druids in Ireland and Canada, we can now calculate response rates for each country. The response rates were calculated simply by dividing the number of completed surveys returned from each country by the estimated number of Druids residing there. The results are presented in the right-hand column of the table, above.

According to these calculations, the response rates for the British Isles, Canada, and Australia were comparable, with survey response rates of about 3-4% of the estimated national population of Druids. Druids in the United States under-reported in comparison, with a national response rate of only 0.69%. New Zealand and Ireland both showed better than average survey response rates of roughly 12-15%.

APPENDIX B NOTES & REFERENCES

1 As noted in: Hutton, R. (2009). *Blood and Mistletoe: The History of the Druids in Britain*. New Haven; London: Yale University Press. pg. 405-406.

2 Aldhouse-Green, M. (2010). *Caesar's Druids: Story of an Ancient Priesthood*. New Haven; London: Yale University Press. pg. 265.

3 For detailed analysis in support of this point, see *Chapter 3: Privacy and Safety Concerns of Modern Druids*.

4 *"What is your Religion?" Office for National Statistics, U.K. (2015)* https://www.ons.gov.uk/peoplepopulationandcommunity/population-andmigration/migrationwithintheuk/articles/whatisyourreligion/2015-01-15

5 For detailed analysis in support of this point, see *Chapter 5: Religions and Spiritual Traditions Practiced with Druidry*.

6 *"Scotland's Census 2011 - Religion (detailed) All people."* National Records of Scotland. (2013) http://scotlandscensus.gov.uk

7 *"E8009: Population Usually Resident and Present in the State 2011 to 2016 by Ethnic or Cultural Background, Religion, Sex and Census Year"* Central Statistics Office, Ireland. (2017) https://www.cso.ie

8 Kosmin, B.A., Mayer, E., and Keysar, A. (2001). *The American Religious Identification Survey (ARIS) 2001*. New York: Graduate Center of the City University of New York.

9 Kosmin, B.A. and Keysar, A. (2009). *American Religious Identification Survey (ARIS 2008) - Summary Report*. Hartford, Connecticut: Trinity College.

10 Statistics Canada, *2011 National Household Survey*, Statistics Canada Catalogue no. 99-010-X2011032.

11 Australian Bureau of Statistics, *Census of Population and Housing, 2011, TableBuilder*. (https://guest.censusdata.abs.gov.au/webapi/jsf/tableView/tableView.xhtml)

12 Statistics New Zealand. (2013). *2013 Census Totals by Topic - tables*.

13 Schmeets, H. (2016). *De religieuze kaart van Nederland, 2010-2015*. Centraal Bureau voor de Statistiek.

14 Statistische Ämter des Bundes und der Länder. (2011). *Zensusdatenbank – Ergebnisse des Zensus 2011 – Personen nach Religion (ausführlich) für Deutschland*.

15 Instituto Brasileiro de Geografia e Estatistica, Sistema IBGE de Recuperação Automática - SIDRA. (2010). *Censo Demográfico, Tabela 2103 - População residente, por situação do domicílio, sexo, grupos de idade e religião.*

Appendix C: Participating Druid Groups

This appendix lists the 147 Druid groups identified by *World Druidry Survey* respondents as being active at the time of the survey (between 30 October 2018 and 20 May 2019). The groups are listed first in descending order of prevalence within the survey data, and then in alphabetical order.

Active World Druidry Groups, circa 2020 c.e.

Druid Group	# of Druids	% of Druids
Order of Bards, Ovates, and Druids (OBOD)	413	57%
Unaffiliated, Solitary Druids	131	18%
Ár nDraíocht Féin: A Druid Fellowship (ADF)	85	12%
Ancient Order of Druids in America (AODA)	56	8%
British Druid Order (BDO)	40	6%
The Druid Network (TDN)	28	4%
New Order of Druids (NOD)	16	2%
Grove of the Summer Stars (New Zealand)	10	1%
Anglesey Druid Order (ADO)	8	1%
Pagan Federation	8	1%
Reformed Druids of Gaia (RDG)	8	1%
Order of the Yew	7	1%
World Fellowship of Druids	7	1%

table continues...

Active World Druidry Groups, circa 2020 c.e. (cont'd)

Druid Group	# of Druids	% of Druids
Henge of Keltria	6	0.8%
Reformed Druids of North America (RDNA)	6	0.8%
an unspecified "local group"	5	0.7%
Druids Down Under	5	0.7%
Druidical Order of the Golden Dawn	4	0.6%
Green Mountain Druid Order (GMDO)	4	0.6%
Sylvan Grove	4	0.6%
Anderida Gorsedd	3	0.4%
Druid Clan of Dana	3	0.4%
Flame and Well Grove	3	0.4%
Isle of Wight Druid Order	3	0.4%
Keepers of Dragon Knowledge Grove	3	0.4%
Mystic River Grove	3	0.4%
Sisterhood of Avalon	3	0.4%
Clareira Druídica da Borda do Campo	2	0.3%
Conclave do Povo Livre (Brasil)	2	0.3%
Conselho Brasileiro de Druidismo e Reconstrucionismo Celta	2	0.3%
DRAOï	2	0.3%
Druid College	2	0.3%
Druids of Western Australia	2	0.3%
East Bay Druids	2	0.3%
Facebook Group: Discover Druidry	2	0.3%
Fellowship of Druids Aotearoa	2	0.3%
Fellowship of Isis	2	0.3%
OBOD Portugal	2	0.3%

table continues...

Active World Druidry Groups, circa 2020 c.e. (cont'd)

Druid Group	# of Druids	% of Druids
Papatuanuku's Daughters	2	0.3%
Peaceful Earth Druid Grove	2	0.3%
Setantii Grove	2	0.3%
Solas An Iarthair Group	2	0.3%
Welt der Linden pagan community	2	0.3%
"my family"	1	0.1%
Ancient Archaeological Order of Druids	1	0.1%
Ancient Way Druidic Association	1	0.1%
Artio Seed Group	1	0.1%
Awen Seed Group	1	0.1%
Bardic Banter & Druid Drivel	1	0.1%
Bitter Root Grove	1	0.1%
Black Oak Grove	1	0.1%
Blidworth Druids	1	0.1%
Caldeirão das Ondas tribe in Salvador, Bahia, Brazil	1	0.1%
Can y Gwynt Grove	1	0.1%
Cascade Sunstone Seed Group	1	0.1%
Celtic Buddhism	1	0.1%
Celtic Golden Dawn	1	0.1%
Charter Oak Grove	1	0.1%
Chiltern Nemeton Grove	1	0.1%
Circle of Coll	1	0.1%
Clann Bhride	1	0.1%
Clareira Druídica Figueira Branca	1	0.1%
Colegiado Brasileiro Derulug	1	0.1%

table continues...

Active World Druidry Groups, circa 2020 c.e. (cont'd)

Druid Group	# of Druids	% of Druids
Collège International d'Études Celto-Druidiques (CIDECD)	1	0.1%
Comardiia Druuidiacta	1	0.1%
Coventia Seed Group Northumberland	1	0.1%
Dancing Waters Protogrove	1	0.1%
Daughters of the Morrigu	1	0.1%
Defence Pagan Network	1	0.1%
Dobunni Grove	1	0.1%
Doire Bhrighid Seed Group	1	0.1%
Druid Fellowship of the Green Path	1	0.1%
Druid Grove of Brighid	1	0.1%
Druidic Dawn	1	0.1%
Druids of the Light	1	0.1%
Duinroos Grove	1	0.1%
Dunderry Park	1	0.1%
Eclectic Light Fellowship	1	0.1%
Facebook Group: Celticae Institute	1	0.1%
Facebook Group: DRUID	1	0.1%
Facebook Group: OBOD New Zealand	1	0.1%
Fellowship of Druidism for the Latter Age (FoDLA)	1	0.1%
Fidnemed an Sid	1	0.1%
Forest Druids of the Cascades	1	0.1%
Forest Tradition	1	0.1%
Gaelic Druid Order (Ashby Grove)	1	0.1%
Gnostic Celtic Church	1	0.1%
Greylock Shadow Protogrove	1	0.1%

table continues...

Active World Druidry Groups, circa 2020 c.e. (cont'd)

Druid Group	# of Druids	% of Druids
Grove de Stenencirkel	1	0.1%
Grove Gort	1	0.1%
Grove of Mannan Mac Lir	1	0.1%
Grove of Red Cedar	1	0.1%
Grove of the Corieltauvi	1	0.1%
Grove of the Poplar Cross	1	0.1%
Hazelwood Grove	1	0.1%
Hearthstone Grove	1	0.1%
House of Blackthorn	1	0.1%
Irish College of Druids	1	0.1%
Irmandade Druídica Galaica	1	0.1%
Keltio Olde Stone Grove	1	0.1%
Keltoi Tradition	1	0.1%
L'Assemblée Druidique du Chêne et du Sanglier	1	0.1%
L'Ordre des enfants de la Terre	1	0.1%
L'Ordre Druidique de Dahut	1	0.1%
Lake Agassiz Seed Group	1	0.1%
Llywyn Swyndig	1	0.1%
Macadamia Grove	1	0.1%
Moor Cottage Stone Circle	1	0.1%
Mountains of Bran Beithe Seed Group	1	0.1%
Nemeton Broceliande Grove	1	0.1%
Nemeton Cruciniacum Seed Group	1	0.1%
Nemeton of the Stars Grove	1	0.1%
Nigheanan Brighde Order of Brighidine Flametenders	1	0.1%

table continues...

Active World Druidry Groups, circa 2020 c.e. (cont'd)

Druid Group	# of Druids	% of Druids
Northern Rivers Grove	1	0.1%
Northern Roots Grove	1	0.1%
Nos Coryn Seed Group	1	0.1%
Oakdale Grove	1	0.1%
OBOD Australia	1	0.1%
One Tree Gathering	1	0.1%
Ord Bridheach	1	0.1%
Ord na Darach Gile	1	0.1%
Order of Celtic Wolves	1	0.1%
Order of Christian Druids	1	0.1%
Order of the Oak	1	0.1%
Order of the Oaken Heart	1	0.1%
Order of the Stone Circle	1	0.1%
Parisi Seed Group	1	0.1%
Prairie Sky Protogrove	1	0.1%
Protogrove of the Valley Oak	1	0.1%
QOBOD	1	0.1%
Red Maple Grove	1	0.1%
Roaming Ravens	1	0.1%
Roharn's Grove	1	0.1%
Seed Group of the Wild Moor	1	0.1%
Silver Branch Seed Group	1	0.1%
Silvereyes Seed Group	1	0.1%
Summerlands Druid Seminary	1	0.1%
Sun Spiral Grove	1	0.1%

table continues...

Active World Druidry Groups, circa 2020 c.e. (cont'd)

Druid Group	# of Druids	% of Druids
Sylvan Celtic Fellowship	1	0.1%
Tamesis Seed Group	1	0.1%
The Draegons	1	0.1%
Three Cranes Grove	1	0.1%
Tuatha de Bridget	1	0.1%
Wayist Druid	1	0.1%
Well of Segais	1	0.1%
Wexford Ireland Seed Group	1	0.1%
White Dragon Seed Group	1	0.1%
Witte Raven Seed Group	1	0.1%

GLOSSARY

This glossary provides brief descriptions of all deities and legendary figures, holidays, religious traditions, magical traditions, spiritual paths, and other technical terms used in this book, which might be unfamiliar to the general reader. It would be impossible to include full descriptions of all aspects of any of these items, here. These entries are meant to serve as a launching pad for further reading, elsewhere.

ADF
acronym for the Druid organization Ár nDraíocht Féin

ADO
acronym for the Anglesey Druid Order

Advent
a four-week Christian festival held in anticipation of the Nativity of Jesus

Aesir
a set of twelve Norse sky deities

African-matrix religions
religious traditions of the Americas that blend traditional African religions with those of the Catholic host culture

Agni
Vedic god of fire, sun, lightning, and knowledge

Ahura Mazda
Zoroastrian creator-god, Lord of Wisdom, creator of all good

Áine
Irish goddess of love and fertility

Airmid (also Airmed)
Irish goddess of magical herbs and healing

Alban Arthan (also Alban Arthuan)
a term for the Winter Solstice, often translated by contemporary Druids as "light of the bear," or "light of Arthur"

Alban Eilir
a term for the Vernal Equinox, often translated by contemporary Druids as "light of the earth"

Alban Elfed (also Alban Elfan, or Alban Elued)
a term for the Autumnal Equinox, often translated by contemporary Druids as "light of the water"

Alban Hefin (also Alban Heruin)
a term for the Summer Solstice, often translated by contemporary Druids as "light of the shore"

Álfablót
Norse/Heathen end-of-harvest-season celebration.

Alvorada da Terra
Galician term for "Dawn of the Land," used to refer to the Vernal Equinox

Ancamna
Gallo-Roman goddess of the Moselle River Valley

Ancestors of blood
deceased people of the genealogical/ ancestral lines of a Druid's family

Ancestors of place
deceased people who once lived and cared for the land where a Druid now resides

Ancestors of spirit
deceased people whose lives and/or teachings have inspired a Druid, and helped them to become who they are

Andarta
Celtic bear goddess

Andraste
British war goddess who helped fight the Roman occupation of Britain; partner of Lenus the healer

Angus Óg (also Aengus Oc)
Irish god of youth and beauty

Animism
system of religious belief in which "spirit" or "soul" is attributed to both human and other-than-human beings, including animals, plants, and other elements of the natural landscape

Anpu
see Anubis

anthroposophy
spiritual philosophy, founded by Rudolf Steiner in the early 1900s, regarding the use of human intellect to comprehend the spiritual world

Anu (also Dana, Danu, or Donn)
Celtic, ancestral mother goddess of the Tuatha Dé Danann; a goddess of fertility

Anubis (also Anpu, or Inpu)
jackal-headed, Egyptian god of the Underworld

ANZAC Day (New Zealand)
national holiday corresponding with Samhain, which shares the thematic element of honoring the dead

AODA
acronym for the Ancient Order of Druids in America

Aotearoa
Māori word for New Zealand

Aphrodite
Greek goddess of love and beauty

Apollo
Greek god of light, music, medicine, and prophesy

Apollo Grannus
Gallo-Roman god of healing hot springs in Germany and France

Aradia
in Neopagan witchcraft traditions, the Queen of Witches

Arapyaú
Guarani word for "the new year," celebrated at the time of the Vernal Equinox in Brazil (September)

Arawn
Welsh king of the Celtic Otherworld

Araymã
Guarani word for "the old year," celebrated at the time of the Autumnal Equinox in Brazil (March)

Archangel
in Judaism, Christianity, and Islam, a senior angel, messenger or assistant of the one, supreme god

archetype
a universal, mental image, concept, or pattern that is present in the collective unconscious

Arianrhod
Welsh moon goddess, also associated with the constellation *Corona Borealis*

Artemis
Greek goddess of the wild hunt

Athena
Greek goddess of wisdom, war, and handicrafts

Arthur
Celtic/British hero-king of myth and legend, associated with Excalibur and the Round Table; the once and future king who sleeps now, but shall return; seen by some Druids as the symbolic Sun King, born at Winter Solstice, growing to strength and maturity in Summer, and cut down at Samhain, to be magically reborn at Winter Solstice.

Artio
Celtic bear goddess (Continental European)

Ásatrú
Icelandic name for Heathenry

Asha (also Asha Vahishta)
in Zoroastrian tradition, an advisor or aspect of Ahura Mazda, in charge of divine law, good thought, and moral order; protector of fire

Astarte (also Ashtart, Astoreth, Inanna, Ishtar)
Near Eastern goddess of love, war, fertility, maternity, earth, grain, date groves, wine, spring, storms, and fate

Athena
Greek goddess of wisdom, war, and handicrafts

Au Sept
Egyptian creation goddess

Ausera
Lithuanian goddess of dawn

Awen (also Imbas)
Welsh word for divine or poetic inspiration; also used to refer to the symbol /|\ representing the three rays of light cast by the rising sun at the solstices and equinoxes

Aya
Assyro-Babylonian goddess of dawn, and the sea

Baba Yaga
Russian/Slavic thunder witch, and deity of the dead

Babd
in Irish myth, a war goddess who often appears as a crow

Bahá'í Faith
monotheistic religion based on the teachings of the prophet, Bahá'u'lláh

Balder (also Baldur)
Norse Sun god, and god of piety and innocence

Bard
a person engaged in works related to music, song, storytelling, or other forms of artistry, within the modern religious tradition of Druidry

Basque (also Euskal Herria)
person/culture/language indigenous to the region at the western end of the Pyrenees Mountains, straddling Spain and France, along the coast of the Bay of Biscay

Bast (also Bastet or Sekhmet)
Egyptian cat goddess of fruitfulness, pleasure, music, dance, and cats

BDO
acronym for the British Druid Order

Bel (also Belenos)
Gaelic god of the dead; also a British mythical king; also the Bright Shining One, god of fire and the sun

Beli Mawr
an ancestral figure of Welsh legend, father of Arianrhod

Belisama
Celtic goddess of the Mersey River; also a sky goddess of fire, the forge, crafts, and illumination; consort of Bel

Beltane (also Beltainne)
Druid Festival celebrated on or around May 1st

Berkano rune
runic symbol representing the birch goddess, a symbol of rebirth

Bertha (also Berchta, Holda, Holla, Frau Holle, Nerthus, or Perchta)
a spirit of spring, the "White Lady" who watches over the souls of unborn children, and children who die before baptism

binary thinking
philosophical approach characterized by thinking in sets of polar opposites

Blodeuwedd
Welsh term for "flower face" or "blooming appearance; refers to the beautiful maiden magically created from the flowers of oak, broom, and meadowsweet, to serve as a wife for Lleu Llaw Gyffes

Boann
Irish goddess of the Boyne River

Bride
see Brigid

Bridie doll
a straw doll representing the goddess, Brigid

Brig
see Brigid

Brigantia
British tribal goddess of the Brigantes. A goddess of seasons, springs, streams, cattle, lambs, hearth, fertility, and women in childbirth

Brigid (also Brighid, Bride, Bridget, Brigit, Brig)
Irish goddess of fire, metalsmithing, fertility, cattle, crops, and poetry, learning, and healing

Buddha
the "Awakened One" who achieved complete enlightenment and might have entered the bliss of Nirvana, but chose instead to returned to the world to share his wisdom

Burns Night
an annual celebration of the life and poetry of the Scottish bard, Robert Burns, on Jan. 25th.

Caer Ibormeith
love interest of Angus Óg, and princess of Connacht

Cailleach (also Cailleach Bheur)
Celtic goddess of winter weather, builder of mountains, mover of islands

Calan Awst
Welsh term for Lughnasadh (literally, First Day of August)

Calan Gaeaf
Welsh term for Samhain/Halloween (literally, First Day of Winter)

Calan Mai
Welsh term for Beltane (literally, First Day of May)

Calas
one of the Three Druid Elements, a term referring to the quality of solidity, hardness, or manifest form

Cale
Greek Grace of beauty

Canol Gaeaf
Welsh term for Imbolc (literally, Middle of Winter)

Ced
in the Druid Revival tradition, the goddess of Earth's biosphere

celebrancy
the act of officiating at ceremonies

Celi
in the Druid Revival tradition, the god of the Heavens

Ceremonial Magic
magical workings performed by way of carefully planned, elaborate formal rituals

Ceres
Roman agricultural goddess of grains, fruit, and flowers

Cernunnos
Celtic god of nature, animals, fruit, grain, and prosperity. Portrayed with a man's body and stag's antlers. Also known as "the horned one"

Cerridwen
Welsh goddess who brews a cauldron of divine inspiration (Awen)

Chaos Magic
a form of magical work in which the magician adopts whatever attitudes and beliefs they feel will be most useful in affecting their desired result, for the magical task at hand

circle casting
marking, purifying, and sanctifying the circular space in which a Pagan or Druidic ritual will take place

clairaudience
ability to mentally perceive sounds out of the range of normal hearing, which are "heard" with the inner ear

clairsentience
the ability to receive messages and teachings from spiritual beings, through sudden, received "knowings"

clairvoyance
ability to mentally perceive hidden objects or objects at a distance which are "seen" with the inner eye

Coatlicue
Aztec Mother and Earth goddess

Contemplative Druidry
a Druidry practice characterized by prayer, meditation, and contemplation rather than by formal ritual or magic

Core Order of Ritual (ADF)
the ritual framework use by Druids of the ADF

Cornwall
region of the United Kingdom on the farthest southwestern peninsula of England

cross-quarter celebrations
set of four Neopagan/Druidic festivals that fall half-way between the solstice and equinox celebrations

Culloden anniversary
annual Scottish commemoration of the Battle of Culloden

Dagda
the Irish "Good God," highly skilled as a warrior, artisan, and magician; the benevolent, omniscient ruler of the Tuatha Dé Danann

Danu (also Dana or Dôn)
Celtic Mother goddess

Dao
see Tao

Demeter
Greek agricultural goddess of grains and vegetation

Dhumavati
aspect of the Hindu Divine Mother goddess associated with inauspicious things like poverty, frustration, and despair

Dian Cécht
Irish god of healing and medicines

Diana
Roman goddess of the moon, the wild hunt, and chastity

Dievs
Baltic sky god

Dionysus
Greek god of wine, revelry, fertility, and drama

Dirona
see Sirona

discursive meditation
meditation practice that takes the form of a structured, internal dialogue on a chosen seed topic or theme

divination
the practice of foretelling future events, or uncovering the hidden truths of things, using tools such as Ogham staves, tarot, or oracle cards

Djehuti
an earlier name for the Egyptian god, Thoth

Dolichenus (also Jupiter Dolichenus)
Roman mystery cult god of fertility and thunder

Donn
Irish ancestor-deity and god of the dead and the Celtic Otherworld

dowsing
using a divining rod to search for underground water sources or mineral veins

Druid
(as a field of endeavor) a person engaged in spiritual leadership, celebrancy, teaching, or justice-related work, within the spiritual tradition of Druidry

Druid Revival
a modern Druidic religious tradition developed in the 1800s, inspired by the writings of Iolo Morganwg (a.k.a. Edward Williams)

Durga
Hindu goddess of death

Dyéus Pter
Proto-Indo-European father and day-light sky god

Ehecatl
Aztec god of wind

Eir
Norse goddess of healing

eisteddfod (pl. eisteddfodau)
a gathering (often a competition) of Bards reciting poetry and performing music

Elen of the Ways
legendary patroness of roads, also seen by some modern Druids as an antlered woodland goddess

Enkidu
Sumerian god of land owners, farmers, and grain growers; a wild man made of mud; foe of Gilgamesh

Entroido
the pre-Lenten carnival as celebrated in the Galician region of Spain, also the Galician term for Imbolc

Eostre
another name for the Vernal Equinox

Epona
Celtic horse goddess

Eris
Greek goddess of discord and strife

Eriu
Irish tutelary goddess; a guardian and protector, or personification of Ireland

Eshu
Yoruban messenger and guardian spirit; a trickster god of discord

Esotericism
see Western Mystery Tradition

Esus (also Hesus)
Gaulish god of vegetation and war; The Woodsman, who tends the trees, pruning deadwood with his axe

eurhythmics
art of harmonious body movement, timed in response to improvised music

Faerie (also the Fair Folk)
name for magical, Otherworld beings, also the Neopagan religious tradition of interacting with those beings

Fand (Queen Fand)
Irish Otherworld queen, wife of the sea god Manannán Mac Lir

Faunus
Roman god of crops, fertility, herding, hunting, and husbandry

Faustina Augusta
a Roman Empress

Festa das Fachas
Galician torchlight festival (Autumnal Equinox)

fire festivals
set of four Neopagan/Druidic festivals that fall half-way between the solstice and equinox celebrations

5Rhythms dancing
a moving meditation technique created by Gabrielle Roth in the 1970s

Flidais
Irish woodland goddess of game, hunting, and wild things

Flora
Roman goddess of spring, fertility, and flowering plants

Forseti
Norse/Teutonic god of justice

Four Elements
air, fire, water, and earth

Freya (also Freyja)
Teutonic goddess of fertility

Freyr (also Frey, or Yngvi)
Norse/Teutonic god of earth, fertility, ruler of dwarves and patron of married couples

Frigg (also Frigga)
Norse/Teutonic goddess of clouds, the atmosphere, and the civilized world

Gabriel (also Jibril)
Archangel of Judeo-Christian-Islamic traditions, who will blow his horn at the end of the world

Gaia
Greek Earth goddess; personification of Mother Earth

Ganesha
Hindu god of wisdom, eloquence, arts, literature, sciences, and skills. God of scribes, remover of obstacles.

Gardnerian practices
the ceremonial, ritual, and magical practices of Wiccans initiated into British Gardnerian covens of witches

Gaul
region of western Europe, which in Roman times was inhabited by Celtic tribes, including all or parts of France, the Netherlands, Belgium, Germany, Luxembourg, Switzerland, and Italy

Gilgamesh
mythic hero/demi-god of ancient Mesopotamia; Sumerian king of Uruk

Gnostic
spiritual path involving the pursuit of esoteric, mystical knowledge

Goddess Tradition
spiritual tradition celebrating principles of the Divine Feminine

Gogyrwen
obscure Welsh term of unclear or disputed meaning, possibly related to Cerridwen's cauldron of Awen

Goibniu
in Irish legend, a weapon-crafting, beer-brewing member of the Tuatha Dé Danann

Gorsedd
a community or gathering of Bards

Great Spirit
in many North American indigenous traditions, the omnipresent, and omniscient creator of the world

Green Man (also Jack in the Green, also Camulos)
war god referred to by Gaius Julius Caesar as "Mars" and the "Dyn Glas" (Green Man); represented as a face surrounded by oak leaves; seen by some Druids as a figure symbolizing the cyclical rebirth of the greening world in spring

Grian
Irish goddess associated with Cnoc Gréine (a hill in eastern Co. Limerick)

Gwion Bach
in Welsh legend, the boy who accidentally won the gift of poetic inspiration from Cerridwen's cauldron, instead of her son, and became the bard Taliesin

Gwyar
one of the Three Druid Elements, a term referring to the quality of fluidity or changeability

Gwydion
a powerful magician in the Welsh legends of the *Mabinogi*

Gwyl Awst
Welsh name for Lughnasadh (literally, Festival of August)

Gwyl Braint
Welsh festival in early February marked by the flooding of the River Braint

Gwyl Forwyn
Welsh name for Imbolc (literally, Festival of the Virgin)

Gwyl Fraid
another name for Imbolc (literally, Festival of Praise)

Gwyn ap Nudd
mythical Welsh King of the Otherworld

haboob
an intense dust storm

Hades
Greek god of death and king of the Underworld

handfasting
Pagan wedding ceremony

Hanuman
Hindu flying monkey god of healing, grammar, poetry, war, and building

Haratua
Māori word for May, used to reference the southern hemisphere's Samhain

Hathor (also Het-Hert)
Egyptian goddess of love, joy, mirth, and the sky and sun

Heathen
a practitioner of Heathenry

Heathenry
a cluster of polytheistic religious traditions derived from Norse, Germanic, and Anglo-Saxon literary and cultural traditions, including Ásatrú, Vanatrú, and Disitrú

Hecate
Greek Underworld goddess of night, darkness, birth, life, death, roads and gates

Hella (also Hela or Hel)
Norse/Teutonic goddess of the Underworld or "Place of Punishment"

Hen Galan
Old New Year in Wales (January 13th)

Henotheism
belief in one, personal, familial, or tribal god, while not denying the existence of other deities

Hera
Greek sky goddess of heaven and of women, childbirth, and marriage

Hercules Saxsanus
Gallo-Roman cult deity of the Brohl Valley, and the old (Roman) quarry of Spitzelofen; patron of quarry workers

Hermes
Greek messenger god of commerce, travelers, shepherds, traders, and thieves

Hermetic tradition
spiritual tradition based upon magical, alchemical, and theosophical writings attributed to Hermes Trismegistus

Herne the Hunter
in English folklore, a ghost of Windsor Forest

Hestia
Greek goddess of fire, hearth and home

Hesus
see Esus

Het-Hert
see Hathor

Hine-Ahu-One
Polynesian/Māori first mother, "the Earth formed Maiden"

Hine-Raumati
Polynesian/Māori personification of Summer, "the Summer Maid"

Hine-Takurua
Polynesian/Māori personification of Winter, "the Winter Maid"

Hogmanay
Scots celebration of New Year's Eve

Holda
see Bertha

Holle, Frau
see Bertha

Holly King
folkloric personification of Winter,
who takes control at Midsummer and
rules over the waning year.

Holy Spirit
one aspect of the Holy Trinity of the
Catholic religious tradition

Horus
falcon-headed, Egyptian sun and sky
god who protects Earth with his wings

Hu Gadarn (also Hu the Mighty)
in the Druid Revival tradition, a
culture hero of the ancient Britons,
who introduced ploughing

Idunn (also Idunna)
Norse/Teutonic goddess who guards
the golden apples of eternal life for the
gods. Celebrated by some Druids at
the Autumnal Equinox

Ietsism
Dutch term for agnostic theism
(literally, "Somethingism")

Imbas
Irish word for divine or poetic inspiration (see also, Awen)

Imbolc
Druid Festival celebrated on or around
February 1st

Inanna
see Astarte

Inpu
see Anubis

Integral
spiritual tradition based on the
Integral Theory proposed by Ken
Wilbur in the 1970s

Ishtar
see Astarte

Isis
Egyptian goddess of earth, protector
of the dead, and patroness of loving
wives and mothers

Jack-in-the-Green
see Green Man

Janus
Roman/Etruscan high god of gates,
beginnings, and endings

Jesus Christ
son of the Christian god, one aspect of
the Holy Trinity of Catholic religious
tradition

Jung, Carl
Swiss psychiatrist who founded the
field of analytic psychology; creator
of psychological concepts including
synchronicity, archetypal phenomena,
and the collective unconscious

Juno Regina
Roman goddess of marriage, protector
of women and childbirth; also goddess
of finance and war

Jupiter Optimus Maximus
Roman god of air, war, and fertility

Kabbalah
spiritual tradition involving a mystical
interpretation of the Old Testament

kāhu
Māori word for a swamp harrier hawk

Kali
Hindu warrior goddess; also a goddess
of fertility, time, mysteries,
destruction, and death

Kami
nature spirits of the Japanese religious
tradition of Shinto

Kano rune
a runic symbol representing fire and
light, the "Rune of Opening"

Kemetic tradition
Neopagan revival of ancient Egyptian
religious traditions

kitchen magic
magical tradition involving simple
charms, herbal remedies, and/or other
magical folk-customs

Kokopelli
Native American fertility deity for
several indigenous peoples of the
southwestern United States; flute-
playing trickster god who chases away
winter and brings springtime and rain

Kore
see Persephone

Krishna
Hindu god of vegetation, love, and
erotic delight

kūmara
Māori word for sweet potato

Lakshmi
pre-Vedic earth goddess in India;
Hindu fertility goddess of fortune and
prosperity

Lammas
another name for Lughnasadh, from the Anglo-Saxon *Hlaef-mass*, the "Loaf Mass," festival of first bread.

Lauraco
Galician god of the Larouco mountain range

Lenus Mars
Celtic healing god of eastern Gaul

Lir (also Llyr)
Irish (Welsh) sea god who lived off the coast of Antrim

Litha
another name for the Summer Solstice

Lleu Llaw Gyffes
Welsh hero of the *Mabinogi*, son of Arianrhod

Llyr
see Lir

Logos
Gnostic version of the son of God (an aspect of Jesus)

Loki
Norse/Teutonic trickster god, and god of strife

Lugh (also Lug or Lugus)
in Irish myth, a celebrated leader of the Tuatha Dé Danann, skilled as a builder, metal smith, poet, historian, harper, magician, physician, cup-bearer, and warrior

Lughnasadh
Druid Festival celebrated on or around August 1st

Maat
Egyptian goddess of truth and justice

Mabon (deity) - (also Maponos)
the Welsh/Romano-British "Divine Youth," son of the goddess Modron

Mabon (holiday)
another name for Autumnal Equinox

Macha
Irish goddess of fertility and war

Maeve (also Medb)
Irish goddess of territory, fertility, and sovereignty; warrior-queen of Connacht

Magusto
Portuguese Autumn harvest festival celebrated November 11th, also the Galician term for Samhain

Mahuika
Māori fire deity (sometimes portrayed as female, sometimes as male)

Maios
Galician term for Beltane

Manannán Mac Lir
Irish sea god and ruler of the Otherworld; in later tradition, a trickster god and magician

Manawydan fab Llyr
Welsh hero of the *Mabinogi*; a skilled craftsman, wheat farmer and magician

Māori
indigenous Polynesian people of New Zealand

Maponos
(see Mabon, deity)

Mara
in India, a god of lightning, seduction, temptation, physical love, and death

Maramma
in India, village guardian deities and household gods

Mari
Basque weather goddess who lives in a high mountain cave

Mari Lwyd
a wassailing folk tradition in Wales, involving a skeletal horse goddess

Mariä Lichtmess
German term for Candlemass, the Christian mass coinciding with Imbolc

Mary
the Christian saint, mother of Jesus, also perceived by some Druids as a mother goddess figure

Matariki
Māori word for the constellation Pleiades, and the season when it first rises, beginning in late May or early June, just before the Winter Solstice

Matronae
a trio of Celtic mother goddesses of fertility; lovers of peace, tranquility, and children

Maui
Polynesian/Māori trickster, sun god, and culture hero who invented fishing, sailing, and ropes

Maypole Dance
folk dance around a flower-garlanded pole, in which ribbons are woven around the pole by the dancers

Meán Earraigh
Irish term for Mid Spring
Meán Fómhair
Irish term for Mid Autumn
Meán Gheimhridh
Irish term for Midwinter
Meán Samraidh
Irish term for Midsummer
Medicine Wheel
symbol or physical metaphor of North
American indigenous peoples, shaped
as a never-ending circle of life, with
"spokes" oriented to the four cardinal
directions
Meliae
Greek tree nymphs associated with
ash trees
Mercury
Roman version of the Greek Hermes
(see Hermes)
Merlin
in Arthurian legend, the famous
magician, prophet, and tutor of Arthur
Metatron
Archangel of Judaic/ Kabbalistic
tradition; the celestial scribe
Miach
Celtic physician deity
Michael
Archangel of Judeo-Christian-Islamic
traditions, who defends good against
evil, and slays the Devil (serpent)
Minerva
Roman version of Athena
Mithra
in Babylonian, Indian, Persian, Greek,
and Roman religious traditions, a sun
and fertility god; a guardian of the
laws of the universe by which nature
is made fruitful; god of contracts and
protector of truth
Modron
the Welsh "Great Mother"
Monad
The One, supreme being, divinity, or
totality of all things
Monism
belief in which there exists only One,
all-pervasive divine essence, and all
other things are aspects or apparent
manifestations of the One
Monotheism
belief in one and only one god

Morganwg, Iolo
Welsh bard, also known as Edward
Williams, whose writings inspired the
Druid Revival Movement; founder of
the Welsh Gorsedd
**Morrigu (also The Morrigan or
Morgan Le Fay)**
in Arthurian legend, the "Great
Queen," and goddess of war
Morris Dance
English folk dance performed in
choreographed sets, often involving
bells on the dancers' shins, and sticks,
swords, or handkerchiefs used to em-
phasize the rhythms
Mothers' Night/Mōdraniht
Heathen celebration on the eve of
Yule, honoring the ancestral mothers
Mount Haemus papers
series of academic papers on Druidry,
sponsored and published by the Order
of Bards, Ovates, and Druids
Mummers Plays
holiday folk plays performed by
informal groups of community players
Nantosuelta
Gaulish Celtic fertility goddess
Nehalennia
Norse goddess of plenty; her symbol
was the cornucopia
Nekhbet
Egyptian goddess of childbirth
Nemain
early Irish war goddess
Nemetona
Gaulish/British goddess of the sacred
grove
Nerthus
see Bertha
New Age
umbrella term used to describe a range
of eclectic, spiritual beliefs and
practices that became popular in the
1970s, drawing upon a variety of
older, occult and esoteric traditions
Nichols, Ross
founder of the Order of Bards, Ovates,
and Druids
Niwalen
in the Druid Revival tradition, the
goddess of dawn and dusk

Njord (also Njorth)
Norse/Teutonic god of riches, wealth, fertility, harvest, fire, and weather

Nodens
British god of healing

Noite dos Lumes
Galician term for "Night of the Fires," the Summer Solstice

Noite Nai
Galician term for Winter Solstice

Northern Traditions
Neopagan traditions inspired primarily by the legends, lore, and mythology of Norse, Germanic, and Anglo-Saxon peoples, but which are more open to blended traditions than Heathenry

Nuada
Irish chief of the Tuatha Dé Danann

Nwyfre
one of the Three Druid Elements, a term referring to life force, energy, or consciousness

Oak King
folkloric personification of Summer, who takes control at Midwinter, and rules over the waxing year.

'Obby 'Oss
a May Day festival tradition in Cornwall, involving two processions, each containing a hobby horse

Obeah
an Afro-Caribbean spiritual-healing and magical justice-making tradition

OBOD
acronym for the Order of Bards, Ovates, and Druids

Odin (also Woden)
Norse/Teutonic Allfather, god of war, intelligence, wisdom, and poetry

Ogham/Ogham staves
ancient Irish alphabet, often engraved on markers or staves. Each letter is associated with a particular tree, and corresponding symbolisms; used by modern Druids as a divination tool

Ogma (also Ogmios or Oghama)
Celtic god of eloquence and language

Oímelc
another name for Imbolc

Oisín
Irish warrior and poet

Omnism
recognition of and respect for all systems of religious belief

oracle cards
a deck of richly illustrated cards, each with particular symbolic meanings, used by some Druids for divination

Osiris
Egyptian god who ruled the earth, bringing laws, religion, agriculture, and viticulture to mortals

Ostara
another name for the Vernal Equinox

Otherworld
a delightful Celtic realm beyond the mortal senses, populated by divine and semi-divine characters and spirits.

Ouroboros
circular symbol of the eternal cycle of birth, life, death, and rebirth, depicted as a snake biting its own tail

Outdwellers
in ADF ritual tradition, spiritual beings outside of the ritual space, who might be troublemakers, and are given an offering to encourage them to leave the Druids in peace during the ritual

Ovate
a person engaged in works of nature study, nature connection, or assorted forms of seership/divination, within the spiritual tradition of Druidry

Pace Egg
a rural English Easter play involving a mock battle, in which the hero is killed and then brought back to life

Pagan
catch-all term referring to a member of any of a variety of nature-reverent religious traditions outside the purview of the Abrahamic religions

Pales
Roman god/dess of cattle

Pan
Greek god of woods, fields, flocks, and wildlife; patron of hunters and shepherds

Panentheism
belief that the universe is a part of a supreme deity who also transcends space and time

Pani-tinaku
in Polynesian/Māori mythology, the
mother of the kūmara

Pantheism
belief that god and the universe are
one and the same

Papatūānuku (also Papa)
Polynesian/Māori Earth Mother

Pavarti
aspect of the Vedic Great Mother
Goddess, Devi, consort of Shiva

Peg Powler
in English folklore, the hag and water
spirit of the River Tees

pentacle
symbol associated with Wicca or other
Witchcraft religious traditions, shaped
as an upwards-pointing, five-pointed
star within a circle, and representing
the five element system of Witchcraft:
air, fire, water, earth, and spirit

Pentecost
Christian holiday commemorating the
descent of the Holy Spirit upon the
Apostles, and other followers of Jesus

Perchta
see Bertha

Perennialism
belief that all religious traditions stem
from a shared, metaphysical truth or
origin

Persephone (also Kore)
Greek goddess of vegetation, spring
flowers, and the Underworld

Plouton (also Pluto)
Roman version of the Greek Hades,
god of the Underworld, ruler of the
deep earth, which gives boundless
riches of crops and mineral wealth

Pluralism
belief that many different religions
can serve as equally valid sources of
truth and moral guidance

Polytheism, Hard
belief in a pantheon of goddesses and
gods who are perceived as objectively
real, individual divine beings

Polytheism, Soft
belief in a pantheon of goddesses and
gods who are perceived as archetypes,
or personifications of natural forces

polytheistic reconstructionism
effort to reconstruct, as far as possible,
the actual beliefs and practices of the
ancient polytheistic religions of the
Celts, Egyptians (Kemetic tradition),
and Greeks (Hellenistic tradition)

Poseidon
Greek god of rivers and the sea

Quakerism
a Protestant Christian denomination
that believes in the ability of evert
human being to directly experience
and access the divine light, within

Quan Yin (also Guanyin)
a Bodhisattva (a person on the path to
Buddhahood) of compassion, and a
goddess of mercy

Quarters, the
the four geographic quarters of the
world: North, East, South, and West

Quetzalcoatl
"The Feathered Serpent," Aztec,
Toltec, and Mayan god of air, clouds,
wind, medicine and healing, fertility,
wealth, thieves, fishermen, farmers,
metalsmiths and builders; inventor of
books, writing, and the calendar

Ra
Egyptian sun god, king of gods and
mortals

Ranginui (also Rangi)
Polynesian/Māori Sky Father

Raphael
Archangel of Judeo-Christian
traditions, responsible for healing

Raunächte
Germanic/Heathen word for the
"Rough nights," or the twelve magical
nights of the Yuletide

Reiki
Japanese form of energy healing

Rhiannon (also Rigatona)
Celtic/Gaulish, horse riding moon
goddess; a major character of the
Mabinogi

Ritona (also Pritona)
Celtic goddess of the Trevery region
of Germany

Rosmerta
from *Ro-Smert-A*, the Gaulish term for "Great Giver Goddess"; Gallo-Roman goddess of fertility, abundance, and motherhood, who carries an axe and a Butter Churn of Plenty

runes
letters in a set of Germanic languages, often engraved on markers or stones, and used by some modern Druids for divination

Rushbearing
English summer festival in which rushes are gathered, carried, and strewn on the parish church floor

Saint John's Day
Christian feast of Saint John, the Baptist, held on Midsummer Day

Samhain (also Samhuinn)
Druid Festival celebrated on or around November 1st

Saturn
Roman god of agriculture, prosperity, and abundance

Saturnalia
Roman pagan festival in mid-December, honoring Saturn

Savitr (also Savitri)
Vedic god of Heaven, giver of life, and father of the sun goddess Surya

Seitura
Galician term for Lughnasadh

Sekhmet
see Bast

Set
Egyptian god of evil and darkness; a weather deity

shamanic tradition
religious tradition in which a person, called a *shaman*, gains the powers needed to heal the sick, communicate with beings in the Otherworld, or to escort human souls through the Otherworld, by engaging in trance or other ecstatic religious experiences

Shamanism
the shamanic tradition practiced by a *šaman* of Manchu-Tungus peoples of eastern Asia

shapeshifting
transforming one's consciousness to perceive, comprehend, and/or behave as a specific plant, animal, or object

Shinto
Japan's indigenous nature religion

Shiva
Hindu god/dess of 1008 names, a creator-deity of the moon, mountains, agriculture, fertility, truth, arts and learning, luck, rivers, forests, death, yoga, and the "cosmic dance"

Sídhe
Irish word for a fairy mound

Sikhism
a monotheistic religion of the Punjab region of India, based on the spiritual teachings of Guru Nanak

Silvanus
Roman tutelary deity of wild woodlands, protector of fields, flocks, cattle, and husbandmen

Simurgh (also Saena or in India, Garuda)
benevolent, magical bird of Persian myth, purifier of land and waters, bringer of fertility, disperser of the seeds of all plants, shaken from the tree of life; source of healing, and wisdom, similar to the phoenix.

Sirona (also Dirona)
Celtic/Gaulish goddess of healing springs

Skadi
Norse/Teutonic goddess of winter

Sköll
Norse/Teutonic giant wolf, god of eclipses and sunsets

Sobek (also Sebek)
Egyptian crocodile god of fertility and death; protector of reptiles

Sol (also Helios)
Roman god of the sun

solitary
a Druid who practices Druidry alone

spirit of nature
"spirit" or "soul" associated with a particular element of the natural world, such as an animal, stone, tree, wind, etc.

spirit of place
"spirit" or "soul" associated with a particular location, such as a city, mountain, river valley, forest, etc.

Spiritism
belief that all living beings, including humans, are immortal spirits which temporarily inhabit physical bodies for a series of incarnations, between which their disembodied sprit may be a benevolent or malevolent influence on the lives of others

Sufism
mystical tradition of Islam

Sul (also Sulis)
British goddess of healing springs

Sumbel
a formal drinking ritual in which toasts are made to the gods

SurveyMonkey
cloud-based computing service which allows for survey administration and data collection via the internet

Tai Chi
Chinese moving meditation practice, based on an old martial art tradition, involving the cultivation and circulation of internal energy (chi)

Tailtiu
Irish earth goddess and mother of Lugh

Taliesin
in Welsh myth, the divinely inspired Welsh bard who, as Gwion Bach, had inadvertently received the blessing of Cerridwen's cauldron of Awen

Tamanuiterā
Māori personification of the sun

Tāne (also Tāne-mahuta or Tāne-nui-a-Rangi)
Polynesian/Māori god of forests and birds, peace and beauty

Tangaroa (also Takaroa)
Polynesian/Māori god of the sea, lakes, rivers, fish, and other water creatures

Taniwha
in Māori mythology, spirits of deep pools, rivers, or the sea, especially in places with dangerous currents

Tao (also Dao)
ancient Chinese philosophical concept meaning The Way, and referring to the underlying natural order of the Universe

Taoism
ancient Chinese religious tradition that encourages living in harmony with The Way (or Tao) of nature

Taranis
Gaulish/British god of thunder

Tarot
a deck of richly illustrated cards, each with particular symbolic meanings, used by some Druids for divination

Tāwhirimātea (also Tāwhiri)
Māori god of weather, including thunder, lightning, wind, clouds, and storms

TDN
acronym for The Druid Network

Tegid Foel
in Welsh mythology, the giant of Pennllyn, husband of Cerridwen

Telluric energy
a grounding energy emanating from deep within the Earth

ternary thinking
philosophical approach characterized by seeking a third perspective that can resolve and find ways to connect polar opposites

Teutates
Celtic tribal god of Gaul and Britain

Thor
Norse/Teutonic god of sky, thunder, lightning, and fertility; a protector of households

Thoth
Egyptian god of wisdom, time, magic, music, astronomy, medicine, writing, drawing, and surveying

Three Druid Elements
a set of three philosophical principles used to describe the essential nature of the universe: Nwyfre, Calas, Gwyar

Three Realms
land, sea, and sky

Thunderbird
in North American Indian myth, a magical spirit-bird of lightning, thunder, rain and vegetation

Tiamat
dragon-shaped, Assyro-Babylonian goddess of the sea, chaos and evil

Tonantzin
Aztec mother goddess, and goddess of Earth

Trinitarian
characterized by the Christian belief
that God is comprised of three distinct
persons: the father, son, and holy spirit, who are all yet essentially one and
the same

triple goddess
a goddess of three aspects, most often
those of the maiden, mother, and
crone

Tripura Sundari
Hindu goddess of creation, protection,
and destruction

triskele (also Triskelion)
Celtic symbol comprised of three,
interlocking spirals, representing the
Three Realms

Tuatha Dé Danann
a legendary race of Celtic gods, also
known as the Children of Danu, Dana,
or Dôn

Twelfth Night
the final night of celebrations in either
the Twelve Days of Christmas, or the
twelve nights of the Yuletide tradition,
which begins at the Winter Solstice
and ends twelve nights later

Two Powers
Above and Below, or Earth and Sky

Tyr (also Tiwas)
Norse/Teutonic sky god of battle, law,
and order

Umbanda
an African-matrix religion of Brazil

Unitarian Universalism
a creedless, liberal religion in which
members derive truth and meaning
from the beliefs and practices of all
major world religions

Uriel
Archangel of Judeo-Christian
traditions, patron of arts, sciences,
judgment, poetry, and the Christian
rite of Confirmation

Venus
Roman goddess of love and beauty

Wadjet
Egyptian goddess of lower Egypt,
symbolizing the forces of growth

Wales
country in the southwestern region of
Great Britain; one of the modern-day
Celtic nations

wassailing (orchards)
visiting dormant apple (or other fruit)
trees, with offerings of poetry, song,
toast and cider, to encourage vibrant
new growth and a good harvest next
year

Wayism
philosophical lifestyle and worldview
similar to that of Taoism, focused on
attaining enlightenment by flowing
with the Way of nature

Wepwawet
Egyptian jackal-headed god of war

Western Mystery Tradition
a cluster of modern philosophies, and
magical and spiritual practices that use
correspondences between inner/outer
or physical/spiritual worlds, and an
assortment of symbols and ceremonial
forms to manifest desired changes

White Tara
in Tibetan Buddhism, a bodhisattva of
compassion and loving-kindness

Wicca
a form of Witchcraft popularized by
Gerald Gardner in the 1950s

wight
in Heathenry, an other-than-human
person, such as a land or sea spirit

wildcrafting
process of deriving something (a food,
medicine, celebration, or ritual) from
the naturally occurring elements found
in one's local landscape

wisdom triads
Celtic literary tradition of poetic
aphorisms composed in sets of three

Witchcraft
duotheistic, Neopagan nature religion
celebrating the cycles of the moon and
sun, and incorporating the practice of
ceremonial or ritual magic

Woden
see Odin

Wuldor
Norse/Teutonic god of winter, skiing,
and archery

Xipe Totec
Aztec vegetation god of seeds, spring,
flowers, goldsmiths, and jewelers;
also a god of suffering and sacrifice

Xochiquetzal
Aztec goddess of flowers and love,
patroness of unmarried women,
weavers, and childbirth

Yahweh (also YHWH)
Hebrew word for the supreme god

Yggdrasil
Norse/Teutonic universal, sacred tree
of life, which connects and shelters all
the worlds

Yngvi
see Freyr

yoga
a set of physical, mental, and spiritual
disciplines developed in ancient India

Yule (also Yuletide)
twelve-day winter festival celebrated
by followers of Heathenry and other
Northern Traditions of Neopaganism;
also sometimes used by Druids as an
alternate name for the Winter Solstice

Zazen
form of sitting meditation used in
Japanese, Zen-Buddhist practice

Zoroastrianism
ancient Iranian religion based on the
teachings of Zoroaster/Zarathustra,
exalting the benevolent, wisdom-deity,
Ahura Mazda

BIBLIOGRAPHY

Agresti, A. (2019). *An Introduction to Categorical Data Analysis (3rd Ed.)*. Hoboken, NJ: John Wiley & Sons, Inc.

Aldhouse-Green, M. (2010). *Caesar's Druids: Story of an Ancient Priesthood*. New Haven; London: Yale University Press.

———. (2015). *The Celtic Myths: A Guide to the Ancient Gods and Legends*. London; U.K.: Thames & Hudson.

Anczyk, Adam. (2014). *The Golden Sickle: An Introduction to Contemporary Druidry*. Katowice, Poland: Sacrum Publishing House.

Ár nDraíocht Féin. (2018). *Dedicant Path Manual*. (members-only publication)

———. (2020). *Core Order of Ritual*. https://www.adf.org/rituals/explanations/core-order.html

Ancient Order of Druids in America. (2019). *Apprentice Guide*. (members-only publication)

———. (2018). *New Candidate Guide*. (members-only publication)

Australian Bureau of Statistics. (2011). *Census of Population and Housing, 2011, TableBuilder*. https://guest.censusdata.abs.gov.au/webapi/jsf/tableView/tableView.xhtml

Bell, Catherine. (1997). *Ritual: Perspectives and Dimensions*. New York, NY: Oxford University Press.

———. (1992). *Ritual Theory, Ritual Practice*. New York, NY: Oxford University Press.

Bettis, J.D. (1975). *Phenomenology of Religion*. London: SCM Press.

British Druid Order. (2018-2019). *Bardic Course.*
(members only curriculum booklets)

Billington, Penny. (2011). *The Path of Druidry: Walking the Ancient Green Way.*
Woodbury, MN: Llewellyn Publications.

Central Statistics Office, Ireland. (2017). *"E8009: Population Usually Resident
and Present in the State 2011 to 2016 by Ethnic or Cultural Background, Religion,
Sex and CensusYear"* https://www.cso.ie

Cooper, Gordon. (2012). "Wild-crafting the Modern Druid."
first appeared in the OBOD's members-only, *Touchstone,* later posted to:
https://druidry.org/resources/wild-crafting-the-modern-druid

Cooper, M.T. (2010). *Contemporary Druidry: A Historical and Ethnographic
Study.* Salt Lake City: Sacred Tribes Press.

Coulter, Charles Russel & Turner, Patricia. (2000). *Encyclopedia of Ancient
Deities (Vol. 1 & 2).* Jefferson, NC: McFarland & Company Publishers, Inc.

Cowan, Tom. (1993). *Fire in the Head: Shamanism and the Celtic Spirit.* New
York, NY: Harper Collins Publishers.

Creswell, J.W. and Plano Clark, V.L. (2018). *Designing and Conducting Mixed
Methods Research (3rd Ed.).* Thousand Oaks, CA: SAGE Publications.

Cunliffe, B.W. (2010). *Druids: A Very Short Introduction.* New York: Oxford
University Press.

Davy, Barbara Jane. (2007). *Introduction to Pagan Studies.* Lanham, MD:
Altamira Press.

Ellis, Peter B. (1994). *The Druids.* London: Constable and Co. Ltd.

Ford, Patrick K. (1977). *The Mabinogi and other Medieval Welsh Tales.* Berkeley,
CA: University of California Press.

Green, M. (1986). *The Gods of the Celts.* Gloucestershire; U.K.: The History
Press.

———. (1997). *Dictionary of Celtic Myth and Legend.* London; U.K.: Thames &
Hudson.

Greer, John Michael (2011). *The Druid Grove Handbook.* Traverse City, MI:
Lorian Press.

———. (2006). *The Druidry Handbook: Spiritual Practice Rooted in the Living
Earth.* San Francisco, CA: Red Wheel/Weiser LLC.

Harrison, P. (2013). *Elements of Pantheism: A Spirituality of Nature and the
Universe (3rd Ed.).* Shaftesbury, Dorset: Element Books.

Harrison, V.S. (2006). "The Pragmatics of Defining Religion in a Multi-Cultural
World." *International Journal for Philosophy of Religion* 59: 133-152

Harvey, Graham. (2017). *Animism: Respecting the Living World (2nd Ed.)*. London: C. Hurst & Co. Ltd.

——. (2011). *Contemporary Paganism: Religions of the Earth from Druids and Witches to Heathens and Ecofeminists (2nd Ed.)*. New York, NY: New York University Press.

Hopman, E.E. (2016). *A Legacy of Druids: Conversations with Druid leaders of Britain, the USA and Canada, past and present*. Winchester, U.K.: Moon Books.

Hutton, R. (2009). *Blood and Mistletoe: The History of the Druids in Britain*. New Haven; London: Yale University Press.

Instituto Brasileiro de Geografia e Estatistica, *Sistema IBGE de Recuperação Automática - SIDRA. (2010). Censo Demográfico, Tabela 2103 - População residente, por situação do domicílio, sexo, grupos de idade e religião.*

Kosmin, B.A., Mayer, E., and Keysar, A. (2001). *The American Religious Identification Survey (ARIS) 2001*. New York: Graduate Center of the City University of New York.

Kosmin, B.A. and Keysar, A. (2009). *American Religious Identification Survey (ARIS 2008) - Summary Report*. Hartford, Connecticut: Trinity College.

Kraemer, C. H. (2012). *Seeking the Mystery: An Introduction to Pagan Theologies*. Englewood, Colorado: Patheos Press.

Lewis, J.R. and Bårdsen Tollefsen, I. (2013). "Gender and Paganism in Census and Survey Data." *The Pomegranate* 15.1-2 (2013) 61-78

MacKillop, James. (1998). *A Dictionary of Celtic Mythology*. Oxford, U.K.: Oxford University Press.

Malory, Thomas. (1998). *Le Morte Darthur: The Winchester Manuscript (Helen Cooper, Ed.)*. Oxford, U.K.: Oxford University Press. (Original work published 1469-70)

National Records of Scotland. (2013). *"Scotland's Census 2011 - Religion (detailed) All people."* http://scotlandscensus.gov.uk

Nichol, James. (2014). *Contemplative Druidry: People, Practice and Potential*. CreateSpace Independent Publishing.

Nichols, Ross. (1992). *The Book of Druidry: History, Sites and Wisdom*. San Francisco, CA: Aquarian Books.

Office for National Statistics, U.K. (2015) *"What is your Religion?"* https://www.ons.gov.uk/peoplepopulationandcommunity/populationandmigration/migrationwithintheuk/articles/whatisyourreligion/2015-01-15

Order of Bards, Ovates, and Druids. (2018). *Bardic Grade.*
        (members only curriculum booklets)

Roller, M.R. and Lavrakas, P.J. (2015). *Applied Qualitative Research Design: A Total Quality Framework Approach.* New York: Guilford Press.

Ross, Anne. (1999). *Druids: Preachers of Immortality.* Gloucestershire; U.K.: The History Press.

——. (2005). *Pagan Celtic Britain.* Chicago, IL: Academy Chicago Publishers.

Saldaña, Johnny. (2016). *The Coding Manual for Qualitative Researchers (3rd Ed.).* Thousand Oaks, CA: SAGE Publications.

Schleiermacher, F. (1893). *On Religion: Speeches to Its Cultured Despisers (John Oman, B.D., Trans.).* London: Kegan Paul, Trench, Trübner & Co., Ltd. (Original work published 1799)

Schmeets, H. (2016). *De religieuze kaart van Nederland, 2010-2015.* Centraal Bureau voor de Statistiek.

Simpson, J.A. and Weiner, E.S.C. (1989). *The Oxford English Dictionary (2nd Ed.).* Oxford, U.K.: Clarendon Press

Statistics Canada. (2011). *2011 National Household Survey,* Statistics Canada Catalogue no. 99-010-X2011032.

Statistics New Zealand. (2013). *2013 Census Totals by Topic - tables.*

Statistische Ämter des Bundes und der Länder. (2011). *Zensusdatenbank – Ergebnisse des Zensus 2011 – Personen nach Religion (ausführlich) für Deutschland.*

INDEX

Larisa A. White, M.S.Ed., Ph.D., is an author, educator, and independent scholar with 30 years' combined experience in mixed-methods sociological research, curriculum design, educational program evaluation, and teaching. She is the founder of Quercus Academy, where she currently teaches. Her research activities focus on the neurobiology of learning, the ways in which people learn, grow, and change under the influence of changing educational contexts and cultures, and the sociology of contemporary, nature-based religions. In her free time, she works on ecological restoration projects in the Coast Range Mountains of California.